June 25–27, 2014
Newcastle Upon Tyne, UK

**Association for
Computing Machinery**

Advancing Computing as a Science & Profession

TVX'14

Proceedings of the 2014 ACM International Conference on
Interactive Experiences for TV and Online Video

Sponsored by:
ACM SIGCHI

Supported by:
BBC and FI content

Association for Computing Machinery

Advancing Computing as a Science & Profession

The Association for Computing Machinery
2 Penn Plaza, Suite 701
New York, New York 10121-0701

Notice to Past Authors of ACM-Published Articles

ACM intends to create a complete electronic archive of all articles and/or other material previously published by ACM. If you have written a work that has been previously published by ACM in any journal or conference proceedings prior to 1978, or any SIG Newsletter at any time, and you do NOT want this work to appear in the ACM Digital Library, please inform permissions@acm.org, stating the title of the work, the author(s), and where and when published.

ISBN: 978-1-4503-2838-8 (Digital)

ISBN: 978-1-4503-3115-9 (Print)

Additional copies may be ordered prepaid from:

ACM Order Department
PO Box 30777
New York, NY 10087-0777, USA

Phone: 1-800-342-6626 (USA and Canada)
+1-212-626-0500 (Global)
Fax: +1-212-944-1318
E-mail: acmhelp@acm.org
Hours of Operation: 8:30 am – 4:30 pm ET

Printed in the USA

TVX 2014 Chairs' Welcome

It is our great pleasure to introduce the *2014 ACM International Conference on Interactive Experiences for Television and Online Video – ACM TVX 2014.*

ACM TVX is a leading annual conference that brings together international researchers and practitioners from a wide range of disciplines. We provide a common discussion space about the future of online video and TV experiences. Particular topics of interest include technology and systems; interaction design; media studies; data science; business models human-centric and experience-focused research.

We are very pleased with the final program, since it provides a broad overview of the current challenges for online video and television research. The program covers a diversity of topics ranging from content production to consumption and in particular, papers discuss relevant research about how to support interactive experiences and evaluate them in real environments. They explore as well novel interaction mechanisms and multi-screen solutions, and provide insights on large-scale analysis of user feedback.

This year the conference attracted 80 paper submissions. A total of 29 Associated Chairs (AC) and 205 reviewers served on the technical program committee representing internationally renowned scientists from academia and industry. Each paper received at least three peer reviews of high quality, as well as an additional meta-review by the assigned AC. All ACs joined the discussions at the program committee meeting. This provided the opportunity for the papers and reviews to be discussed in detail and all final decisions to be agreed.

The outcome of this process was that 20 of the 80 submissions were accepted (25%) for inclusion in the final program. All the accepted papers were presented in Newcastle upon Tyne in June 2014. In our commitment to continuously improve the quality of program, 4 papers have been given special recognition for their excellence and have been nominated for consideration as a Best Paper. The winner of Best Paper Award will be revealed at the conference in June.

This year we have put serious effort into inclusion at the event, spearheading two primary initiatives. Firstly, we have introduced an open application process for becoming ACs, in which 10 members were appointed as a result. Secondly, during the ACM TVX submission process, we provided the opportunity to bring the experience of established researchers to new researchers through mentorship. Four authors participated in this process, resulting in two accepted papers.

We are pleased to present two distinguished keynote speakers. These valuable and insightful talks provide us a better understanding of the present and can guide us to the future:

- Dick Bulterman
  (FX Palo Alto Laboratory & VU University Amsterdam)

- Dale Herigstad
  (Chief Interaction Officer at POSSIBLE and Co-Founder of SeeSpace)

Putting together TVX 2014 was a team effort. We would like to express our gratitude to all the contributors, program committee and volunteers who have made this conference possible.

We also thank the authors for providing such high quality content for the 2014 program and we are extremely grateful to the program committee who worked very hard in reviewing papers and providing feedback for authors. This conference could not have happened without our committee putting their time and effort in making this process a success. We thank the various institutions of our ACs for sparing their time to help us move this important research field forward.

Special thanks also go to: Elizabeth Churchill (Executive Vice President of ACM SIGCHI) and Philippe Palanque (SIGCHI Adjunct Chair for Specialized Conferences) for their infinite commitment with the conference and for shepherding us in the process of bringing this conference under the umbrella of the ACM; to Ashley Cozzi from ACM for helping us navigate contracts and budgets; to the TVX Steering Committee for their support and guidance; and to Lisa Tolles from Sheridan Proceedings Service for helping us pull the content together. Finally, we extend our deepest gratitude to our sponsor, ACM SIGCHI, for taking the risk to support this conference, and to our generous corporate supporters, BBC, FIContent whose endorsement and support were essential in pulling this conference together, and in particular, the Digital Interaction Group at Newcastle University for sharing their time and resources in producing the event.

We hope that you will find this program interesting and thought-provoking, that the conference will provide you with a valuable opportunity to share ideas with other researchers and practitioners from institutions around the world, that you will consider sharing with others who could not be here the ideas, inspirations and provocations you experience and that you will consider supporting this conference series with your contributions in the future.

Patrick Olivier,
Peter Wright and
Tom Bartindale
TVX 2014 General Chairs

Marianna Obrist,
Pablo Cesar and
Santosh Basapur
TVX 2014 Program Chairs

Table of Contents

Session 5: Consumption: Multiple Screens and Attention

Session 6: Interaction: Tablets, Gestures, and Tables

Session 7: Keynote Address

Author Index

TVX 2014 Conference Organization

General Chairs: Patrick Olivier *(Newcastle University, UK)*
Peter Wright *(Newcastle University, UK)*
Tom Bartindale *(Newcastle University, UK)*

Program Chairs: Marianna Obrist *(Newcastle/Sussex University, UK)*
Pablo Cesar *(CWI, Netherlands)*
Santosh Basapur *(Institute of Design, IIT, USA)*

Steering Committee: Pablo Cesar *(CWI, The Netherlands)*
David Geerts *(CUO/iMinds/KU Leuven, BE)*
Jens F. Jensen *(Aalborg University, DK)*
Artur Lugmayr *(Tampere University of Technology, Finland)*
Konstantinos Chorianopoulos *(Ionian University, Greece)*
George Lekakos *(Athens University of Economics and Business, Greece)*
Marianna Obrist *(Newcastle/Sussex University, UK)*
Hendrik Knoche *(Aalborg University, DK)*

Associate Chairs: Xavier Amatriain *(Netflix, USA)*
Frank Bentley *(Yahoo! Labs, USA)*
Petter Bae Brandtzæg *(SINTEF, Norway)*
Rodrigo Laiola Guimarães *(IBM Research, Brazil)*
Mike Darnell *(Samsung SRA, USA)*
Aisling Kelliher *(Carnegie Mellon University, USA)*
Diego Martinez *(University of Bristol, UK)*
Florian 'Floyd' Mueller *(RMIT University, Australia)*
Janet Murray *(Georgia Tech, USA)*
Frank Nack *(University of Amsterdam, The Netherlands)*
Omar Niamut *(TNO, The Netherlands)*
Corinna Ogonowski *(University of Siegen, Germany)*
Bhavan Gandhi *(ARRIS, USA)*
Cyril Concolato *(Telecom ParisTech, France)*
Giuseppe Pascale *(Opera Software, Germany)*
Radu-Daniel Vatavu *(University Stefan cel Mare of Suceava, Romania)*
Sara Kepplinger *(Technische Universität Ilmenau, Germany)*
Marco de Sa *(Yahoo! Labs, USA)*
Paul Marrow *(Universität Paderborn, Germany)*
Christian Geiger *(Duesseldorf University of Applied Sciences, Germany)*
Marie-Jose Montpetit *(MIT Media Lab, USA)*
Nuno Correia *(New University of Lisbon, Portugal)*
David Geerts *(KU Leuven, iMinds, Belgium)*
Yiqiang Chen *(Chinese Academy of Sciences, China)*
Teresa Chambel *(LaSIGE, University of Lisbon, Portugal)*

Associate Chairs (continued):

Jean-Claude Dufourd *(Telecom ParisTech, France)*
Takashi Matsumoto *(Kyushu University, Japan)*
Shaun Lawson *(University of Lincoln, UK)*
Niloofar Dezfuli *(Technische Universität Darmstadt, Germany)*

Demo Chairs:

David Ayman Shamma *(Yahoo! Research)*
David Green *(Newcastle University, UK)*

TVX in Industry Chairs:

Mike Evans *(BBC Research and Development, UK)*
Patrick Huber *(Sky Deutschland, DE)*

Workshop Chairs:

Gina Venolia *(Microsoft Research, USA)*
Jonathan Hook *(Newcastle University, UK)*

Inclusion & Accessibility Chairs:

Reuben Kirkham *(Newcastle University, UK)*
Alistair Edwards *(University of York, UK)*

Work in Progress Chairs:

Regina Bernhaupt *(Ruwido, Austria)*
Guy Schofield *(Newcastle University, UK)*

Grand Challenge Chairs:

Ian Kegel *(BT, UK)*
Robert Strzebkowski *(Beuth University, DE)*

Course Chairs:

Maria da Graca Campos Pimentel *(University of Sao Paulo, Brazil)*
Daniela Busse *(Samsung Research, USA)*

Sponsor Chair:

David Geerts *(CUO/iMinds/KU Leuven, BE)*

Doctoral Consortium Chairs:

Hendrik Knoche *(Aalborg University, DK)*
Nicholas Race *(Lancaster University, UK)*

Media Chairs:

Andrew Garbett *(Newcastle University, UK)*
Jochen Huber *(MIT Media Lab, USA)*

Program Committee (continued):

Rene Kaiser
Santosh Kalwar
Amela Karahasanovic
Ian Kegel
Aisling Kelliher
Lyndon Kennedy
Sara Kepplinger
Mohammadreza Khalilbeigi
Jeeeun Kim
Jarrod Knibbe
Hendrik Knoche
Werner Kriechbaum
Artus Krohn-Grimberghe
Rodrigo Laiola Guimarães
Effie Law
Shaun Lawson
Jean-Yves Lawson
Jean Le Feuvre
Young Lee
Alvin Lee
George Lekakos
Judith Liebetrau
Pengfei Lu
Marika Luders
Benedita Malheiro
Matei Mancas
Hiren Mandalia
Marcelo Manzato
Paul Marrow
Diego Martinez Plasencia
Larry Marturano
Judith Masthoff
Takashi Matsumoto
Daniel McDuff
Mark McGill
Richard Medland
Britta Meixner
Erick Melo
Bernard Merialdo
Kate Miltner
Pejman Mirza-Babaei
Antonio Molins
David Monaghan
Andres Monroy-Hernandez
Mario Montagud Climent
Marie-Jose Montpetit
Christiane Moser

Mu Mu
Florian Mueller
Frank Nack
Nitya Narasimhan
Sheau Ng
Omar Niamut
Corinna Ogonowski
Jean Ostrem
Giuseppe Pascale
Celia Quico
Nicholas Race
Stefan Radomski
Umar Rashid
Janet Read
Holger Reckter
Ulrich Reiter
Yosra Rekik
Jan Riemann
Teresa Romão
Remi Ronfard
Stevan Rudinac
Jonathan Ruff
Javier Ruiz-Hidalgo
Alireza Sahami Shirazi
Antti Salovaara
Celso Santos
Mark Schlager
Kai Schubert
Sue Ann Seah
Julian Seifert
David Shamma
Luiz Fernando Soares
Joakim Soderberg
Emilija Stojmenova
Christian Sturm
Steve Szigeti
John Tang
Christian Timmerer
Marko Tkalcic
Konrad Tollmar
Deborah Torres
Pauliina Tuomi
Marian Ursu
Dimitar Valkov
Jan Van den Bergh
M. Oskar van Deventer
Maarten Van Mechelen

TVX2014 Sponsor & Supporters

Sponsor:

Supporters:

Hosted by:

Digital Interaction
at Culture Lab

Interacting with Third-Party Content: Is a Second Screen Enough?

Prof.dr. Dick Bulterman

FX Palo Alto Laboratory & VU University Amsterdam

Abstract

Creating compelling multimedia content is a difficult task. It involves not only the creative process of developing a compelling media-based story, but it also requires significant technical support for content editing, management and distribution. This has been true for printed, audio and visual presentations for centuries. It is certainly true for broadcast media such as radio and television.

A broadcast model of content distribution is based on maximizing the appeal of content while minimizing the 'cost' per viewer. This 'one size fits all' model has lost some of its appeal as more content distribution channels has developed and as an increased desire for content personalization has manifested itself. Simply put, modern content needs to be accompanied by an increased degree of personal interaction with that content.

Several technologies have been developed to increase the degree of personal interaction with content. One of these is the secondary screen: a device that lets users select adjunct information or provide feedback to (and with) other content viewers. At present, the secondary screen helps viewers *discuss* content, but it provides only limited support for *influencing* content. This makes the secondary screen a transitional technology.

An important trend within media production that will likely drive increased content interaction in the future is *content personalization*. Personalization, as considered in this talk, has two aspects: having the viewer transition to being the supplier of content, and having the viewer (in the small) becoming the determinant of content. An example of the first instance is having a viewer of an event share content from this event with others. An example of the second instance is tailoring the content to a particular audience: the story you share with Mom about the event may be different than the version you'd like to share with your friends. (It also may be different from the version you'd like to tell your own children 15 years after the event had taken place.) This makes media interaction a context- and time-sensitive problem. No wonder most researchers analyze media instead of create it!

Permission to make digital or hard copies of part or all of this work for personal or classroom use is granted without fee provided that copies are not made or distributed for profit or commercial advantage, and that copies bear this notice and the full citation on the first page. Copyrights for third-party components of this work must be honored. For all other uses, contact the owner/author(s). Copyright is held by the author/owner(s).

TVX'14, June 25–27, 2014, Newcastle Upon Tyne, UK.
ACM 978-1-4503-2838-8/14/06.
http://dx.doi.org/10.1145/2602299.2603000

The talk will survey several approaches to describe and manage media interactions. We will focus on the temporal modeling of context-sensitive personalized interactions of complex collections of independent media objects. Using the concepts of 'togetherness' being employed in the EU's FP-7 project *TA2: Together Anywhere, Together Anytime*, we will follow the process of media capture, profiling, composition, sharing and end-user manipulation. We will consider the promise of using automated tools and contrast this with the reality of letting real users manipulation presentation semantics in real time.

The talk will not present a closed form solution, but will present a series of topics and problems that can stimulate the development of a new generation of systems to stimulate social media interaction.

Categories and Subject Descriptors

H.4.3 [**Information System Applications**]: Communication Applications - Computer conferencing, teleconferencing, and videoconferencing.

Keywords

Personalization; shared content; media browsing.

Short Bio

Dr. Dick Bulterman is President of the FX Palo Alto Laboratory (FXPAL) and professor of computer science at the VU University in Amsterdam. Before joining FXPAL in 2013, he was a senior researcher at CWI in Amsterdam, where he founded the Distributed Multimedia Languages and Interfaces group. In 1999, he started Oratrix Development BV, a CWI spin-off company that transferred the group's SMIL-based GRiNS software to many parts of the civilized world. Prior to joining CWI in 1988, he was on the faculty of the Division of Engineering at Brown University, where he was part of the Laboratory for Engineering Man/Machine Systems. Dr. Bulterman received a Ph.D. in computer science from Brown University (USA) in 1982. In 2013 he was awarded the ACM SIGMM Lifetime Technical Achievement Award. He is a member of Sigma Xi, the ACM and the IEEE.

Companion Apps for Long Arc TV Series: Supporting New Viewers in Complex Storyworlds with Tightly Synchronized Context-Sensitive Annotations

Abhishek Nandakumar, Janet Murray
Experimental Television Lab
Digital Media Suite,
Georgia Institute of Technology,
Atlanta, GA - 30308
{abhishekn, jmurray} @gatech.edu

ABSTRACT

As television merges with digital technology, storytelling is becoming increasingly complex. Use of a second screen has become common, but academic research has focused on social applications and commercial applications have stressed community-building and trivia questions. Our survey of viewers reveals an unmet need for tightly synchronized second screen applications that can help them to enter and keep track of dramatic series with multiple recurring characters and multi-episode story arcs. We employed an iterative design process to create a second screen companion application for the critically acclaimed series *Justified* that was tightly synchronized, context-sensitive, and character-focused. Our usability testing indicated that use of the companion app enhanced comprehension for first-time viewers of a late season episode, and was especially effective in supporting understanding of character relationships, while also surfacing design considerations for future applications.

Author Keywords

Agency; second screen companion design; narrative; interactive television.

ACM Classification Keywords

H.5.2 [Information Interfaces And Presentation]: User Interfaces - User-centered design.

INTRODUCTION

Television narrative is designed to capture viewers' attention and to preserve their interest through multiple episodes and across seasons. The advent of digital recorders and streaming video sites has made producers more aware of viewers' demand for continuity and consistency across episodes. They have led to the creation of shows with a dozen or more frequently recurring characters and with story arcs that last over and across entire seasons, building toward a multi-year series finale [22]. Viewers are therefore rewarded for close attention and challenged to follow plot developments from episode to episode.

The TV series *Lost* was an important turning point, in which fans created their own online Lostpedia to keep track of characters and events. *Lost* fans included many who identified as "shippers," i.e. viewers interested primarily in the relationships between characters rather than in the science fiction aspects of the story world [9]. The *Lost* writers responded to this interest by expanding the cast of characters, and increasing the possible structures of relationships by creating an alternate timeline. The intense interest in the characters can be seen as an illustration of the psychological theory that narrative is an adaptive cultural practice that allows us to produce mental simulations of human relationships [21, 27]. It is understandable therefore that viewers would be attracted to sustained fictional storyworlds with recurring characters in changing situations, while at the same time needing help in keeping in mind all the character and plot details.

Since the 1980s when television writers started to explore longer-form story arcs that did not resolve at the end of a single weekly episode, TV shows have addressed viewer confusion by starting each new episode with a retrospective montage, introduced by the voice-over words "Previously on….". These recap sequences serve three purposes: to remind regular viewers of events from recent or long past episodes that are particularly relevant to the current episode, to update viewers who have missed some episodes, and to provide new viewers with important context about the show [16]. Our research began with the observation from our own viewing that the short (under 1 minute) recap montage was inadequate to help us follow, as new or regular viewers, an episode of a complex series such as *The Wire, the Sopranos,* or *Mad Men* – exactly the ones that were hailed as important cultural achievements. Through our research, we wanted to see if presenting viewers with context-sensitive streams of synchronized information could improve their understanding of long form narrative. We prototyped a companion second screen application for TV, which viewers could use as they watched a show. For this purpose, we chose the Peabody award winning American FX channel series *Justified* because it had a particularly strong extended story arc over its first season. We also conducted a separate survey about TV viewing habits, which helped us inform our design decisions as we created multiple iterations of the second screen application. In this paper, we document our design research process, and present the results of our survey and usability testing. We then use these results to suggest areas for further research and some tentative design guidelines for the evolving genre of second screen applications.

PREVIOUS WORK
The methods of consumption of television content have changed tremendously in the past ten years. In addition to broadcast and cable television channels and inputs from our DVRs, our televisions now provide us with computational capabilities while being able to host a series of internet-connected applications. Researchers have noted that TV interactivity offers the viewer rich opportunities to edit, share or control the playback compared to traditional, less viewer-active models of production, delivery and consumption [3]. Pablo Cesar and Dick Bulterman identify second screen interaction with TVs as having four major uses: to control, enrich, share, and transfer conventional television content [4]. Popular culture theorist Henry Jenkins also stresses enrichment and sharing, hailing a new age of "convergence media" and "transmedia" storytelling in which the experience of watching TV shows is unchanged, while the content becomes more "spreadable" across platforms, for deeper story development, and beyond corporate control for greater fan participation [13-15]. Similarly, the focus of much second screen research has been on the integration of social media services to accommodate affordances for communication with friends and family [8, 10-13, 20].

As increased bandwidth has made internet streaming more widely available, services like Netflix, Amazon Instant Video, Hulu Plus and Vudu have become popular alternative sources for episodic television content. Recently, Netflix usage accounted for 33% of peak downstream internet traffic [32, 36] in the United States. The proliferation of streaming has seen Smart TVs, and devices like Roku and AppleTV integrate many of these services to bring them from traditional interfaces that use a mouse, keyboard and web browser to the convenience of the 10-foot experience allowing users to browse and consume streaming content on their television. They also provide users with second screen applications on phones and tablets, but their functionality has been limited to social

features and the interaction modes of a traditional remote control – playback and content selection. One such popular application, IntoNow (now Yahoo SmartTV), allows users to sync with a current show and share personalized clips from the show with friends. It also provides them with stats for sports, and information about the cast in movies and TV shows [2, 7]. In addition to streaming content, these devices also allow viewers to use clients for web-hosted media, and interactive applications on their TVs, further blurring the boundaries beyond television-based and computer-based functionality.

But though research and commercial development has tended to focus on computer-based applications as communication devices for sharing or commenting on television content, our work has focused on the computation as a means for navigating complex narrative story structures[20, 23-25]. This is based on a theoretical position that sees the new digital medium as offering the possibility of enhanced human expression through more complex and interactive forms of storytelling [26]. Even before second screen applications for narrative became common, there was some empirical evidence that viewers were looking for greater functionality. For example, in a 2009 study of user practices, viewers asked about the features of DVRs and online streaming expressed a dislike for traditional electronic program guides, and showed interest in a television experience that is more focused on the content [1]. Other studies of television use in the home have suggested that by integrating digital technology with specific television content, designers can provide users with a more synchronized and immersive experience [29, 31].

Within the industry, discussions of interactive television have been characterized for over a decade by reference to the tension between "lean back" and 'lean forward" experiences [33], a genre dispute that has mirrored digital media controversies over games versus narrative. A recent evaluation of game controllers and tablets revealed that users prefer TV interaction modes that do not require mastery, and are therefore less likely to result in user error [6]. Industry leaders have been drawn closer to interaction as they have seen it as a source of additional revenue and a means of demonstrating audience involvement to advertisers, and they have favored applications that require a single button click often based on multple choice answers with immediate feedback. Network-affiliated application designers have used synchronized second screens to elicit the users' input in trivia tests, guesses about future plot developments, or expressions of allegiance to one character or another [6, 28]. For example, the second screen application for the TV show *Leverage* from Turner Networks tests users' knowledge of story details, such as where a particular went to school or what they are most afraid of, and provides quick polls with immediately tabulated results [38]. Another approach for synchronized content is to provide viewers with alerts that link to explanatory or production information about something just

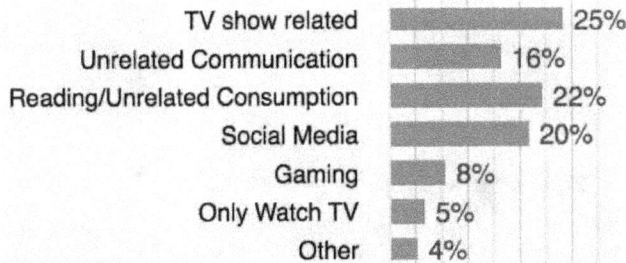

Fig 1.a. Second screen usage distribution.

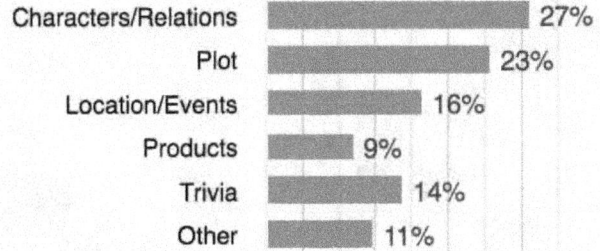

Fig 1.b. Categories of show-related searches.

seen. The HBO Go application [37], available on desktops and mobile devices for showing television content to subscribers across platforms, offers a card-like sidebar for longer annotations synchronized with streamed content. Viewers can pause an episode of *Game of Thrones,* to read a paragraph about one of main characters or view a short video about the production process for one of the intricate fantasy-medieval weapons. The HBO Go application also allows viewers to lean back and watch the show uninterruptedly and then browse through the stack of annotations separately. Though these annotations are synchronized with the TV show, the character descriptions are general and not contextualized to the particular episode or dramatic moment, and the production information, like much of the trivia content common to second screen applications, often breaks the fourth wall by calling attention to the production process or the actors rather than focusing on the fictional world and the characters[5].

In short, companion applications for long-form television narratives offer a rich field for interaction design that is at an early stage of development, both commercially and as a focus of research. Existing conventions for synchronized content raise questions of immersion and agency, of what to provide and how to provide it, that go beyond the current landscape of social networking, trivia questions, and generic "enhancements." One way to address these questions is by designing research prototypes that provide a finer granularity of narrative reference, and a more explicit recognition of the increasing complexity of television narrative than currently available. Building on the increasing convergence of television and computation but free of the limitations of any particular delivery platform or revenue model, academic design teams have the opportunity to focus on the intersection of narrative curiosity and interaction design.

TV VIEWING HABITS AND SECOND SCREEN USE
To be able to better understand what kinds of information viewers seek about shows they follow, we designed a web survey with 20 questions about television viewing habits. Members of the lab shared the survey over email, Facebook and Twitter. We captured the following information: demographics, the number of hours spent watching TV

content, content genres and categories, whether individuals used cable, DVRs or streaming services, the major use cases of second screens (smartphones, tablets or computers) with TV (see fig 1.), the nature of company and social interactions, habits of re-watching television, the kind of information viewers tried to seek online, and a wish list of what viewers felt they might want to find more easily.

We had 98 responses to our survey with 63% male and 37% female respondents, from a variety of age groups with 45% being between ages 17 and 30, 27% being between ages 31 and 40, 23% between ages 41 and 60 and 4% above the age of 60. We tried to gauge the frequency with which TV viewers used website resources to follow TV shows. We asked respondents about how they resumed watching a show after having missed previous episodes. 34% said that they tried to infer the story and characters from the context of the episode they had resumed watching the show from, 24% looked up resources on the web, 22% would simply watch previous episodes, 10% asked peers who followed the show for an explanation, and 10% stopped following the show. 66% of respondents said that they liked to watch TV episodes more than once. We asked them why they liked to watch episodes again: 40% said they did because their quality was predictable, 33% watched it to see important details they felt they had missed, 17% did to introduce the show to someone else and 10% used liked to keep their favorite shows on in the background as they did other work.

We also found out that 81% of our respondents were accustomed to using second screens in front of their televisions, and 86% used online resources for the specific purpose of getting more information about shows they followed, either during or after the show. Wikipedia, IMDB and other show-specific wikis were the primary sources for information about plots and characters. Half of all respondents wished they had an easier way to find character and plot information for specific episodes of TV shows they were watching. 65% of participants preferred to use on-demand content and online streaming over traditional cable network access. According to our survey, email and social media usage accounted for 20% of second screen interaction, and 25% of all second screen interaction

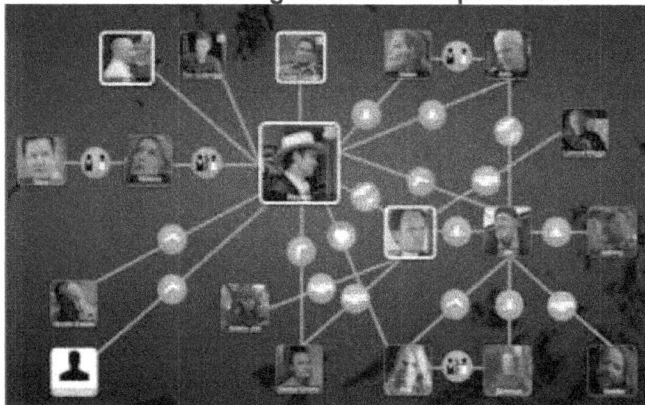

Fig 2.a. Story map of Justified Episode 11.

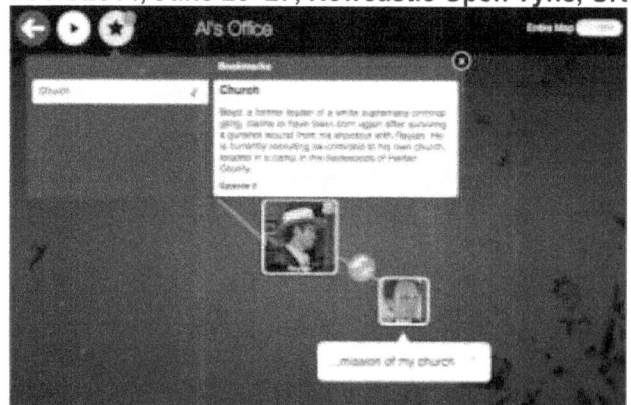

Fig 2.b. Annotations of specific events in a scene.

focused on communication or information retrieval specifically about the show.

DESIGN OF SECOND SCREEN

The goal of our second-screen application was to provide useful information to viewers of a complex television drama in a synchronized second-screen experience that would not disrupt the viewing experience. We chose the show *Justified* (Season 1) [34] because it displayed a consistent story world with many recurring characters and a season-long story arc over a manageable 13-episode season. *Justified* was run by a head writer/producer Graham Yost whom we interviewed about his writing approach. Yost described the process as setting out a five act structure over the course of the season, with a turning point in the middle of the third act[35]. In interviews with us and with others he described his fidelity to the novelistic world of Elmore Leonard, whose crime novels were widely respected for their depiction of memorable characters in well-observed dialog. The lead character of *Justified,* Raylan Givens, appears in several of Leonard's works [17-19] .

We began by prototyping a version of the application that included synchronized information to accompany the most exposition-heavy introductory scene of the first episode and the last action sequence of the last episode. For the early scene we demonstrated the helpfulness of displaying character images on the second screen to reflect who was in the scene and also who they referred to, together with spatial cues that indicated the relationship of the characters to one another. For the final scene we demonstrated the appropriateness of a recap of a crucial story-thread involving the hero, Raylan, and the anti-hero, Boyd, since

the first season ends with a very meaningful and dramatic interaction between them, which would make a regular viewer want to go back and see some of the earlier scenes again. We demonstrated these functionalities to eTV researchers and industry visitors [23], and the response encouraged us to annotate a complete episode.

We focused on episode 11 since it focused on the longer story arc, and drew on considerable knowledge of previous episodes. As we annotated episode 11, we used a timeline spreadsheet to list all characters on screen or referred to in dialog as the episode progressed. As for our earlier prototype, we translated this chart into a story map, using photo thumbnails to represent characters, along with the combination of lines and iconography between two characters to describe their relationship (see figure 2.a.). A character was displayed on the iPad only if they were present or mentioned in the current scene of the episode. Tapping on a character on the second screen allowed viewers to see a short character description.

We conducted a pilot session with 4 participants. Each participant was a member of our lab, but had never watched *Justified* before. It was observed that participants were unable to follow the story despite having names and descriptions available for each character, and having them displayed in groups that separated the lawmen from the outlaws, with icons showing family relationships and who was fighting with whom.

We realized that we had to increase the depth and granularity of our annotation to support new viewers. For our second prototype of Episode 11 we added context-sensitive descriptions of the characters' situation that

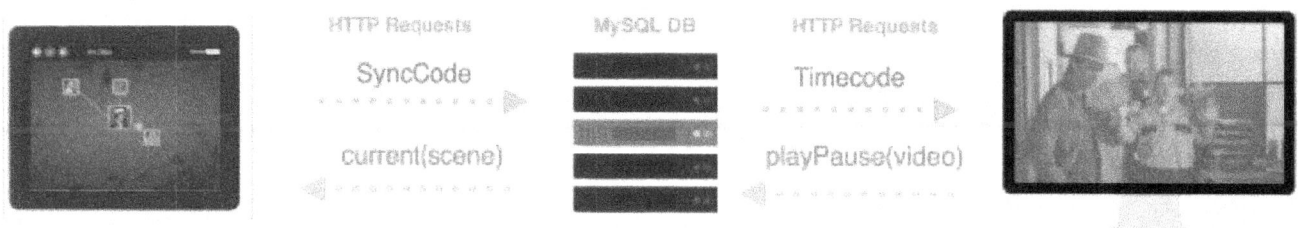

Figure 3. Communication between components used to build prototype of second screen experience.

changed as the episode progressed, as well as brief video montages that introduced the characters with key moments from earlier episodes. We also added annotations to explain confusing references in the dialog with either text or, when necessary, with more video montages. We limited these montages to three minutes, which had long been our own rule of thumb in the lab, and has recently been reported as the YouTube ideal as well [30].

One of our design goals while creating this application was to maintain agency – to provide viewers with useful information about the show through the companion application without trying to move their attention away from the show. In our second prototype, we focused on moments when the viewer would experience confusion or curiosity because of a specific story beat, such as a dramatic reference to an unsolved crime. For each such curiosity-inducing story beat, we used a speech callout icon quoting the key part of the dialog (see figure 2.b.). When the viewer tapped the callout, we provided them with information about the event to be able to continue watching the show. Viewers who chose to learn more about a particular character could tap on their image on the map to access the relevant video montage. The TV was paused automatically for the duration that the montage was played back on the iPad, and then automatically resumed.

TECHNICAL IMPLEMENTATION
We used an Sony Smart TV with Android OS and an iPad to prototype our second screen design. The TV application and the iPad application were both developed using HTML5, CSS3 and JavaScript. We also developed a server application using MySQL and PHP which formed the data store to synchronize timing information between the TV and iPad applications. As the video played back on the TV, the HTML5 video player would send video time codes to the server(see figure 3). The iPad application queried the server and used these time codes to display information that was relevant to and in sync with the current state of the episode being played back.

The iPad application used a local database to retrieve information based on time codes from the episode being played back. One database table listed all the events mentioned in the show, the characters appearing or being mentioned in each episode as well as how the relationships

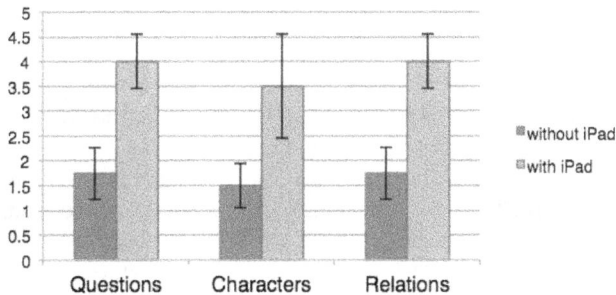

between these characters changed as the show progressed. A separate table was created in the database to describe events and related pieces of backstory, along with links to video montages created from previous episodes to provide viewers with more context about each event. The tables contained information about the characters on screen, as well as about the characters and events mentioned throughout the episode. Each table had a column, which provided a range of time codes between which corresponding information would be made available on the second screen. When information about a past event or backstory was mentioned in the show, a speech bubble appeared with a link which when tapped would display a short description as well as an optional short video clip about the event. If the viewer chose to watch the video clip, the iPad application requested that the TV application pause playback. After pausing playback, the video on the iPad would start playing back. During resumed playback, as new events were shown in callouts, previous descriptions and video about events were archived and available for access from the annotations menu. The annotations menu used the TV timecode to display information about events only if they had already occurred. This design decision was made consciously to prevent information about the show from being revealed prematurely. This information became available only after viewers saw relevant portions of the story unfold as the episode progressed.

PRELIMINARY USABILITY TESTING
We invited 8 participants who had never seen the show before to participate in our usability testing sessions. The participants were required to watch twenty minutes of *Justified, Season 1 Episode 11 with our application,* and then to answer questions about the episode. To gauge the utility of the application, we invited 8 additional participants to watch the show as they normally would. All participants were students who frequently used another device while watching television. Participants were compensated with a $5 Starbucks gift card for their time. The questionnaire included 17 questions about specific events in the episode, along with additional questions about specific user preferences while using the application. The group without the companion app did poorly in answering questions about the story segments they had just viewed, with an average of 4.9/17 correct answers. None of these participants chose to look up information online while watching the show. When we asked participants about this, they responded by saying, "...won't want to break away from the show to find that...", "...it takes too much time.", and "...usually get more info during commercials...". The group that used the companion app did much better (11.5/17 correct answers), and showed particularly good scores in identifying the relationships between the characters with 4/5 correct answers compared to 1.7/5 for those without the iPad (see figure 4).

On asking participants to rate how helpful they found the iPad application on a scale of 1 to 10 (with 10 being the most helpful) responses averaged 5.2. Participants said that while they found the iPad extremely useful in being able to understand the context of the show, they found it less helpful because of the test environment, and they rated its distraction effect as 3.1 on a scale of 1 to 10, with 10 the most distracting. One participant said, "I find myself looking up characters all the time. Not holding it in my hand but having it ready by my side would make it very helpful. More so, than in this study." Testers felt that in normal usage, they would not have been as conscious about the iPad application, and used it only when there was a moment of curiosity. It is important to note that while the group with the iPad rated the helpfulness of the second screen as 5.2/10, 7 out of 8 participants also used words like "very helpful" and "extremely useful" to describe the application. Participants acknowledged that they would normally seek this information during commercial breaks or after an episode had ended. For comparison, one participant described the 'HBO Go' application: "…it provides some information for Game of Thrones, but relationships are important…it does not describe them at all.". Users found the synchronized relationships and event montages the most useful features in the application.

We asked participants for which shows they wanted such an experience to be made available. The top three responses were Mad Men, Game of Thrones and ESPN.

DISCUSSION

The application proved most effective in increasing comprehension of the relationships between the characters. This is consistent with the theoretical position that fictional narratives allow us to create mental simulations of human relationships[22, 27]. It also is consistent with the "shipper" internet activity around *Lost,* and the responses of surveyed viewers who reported that characters were a major focus of their show-related second screen use.

It was also evident from the survey and the usability testing that in addition to getting additional information about key characters and their relationships over the course of the season, viewers wanted to be able to find specific plot details relevant to the present dramatic situation of the show. They wanted efficient summaries of previous events that contextualized the action they were watching without "spoilers" giving away plot developments they had not yet seen.

Summarizing the features of our application that users described as helpful:

1. **Annotations:** New viewers were able to instantly identify characters in the show, and to understand dialog allusions to previous events by calling up short text explanations. This feature was used spontaneously by all the testers, and helped provide context when there were references from previous episodes.

2. **Video montage for key events:** When short text descriptions were insufficient to provide context, users were able to call up a 3-minute clip that replayed important segments of previous episodes that provided background for the action. Users responded positively to the feature saying things like "…ah so that's what they meant", and "I had no idea about that murder before this".

3. **Video montage for important characters:** For users who had never seen or read about the series, episode 11 presented a challenge because of the complex relationships among the characters, in a fictional world in which family members, lovers and friends were often on different sides of the law, and actively deceiving one another. The relationships were too complex to be summarized with the rapid clips of a typical "Previously on" review, the standard for non-interactive television. The Story Map home screen linked characters with expressive icons like a gun or a heart which led to relationship-focused video montages that offered key dramatic scenes between the two characters leading up to the current action. Viewers were particularly interested in understanding relationships, because they did not think that current websites and synchronized applications are sufficiently helpful: "ABC doesn't explain anything, HBO does…but you have to keep searching…" and "…you can even see characters change through the season".

4. **Expanded Map:** The application provided an option, which displayed the entire map of character relationships in that episode. New viewers were able to understand how certain characters were more important to the show than others by looking at the number of relationship lines fanning out from each character. While looking at the entire map, one user immediately described Raylan as a "…character who must be central to the show". Another user appreciated the feature saying, "the visual overview tells me who plays a bigger role…whom to pay attention to".

Among the problems that we are correcting in future designs are:

1. Viewers who paused the show to view the video montages and found them valuable wanted to gain the information more quickly. Some of the responses we received for the character montages were "helpful in understanding a character's motivations", "that explains why Boyd behaves like that". When asked about the length of the montages, a common suggestion was to limit them to "less than 30 seconds". The longest continuous interaction with the iPad in the TV show's paused state was 48 seconds. These requests suggest that their model is the "Previously on" television convention. On the other hand, craft practice would suggest longer intervals of 2.5 to 3 minutes for on-demand video such as

YouTube segments [30]. We see this as an area for further research.

2. Viewers wanted control of when the TV video stopped and started, rather than having it stop automatically when they clicked on a video on the iPad. They were concerned that stopping the main video would be too disruptive if they were watching it with someone else. Users liked the option of a pause button on the application, which could be used while interacting with the iPad. They wanted a control that allowed them to enable or disable automatic pause/playback. They said the decision to use this feature would also depend on whether or not they were watching TV alone. When they had others watching TV with them, they said they would prefer to turn automatic pausing off, so that they do not disrupt the experience for other viewers. This result is consistent with the design goal of maximizing user agency. We had considered a bookmarking feature but disabled it for this round of testing. The testers' responses point to the importance of supporting story comprehension in viewers watching in groups with varying familiarity. Future research will examine various strategies for meeting this need including bookmarking, and more efficient and perhaps silent montage strategies.

When users resumed playback of content, they wanted to be able to move back the play head, so that they are able to hear any important dialog that they paused midway. In addition to being able to rewind the video, they wanted the ability to jump to specific scenes in the episode. Users did not want to use an additional remote to access playback, rewind and fast-forward options. While it makes sense that a commercial implementation of the system would include this expected functionality, this request raises further design issues about the future hardware/software configurations.

CONCLUSION
Our prototyping and testing confirmed the survey results that users would welcome second screen applications that helped them to enter long-form TV narratives mid-season or to follow them from the beginning with the close attention of the habitual viewer. We are optimistic that with further research and refinement of design, the kinds of aids tested here can provide viewers with contextualized information on a second screen that directly reflects the events, characters, and relationships enacted or referred to at the synchronized moment in a non-distracting manner with viewers free to pursue greater depths of information as needed.

Data from our survey reinforced the observations we made in testing this system, which we present as a tentative set of guidelines for the design of tightly synchronized companion applications:

1. **Opt-in interruptions:** While designing second screen interactions, it is important to give users complete control over playback to minimize disruption during a shared TV viewing experience. This includes providing the user with an option to choose whether or not to automatically pause the show while interacting with the second screen for extended periods of time.

2. **Companion experience synchronized with present context.** Presenting users with an opt-in companion that aids viewers during moments of curiosity is helpful in maintaining agency. Additionally, the companion should "listen" to the show, and display information relevant to the events and characters in the current episode's context to minimize time spent in navigation and search by the user.

3. **Emphasis on characters (like many online aids now provide) and relationships between characters (which our application added):** In order to do this effectively, with the right level of context-sensitive detail and without spoilers, it is important to have a framework that updates with each episode and even with scenes within an episode. This is becoming more challenging but also more needed by viewers as television series expand the casts of significant continuing characters.

4. **Events:** Provide concise descriptions of events that have taken place in the past if they are explicitly referred to in dialog.

5. **Social Context:** Take into account the situation in which multiple simultaneous co-located viewers have different knowledge levels, and no one can stop the playing of the current episode without impacting the experience of the others.

The last two areas offer rich possibilities for future research focused on the widely available and often used second screens of current television viewers. Other more general areas that are promising for further design research are the differences in narrative mental models between new viewers, habitual viewers, and committed fans re-viewing a familiar episode; overview strategies for representing relationships with readable spatial arrangements and iconography; strategies for navigating discrete story threads within a multi-threaded story world; and integration of social television applications with narrative-focused applications. In addition the strategies that we are researching could be investigated in the framework of non-fictional television forms such as news or historical documentaries, and from the vantage point of the creators of long-form episodic story worlds, who, like their viewers, are increasingly challenged by the complexity of twenty-first century storytelling.

REFERENCES
1. Barkhuus, L. and B. Brown. Unpacking the television: User practices around a changing technology. In ACM Transactions on Computer-Human Interaction (TOCHI) (2009). 16(3): p. 15.

2. Blanco, R., Morales, G.D.F, Silvestri, F. Towards leveraging closed captions for news retrieval. In Proc. WWW 2013 (Companion V olume), pp.135-136.

3. Cesar, P. and K. Chorianopoulos. The evolution of TV systems, content, and users toward interactivity. In Found. Trends Hum.-Comput. Interact (2013). . 2, 4, 373-95

4. Cesar, P., D.C.A. Bulterman, and A.J. Jansen. Usages of the secondary screen in an interactive television environment: control, enrich, share, and transfer television content, in Changing television environments. Springer (2008). p. 168-177

5. Chuang, Y.-L., et al. Use Second Screen t Enhance TV Viewing Experiences, in Cross-Cultural Design. Methods, Practice, and Case Studies. Springer (2013). p. 366-374.

6. Cox, D., Wolford, J., Jensen, C., & Beardsley, D. An evaluation of game controllers and tablets as controllers for interactive tv applications. In Proc. ICMI 2012. (pp. 181-188). ACM (2012).

7. Doughty, M., Rowland, D, Lawson, S. Who is on your sofa?: TV audience communities and second screening social networks. In Proc. EuroiTV 2012. ACM Press (2012).

8. Geerts, D. and D. De Grooff.. Supporting the social uses of television: sociability heuristics for social TV. In proc. CHI 2009, ACM Press (2009).

9. Geisler, G., G. Willard, and C. Ovalle, A crowdsourcing framework for the production and use of film and television data. New Review of Hypermedia and Multimedia, 2011. 17(1): p. 73-97.

10. Harboe, G., et al. Ambient social tv: drawing people into a shared experience, In Proc. CHI 2008, ACM Press (2008).

11. Hess, J., et al. Jumping between devices and services: towards an integrated concept for social tv. In Proc. 2012 EuroITV 2011, ACM Press (2011).

12. Hess, J., et al. Bridging among people, places & devices by integrated, ambient and playful socialmedia approaches. In Proc. EuroiTV 2010, ACM Press (2010).

13. Jenkins, H., Transmedia storytelling. Volume (1) (2009). p. 56.

14. Jenkins, H. Convergence culture: Where old and new media collide. NYU press (2006).

15. Jenkins, H., et al. Spreadable media: Creating value and meaning in a networked culture. NYU Press (2012).

16. Lesser, W. How TV Tells Us What Went Before, in The New York Times (2013).

17. Leonard, E. Pronto. HarperCollins (2009).

18. Leonard, . Riding the rap. HarperCollins (2009).

19. Leonard, E. Raylan. Hachette UK (2012).

20. Lochrie, M., Coulton, P. Mobile phones as second screen for TV, enabling inter-audience interaction. In Proc. ACE 2011, Article 73, ACM Press (2011)

21. Mar, R.A. and K. Oatley, The function of fiction is the abstraction and simulation of social experience. Perspectives on psychological science, 2008. 3(3): p. 173-192.

22. Mittell, J., Narrative complexity in contemporary American television. The Velvet Light Trap, 2006. 58(1): p. 29-40.

23. Murray, J., et al. 2012. Story-map: iPad companion for long form TV narratives. In Proc. of Euro ITV 2012, ACM,Press 223-226.

24. Murray, J., Goldenberg, S., et al. StoryLines: an approach to navigating multisequential news and entertainment in a multiscreen framework. In Proc. ACE 2011, ACM Press (2011).

25. Murray, J. Transcending transmedia: emerging story telling structures for the emerging convergence platforms. In Proc. EuroiTV 2012. ACM Press(2012).

26. Murray, J. Hamlet on the Holodeck: The future of narrative in cyberspace. Simon and Schuster (1997).

27. Oatley, K. 2011. Such stuff as dreams: the psychology of fiction. Wiley-Blackwell.

28. Simon, H., E. Comunello, and A. von Wangenheim. Enrichment of Interactive Digital TV using Second Screen. International Journal of Computer Applications, 2013. 64(22): p. 58-64.

29. Simons, N. Television audience research in the age of convergence: challenges and difficulties. In Proceedings of the 9th international interactive conference on Interactive television (pp. 101-104). ACM Press (2011).

30. Stark, C. What's the ideal length for a YouTube video? Stark Insider (2013).

31. Tsekleves, E., et al. Investigating media use and the television user experience in the home. In Entertainment computing, 2011. 2(3): p. 151-161

32. Vance, A. 2013. Netflix, Reed Hastings Survive Missteps to Join Silicon Valley's Elite, in Bloomberg Businessweek (2013).

33. Winkle, P.V. Lead Us Not Into Temptation: The Second Screen Addiction, in Oz Magazine. Oz Publishing, Inc (2013).

34. Yost, G. Justified, FX Network (2010-now)

35. Yost, G. Culver City Interview with J. Murray, Feb 18, 2012

36. Global Internet Phenomena. Sandvine Report.

37. HBO GO. Game of Thrones Interactive Experience (2013).

38. Leverage app for iOS and Android. Turner Broadcasting(2012). http://www.tntdrama.com/series/leverage/display/?cont entId=244273

Enhancing Interactive Television News

Dan R. Olsen Jr., Benjamin Sellers, Trent Boulter
Computer Science Department, Brigham Young University
olsen@cs.byu.edu, bsellers@gmail.com, trentboulter@gmail.com

ABSTRACT

A prototype system for interactive television news is described. It supports the full production cycle for interactive news, including assembly of clips into stories and stories into newscasts. A variety of interactive techniques are offered to the viewer. These include expressing likes and dislikes of headlines, skipping out of stories, requesting additional content and selection of stories from a menu. This system was deployed into homes for two weeks using fresh television content. User control events were logged and evaluated to understand interactive viewing behavior.

Author Keywords
Interactive Television; Television News; Network Video;

ACM Classification Keywords
H.5.1 Multimedia Information Systems

INTRODUCTION
This paper describes an interactive television news service that was delivered over the network into the homes of test users. This is the second such trial that we have performed. In the first effort [10] it was clear the people liked and used the interactivity. However, a variety of failings were identified. We completely redesigned the system to address these challenges. In this paper we report our response to earlier insights and the resulting behavior when actually used in homes. We have also redone the production process to exploit the capabilities of internet television.

The system we will describe here provides interactivity in three basic ways:

1. Story-by-story choice of what to watch
2. Ability to skip out of a story at any time
3. Ability to dive deeper into additional material on a particular topic

With a technology such as interactive television, a laboratory experiment is not appropriate. Television is engaged with the way people live. In particular, television news must be fresh in order to realistically engage viewers.

Because of these requirements, in-home deployments of such systems are highly important to user interface design

experimentation. In this work, we deployed into 10 homes and logged the viewers' interactive behavior. The results are formative rather than summative but provide important insights into the structure of such interactive systems.

We have pursued two key questions:

1. What software architecture is required to produce an interactive newscast? News is not only interactively consumed but must be realistically produced.

2. What are the interactive usage patterns during viewing? Previously, viewers made little use of the additional material we provided. In this work, we have tried different interaction techniques and produced much higher utilization.

An additional question for interactive television is revenue. We largely ignored this issue. We removed all advertising from our experiments. We did, however, assume that longer viewing time would mean more revenue either in advertising or in subscription shares.

PREVIOUS WORK

There have been a variety of studies that have shown that television and the Internet are converging [5]. Studies show that there is significant consumer interest in more interactive television experiences [11].

News interaction as an algorithm
Informedia [3] pioneered an approach that framed the news experience as an information retrieval problem. Their work was focused on extracting appropriate information from a variety of sources that could be used to retrieve video for user consumption.

Similarly, the MyInfo[13] project used speech recognition, closed captions and features extracted from the video itself to automatically segment a newscast into stories. Based on their recognition algorithms, they would perform web searches to find additional material to augment the story. The user interacts with this system by selecting materials from a play list.

In a similar vein, the MyNewsMyWay[6] project used a profile of viewer interests. The system would then match the profile against news stories to select what was viewed. From the point of view of news producers there is little control of the experience or the story. It is simply a matter of adding tags for the algorithms to exploit. The "News at Seven" project [xx] also provides algorithms for generating the news.

There are many examples of technologies which automatically or semi-automatically process video to produce an experience that provides a viewer with a choice of what to watch. Image processing and video technology proceedings are full of such papers. We have three problems with this algorithmic approach.

The first is that many of these systems assume that news lives in a historical database as simple video files. Real news is fresh. It is current. It is about what is happening in the world now. That is why it is called the news. Secondly, there is no need for automated segmentation of a newscast. The news is created in segments. It is only assembled as a whole at the last minute when broadcast. Rather than use unreliable recognition problems on assembled newscasts we modified the news production process to capture segmentation at the source. Lastly, the news is a human-to-human experience. Viewers develop para-social relationships with newscasters [4]. It is a process of news professionals gathering, filtering, summarizing and humanizing the facts of the world [1]. Algorithms do not do this well.

Interactive video
The BBC [8] introduced a limited form of interactive video using standard broadcast channels. The Red Button on their remote control allows them to skip among a fixed number of different news feeds.

A notable attempt to move away from algorithms and into a more creative and interactive model is Hyper-Hitchcock [2]. In this system the user is presented with a timeline of the current video. Below the timeline, viewers are shown thumbnails of other linked videos that are related to that portion of the core video. The essential idea is hyperlinking sections of a video to other video. The Hyper-Hitchcock approach is very general in its applicability but not focused specifically on the news experience. It did, however, strongly influence our work.

Our previous experiment
The work reported in this paper is an outgrowth of [10]. In the prior work, a major local news station was recruited and consented to modify their news production processes for one week. The body of the interactive news was a sequence of stories ordered by the headline responses. While watching, the primary control was to skip out of a story early and move on to the next story. In addition, viewers had access to a play list of all of the stories so that they could select what they wanted directly. On stories for which additional material was provided, a label would appear in the upper left corner of the screen indicating the presence of additional material. The viewer could then select to watch this material.

The production system worked well and did not impede the newsroom processes. Reporters were somewhat reluctant to spend much effort on creating the additional material. They were supportive of the experiment but did not see this as part of their job. This resulted in only 21% of the stories having any additional material and some of the material was of low quality.

We deployed computers running our viewer software into 10 homes and recorded their interactive behavior. The interactive viewing mechanism was a success and is reused in this experiment. Users performed some form of news navigation every 79 seconds on average, which indicated a high level of engagement. The most common form of interaction was to skip to the next story.

The use of additional story content was very low. We believed that this was due to:

- relative rarity of additional content,
- low quality of some of the content,
- the label indicating the content was easily missed
- the whole idea of additional content is unexpected

PROJECT STRATEGY

In this project, we wanted to explore new ways to get viewers to watch additional content. Watching extra news content is important not only because we believe it enriches the viewer's experience but for financial reasons. If the primary interactive behavior is for viewers to skip over news content, then the total news viewing time is reduced. In most revenue models, lower viewing time means lower income. Lower viewing time means watching less advertising. In subscription systems, lower viewing time means a smaller share of the subscription income.

In this project we addressed two main issues. The first was to create a deeper, richer and more collaborative model for interactive news production. The second was to increase the amount of additional material that was viewed. To achieve this we wanted to greatly enrich the quantity and kind of additional material. The reporter-generated material is still possible in our new system, but we focused on two other kinds of material: stories from competitive news programs and historical material. Because the video lives on a server, all of the prior news stories can be stored and made available. If a particular dictator is being toppled today, there are probably previous stories on that country and that individual.

Our key production contributions are 1) new sources and styles of interactive content to draw viewers into that content and 2) a more open and collaborative model for acquiring news content for delivery.

SYSTEM ARCHITECTURE
The news production workflow is shown in Figure 1. Video feeds come from a variety of sources including reporters, competitors, contributing newsmakers or others. This reflects more of the way newscasts are currently assembled than the way in which they are presented.

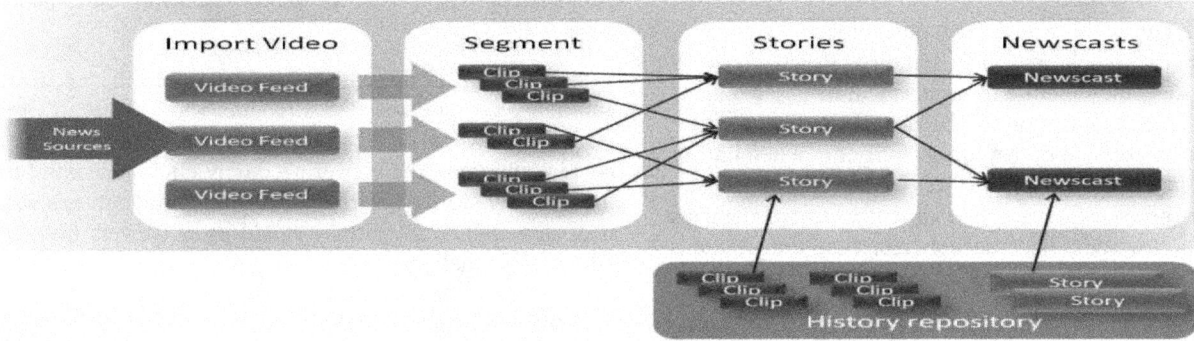

Figure 1 – Newscast production flow

Segmentation

Video feeds are segmented into clips, which consist of a video feed and a start and end point within that feed. Video can be chopped into many clips to be used for a variety of purposes. Clips may also overlap because the video is not actually cut.

Stories and newscasts

Clips are then assembled into stories and stories are assembled into newscasts. The assembly of stories and newscasts are where newscasters exert their creative influence. They can add clips from their own video feeds and juxtaposition various viewpoints when creating a coherent story. The collection of stories into newscasts creates a particular view of today's world.

If the video feed and clip databases are generally available under suitable revenue sharing terms, it now becomes possible for a newscaster to have no news reporting staff at all. A possible newscaster role would be to select and interpret from material made available by others. News based on a large (possibly national or international) news repository rather than video tape and broadcast channels can radically change the way television news is crafted. This contributory model for assembling the news is sharply different from our previous newscast-centric approach.

The contributory model also supports freelance reporters who follow particular interests or regions. They can make contributions to the database of stories from which newscasters can select what they will show and what they will emphasize.

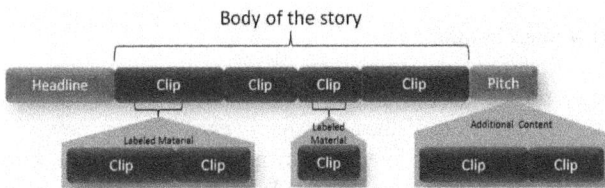

Figure 2 – News story structure

Figure 2 shows the basic structure of a story. The body of the story is composed of a sequence of clips to be played one right after the other. The presence of clips is invisible to the viewer. It just feels like one story. However, to the production team, the assembly from clips is a basic production technique that is currently used in professional news organizations. At the beginning of a story is an optional headline clip. This is played (typically at the beginning of the newscast) to advertise the story and solicit interest. This mirrors the "tease tracks" of most professional newscasts.

There are an optional number of labeled segments that can be attached to a story. The label is descriptive text that is shown to the viewer to invite them to watch some additional material. The label is associated with a time range in the story. The additional material is a sequence of clips. These labels form prompts for the viewer to select additional material.

At the end of the story is an optional pitch clip. The pitch clip is a short segment of video that invites the viewer to watch some additional material. This is new for this system. It mirrors what one sees in many newscasts today where the news anchors will describe additional material and tell viewers that they can reach this material at the news station's web-site. One of our hypotheses was that actively inviting viewers to watch the new material would be more effective than an unobtrusive label.

A story is essentially a data structure which can be created by the production software and traversed by the viewer software.

NEWS PRODUCTION

Our news production tools are web-based with the video stored in the cloud. We used Windows Azure [7] to provide the streaming service. Production of the news is relatively straightforward. Video feeds are uploaded from various sources and transcoded for streaming. At the time of upload, metadata is entered describing the feed's source and subject matter. From there three interleaved processes are used to assemble a news cast.

• Feeds are cut into clips
• Clips are assembled into stories

• Stories are assembled into newscasts

Though Figure 1 shows a sequential process, real news production is asynchronous and iterative. Production of a coherent story may require the adjustment of clip length as well as the acquisition of other material. Production of a particular newscast may require simplifying, extending or creating new stories to fit the overall structure of a particular newscast. Assembly of basic story elements might be followed by news anchors recording introductions and connective commentary to stitch a story together.

Story construction is timeline based. Clips are dropped into the timeline in the order they should appear. This is the most creative part of the news production process. This is where the raw material is formed into a cohesive story.

Headlines
For a given newscast, you only want a subset of the stories to appear in the headlines. If the headlines take too long, the viewer becomes bored with lots of headlines and no solid information. This creative choice is exerted by deciding which stories should have headline clips.

Labeled extra content
One of our hypotheses was that the rarity and novelty of additional content led to low usage in our previous experiments. Because there was so little additional content, people may have just not expected it to be there and may not have been aware of it. For some additional content, we envision a future system where newscast owners and news story creators share revenue. The newscast owner can fill out their offerings with the viewpoints of others at little cost to themselves. This makes their offering much bigger and richer with only a little editing effort.

For a news creator, having their story included in someone else's newscast, even that of a competitor, provides new viewers and new revenue at little additional effort to themselves. Historical content is easily added from the story database of previous newscasts.

To add labeled content, clips or other stories are assembled into the body of the supplementary segment. The supplement is given a textual label and then placed on a time period in the main story's timeline.

One of the challenges faced by those assembling a newscast is locating clips that should be included. There are many services for such searching. Wagner, et. al. [12] provide some interesting insights into how to find stories that provide context. We have focused on assembling the interactive experience.

Pitches
Because of our previous deployment's failure to entice viewers into additional material, we revisited the structure of our interactive television newscasts. Many newscast stories include an invitation for viewers to seek more

information by going to the station's web site. This is a cumbersome idea, but it seems to work for many newscasters.

Our innovation in this system was to embed the pitch for additional content into the structure of the story. Every story can have a pitch at the end with some additional content attached. The viewer need only click the control to immediately see the additional content. Our hypothesis was that such explicit invitations would draw viewers into the additional invitation.

THE VIEWING EXPERIENCE
In prior experiments, users responded that they preferred a one-handed controller rather than two-handed for a more relaxed experience. For our prototype viewing software we used a wireless mouse like that shown in figure 3. We did not use the mouse capabilities, only the buttons.

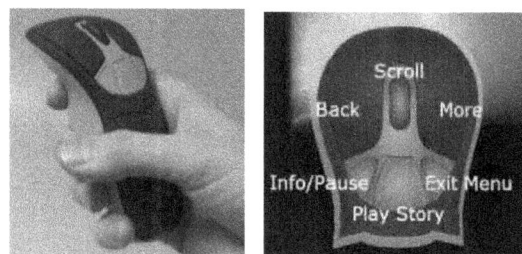

Figure 3 - Interactive Controller

One of the problems with the interactive news is that there are many more options than fit into a simple controller and new viewers have little idea how to get the behavior they want. Also shown in figure 3 is a technique we call *control overlays*, which we had used previously with great success. When the viewer pulls the trigger with their forefinger, an overlay like that shown in figure 3 appears on the screen. The overlay looks similar to the controller, making the mapping intuitive. It is easy for a viewer to pull the trigger; stay focused on the screen and hit the desired button without looking at the controller. In our experience, users learn the controls rapidly and stop using the overlay assistance. As the interactive context shifts we keep analogous functions on the same buttons. Once viewers were told about the trigger, we had no need to give further instruction. Subjects regularly used all of the controls with no help video or other instruction aids.

Newscast headlines
The first form of interaction is when headline clips are being presented. While watching a headline the viewer sees the title and icon. If they pull the overlay trigger they will also see the control overlay shown at the bottom. The icon is a visual reminder of expected actions, with the overlay providing more clarity about what the left and right button will do. A viewer can "like" or "dislike" a story or not act at all. Viewer's actions on headlines are used to reorder the

stories by pulling "liked" stories to the front of the playlist and pushing "disliked" stories to the end. This headline presentation is built dynamically from the newscast's list of stories and the stories that have headline clips.

In-story interaction

After the headlines, the newscast stories are played in order as determined from the viewer's headline preferences. If there is additional material, the title and icon is shown in the upper left. The icon in the upper left also shows the button that will play this content.

Playlist interaction

Another button shows a playlist menu. This shows a list of all of the stories in the newscast. The viewer can scroll through this list and pick particular stories to watch. We specifically included this form of interaction to test viewer preferences. We wanted to see if they would use the more sequential controls like "next" and "previous" or would browse a list for selecting specific stories. Many stories have additional content associated with them. Selecting the additional content brings up an additional menu like that shown in figure 4. These are links to other stories and to historical content from previous newscasts. These links are added manually when producing the interactive newscast. This position of the historical content in the playlist menu impacted some of the results that we report in the next section. Unlike our previous deployment that only provided additional content on a very few stories, we were able to provide additional materials on virtually every story. Many stories had multiple supplements available through the playlist as shown in figure 4.

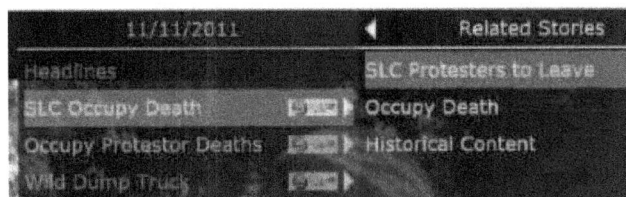

Figure 4 – Additional content from playlist

Pitches

At the end of some stories there can be a video clip inviting viewers to view additional material on the story just completed. A simple click takes the viewer into the additional material from which they can return to the main newscast at any time. We did not have access to news anchor talent to record these pitches. Instead we used a generic pitch clip recorded by a student from the news and communications department. We were concerned our generic prerecorded pitches would reduce their effectiveness. As will be seen in the experimental data, this was not a problem.

DEPLOYMENT

The study of how people use interactive television news is particularly problematic because it is news. The content must be fresh and relevant in order to get any understanding of viewer behavior. The use of news cannot be effectively studied in a laboratory setting because the way people consume their news is very much tied up in how they live their personal lives.

In-home deployments of technology are expensive and cumbersome to carry out. Of necessity, they have a small number of viewers. The result is that the data collected is more formative than summative. Interactive television is in its infancy. We are trying to understand broad directions that can guide more extensive, commercial deployments that will yield more definitive data.

For this trial, we delivered 10 newscasts over a two week period (Monday-Friday). Viewers were provided with the current day's newscast and an archive of the previous 4 newscasts. We kept the archive short so as to not clutter the user interface. Television screen space is a scarce resource. There were two parts to this experiment: 1) the production of an interactive newscast and 2) the in-home viewing of that experience.

News production

Our interactive newscasts were driven by the 5PM news broadcast of KSL television. For several weeks before our trial we recorded the news and chopped it into clips. This formed the basis for our historical content. When we started the trial, we had a historical base of over 1,000 stories. For each story in the newscast, we were able to provide an average of 25 historical stories that were related. This is far richer than what was done in [10]. We chose to create clips from an actual newscast so that our content would be fresh and identical to existing newscasts.

Each night we recorded the KSL news broadcast, converted it to digital form and segmented it into clips and stories. We removed all commercials and all promotions of other television content. The result was that each newscast had between 17 and 25 minutes of news content. Each newscast had between 14 and 22 separate stories. For additional content we used stories from other news channels that provided alternative viewpoints. In our previous study, we provided additional content for 21% of the stories. In this study, 95% of all stories had additional related content.

For the headline clips we used the tease promotions that all television newscasts include. News organizations will frequently promote a story before going to commercial in order to encourage viewers to stay on the channel. We extracted these clips from the newscast and used them for our headline clips. Every newscast had an average of 3.5 headline clips.

Our pitch clips were constructed using still images and voice-overs recorded by students from our university's broadcast communications department. Every newscast had an average of 6.4 pitch clips to invite viewers into additional material.

Production process

Our production process involved recording newscasts from broadcast television. These were digitized and passed to 3 student production assistants who segmented the clips and assembled the stories. A graduate student from broadcast communications served as the producer for our interactive newscasts. None of these production people were from technical fields of study. We wanted to see if non-technical staff could produce interactive news using our tools, without technical training.

We ran news production for two weeks before the in-home trials so that the production team could practice and refine their processes. We found that the tools were easy to learn. What was difficult for the production staff was to understand the structure of an interactive newscast. It took some time to refine the process of collecting, finding and assembling material into a credible interactive form. Nothing in their previous training had taught them how to think about interactivity in the news. The good news is that after the initial two weeks, the process worked smoothly every night. Two weeks of training seems like a small cost. We are confident that these processes would be easy to teach within a standard broadcast communications curriculum.

Each night the process began with the 5PM broadcast. We delivered an interactive newscast by 8PM. We did not actually need the full three hours but we wanted to promise our viewers a specific availability time that we knew we could meet. 8PM is also a better time for a more focused interactive experience than 5PM.

The primary cause of production delay was the time required to digitize, upload and convert the video. We know from prior work that this time can be sharply reduced by more specialized equipment than we had available.

Home deployments

Our equipment and staffing required that we limit our trial to 10 homes. We sent out a survey through email and social network contacts reaching over 2,000 people in our geographic area. Of these, 128 met our criteria of being older than 18 (we were not interested in children's news) and willing to participate. Most of those we contacted were not willing to participate. From these 128 we chose 10 that had good internet connections in their home, were easily accessible for hardware installations and reported an active interest in television news. To simulate a set-top box with appropriate software we used a Dell Studio or a Mac Mini depending on the kinds of connections available on their television. This was connected to their primary television.

A summary of the viewer data that we collected is shown in figure 5. Out of the 10 installations, 8 actually watched the news. During the first week, 7 watched and 8 watched during the second week. Though the other 2 agreed to watch and accepted an installation, they never turned it on. Every day of the 10-day trial, we sent emails to each

participant, reminding them of the availability of the news at 8PM.

Homes deployed	10	
Days of news	10	
Sessions watched	96	
View minutes per newscast	10.5	52%
View minutes of additional content	1.4	
Stories with additional content		95%
Pitches activated		55%
Prompts activated		23%
Pitches per newscast	6.4	
Playlist selections		22%
Headlines per newscast	3.5	
Headlines rated		84%
PlayNext selection		77%
PlayPrevious selection		8%
Playlist selection		15%

Figure 5 – Summary of data collected

Because our interactive newscast uses HTTP-based protocols, it is easy for us to track and log all interactivity on a per-home basis. We segmented the log data into sessions. A session lasted from the time a viewer started a particular newscast until they left that newscast. We discarded any session of less than 1 minute of viewing. We assumed that such viewing was some kind of a false start rather than actual viewing. During the first week we logged 51 sessions and during the second week we logged 45.

Figure 6 shows the dates of the various newscasts (x axis) and the times when those newscasts were actually viewed (y axis). There is a mark for every unique session. Marks on the diagonal show normal viewing just as the news is available. However, a large amount of the viewing is much later than the actual availability. There is a very strong pattern of viewers watching news when it is convenient for them rather than on schedule. This is true even when the news is more than a day old. Of particular interest are the horizontal patterns. These are people watching several newscasts at the same time. The red dots are one individual watching a lot of news (much of it a week old) at the same time. The average session was viewed 35 hours after its original production. There is a clear pattern of finding a convenient time and then "getting caught up." A possible alternative interpretation of the data is that viewers felt guilty about not watching as they agreed. Post experiment interviews supported the "getting caught up" interpretation. This may be encouraged by the fact that they can readily skip news that they are already aware of, spending catch up time only on what they truly missed.

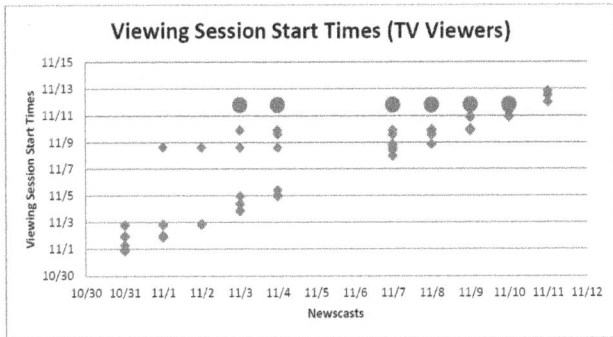

Figure 6 – Viewing times

Viewing time
Of key importance to news agencies is the time that viewers will spend watching. If giving the viewer control means that they watch less, there is potentially less advertising revenue. The average combined length of the base stories of our interactive newscasts was 20 minutes. Out of this time, viewers watched an average of 9.11 minutes. This is less than half. We knew that viewers would skip over uninteresting stories and we hoped to make that up by enticing them to watch extra content. On average they watched 1.41 minutes of extra content per session for a total viewing time of 10.52 minutes per session or 52%. This is not good news for advertising-based revenue. This is mitigated in three ways: 1) advertising can be more targeted to individual viewers and thus command higher prices or 2) traditional television news consumption is not a continuous behavior, or 3) interaction creates a more focused viewer experience as will be discussed in the next section.

On the level of an individual story, viewers watched an average of 62% of the story. People are watching enough to get the essence of the story and then regularly making the decision to move on.

Interactive features
Our deployment included a number of interactive features. By logging behavior on the server, we are able to measure the usage of those features. Of all headlines presented, viewers interactively rated 84% of them. This was a very popular feature. It gave viewers a quick way to decide what they wanted to watch. In this study, viewers were more than twice as likely to rate a headline positively than negatively. On average our viewers exerted some interactive choice during every single newscast. They are definitely interactively engaged. On average, they activated one or

more of the choice options every 57 seconds. In our earlier study, this was every 79 seconds. In this latest deployment, there were many more content options available than before.

Anecdotal reports from our news partners indicate that much of traditional television news consumption does not involve actually sitting in front of the television. People frequently wander around and do other things. In this deployment the high rate of interactivity indicates viewers that are heavily engaged rather than wandering off leaving the television playing but unwatched.

There are three basic navigation controls: PlayNext, PlayPrevious and Playlist. These were used in 95% of the sessions watched. For an average session PlayNext was used 77% of the time, PlayPrevious 8% and Playlist 15%. Clearly the most popular control was to skip to the next story. The use of PlayPrevious was down from the 33% of our previous study (we have no explanation). The use of the Playlist was also down significantly from the 26% of the previous study.

Extra content
For the commercial reasons that we have described, we were very interested in boosting viewer's use of extra content. Our key changes were to provide much more extra content and to directly pitch the extra content as part of the newscast. In our previous study, there were 0.32 views of extra content per session. In this study there were 1.23 extra content views per session. This is much better performance.

To better understand what made the difference we logged three ways in which a viewer might choose additional content. Pitches, where a specific video invitation is included at the end of a story accounted for 55% of the selections. This feature did not appear in our prior study. Prompts, in the upper left of the screen, accounted for 23% of the choices. Prompts were the primary extra content mechanism in our previous study. Playlist menu selections accounted for 22%.

We divided the logs into week 1 and week 2 to see if there were changes in behavior as viewers gained experience with the viewing interface. During week 2, pitches moved up to 72% of the choices with the menu dropping to 6%. It is quite clear that viewers like to be invited to view additional material rather than a more passive offering that they can select. We are convinced that the introduction of pitches along with the larger amount of available material led to the increased usage of extra content.

Interview feedback from viewers showed that the quality of the additional content is still an issue. Because we were not producing any content but rather scavenging it from existing sources we were using video for other than its original purpose. The comments indicate that viewers want deeper analysis of a story when they chose the additional content. This would require a very different level of professional production involvement than either of our two studies has been able to accomplish.

Historical content

We were disappointed to find that only 10% of the additional content came from our historical content. We had hypothesized that viewers would want deeper background on stories. We believe that part of the problem was that historical content was rather deep in the playlist menu system and simply got lost.

However, viewing patterns showed an interest in historical content, just not in the way we had hypothesized. Figure 6 shows when various newscasts were viewed. There is a very strong pattern of viewers wanting to catch up on newscasts they had missed even though this was no longer current news. This area needs more exploration.

CONCLUSIONS

News production was easy to learn and it was easy to produce complex interactive newscasts using non-computer science news people. We have again confirmed the popularity of interacting with the news and the use of headline like/dislike choices as a means of tailoring the newscast. Skipping out of a story also remains popular.

We have demonstrated new sources for additional content to augment stories of interest to a particular viewer. We have also shown that specific invitations to watch are the most effective means for drawing viewers in. Post-trial interviews also indicated that viewers did not like the way that following a prompt to additional story material would interrupt the main story. They liked their additional material at the end of the story, as with the pitches. This is also helpful guidance of future implementations.

Even with the extra content, viewers are watching news for less total time. The extra content viewed does not make up for the amount of content that viewers skip over. This is balanced, however, by the fact that viewers are continuously, interactively engaged. They are watching less time, but they are focused on the news rather than wandering around doing other things. We have no idea whether this balances out the prospective impact on advertising.

It is also clear that although our attempts at prototyping an interactive news experience have been successful, viewers want more carefully developed interactive material. In our own production process, we found ourselves developing new work models to handle the more dynamic structure. There is an interesting future of viewer engagement with their news that is ahead of us.

REFERENCES

1. Domingo, D. Interactivity in the Daily Routines of Online Newsrooms: Dealing with an Uncomfortable Myth. Journal of Computer-Mediated Communication 13, 3 (2008), 680-704.

2. Girgensohn, A., Wilcox, L., Shipman, F., and Bly, S. Designing Affordances for the Navigation of Detail-on-Demand Hypervideo. AVI, (2004), 290-297.

3. Hauptmann, A.G. and Witbrock, M.J. Informedia: News-on-Demand Multimedia Information Acquisition and Retrieval. Intelligent Multimedia Information Retrieval. AAAI Press, 1997, 213-239.

4. Houlberg, R. Local Television News Audience and the Para-Social Interaction. Journal of Broadcasting 28,4 (1984), 423-429.

5. Klinenberg, E. Convergence: News Production in a Digital Age. The ANNALS of the American Academy of Political and Social Science 597, 1 (2005), 48-64.

6. Larsson, H., Lindstedt, I., Löwgren, J., Reimer, B., and Topgaard, R. From Time-Shift to Shape-Shift: Towards Nonlinear Production and Consumption of News. Proc. of 6th Euro. Conf. on Changing Television Environments, Springer-Verlag (2008), 30-39.

7. Nichols,N. and Hammond, K. Machine-Generated Multimedia Content. In Proceedings of the 2009 Second International Conferences on Advances in Computer-Human Interactions (ACHI '09). IEEE Computer Society, (2009) 336-341.

8. Windows Azure, http://www.windowsazure.com 2012.

9. Merialdo, B., Lee, K.T., Luparello, D., and Roudaire, J. Automatic Construction of Personalized TV News Programs. Proceedings of the Seventh ACM International Conference on Multimedia, ACM (1999), 323-331.

10. Olsen, D. R., Bunn, D., Boulter, T., and Walz, R. "Interactive Television News" ACM Transactions on Multimedia Computing and Communications Applications. Vol 8 (2), (May 2012).

11. Purcell, K., Rainie, L., Mitchell, A., Rosenstiel, T., and Olmstead, K. Understanding the Participatory News Consumer. 2010.

12. Wagner, E., Birnbaum, L., and Forbus, K. Modeling multiple-event situations across news articles. In Proceedings of the fifth international conference on Knowledge capture (K-CAP '09). ACM, 207-208.

13. Zimmerman, J., Dimitrova, N., Agnihotri, L., Janeyski, A., and Nikolovska, L. Interface Design for MyInfo: a Personal News Demonstrator Combining Web and TV Content. INTERACT, IOS Press, (2003).

RedTag: Automatic Content Metadata Capture for Cameras

Tom Bartindale, Daniel Jackson, Karim Ladha, Sebastian Mellor, Patrick Olivier, Peter Wright

Culture Lab, Newcastle University

Newcastle upon Tyne, UK

{tom.bartindale, d.g.jackson, karim.ladha, s.j.i.mellor, p.l.olivier, p.c.wright}@ncl.ac.uk

ABSTRACT

RedTag is an optical tagging system that provides time based identification of objects, people or devices via small low cost infrared transmitters and receivers. We have developed RedTag as a cheap and flexible method of augmenting existing video capture equipment with an additional temporal metadata output of content based information. In this note, we describe the technology behind RedTag and demonstrate the interaction opportunities that arise through access to temporal metadata.

Author Keywords

Film; metadata; infrared; DTMF; editing; production; electronics.

ACM Classification Keywords

I.4.8 IMAGE PROCESSING AND COMPUTER VISION: Scene Analysis (Tracking)

INTRODUCTION

There are many uses for a low cost and flexible system for tagging physical objects and people for remote identification, specifically within a specific spatial frame of reference (such as that dictated by a camera's field-of-view). Within video production, temporal, content based information about each video clip is vital metadata that it is currently not possible to automatically generate, especially at the point of capture. The identification of actors, participants or objects within a video clip is vital for later categorization and identification during post-production. Professional teams often employ a Script Supervisor to manually gather this data, which is reconciled in post-production, but this is often not possible for smaller, non-professional teams. A system that integrates with existing camera equipment and workflow tools would avoid unnecessary expense and change to existing workflows. RedTag can capture content based metadata about the visible infrared tags which is then recorded onto existing camera equipment using an unused audio recording channel, providing content based metadata about the frame context with implicit temporal synchronization. No additional or non-standard camera equipment is required except a small RedTag receiver and audio cable. RedTag components are

small, wireless, cheap to manufacture and deploy, robust, flexible and offer sensing within a cameras field-of-view.

VIDEO METADATA

New forms of media delivery, user interaction, branching narrative, multi-format content and second-screen content are emerging as key outputs of a production. Rich and accurate metadata on source footage is key to creating value in such content. Metadata allows footage to be re-purposed, re-edited and matched with additional content without direct human intervention. It is also key for making content accessible, providing triggers for audio-description, subtitling and re-mastering of content. Video files already support native attachment of metadata through MXF [3] and many video cameras automatically record static technical information about shot and camera setup, however, these formats do not generate or store temporal context or content identification. RedTag augments objects, props, scenery and actors to automatically recording when these items enter and exit frame. The practice of accompanying 'rushes' (dumps of footage from the cameras) with notes on shot content from a Script-Supervisor (or other member of the crew) is common practice, and this data is used by the post-production team to more easily interpret footage. The automatic availability of this metadata facilitates a number of processing opportunities with the captured footage for post-production and additional content which are not possible with the data provided by manual annotation techniques both for professional and amateur video producers:

Editing: Video metadata can be used to either automatically mark in and out points in clips depending on the entry, exit or presence of specific objects or persons, or be used as an indicator for the editor as a time-based overlay on the editing surface. Rough or 'rush' edits can then be created with little effort ready for clip review or further editing.

Continuity Checking: Continuity checking across multiple scenes, shots and locations is key to producing believable content. Content based metadata regarding props in shot, costumes or extras within each shot can support automatic highlighting of inconsistencies and possible problems.

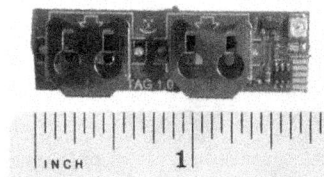

Figure 1 A RedTag Transmitter

Segmentation: Content based metadata supports the segmentation of video into semantically meaningful chunks, and subsequent efficient identification and contextualizing of footage. Temporal metadata allows sub-segments of clips to contain meta-information without segmenting clips into individual files, supporting increased temporal granularity for capturing contextual metadata and allowing for time based tagging of content within the scene. This can be used for providing time-based second screen content during broadcast.

Searching: Often individuals and organizations produce and archive all of their footage for audit or future use. Time-based content based metadata supports searching large archives for specific objects, locations or persons as well as retrieving the specific point within a clip that the search term was found.

Annotation: Clips that are augmented with time-based metadata of the appearance of objects, people and locations can be used to automatically segment clips for on screen overlays, subtitling and audio description. In live broadcasts, metadata could provide automatic titling of presenters or interviewees, whilst simultaneously generating live audio description about the presence of objects, locations or people who are silent in the scene.

PREVIOUS WORK
Systems such as iBand [4] nTag, GroupWear [1], SpotMe[1] and Poken[2] all provide wireless technologies for tagging people or objects, but these systems are design for enabling social interaction between participants through facilitating social connections within shot distances. Longer range wireless tagging has been successful for indoor localization: The ActiveBadge [6] system uses Infrared (IR) beacons worn by people in a building which transmit a unique code at 15s intervals. Transmissions are detected by sensors placed throughout the building to determine the wearer's position. Similarly, Digital Assistant [5] IR badges can identify people to specific interaction points by transmitting unique codes to worn receivers, and Meme Tags can exchange short messages using IR for two way-communication but these solutions do not take into account the camera frame as a reference. Similarly Intellibadge [2] is a system for adding value to social interaction at live events through augmenting attendees with RFID aware device and fixed RF beacons in specific locations in the venue, combining the personalization of Poken with the indoor localization and contextual control of media demonstrated by the Active Badge and Digital

Assistant. Although these technologies provide temporal identification of subjects in a location, they do not integrate with the field-of-view of a camera or recording equipment within the space. These technologies make use of IR technology for identification of people and objects from a distance but without considering camera field of view or recording of this data without additional hardware. Optical technologies such as QR codes or AR tags however have proved successful in tagging objects within video, but have the obvious disadvantage of visibility within the scene, negating their use in broadcast media.

THE REDTAG SYSTEM
The RedTag system consists of multiple low-power infrared emitters, and rechargeable receivers (see Figure 2) leveraging robust proven IR technology. Each small transmitter is programmed with a unique identifier (ID) and affixed to a person, object or at a fixed location. Receivers are mounted on camera equipment orientated in the same direction as the lens and connected to the secondary audio recording input. Tags regularly 'chirp', transmitting their ID via infrared. These codes reach the receiver only when within the camera field-of-view and are output as DTMF tones representing the visible tag's ID and are recorded onto the camera audio feed. Simple DTMF decoding software is used to return the ID and relative timestamp of each tag in the recording.

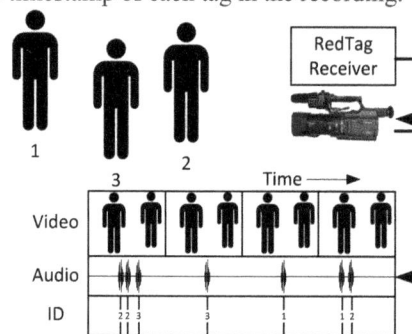

Figure 2 RedTag System Functional Workflow

RedTag transmitters use a modulated IR signal, similar to TV remote controls. Emitters are designed to be low cost, small consumables which can be embedded into objects. In one implementation, each emitter is powered by two replaceable coin-cell batteries, giving it a lifespan of around 3 weeks. In the most common configuration, a RedTag receiver emits each code that it receives from multiple RedTag transmitters as a stream of DTMF tones, which is recorded onto a cameras additional audio channel.

Transmitter
A RedTag transmitter (Figure 1) may consists of just seven or less components on a single layer PCB, including: a 6-pin PIC 8-bit microcontroller, Infrared emitter (850nm wavelength, modulated at 455 kHz), appropriate resistors and one or two coin-cell batteries. Even in small scale production, the unit cost for each transmitter when mass produced is under $3, allowing transmitters to be used as non-returnable consumables in large scale deployments. During operation, the tag waits a pseudo-random interval (around 1 second)

Figure 3 RedTag Receiver (in a camera mounted enclosure with an aperture matching the camera lens)

before transmitting its 16-bit payload (ID). This jitter prevents any tags' chirp from falling into phase with another and repeatedly colliding which would prevent successful reception. To prevent spurious or misidentification of tags, Manchester coding is used to transmit the payload, which helps to identify collisions with other transmitters. As an additional measure, the 16-bit payload consists of a 10-bit unique identifier and a 6-bit CRC (using the ITU 6-bit CRC) to protect against ID corruption. Given the 22.75 kbaud (455 kHz carrier, 20 cycles per bit), each 16-bit ID takes 1.76ms to transmit. Given perfect synchronization between transmitters this allows 568 transmitters to be detected a second. However, as no synchronization (or two-way communication) exists between transmitters or receivers, the collision rate increases with the number of transmitters visible. With 100 transmitters in use, all transmissions with 1.76ms duration are randomly allocated within a 1s intervals, and the probability of any one transmission avoiding collision with 99 others in one second is $P(no\ collision|T = 1) = (1 - 0.00176)^{99} \approx 0.84$. Thus the probability of one transmission avoiding collision at least once in 5 seconds (a contextually useful time window) is $P(no\ collision|T = 5) = 1 - (1 - 0.84)^5 \approx 0.9999$. A statistical simulation of collisions shows that we can reliably ($P(success) \approx 0.99$) receive the tag ID of 60 transmitters within a 5 second window.

Receiver

Each RedTag receiver (Figure 3) features a 16-bit microcontroller, infrared receiver, a re-chargeable battery and combination 3.5mm audio jack and USB connector. Receivers are mounted in an enclosure of IR blocking material with an aperture directly in front of the IR receiver. The aperture size is calculated to provide the same field-of-view to that of a camera (see Figure 4). When a transmission is received, the RedTag code received is output via the audio jack as DTMF audio tones which are still identifiable through any compression used. Each code is emitted as four DTMF[3] symbols: a '#' symbol, used as a delimiter between records, followed by a three digit number. Each tone is played for 40ms with a 50ms interval, allowing three newly seen devices to be identified each second. The receiver operates a memory queue to buffer incoming codes, and ensures that newly observed codes are reported in a first-in-first-out order as soon as possible and duplications in the queue have lower precedence than unique entries. In this way, the receiver maintains a current list of observed transmitters, and only fails to pass on this data through DTMF if the queue overflows. Although using DTMF codes means that there may be a slight temporal delay between the receiver observing the transmitter, and emitting the DTMF code for it, this queue method ensures that all of the observed devices will be recorded within a temporally relevant period. By attenuating the transmitters in firmware or optically, the effective range of the transmitter can be adjusted from 5m to

---

[3]http://en.wikipedia.org/wiki/Dual-tone_multi-frequency_signaling

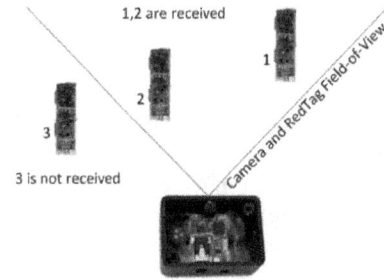

Figure 4 RedTag Receiver with a Camera Aperture

100m, depending on the sensitivity required. Transmitter range is particularly directional and subject to multi-path reflection to receivers however this can be advantageous when applying apertures to RedTag receiver units to match a camera's field-of-view. To retrieve RedTag data from a camera recording, the relevant audio channel is extracted and passed through a software DTMF decoder which outputs the ID and timestamp of each detected RedTag. Before post-production, software is used to batch process clips, separating the additional audio channel and detecting the tones (tags id's) alongside a timestamp within the stream. Each ID is replaced with a description of where the tag was located (provided by the crew) and the information is saved back to the source file as XMP metadata. If required, RedTag data (as audio) is maintained through subsequent manipulation (cutting, editing and mixing) and stripped out later.

EVALUATION

We tested RedTag in a controlled setting to determine its spatial and technical limitations. In a single tag test, the effective range of a RedTag was tested to be 6±0.1m, and the effective angle of rotation from the receiver before losing signal was 185° from the horizontal. In two standard camera shots (close shot and mid-shot), with an $f/4$ lens, RedTags are received within +=3° outside of the camera frame bounding box, whereas in a wide shot, RedTags are only received within with center 40% of the camera frame, due to the fixed sensor aperture. We accepted this limitation of a fixed aperture due as we had configured the receiver for close, interview style filming. To evaluate the effectiveness in a real world scenario, we setup a 3 key use-cases as controlled tests: an interview or presentation scenario with 1 or 2 people in frame and a fixed camera; social coffee break scenario, with multiple small groups of people and a moving camera; a film acting style scenario, with a fixed camera, and acting towards the camera. For each one, we analyzed: the **correctness** of generated metadata (false positives for transmitters not present); **temporal instability** (is the transmitter data recorded within a useable timeframe of sensing the transmitter); **maximum tags**; **range constraints** and **data accuracy** (e.g. missing people from clip). For the test, a single RedTag receiver was mounted underneath the lens of a Panasonic AF101 camera and plugged into the secondary audio input channel, and each of 11 participants wore a transmitter inside in a badge on a lanyard. 10 videos were captured in various filming scenarios. The transmitter id's from the resulting video were retrieved and compared against the same footage which had been annotated by hand to provide a ground truth of people in the camera frame. Overall, no false positives were experienced. In clips with a static camera and a single person in frame, their RedTag was received on a regular schedule (2s) throughout the clip. In clips with more action and moving cameras we see 90% and 84% discovery for film style and coffee break style respectively – we sample only the transmitters visible for at least 2 seconds and require the detection to occur while it is visible. When allowing for delays in detection we detect 87% and 99% of transmitters within 1 minute of visibility. This is appropriate for identification of people within multiple clips but negates specific temporal identification. It was noted that for 2 people in the scene, no transmissions were received, suggesting hardware failure. In most cases, including those with larger groups of people, there were usually only 2 or 3 people facing towards the camera while others faced away or side on. A slow sweeping motion or several steady shots into the group generally captured all participants. With our placement of transmitter (in a neck worn badge holder) they are relatively low on the body but were often still be detected as the receiver was mounted below the lens and provides a non-rectangular field of view, slightly larger in the vertical direction. In practice, 10% of cases where the a person was visible in shot resulted in failure to detect their transmitter due to orientation to the camera, in addition to brief appearances (less than 1s) and transmitters occluded by arms, hands, or objects, as expected. Whether deliberate or not, this prevented identification within the scene and is a critique on the lanyard mounting method.

DEPLOYMENT

We have deployed RedTag during three academic conference events with ~200 attendees each. At each event, attendee badges contained a transmitter pre-linked to their event registration information. RedTag was used to augment video footage taken of talks and interviews to segment and label footage for rapid editing. Eight cameras used throughout the venue were equipped with a receiver. During editing the associated metadata was retrieved and mapped onto attendee registration information and displayed as a visual overlay on the editing timeline aiding rapid segmentation and identification of specific clips, as well as automatic tagging of interviewees and speakers. This information was also used to overlay associated captions and information on all playback and output streams.

DISCUSSION

Our technical evaluation and subsequent deployment has highlighted practical considerations for RedTag in practice which are key to discuss:

Reliability: In scenarios with large numbers of transmitters, RedTag may not receive temporally correct data, but depending on the length of capture will receive the transmitter at some point. This is useful for identifying if a transmitter exists in a video, but negates the use of time-based data to locate it. In choreographed capture scenarios however, transmitters can be mounted to face the camera and thus can be used to reliably determine time based frame entry and exit information about the transmitter. Some materials reflect IR light, as such false positives are a possibility. Due to the hardware auto-gain control and receiver aperture however, this scenario is unlikely and did not occur in either our study or deployment.

Occlusion: Although operating with line-of-sight IR, transmitters can be hidden in clothing or objects to avoid their appearance in shot as long as the material is IR transparent and many different materials have such properties. Occlusion by other objects however will prevent reception, thus production crew must be aware of this property when mounting transmitters. In some cases however, this can be advantageous, such as for generating audio description of items visible in a scene. In our deployment, the primary cause of occlusion was the user covering their badge accidentally, and this could be controlled by alternative mounting of the transmitters.

Human Effort: The addition of RedTag to the production workflow requires management of transmitter IDs and associated metadata. As managing cast, props and locations are already performed by roles within a production team, this responsibility could be shared amongst the crew, resulting in little extra overhead. In conclusion, the RedTag system provides a method of automatically capturing content based temporal metadata, storing this data as part of the video media for later use in post-production.

REFERENCES

1. Borovoy, R., Martin, F., Resnick, M., and Silverman, B. GroupWear. *In Proc. CHI '98*, ACM Press (1998), 329–330.
2. Cox, D., Kindratenko, V., and Pointer, D. IntelliBadge TM: towards providing location-aware value-added services at academic conferences. *In Proc. UbiComp '03*, (2003).
3. Devlin, B. What is MXF? *EBU Technical Review*, (2002).
4. Kanis, M., Winters, N., Agamanolis, S., Gavin, A., and Cullinan, C. Toward wearable social networking with iBand. *In Proc. CHI '05*, ACM Press (2005), 1521.
5. Sumi, Y. and Mase, K. Digital assistant for supporting conference participants: An attempt to combine mobile, ubiquitous and web computing. *In Proc. Ubicomp '01*, (2001).
6. Want, R., Hopper, A., Falcão, V., and Gibbons, J. The active badge location system. *ACM Transactions on Information Systems 10*, 1 (1992), 91–102.

Playout Delay of TV Signals: Measurement System Design, Validation and Results

Wouter J. Kooij
TNO
Delft, The Netherlands
wouter.kooij@gmail.com

Hans M. Stokking
TNO
Delft, The
Netherlands
hans.stokking@tno.nl

Ray van Brandenburg
TNO
Delft, The Netherlands
ray.vanbrandenburg@tno.nl

Pieter-Tjerk de Boer
University of Twente
Enschede,
The Netherlands
p.t.deboer@utwente.nl

ABSTRACT

Due to new interactive TV services, synchronizing the playout of content on different TVs is becoming important. To synchronize, knowledge of delay differences is needed. In this study, a measurement system is developed to gain insight into the magnitude of delay differences of different TV setups in an automated fashion. This paper shows the measurement system, which is validated for precision and accuracy. Preliminary measurements results show that regular TV broadcasts differ up to 6 seconds in playout moment and that web based TV broadcasts can introduce more than a minute delay. Furthermore, we measured a broadcasting before encoding and modulation, which resulted in a time about 4 second before the fastest receiver. On a side note, while developing the measurement system we found out that GPS timing on consumer Android devices was inaccurate, with fluctuations of up to 1 second.

Author Keywords

TV; broadcast; media synchronization; delay; Android

ACM Classification Keywords

H.5.1 [**Multimedia Information Systems**]: Video, Broadcasting

BACKGROUND

The following scenario might sound familiar: imagine you are watching an exciting soccer match, such as a world cup game. The team you are supporting is in ball possession and is setting up an attack when you suddenly hear loud cheering noises coming from your neighbors. A little later you see where this cheering came from: a goal was scored. This is an example often given to illustrate a playout difference. A playout difference is the difference in delay between the displaying of a certain piece of content on different TV systems, possibly using different techniques or obtaining content from different content providers. These playout differences have been shown to be noticeable or annoying, even for differences as small as just 1 second [1].

A playout difference is not just annoying when watching football, there are other applications where playout differences cause problems. Examples of this are applications that involve real time content or user interaction through television. Sources such as [2] and [3] report or expect an increase in the use of these kind of advanced television services.

Knowledge of playout differences is essential for the design of such services. An example where this is essential is a second screen application for live TV quizzes that require live viewer interaction. Knowing the playout delays make it possible for service developers to account for this in their design. It will also be interesting to know if there is delay dispersion for geographically different locations or different moments in time.

Thinking one step ahead, knowing or being able to quickly measure these delays might even be a step in the direction of a possible synchronization of TV broadcast chains. In this paper, we report on a system we have developed that can measure playout differences in an automated fashion using smartphones as measurement devices, and using a technique called audio fingerprinting. We have validated the system's accuracy, and report on (preliminary) measurement results.

RELATED WORK

For media synchronization, a good overview is given in [4], explaining and discussing intra-media synchronization, inter-media synchronization (i.e. lip-sync) and inter-destination media synchronization. Our paper focusses on playout differences, which are mostly relevant for both inter-media synchronization and inter-destination media synchronization (IDMS), topics discussed extensively in [5]. More recently, various synchronization use cases are presented in [6], showing synchronization requirements ranging from very high (<10ms) to low (< 2 sec) for various IDMS use cases, while [7] recommends synchronization of approximately 1 second for a seamless shared experience. The results presented in our paper will show that current playout differences can be much larger than this, and thus synchronization solutions will be required for many interactive TV services.

The accuracy of our measurement system depends largely on the accuracy of the clock synchronization. [8] contains a number of recommendations on how to achieve such accuracy, among which the recommendation to use a single time server and the recommendation to first achieve a good so-called difference clock, i.e. a good internal clock.

Furthermore, an overview of applications that fit into the social TV paradigm, including examples where synchronization is needed, can be found in [9]. More examples of such applications involving real-time interaction through a TV can be found in [10] and [11].

As far as the authors know, no large scale measurement of TV playout delays in an automated way has been performed before. Similar studies were performed that measured TV playout differences on small scales or in a non-automated fashion, such as [1] and [12]. These studies have shown that playout differences of up to a few seconds are possible between different TV broadcasts within the same region. At that time, only regular broadcasts were studied, i.e. web players and tablet-based television broadcasts were not included. There are also other systems for managing delay, such as presented in [13]. But this work is not applicable here, as it requires access to both the ingest and playout point

TV BROADCASTING DELAY

Different TV broadcasting techniques have different distribution channels and techniques. This imposes a difference in delays between the broadcasting moment and the delivery of content via different broadcasts. It can often be seen in practice that analog television is faster than digital television. This is because digital television has more delay introducing steps such as encoding or transcoding.

Furthermore, the transmission technique used for broadcasting influences the amount of delay introduced in a TV broadcast. For example, television from satellite (DVB-S) imposes a delay introduction of at least some hundreds of milliseconds of delay, just from the delay introduced by the signal propagation to and from the satellite at the speed of light. Other broadcasting techniques such as cable television (DVB-C) or terrestrial broadcasts (DVB-T) have a much smaller lower boundary of the minimum transmission time in terms of what is physically possible. And, depending on the format of the original signal, HD and SD signals will differ as one has to be transcoded to the other.

Apart from this, TV broadcasting with Internet Protocol TeleVision (IPTV) has other Quality of Service (QoS) or Quality of Experience (QoE) related techniques that influence the delay of the broadcast. Examples of these are error correction or retransmission schemes used.

To get an idea where these delays in a television network arise, Figure 1 presents a global overview of delay introducing factors in a general TV broadcasting chain. This figure includes the chain structure of both the scenario depicting live broadcasts and the scenario where pre-

recorded content is broadcasted. The aforementioned elements encoding and transmission are theoretically the largest causes of delay. In practice there might be additional or different provider-specific steps involved. The actual amount of delay introduced in a TV broadcast can depend on many other factors such as the usage of specific hard- and software and the associated configuration that comes with it.

This paper focusses on the delay introduced by the distributor, the transport and the user side, i.e. the boxed region in Figure 1.

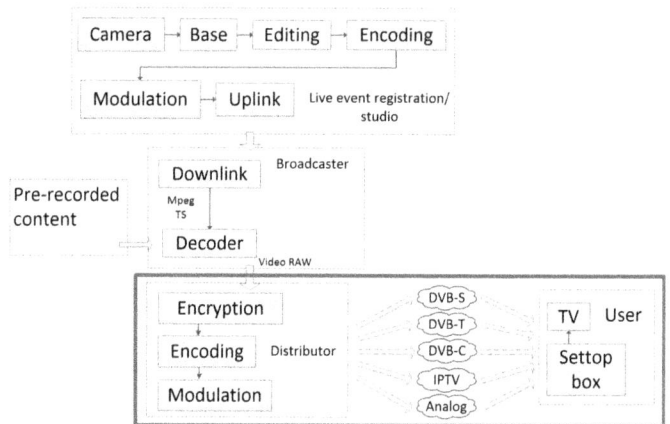

Figure 1: Chain structure of a TV content delivery chain

MEASUREMENT SYSTEM

To measure the playout delay of a TV broadcast, we use a technique called audio fingerprinting. Audio fingerprinting techniques make use of so-called fingerprints that digitally summarize the content of audio. These fingerprints are then matched against a previously calculated (or in case of live TV fingerprinting a real-time calculated) set of reference fingerprints in a fingerprint database. The general principle is more or less the same as for example the popular app Shazam, of which the workings are globally described in [14]. Our system makes use of the freely available live TV fingerprinting platform "Entourage" provided by the company Gracenote [15]. This TV fingerprinting platform provides real-time recording and fingerprinting of live TV channels done by Gracenote. This acts as the reference that we use for comparing a locally (i.e. a normal TV) recorded fingerprint (and the corresponding starting moment in time) with. The platform of choice is Android, which allows for performing easy measurements, not only by ourselves but also by people that are not familiar with our measurement system.

More specifically, an Android device records audio from a TV through its internal microphone, calculates an audio fingerprint and compares this with the mentioned reference. The playout difference is then calculated as the difference in time between the recording of both audio fingerprints.

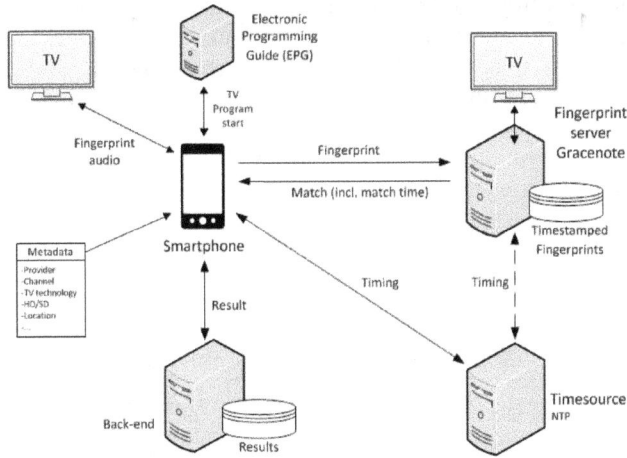

Figure 2: Architecture of the measurement system

Furthermore, our measurement application allows for input of metadata such as the broadcaster name, channel name, TV technology, TV quality (HD/SD) and location. A measurement of the playout difference combined with this manually entered metadata is submitted to a back-end database server on which the measurements are stored.

To accurately compare the moment the fingerprint is recorded on the smartphone with the moment the fingerprint is recorded on the reference, both sources need to have an accurate notion of time. To accomplish this, the smartphone obtains a timestamp by querying an NTP server.

To make sure the time obtained with NTP is accurate and consistent for individual measurements, we use a single stratum 1 NTP server managed by ourselves. To reduce the influence of congestion spikes, the smartphone performs multiple timestamp requests to this server and only uses the response with the lowest round-trip-time (RTT). This is done according to the recommendations from [8]. If the delay of the RTT is lower, the "quality" of the timestamp is better. The server side fingerprinting mechanism that assigns fingerprints a timestamp is assumed to be sufficiently accurate. This is validated as well, as can be seen from the accuracy measurements later in this paper.

An architectural overview of the system can be found in Figure 2. The smartphone application acts as the center of communication between the mentioned components. The smartphone application records sound from a TV, queries the NTP server for a timestamp and starts creating a fingerprint right at this moment. Next, the created fingerprint is submitted to the reference server of Gracenote which compares the fingerprint with its database of live, continuously created fingerprints of its own TV source. If a match is found, the time offset (relative to the start of matching TV program) is returned to the smartphone.

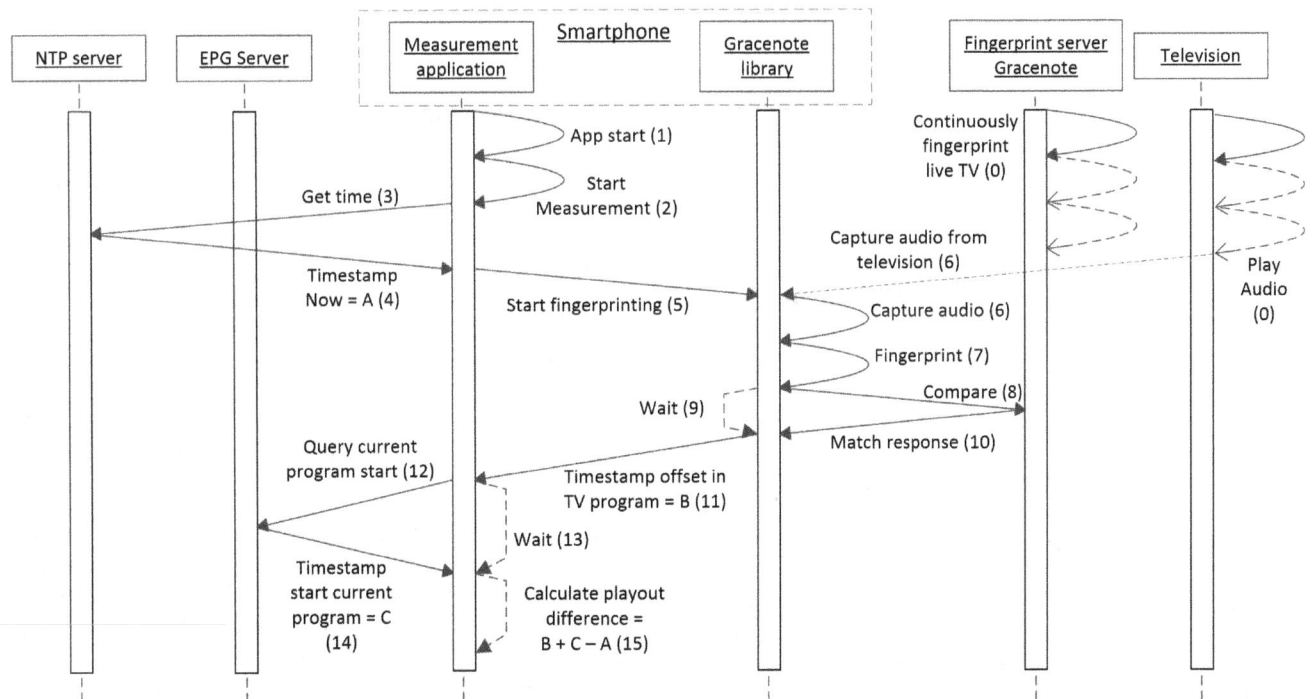

Figure 3: Measuring playout difference

Next, the smartphone queries the EPG server to determine the absolute moment in time the fingerprint was recorded on the reference. The moment of local fingerprint recording and the moment of reference fingerprint recording are compared against each other to obtain the playout difference. Finally, combined with manually entered metadata, the playout difference measurement is submitted to a back-end database, storing the results. For a better understanding and to get an action sequence overview, shows a sequence diagram of this process.

MEASUREMENT SYSTEM PERFORMANCE

Factors in performance

This section shows the test results of performance (for precision and accuracy) of the measurement system as a whole and for some of the individual parts of the measurement system. Factors influencing the performance of the measurement system include the internal clock accuracy of Android, the server-side fingerprint offset matching timestamp accuracy, EPG program start timestamp accuracy, the reference time source (NTP server) accuracy and measurement outliers. Of these factors, the Gracenote servers provide fingerprint offset matching and EPG program start times. The fingerprint matching seems to give us some outliers, see the section on outliers. The EPG program start times seem quite stable, i.e. we did not notice any large jumps in playout difference when measuring delays during different programs.

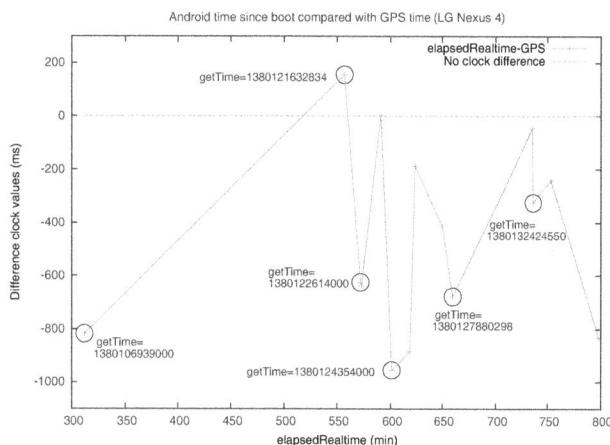

Figure 4: Inconsistency of GPS timing on an LG Nexus 4

No time related accuracy measurements are possible without an accurate time source. Using the timestamp obtained from the GPS receiver on Android turned out to be inaccurate, or at least it was on the specific test device (an LG Nexus 4 smartphone). This was tested by comparing the internal clock with the GPS time as obtained through the Android API. The time obtained this way on the specific test device through the Android API can be wrong by up to a whole second. More details on this test can be found in [16]. The accuracy of GPS timestamp information seems to be device-, firmware- and hardware-specific. Because of

this, direct GPS timestamp information on Android is not an option for obtaining consistent and precise timing information.

In Figure 4, the inaccuracy and inconsistency of the GPS timing on the test device is shown. The GPS timing clearly deviates from the line that represents a situation where the GPS timing would be in sync with the internal clock of Android (elapsedRealtime). The latter is shown to be monotonic with a small linear drift in the next section. Even when this drift is compensated for, we must conclude that the GPS timing information on Android is not accurate enough for our purposes.

Since GPS timing on Android turns out to be too inaccurate, we chose to use NTP (Network Time Protocol). We set up our own Stratum-1 NTP server using a GPS receiver as its reference. For more detail on this, see [16].

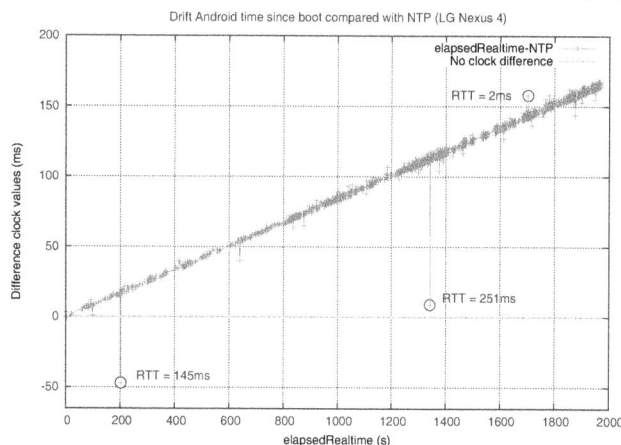

Figure 5: Accuracy internal clock Android (LG Nexus 4)

Internal clock Android

The Android internal clock (relative to the start of the device, in the API called "elapsedRealtime") is used for calculating several time deltas and for keeping track which operation was started when. More specifically, it is used to correlate the NTP time with the moment of a fingerprint creation, in order to obtain the exact timestamp of the fingerprint. This is especially important, since the measurement system performs multiple NTP requests and only uses the one with the lowest round-trip-time. For the app to be accurate the internal clock must be sufficiently accurate.

In order to verify the accuracy of the internal clock, we created a wireless network with a NTP server, a router and an Android smartphone. No other devices were connected to this network. This allows the smartphone to communicate with the NTP server directly without interference of other network traffic. This way, the smartphone can obtain timestamps from the NTP server with maximum accuracy. To test the accuracy of the internal clock of Android on the test device, a series of timestamps requests to the NTP server were performed over a period of about 30 minutes. The timestamps obtained this way were then compared with the time of the internal clock by calculating the time difference elapsed since a fixed starting point for both timestamps. The differences between both values were then compared with each other and indicate the accuracy of the internal clock of Android. The results of this test are displayed in Figure 5. The test device used here, and for the remainder of this paper is an LG Nexus 4, using a native version of Android 4.2.

These test results show that the internal clock in Android is monotonic with a small linear drift. The slope of the line that runs through the middle of all points represents the amount of linear drift of the clock. This line has a slope of 84.23µs/s. For the purpose of the measurement system, this is accurate enough. We require the clock to remain accurate during a single measurement. As a measurement last about a couple of minutes, the inaccuracy remains in the order of magnitude of 10s of milliseconds. As the expected measurement results are in the order of seconds of difference, this is acceptable for the internal clock.

Outliers

While using the app for measuring, correct measurements were usually obtained, but there were also moments where the measurement system would provide a value that was clearly not correctly representing the playout difference at that moment. These incorrect measurements, which are called outliers from here on, occurred on more or less random moments. These outliers are usually a fixed value roughly 3 seconds off from the real value (as determined by the accuracy test later in this paper). What might be going on here is that a sub-fingerprint next to the matching fingerprint is invalidly marked as match (a false positive), although this is speculation on our part. The mechanism used for dealing with these outliers operates by performing multiple measurements and only keeping the median value of the measured values. For this purpose, we have performed 8 measurements each time, and kept only the 5th lowest, as we saw more outliers on the low side. This is a very severe outlier removal mechanism, but ensures proper measurement results in practice. If the distribution of outliers would follow a normal distribution, the chance of an outlier would be as good as zero. This is not the case however, and there is still a slight chance that the system might provide an occasional outlier, despite the outlier removal mechanism.

Precision

Next, the measurement system was tested for overall precision, i.e. closeness of agreement to which subsequent measurement show the same value under the same circumstances. The test setup is shown in Figure 6. This test uses two smartphones with the app installed to calculate the playout difference at roughly the same moment. The overall precision error is then calculated as the difference in playout differences calculated by both smartphones.

The results of the precision test can be found in Figure 7. This obviously contains outliers. We watched the TV show during the measurements, and no actual jumps in the playout were seen. So, we applied our previously described outlier removal, with the results displayed in Figure 8. After the outlier removal, the precision error is found to be at most 200ms in this test. This is adequate for our measurement application, as we are expecting to measure playout difference in the order of magnitude of seconds.

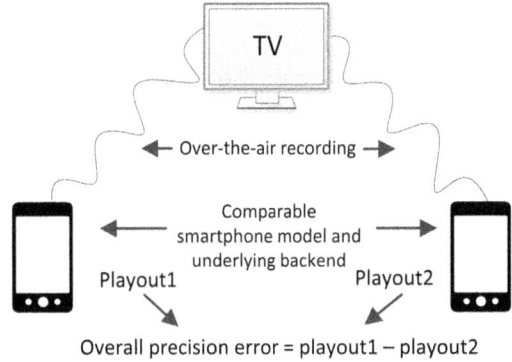

Figure 6: Precision measurement setup

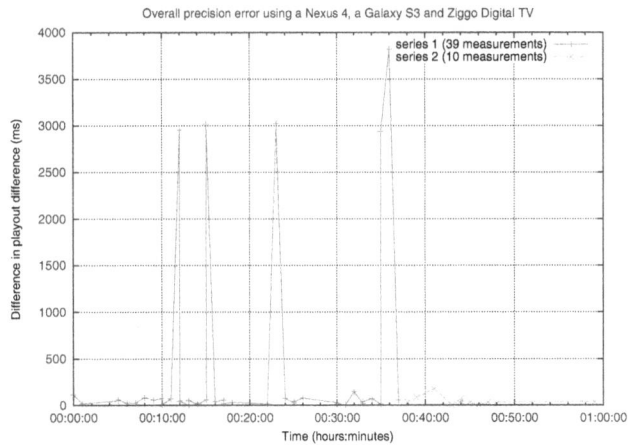

Figure 7: Overall precision error of the system.

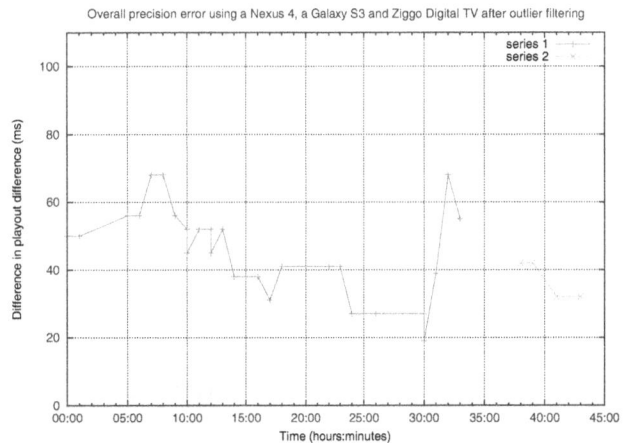

Figure 8: Precision error, after outlier removal

Accuracy

Figure 9 shows the test setup used to test the system for overall accuracy. This setup is a bit more complicated than the precision test setup. It includes two TVs, two smartphones and an audio interface. The goal of this test is to measure the degree to which measured playout differences correspond with the actual playout differences. Without access to the actual TV reference, this test is not straightforward. The difference in playout times of the actual audio (as locally recorded from two TVs) is compared with the difference in playout differences obtained by two similar smartphones using the application. This way, the calculated accuracy error constitutes again the error introduced by both phones.

In this setup, the actual difference in audio between both TVs is measured by connecting a PC using the audio interface that has a direct connection to the 3,5mm headphone connections of the TVs. It records both audio signals as two mono signals combined into one stereo signal. This audio was then aligned manually by looking at a graph of the audio signals. In this way, we manually determined the playout difference between both TVs.

The test results for the accuracy test, after outlier removal as previously discussed, are presented in Figure 10. In this graph, one line represents the actual difference in audio (as is measured directly from the TV audio, Δ audio in Figure 9) and the other line represents the measurement difference between the two simultaneous smartphone measurements (Δ measurement in Figure 9). The actual difference (Δ audio) is measured for every tenth smartphone measurement, to deal with possible audio hick ups from the TV (caused by frame skipping) and to reduce the chance of a human reading error.

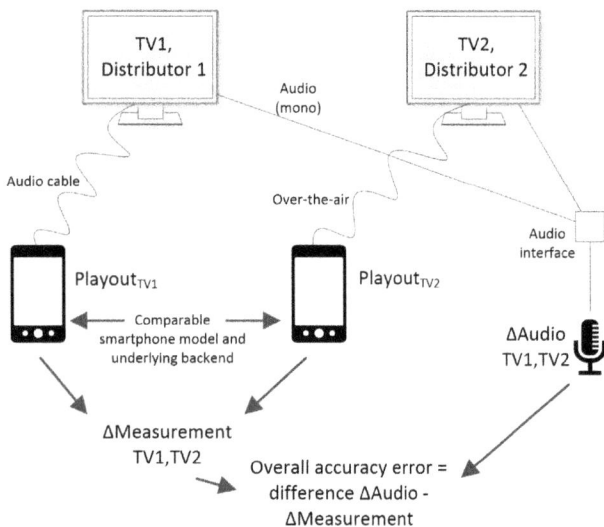

Figure 9: Accuracy measurement setup

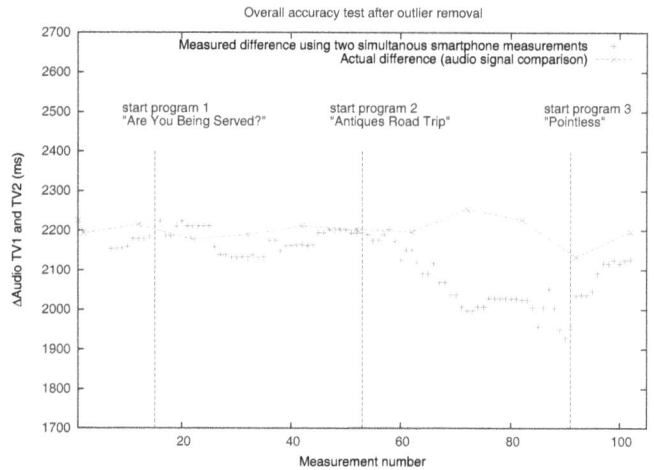

Figure 10: Accuracy error after outlier removal (using the median of a sliding window of 7 measurements)

The degree to which both values agree indicates the accuracy of the measurement system. Note that the distance between the smartphone and the TV is neglected as the goal is not to provide frame-accurate measurements. As can be seen from this figure, the maximum combined overall inaccuracy error for both phones is 250ms. Of course, on average the accuracy is much better compared to the maximum inaccuracy.

The program names indicating the start of different TV programs are also included in the picture. Recall that the system queries an EPG server to determine the start time of a TV program. Since a fingerprint matching results only delivers the offset in time of a match in a current TV program, using the EPG data allows for having an absolute time of the occurrence of the measured piece of audio. This in turn allows it to be compared with the absolute moment in time as measured using the NTP server representing the moment the piece of audio was fingerprinted locally.

Between around measurement number 60 and 90, the accuracy becomes less than in earlier measurements. This seems to be right in between the start of program 2 and program 3. A reason for this might be that the server side of the fingerprinting is experiencing clock drift at this moment. After the start of program 3, the measurements become more accurate again. Again, the accuracy seems adequate for the measurements we want to perform.

RESULTS

The application has been used to perform playout difference measurements mainly in the Netherlands and also in the UK. The results of these measurements, independent of geographical location or time can be found in Figure 11. Remember that the reference is the live fingerprinting TV server from Gracenote, which is the reference to which all measurements were compared with. Therefore the playout difference of the reference with itself is logically zero. This figure displays the average of the measured combination of broadcaster, subscription (technology) and quality (HD or SD) for both the channels BBC One and BBC Two combined. Experience shows that the playout delay for these channels is the same.

One thing that can be seen from these measurements is that analog delivery is faster than other delivery mechanisms s from the same broadcaster. The reason for this is probably in the encoding part, which makes digital TV slower than analog TV.

Furthermore, in general HD broadcasts are slower than their SD equivalents. This also seems logical, because HD broadcasts introduce more encoding delay (due to multi-pass encoding for example) and are therefore more likely to introduce delay in the broadcast.

Looking at the absolute values, it can be seen that playout differences of up to almost 5 seconds are possible in TV broadcasts in the Netherlands. International playout differences are larger when measurements from the UK are also included. These measurements are the fastest, and compared with the slowest measurement in the Netherlands (excluding internet streaming TV), playout differences can become almost 6 seconds.

Also, with the help of the BBC, a measurement was performed at the broadcasting chain prior to coding and multiplexing. This is indicated as "internal" in Figure 11. Comparing the playout difference between this internal measurement and the fastest measured average playout difference, we see that there is a difference of around 4 seconds. This value consists of the delay caused by encoding, modulation and also distribution to the fastest receiver (which is terrestrial and SD quality). Since it is not known which part of this value is broadcasting delay, we

can only conclude that in this case the encoding and modulation at the BBC takes at most around 4 seconds.

Furthermore, the measurements clearly show that the playout delay in the United Kingdom is lower than in the Netherlands. This is not surprising as it is broadcasted from the UK itself, although analog delivery can be faster than the slower broadcasts in the UK (such as HD or Satellite).

Something else that can be seen from these measurements is that internet streams (KPN ITV Online, BBC iPlayer) are much slower than normal television. These streams can be around 20 seconds or even more than a minute slower than a regular TV broadcast. This is not very surprising and is something that could be expected since content for internet streams is normally prepared separately and is distributed separately as well. The underlying techniques and systems that deliver these streams can vary greatly, both in terms of architecture as well as in terms of delay. E.g. in case MPEG-DASH is used for delivering the internet streams, the content is segmented and encoded in several versions, and usually delivered using Content Delivery Networks.

A geographical delay dispersion analysis at a national level, where exactly the same broadcaster and setup combination (subscription type/quality) are directly compared with each other was not performed due to a lack of data. We did notice that there is definitely some playout differences between geographically distributed measurements with the same setup. But without sufficient geographically distributed measurements of the same broadcaster and setup combination, no clear conclusion can be drawn. Apart from this, the fact that different TVs or settop boxes will cause some variance in the measured delays will only make it harder to draw a conclusion on this.

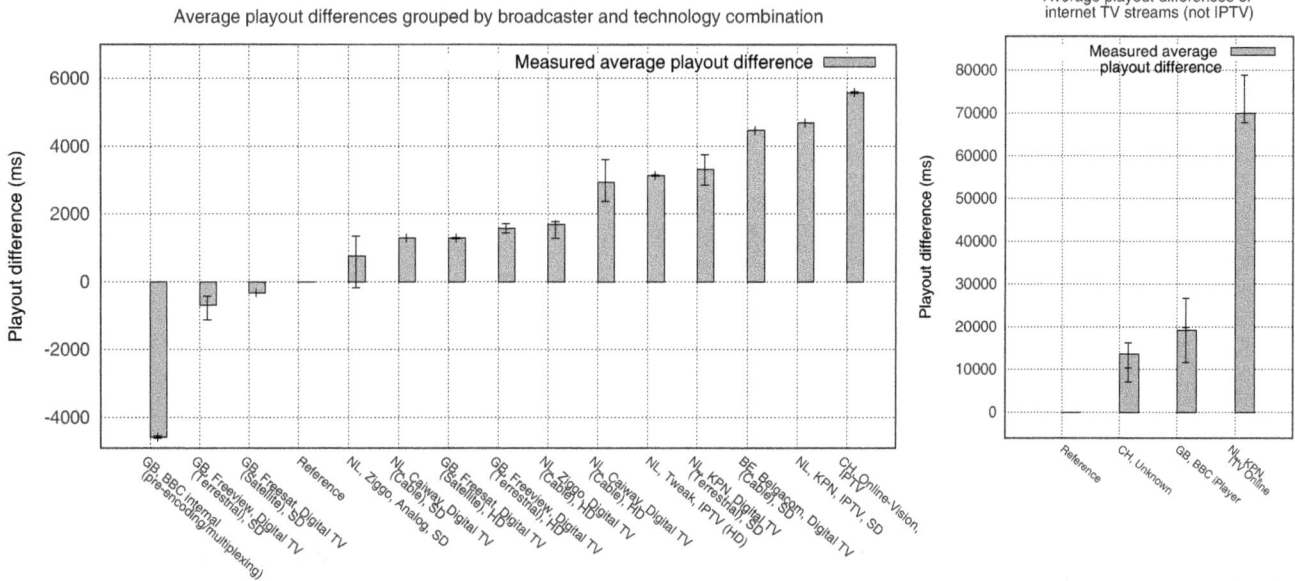

Figure 11: Playout differences by provider setup for regular TV (a, left) and for internet streams (b, right)
The error bars indicate maximum and minimum measurements. The measurements that seem very accurate only contain one or two measurement results. The total number of measurements is 182.

CONCLUSION

A measurement system that is able to automatically measure playout differences of TV content compared to a reference is presented. The system is able to measure the TV playout accurately, although in a rare occasion the system may mistake an outlier as a valid measurement. The system is not so accurate that it allows for frame accurate synchronization, but it is adequate to give a good overview of the order of magnitude of playout differences of TV signals. This is something that has not been done before on a large scale, as far as the knowledge of the authors goes.

The measurement results show that analog delivery is delivered faster than non-analog delivery in general. Also, in general, HD broadcasts seem to be slower than SD broadcasts. Furthermore, internet streams of TV can be more than 1 minute slower than a "regular" TV broadcasting technique. Also, we measured a broadcasting before encoding and modulation, which resulted in a time about 4 second before the fastest receiver.

FUTURE WORK

To gain a better insight in the geographical distribution of specific TV setups (broadcaster and technology), more geographically distributed measurements are needed. Furthermore, as a means of verification, cross-checking the system with latency measurements on an SFN network is something that will be useful.

ACKNOWLEDGEMENTS

The work by TNO is partially funded by the European Commission's 7th Framework Programme under grant agreement no. 318343 (STEER project).

REFERENCES

1. Rufael Mekuria, Pablo Cesar, and Dick Bulterman. 2012. Digital TV: the effect of delay when watching football. In Proceedings of the 10th European conference on Interactive tv and video (EuroITV '12). ACM, New York, NY, USA, 71-74.

2. Evelien D'heer, Cédric Courtois, and Steve Paulussen. 2012. Everyday life in (front of) the screen: the consumption of multiple screen technologies in the living room context. In Proceedings of the 10th European conference on Interactive tv and video (EuroITV '12). ACM, New York, NY, USA, 195-198.

3. Lochrie, M., & Coulton, P. 2012. Tweeting with the telly on!. In Consumer Communications and Networking Conference (CCNC), 2012 IEEE (pp. 729-731). IEEE.

4. Ud Din, Shahab, and Dick Bulterman. "Synchronization Techniques in Distributed Multimedia Presentation." MMEDIA 2012, The Fourth International Conferences on Advances in Multimedia. 2012.

5. Fernando Boronat, Jaime Lloret, Miguel García, Multimedia group and inter-stream synchronization techniques: A comparative study, Information Systems, Volume 34, Issue 1, March 2009, Pages 108-131, ISSN 0306-4379, Oxford, UK.

6. Montagud, M., Boronat, F., Stokking, H., & van Brandenburg, R. (2012). Inter-destination multimedia synchronization: schemes, use cases and standardization. Multimedia Systems, 18(6), 459-482.

7. Geerts, D., Vaishnavi, I., Mekuria, R., Van Deventer, O., & Cesar, P. (2011, May). Are we in sync?: synchronization requirements for watching online video together. In Proceedings of the SIGCHI Conference on Human Factors in Computing Systems (pp. 311-314). ACM.

8. Julien Ridoux and Darryl Veitch. 2010. Principles of Robust Timing over the Internet. Queue 8, 4, Pages 30 (April 2010), 14 pages.

9. Pablo Cesar and Konstantinos Chorianopoulos. 2009. The Evolution of TV Systems, Content, and Users Toward Interactivity. Found. Trends Hum.-Comput. Interact. 2, 4 (April 2009), 373-95.

10. Pedro Almeida, Jorge Ferraz, Ana Pinho, and Diogo Costa. 2012. Engaging viewers through social TV games. In Proceedings of the 10th European conference on Interactive tv and video (EuroITV '12). ACM, New York, NY, USA, 175-184.

11. Goranka Zoric, Louise Barkhuus, Arvid Engström, and Elin Önnevall. 2013. Panoramic video: design challenges and implications for content interaction. In Proceedings of the 11th European conference on Interactive TV and video (EuroITV '13). ACM, New York, NY, USA, 153-162.

12. van Deventer, M.O., Stokking, H.M., Niamut, O.A., Walraven, F.A., Klos, V.B., Advanced interactive television services require content synchronization. In Proceedings of the 15th International Conference on Systems, Signals and Image Processing, pp.109-112, 2008.

13. Jansen, J., & Bulterman, D. C. (2013, February). User-centric video delay measurements. In Proceeding of the 23rd ACM Workshop on Network and Operating Systems Support for Digital Audio and Video (pp. 37-42). ACM.

14. Wang, A.L. An industrial-strength audio search algorithm, 2003.

15. Gracenote. https://www.gracenote.com/

16. Kooij, W. Playout delay of TV broadcasting, University of Twente, the Netherlands, Master Thesis, 2014.

A Large-scale Exploration of Group Viewing Patterns

Allison J.B. Chaney[*]
Princeton University
achaney@cs.princeton.edu

Mike Gartrell[*]
University of Colorado Boulder
mike.gartrell@colorado.edu

Jake M. Hofman[*]
Microsoft Research
jmh@microsoft.com

John Guiver
joguiver@microsoft.com

Noam Koenigstein
noamko@microsoft.com

Pushmeet Kohli
pkohli@microsoft.com

Ulrich Paquet
ulripa@microsoft.com

ABSTRACT

We present a large-scale study of television viewing habits, focusing on how individuals adapt their preferences when consuming content with others. While there has been a great deal of research on modeling individual preferences, there has been considerably less work studying the preferences of groups, due mostly to the difficulty of collecting group data. In contrast to most past work that has relied either on small-scale surveys, prototypes, or a relatively limited amount of group preference data, we explore more than 4 million logged household views paired with individual-level demographic and co-viewing information. Our analysis reveals how engagement in group viewing varies by viewer and content type, and how viewing patterns shift across various group contexts. Furthermore, we leverage this large-scale dataset to directly estimate how individual preferences are combined in group settings, finding subtle deviations from traditional models of preference aggregation. We present a simple model which captures these effects and discuss the impact of these findings on the design of group recommendation systems.

ACM Classification Keywords

H.5.3. Group and Organization Interfaces: Collaborative Computing; H.3.3. Information Search and Retrieval: Information Filtering

Author Keywords

Group recommendation; group viewing patterns.

INTRODUCTION

We are in the midst of an industry-wide shift, wherein the primary means of home broadcast video entertainment is moving from traditional television sets to online and Web services (e.g., Netflix, Hulu, and Xbox) that contain a rapidly expanding catalogue of content. While there is a substantial body of work on understanding the preferences of individuals in these settings—largely for the purpose of aiding users in discovering relevant and novel content within these catalogues—there is a comparatively small amount of research on modeling

[*]Authors contributed equally.

TVX 2014, June 25–27, 2014, Newcastle Upon Tyne , UK.
Copyright is held by the owner/author(s). Publication rights licensed to ACM.
ACM 978-1-4503-2838-8/14/06 ...$15.00.
http://dx.doi.org/10.1145/2602299.2602309

group viewing habits, mostly owing to the difficulty of collecting co-viewing data. Absent this data, group preferences are often modeled via simple aggregates of the underlying individual preferences. While such approaches are somewhat successful, they obscure more subtle group dynamics and interactions that affect group decision making—for instance, the preferences of a parent and child together may be difficult to determine from what each watches alone.

As reviewed below, previous studies often rely on small-scale, self-reported viewing data to draw qualitative conclusions about group viewing, and most existing large-scale log datasets contain group preference data for only several hundred groups [19, 18]. In contrast, we use a dataset that contains both individual and group viewing patterns from a representative panel of more than 50 million U.S. viewers—in over 50,000 groups—automatically recorded by Nielsen[1]. Hence, our work presents one of the first attempts at understanding the relationship between viewing patterns of groups and their constituent individuals from direct, logged data at scale. Our findings indicate that group context substantially impacts viewer activity and that knowledge of the group's composition can be informative in determining group interests.

Our study makes three key contributions: first, we provide a large-scale analysis of viewing patterns with an emphasis on differences between groups and individuals; we break down what users watch alone, how often they engage in group viewing, and how their preferences change in these contexts. Second, we analyze how individual preferences are combined in group settings. Finally, we propose an approach to group recommendations based on the demographic information of the group's constituent individuals. By capturing interactions between the constituents' preferences, our approach predicts group preferences more accurately than existing group recommendation methods. This calls for more sophisticated non-linear aggregation functions that can better estimate the interplay between individuals within a group.

RELATED WORK

Historic TV Viewing Studies. In the early eighties, Webster and Wakshlag [23] analyzed viewing patterns of groups and individuals. Groups that did not change their composition over time showed more program-type loyalty, similar to individual users. Group composition was not considered, however, and to our knowledge, this has remained unstudied.

Most historic studies of viewing behavior rely on self-reported diary surveys [8, 23] that have a few hundred respon-

---

[1] www.nielsen.com

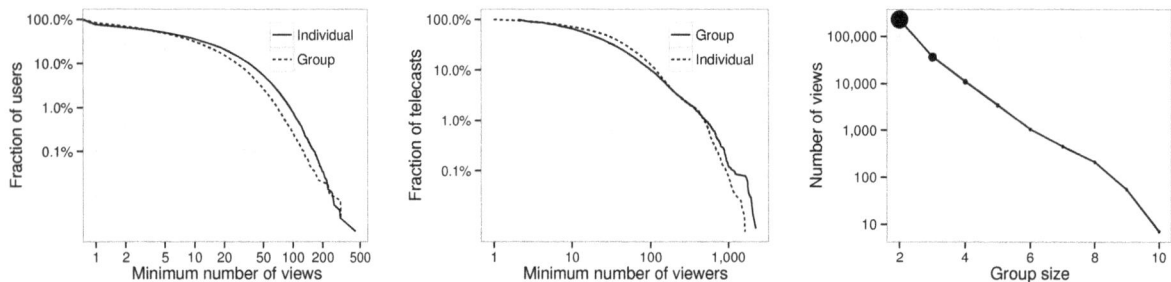

Figure 1. (a) Cumulative distribution of user activity split by individual and group views. (b) Cumulative distribution of telecast popularity by number of viewers. (c) Number of views by group size.

dents, most likely resulting in subject selection biases. Later studies [14] show that television viewing behavior is affected by the demographic characteristics of viewers.

Recommendation Systems for Groups. The problem of group recommendation has been investigated in a number of works [1, 4, 5, 11, 16, 20, 22, 24]. Various techniques target different types of items (e.g., movies, TV programs, music) and groups (e.g., family, friends, dynamic social groups).

Most group recommendation techniques consider the preferences of individuals and propose different strategies to either combine the user profiles into a single group profile, and make recommendations for the pseudo user, or generate recommendation lists for individual group members and then merge these lists for the group. Jameson and Smyth's three main strategies for merging individual recommendations are *average satisfaction*, *least misery*, and *maximum satisfaction* [11], These form the bedrock of group recommendations [1, 5, 13] and we refer to them as "preference aggregation functions." Average satisfaction assigns equal importance to each group member and is used in several group recommendation systems [4, 24, 25]; both average satisfaction and least misery are reasonable candidates for group decisions [13]. Different user weights, dissimilarity among group members, and social connections are also used in aggregation models [3, 1, 6]. If the group is guaranteed to remain static, the dynamic aspect of groups can be ignored [22]. All of this work involves relatively small-scale studies or prototypes; related research on group recommendations relies on synthetically generated data from the MovieLens dataset [2, 12, 15].

Smaller practical recommender systems include PolyLens, a group-based movie recommender that targets small, private, and persistent groups [16] and considers the nature of groups, rights of group members, and social value functions. PartyVote provides a democratic mechanism for selecting and playing music at social events [20].

Larger group preference datasets are beginning to emerge. The 2011 Challenge on Context-Aware Movie Recommendation (CAMRa 2011) used a dataset from the Moviepilot Web site consisting of about 170,000 users, 24,000 movies, and 4.4 million ratings [18]. This dataset also provides household membership identifiers, but this "group" component is substantially smaller: it accompanies a user's rating for only 290 households. Many group recommendation approaches have been proposed and evaluated using this dataset [7, 9,

10]. Similarly, a large-scale dataset from the BARB organization is used in [19], which consists of about 15,000 users, 6,400 households, and 30 million TV program views. However, only 136 of these households are used in [19], since the rest lack sufficient group activity.

In contrast to prior work, our work uses a dataset containing hundreds of thousands of implicit group preferences, along with substantial metadata for individuals, households, and programs. This dataset has been actively recorded, and contains detailed demographic information for a large representative sample of viewers. We present further details below.

DATASET
The Nielsen Company maintains a panel of U.S. households and collects TV viewing data through both electronic metering and paper diaries. In the month of June 2012, Nielsen recorded 4,331,851 program views by 75,329 users via their electronic People Meter system, which records both what content is being broadcast and who is consuming that content. We restrict this dataset to events where at least half of the program was viewed[2], resulting in a collection of 1,093,161 program views by 50,200 users. These views are comprised of 2,417 shows with 16,546 unique telecasts (e.g., individual series episodes, sports events, and movie broadcasts). Each program is associated with one of 34 genres and other metadata, including the distributor and optional sub-genre.

Users also have associated metadata, including age and gender, and are assigned to households, allowing a simple heuristic for identifying group viewing activity. We define a group view as one where at least two members of a household each watch at least half of the same telecast on the same day. There are 279,546 such group views in our dataset. When a user watches the majority of a telecast alone, we define this an individual view; 813,615 individual views are present. Due to the large number of views all viewing pattern results presented later in this paper are statistically significant.

The number of programs watched by users exhibit a heavy-tailed distribution, with many users viewing only a handful of telecasts while a few heavy users consume substantially more content. Figure 1a shows that roughly half of all users have viewed at least 5 telecasts individually; likewise, another (probably overlapping) half of users have viewed at least 5

---

[2]This 50% threshold simplifies our analysis so that at most one telecast can be viewed by each user in a given time slot.

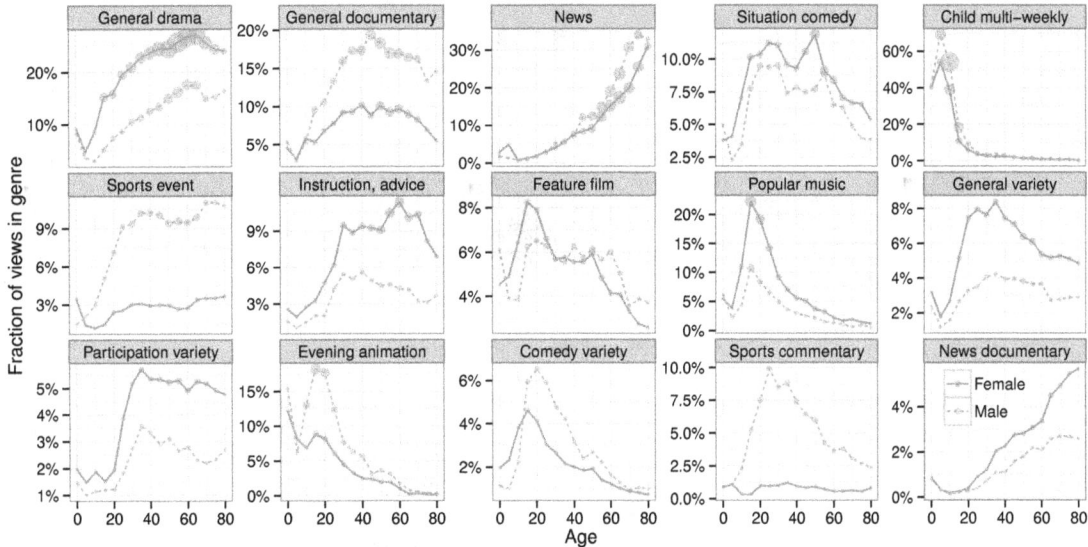

Figure 2. Distribution of views across genres by age and gender.

telecasts in a group. Similarly, most programs are watched relatively infrequently, with a few being very popular. For example, Figure 1b shows that less than 10% of telecasts have been viewed by at least 100 different users. We note that telecast popularity is slightly higher in group settings because each individual in a group view is counted separately here, so that a show watched by a pair of individuals is counted as two views for that broadcast. Finally, as shown in Figure 1c, upwards of 80% of co-viewing occurs in groups of size two, with larger groups occurring substantially less frequently. Most (78%) of couple views are by two adults, with 86% of such groups comprised of one male and one female.

INDIVIDUAL VIEWING PATTERNS

In this section, we analyze how individual viewing behavior varies with age and gender. For this purpose, we compute the genre-specific view counts in the context of demographic information. Figure 2 depicts how users of varying age and gender distribute their attention across genres at the aggregate level. Panels are ordered by decreasing overall genre popularity, and point size shows the relative fraction of overall views accounted for by each demographic group in each genre.

We observe strong age effects for the viewing of certain genres like general drama, child multi-weekly, evening animation, news, popular music, general variety and news documentary. For instance, we observe that older viewers spend a large fraction (about 20-30%) of their time watching news relative to teenagers, who consume little of this genre and devote substantially more of their attention to popular music shows. Likewise, general documentaries are more popular with adults and seniors than with children, while child multi-weekly programs are popular for children and much less popular with adults and seniors, as one would expect. General dramas are quite popular for every age and gender demographic we examined.

We also see gender differences in individual preferences, with females spending more of their time watching talk shows,

drama, and music relative to males, who prefer animation, documentaries, and sports. Sports events tend to be more popular with males than with females, across all ages.

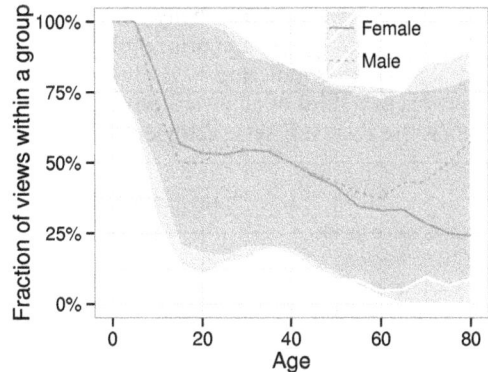

Figure 4. Fraction of views within a group by age and gender.

GROUP VIEWING PATTERNS

Having briefly investigated individual viewing activity, we turn to the main analysis of the paper and analyze group viewing patterns. We examine engagement in group viewing by group and program type, how groups of various types distribute their viewing time, and how individuals modify their viewing habits in group contexts.

Group Engagement

As noted above, roughly a quarter of all views in our dataset occur in groups of size two or larger, comprising a sizable fraction of total activity. To gain further insight into the composition of groups, Figure 4 shows the relative amount of group viewing by users of different ages and gender. The solid lines indicate the median fraction of group views for the specified demographic, with the top and bottom of the surrounding ribbon showing the upper and lower quartiles, respectively. We see that younger users spend the majority (~75%) of their time viewing in groups compared to older viewers. Viewers in their 20s and 30s spend roughly equal

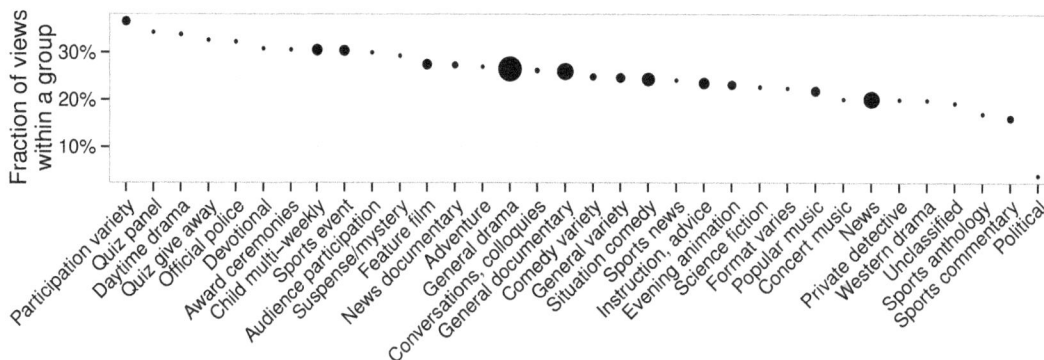

Figure 3. Fraction of views within a group by genre.

amounts of time viewing alone and in groups, whereas older viewers generally spend slightly more time watching individually. We observe small gender effects for younger individuals and larger gender effects for older individuals, with younger females and older males displaying a higher rate of group views relative to their counterparts.

Next we investigate the type of content consumed by these groups. As shown in Figure 3, the relative fraction of group viewing varies significantly by genre. While more than a third of views on quiz shows, drama, and sports events are within groups, only 20% of music, news, and politics views occur in groups settings. We note that many of the genres that are likely to be viewed by groups comprise a relatively small fraction of total activity, as indicated by point size. For example, while upwards of a third of all award ceremony views are in groups, there are relatively few such views overall.

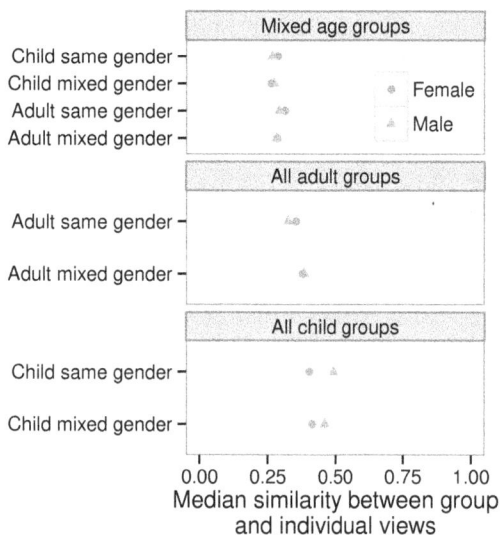

Figure 5. Similarity between group and individual viewing distributions.

Individual vs. Group Viewing

With this understanding of group engagement, we turn our attention to how individual viewing habits change in group settings. To do so, we compute viewing profiles for each user in the dataset under various group contexts and compare their individual and group profiles. Specifically, we characterize each user as either an adult or child (over/under 18, respectively) and male or female; likewise, we categorize each

group view by its gender (all male/mixed gender/all female) and age (all adult/mixed gender/all child) breakdowns. For each user, we compute the fraction of time they spend viewing each genre alone and in each of these nine possible group types. We then quantify the similarity between each user's individual and group view profiles using Hellinger distance, a metric over probability distributions.[3] Finally, we aggregate by user and group type and report the median similarity across users in each demographic when viewing in each group setting, as shown in Figure 5. From this plot we see that the similarity between individual and group viewing patterns varies substantially with the age composition of groups and less so with gender breakdown. For example, the bottom panel shows that activity by groups of all children looks most similar to views by individual children, compared to the mixed age groups in the top panel, which display the largest deviations from what members of those groups watch individually. Thus, the younger and more homogeneous the group, the higher the similarity between group and individual views.

For more details on how preferences shift in individual and group settings, Figures 6 and 7 show how attention is redistributed across genres with different age and gender audience compositions, respectively. For example, Figure 6 reveals that feature films are more popular among mixed age groups than they are either for individuals or groups of the same age. Likewise, we see that children devote substantially more of their time to child multi-weekly shows when viewing in groups (~50%) compared to viewing alone (~30%). Adults watch more dramas, documentaries, and sports events in groups with other adults, and are more likely to watch news, sports commentary, and advice shows alone. We also see that adults and children both compromise on certain genres: one group watching more than usual and the other watching less. This occurs for many genres, including dramas and documentaries, where adults watch less than usual and children watch more, as well as popular music and evening animation, where children watch less and adult watch more together than they do separately. We see little compromise for adults on sports events and participation shows, possibly due to time sensitivity; in both of these cases, adults watch just as much as they do in groups with other adults, and children watch far more than they otherwise would.

---

[3]Hellinger distance is normalized to fall between 0 and 1; we measure similarity by the complement of Hellinger distance.

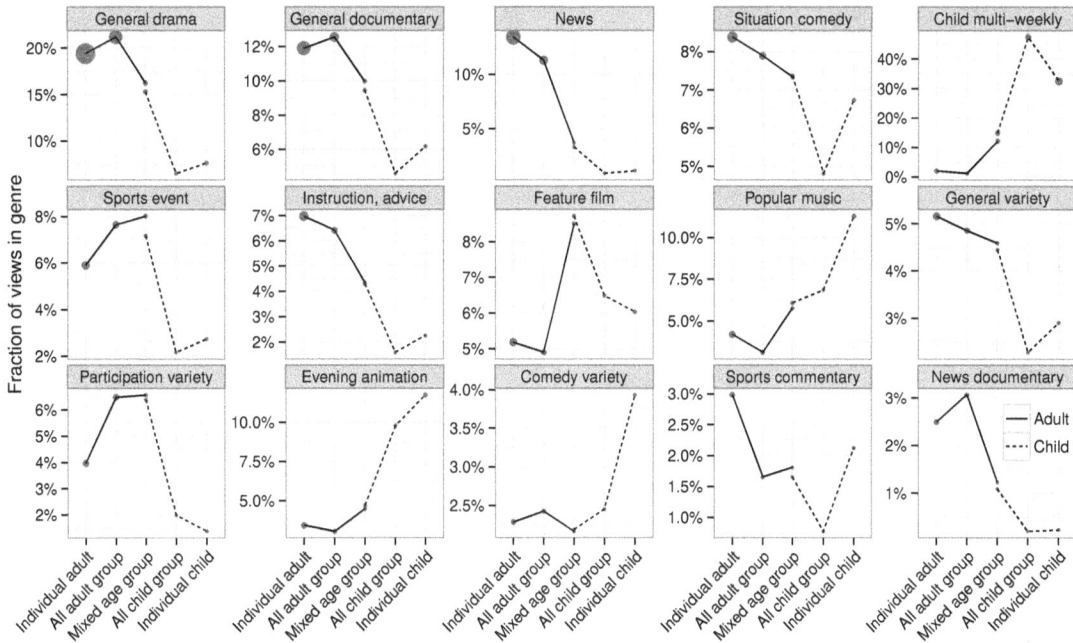

Figure 6. Distribution of views by genre for adults and children in different group contexts.

We also see substantial shifts in preferences as gender composition varies in Figure 7. For instance, feature films are more popular with same gender groups than they are with either individuals or mixed gender groups, whereas the opposite effect is seen for news, which is more popular amongst individual males and females than in groups. We also see that news is more popular in mixed gender groups than in same-gender groups. We speculate that this effect is attributed to passive viewing patterns of couples in the same household, rather than an active desire to watch news as a group. While these changes are fairly similar between men and women, we note that other genres show gender-specific effects. For example, groups of men spend nearly double the amount of their time watching sports compared to individual males, but no such difference is seen for females. Likewise, all female groups spend substantially more of their time viewing popular music shows than do individual females. Finally, as with age effects, mixed gender groups appear to compromise on many categories. For dramas, advice, and sitcoms, men watch more and women watch less together than when in homogeneous groups. We see the reverse effect for documentaries, evening animation, and sports shows, with women watching more and men watching less.

GROUP RECOMMENDATIONS

The previous section explores the differences between a group's preferences and those of its individual constituents. While these effects are large at the aggregate level, both groups and individuals have substantial variability in their tastes, which can make modeling any particular group's preferences difficult. We investigate this problem in more detail—namely, assuming that we know what the members of a group like individually, how do we aggregate their preferences to predict what the group will view?

We approach this problem in two steps. First, we fit a matrix factorization model to approximate individual preferences, which demonstrates good empirical results in predicting individual views. Next, we evaluate popular baseline methods for aggregating each individual's modeled preferences to predict group activity. We find that three of the traditional aggregation methods fail to capture subtle non-linearities and interactions between individual preferences, which we are able to estimate directly from our large-scale dataset. We propose a relatively simple model to account for these features that provides further insight into group decision making.

Modeling Individuals

To examine how to best combine preferences of individuals in a group, we first need a means of determining each individual user's interest in each telecast in our dataset. We use the Matchbox recommendation system [21] without features, which fits a matrix factorization model to user's individual viewing activity to approximate these preferences.

Fitting such a model requires information about both "positive examples"—the telecasts that a given individual viewed—and "negative examples"—telecasts that were available to individuals but not consumed. Unfortunately our dataset lacks negative examples, so we approximate this set as follows: for each telecast viewed by an individual, we consider all simultaneously broadcast telecasts on all channels in a user's viewing history as potential negative examples. This results in roughly 16 negative examples for every positive example across the dataset. To keep a balanced number of positive and negative examples in our training set, we sample one negative example for each positive one, weighting telecasts by overall popularity [17].

We train Matchbox using this dataset with $K = 20$ latent trait dimensions on a randomly selected training set composed of

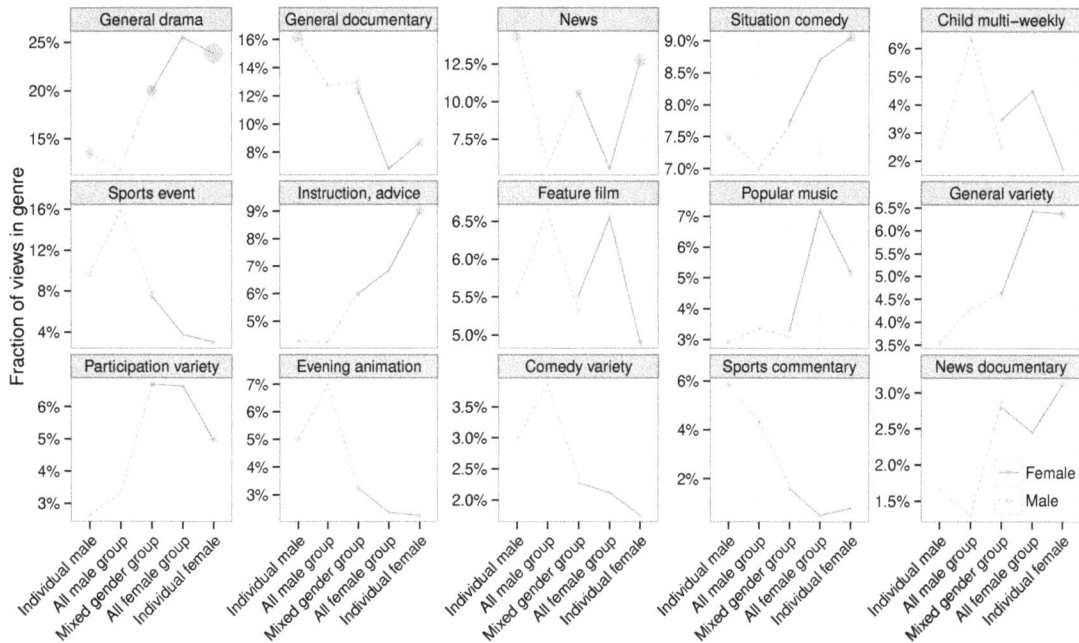

Figure 7. Distribution of views by genre for men and women in different group contexts.

80% of the individual view data set, with the remaining 20% of individual views used for the test set. We set the user threshold prior and noise variances to 0, assuming a time-invariant threshold and a binary likelihood function. We place flexible priors on users and items by setting the user trait variance and item trait variance hyperparameters to $\frac{1}{\sqrt{K}}$, and the user bias variance and item bias variance hyperparameters to 1. The best-fit individual model found by Matchbox has an AUC of 88.3% on the held-out test set. Given this performance, we consider the model to be a reliable approximation to individual preferences and next investigate the group recommendation problem.

Preference Aggregation

As noted in our overview of related work, there are many approaches to aggregating individual preferences. Here we investigate three of the simplest, which are commonly used: least misery, average satisfaction, and maximum satisfaction. Denoting individual preference that user u has for item i by p_{ui}, these methods predict group preferences as follows:

$$\text{least misery}: \quad \min_{u \in G} p_{ui}$$
$$\text{average satisfaction}: \quad \frac{1}{|G|} \sum_{u \in G} p_{ui}$$
$$\text{max satisfaction}: \quad \max_{u \in G} p_{ui}.$$

Least misery aims to minimize dissatisfaction of the least satisfied individual, maximum satisfaction to maximize enjoyment of the most satisfied, and average satisfaction takes an equal vote amongst all members.

After learning individual preferences with Matchbox, we evaluate each of these aggregation methods on all group views in our dataset. We find a strict ordering in terms of performance, with maximum satisfaction slightly outperforming average satisfaction, and both dominating least misery,

across and within all group types. We find an overall AUC of 83.0% for maximum satisfaction, 82.6% for average satisfaction, and 79.7% for least misery. In further examining the quality of group predictions by group type, we see that mixed age and mixed gender group views are the most difficult to predict, with an AUC of 81.3%. Likewise, groups of all children are easiest to model, with performance on all male groups being considerably higher compared to all female groups (AUCs of 89.7% and 84.1%, respectively). Note that these results are obtained with maximum satisfaction and are largely consistent with the individual-to-group similarity comparison in Figure 5.

While some work on preference aggregation has been constrained to these relatively simple functions over individual preferences, our large-scale dataset of hundreds of thousands of group views enables us to conduct a direct examination of group preference landscapes. For simplicity, we limit this analysis to groups of only two members (which comprise 80% of all group views). For each group viewing event in our dataset, we bin the individual predicted probability for each member of the group to the nearest ten percent and aggregate views to examine the empirical probability of a group view within each bin. Panel 3 of Figure 8 shows the result for adult mixed gender couples, with the binned male's and female's preference on the x- and y-axis, respectively, and the probability of a group view on the z-axis. The predicted landscape for average satisfaction and maximum satisfaction are shown in the first two panels for comparison, from which it is clear that these traditional aggregation functions are overly simple, missing crucial interactions and non-linearities in the group preference landscape.

The empirical landscape appears to be a mixture of the average and maximum satisfaction functions, but differs from both of these functions along the diagonal, where users share

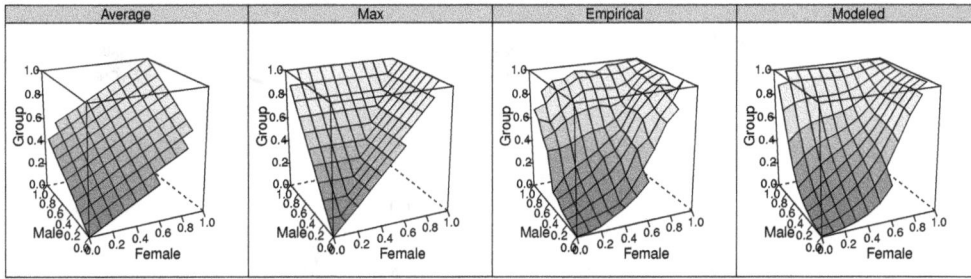

Figure 8. Modeled and actual probability of group viewing as a function of individual viewing for 2-person, mixed-gender adult couples.

identical individual preferences. For example, when both individuals equally dislike a program, there is a lower probability that the group will view the show than traditional approaches suggest. This difference is highlighted in Figure 9a, where the dotted line indicates the (identical) predictions made by average satisfaction, least misery, and maximum satisfaction, whereas the points show the empirical probabilities of group viewing. We see a similar deviation when matched preferences are large, showing a slightly higher likelihood of group viewing than naive methods predict. We also see that average satisfaction deals poorly with the extremes: for example, when one individual has a strong preference for a show while the other has a strong preference against it. One explanation for this behavior is a repeated bargaining scenario where groups alternate between satisfying a different individual in each instance.

In addition to differing from the three simple aggregation functions discussed above, the empirical landscape also deviates from predictions made by other popular aggregation methods [13]. For instance, the "average without misery" strategy corresponds to simply zeroing out the average satisfaction landscape below a certain predicted group preference, while the "multiplicative" method would result in a parabolic landscape.

To capture these subtleties, we fit a simple logistic regression with interactions to determine the probability of a group view (p_G) from the individual probabilities:

$$\log \frac{p_G}{1 - p_G} = \alpha_0 + \alpha_f p_f + \alpha_m p_m +$$
$$\beta_f p_f^2 + \beta_m p_m^2 + \gamma_f p_f^3 + \gamma_m p_m^3 + \delta p_f p_m,$$

where p_f is the female's probability of viewing the show individually and p_m is the male's. The β and γ terms accommodate the non-linearities in the landscape, while the δ term accounts for multiplicative interactions. The resulting model fit for two-person, mixed-gender adult couples, shown in the fourth panel of Figure 8, provides an improved approximation to the empirical landscape, with an AUC of 83.1% compared to 82.9% and 82.7% for maximum satisfaction and average satisfaction, respectively, on a randomly selected 20% held-out test set. Importantly, we note that while the differences in these aggregate metrics may seem insignificant, the model performs substantially better in crucial portions of the landscape—for example, traditional methods overpredict in regions where both group members dislike content (e.g., small individual values in Figure 9a), leading to potential dis-

satisfaction and possibly lost of trust in the recommender system. Aggregate metrics understate these improvements due to the non-uniform density of group views along the landscape.

Figure 9b shows further details of the model for mixed-gender adult couples, taken along slices of the landscape where either the male or female is indifferent, corresponding to a individual preference of 0.5. For instance, the blue curve in Figure 9b shows how the probability of a group view changes with the male's individual preference when the female's preference is held fixed at 0.5, and vice versa for the pink curve. This highlights two key observations: first, the modeled curves are far from (piecewise) linear, as traditional aggregation functions would suggest, and second, we see no obvious signs of gender dominance. We contrast this with Figure 9c, which shows the model fit for two-person mixed age groups. Here we see an asymmetry between adults and children, where the marginal increase in a child's interest at low preference levels has higher impact than an adult's.

We note that while we have discussed only mixed gender and age couples here, these same qualitative observations apply to other group types: a simple non-linear group model provides a better fit to the empirical group landscape compared to traditional aggregation functions, which translates to improved performance for group recommendations.

CONCLUSIONS

Throughout this study we have seen that groups are more complex than the sum of their parts. In particular, we saw that viewing habits shift substantially between individual and group contexts, and groups display markedly different preferences at the aggregate level depending on their demographic breakdowns. This led to a detailed investigation of preference aggregation functions for modeling group decision making. Owing to the unique nature of the large-scale observational dataset studied, we directly estimated how individual preferences are combined in group settings, and observed subtle deviations from traditional aggregation strategies.

While we were able to explain observed group behavior with a relatively simple model, these results raise nearly as many questions as they answer. For example, further investigation is required to understand *why* these preference landscapes take the shape they do, with third-order non-linearities. Likewise, untangling the driving forces behind these observations requires more than simple observational data. On one hand, effects could be explained by direct influence of individuals on each other, while on the other hand these outcomes may

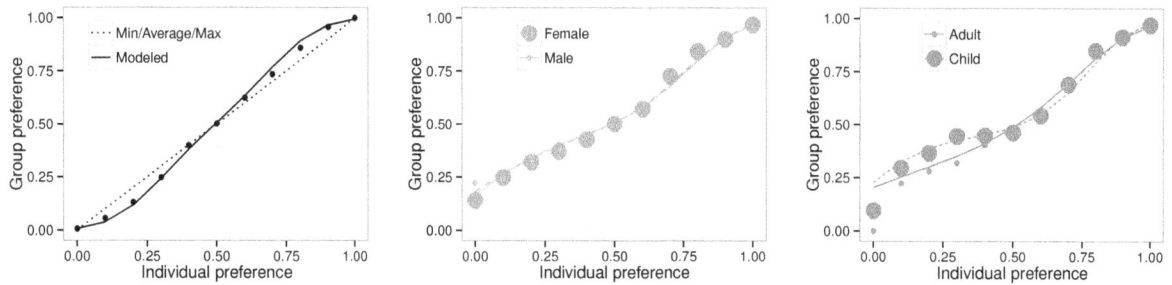

Figure 9. (a) mixed gender adult couples with identical preferences, (b) mixed gender adult couples where one member is indifferent, (c) mixed age pairs where one member is indifferent.

be confounded with homophily, wherein individuals tend to preferentially participate in groups that share their tastes. We leave answers to these questions along with generalizations to arbitrary group settings as future work.

ACKNOWLEDGEMENTS
We thank Nir Nice for acquiring a license for the Nielsen dataset used in this work.

REFERENCES
1. Amer-Yahia, S., Roy, S. B., Chawla, A., Das, G., and Yu, C. Group recommendation: Semantics and efficiency.
2. Baltrunas, L., Makcinskas, T., and Ricci, F. Group recommendations with rank aggregation and collaborative filtering. In *RecSys* (2010).
3. Berkovsky, S., Freyne, J., and Coombe, M. Aggregation trade offs in family based recommendations. In *Australasian Joint Conference on Advances in Artificial Intelligence* (2009).
4. Boratto, L., Carta, S., Chessa, A., Agelli, M., and Clemente, M. L. Group recommendation with automatic identification of users communities. In *WI-IAT* (2009).
5. de Campos, L., Fernández-Luna, J., Huete, J., and Rueda-Morales, M. Managing uncertainty in group recommending processes. *Journal of User Modeling and User-Adapted Interaction 19* (2009).
6. Gartrell, M., Xing, X., Lv, Q., Beach, A., Han, R., Mishra, S., and Seada, K. Enhancing group recommendation by incorporating social relationship interactions. In *GROUP* (2010).
7. Gim, G., Jeong, H., Lee, H., and Yun, D. Group-aware prediction with exponential smoothing for collaborative filtering. In *CAMRa* (2011).
8. Goodhardt, G. J., Ehrenberg, A. S. C., Collins, M. A., et al. *The television audience: patterns of viewing. An update.* No. Ed. 2. Gower Publishing Co. Ltd., 1987.
9. Gorla, J., Lathia, N., Robertson, S., and Wang, J. Probabilistic group recommendation via information matching. In *WWW* (2013).
10. Hu, X., Meng, X., and Wang, L. Svd-based group recommendation approaches: an experimental study of moviepilot. In *CAMRa* (2011).
11. Jameson, A., and Smyth, B. Recommendation to groups. In *The adaptive web: methods and strategies of web personalization* (2007).
12. Kim, H.-N., Rawashdeh, M., and El Saddik, A. Tailoring recommendations to groups of users: a graph walk-based approach. In *IUI* (2013).
13. Masthoff, J. Group modeling: Selecting a sequence of television items to suit a group of viewers. *Journal of User Modeling and User-Adapted Interaction 14*, 1 (2004).
14. McCarty, J. A., and Shrum, L. The role of personal values and demographics in predicting television viewing behavior: Implications for theory and application. *Journal of Advertising 22*, 4 (1993), 77–101.
15. Ntoutsi, E., Stefanidis, K., Nørvåg, K., and Kriegel, H.-P. Fast group recommendations by applying user clustering. In *Conceptual Modeling.* Springer, 2012, 126–140.
16. OConnor, M., Cosley, D., Konstan, J. A., and Riedl, J. Polylens: A recommender system for groups of users. In *European Conference on Computer-Supported Cooperative Work* (2001).
17. Paquet, U., and Koenigstein, N. One-class collaborative filtering with random graphs. In *WWW* (2013).
18. Said, A., Berkovsky, S., and De Luca, E. W. Group recommendation in context. In *CAMRa* (2011).
19. Senot, C., Kostadinov, D., Bouzid, M., Picault, J., Aghasaryan, A., and Bernier, C. Analysis of strategies for building group profiles. In *UMAP* (2010).
20. Sprague, D., Wu, F., and Tory, M. Music selection using the partyvote democratic jukebox. In *AVI* (2008).
21. Stern, D. H., Herbrich, R., and Graepel, T. Matchbox: large scale online bayesian recommendations. In *WWW* (2009).
22. Vildjiounaite, E., Kyllnen, V., and Hannula, T. Unobtrusive dynamic modelling of tv programme preferences in a finnish household. *Journal of Multimedia Systems 15* (2009).
23. Webster, J. G., and Wakshlag, J. J. The impact of group viewing on patterns of television program choice. *Journal of Broadcasting & Electronic Media 26*, 1 (1982), 445–455.
24. Yu, Z., Yu, Z., Zhou, X., and Nakamura, Y. Handling conditional preferences in recommender systems. In *IUI* (2009).
25. Yu, Z., Zhou, X., Hao, Y., and Gu, J. Tv program recommendation for multiple viewers based on user profile merging. *Journal of User Modeling and User-Adapted Interaction 16*, 1 (2006).

Detection of Predictability Ratings of Live Events on TV by Use of Second Screens

Kiraz Candan Herdem

Human Computer Interaction, Department of Electrical and Computer Engineering
Iowa State University, 1620 Howe Hall, Ames, IA, 50011, USA
cherdem@iastate.edu

ABSTRACT

Event predictability, one dimension of human emotion description, indicates to what extent sequences of events in videos are predictable for viewers. This study adopts second screening style of Social TV viewing model, where viewers text about live events on TV via social media app on mobile second screen. 14 instances from different TV content types are presented to 19 viewers on TV-like screen. While texting, custom Twitter application collects touch and inertial sensors' data of which features are extracted to model viewers' physical interaction with mobile screens. Viewers self-reported their predictability ratings via a slider with 9 scales, which later are divided equally into three levels indicating whether viewers describe events in videos as unpredictable, medium or predictable. Bayesian networking classifier is created to recognize the three predictability labels from features described in physical interaction model. The study result shows that the predictability labels are recognized with 85.7% average accuracy.

Author Keywords

Social TV viewing; mobile second screens; event predictability ratings; mobile physical interaction.

ACM Classification Keywords

H.5.2. Information interfaces and presentation (e.g., HCI): User Interfaces: Input devices and strategies.

INTRODUCTION

Sensing how the viewers perceive live programs on TV in real time could enable the design of social TV systems presenting more interesting and enjoying programs to the media consumers. However, viewers are interested more with social communication of their viewing experiences via second screen social media apps[27] than interacting with second screen TV app[28].

How people perceive the instances of TV content is explored through social media messages[32] or usage analysis of second screen apps enabling users to interact with each other[25,31]. Main disadvantage of those techniques is difficulty of processing the big data and presenting the results in real time.

Events are part of viewers' emotional experience[24] that causes them to feel certain emotions and message generation to express them on social media. Previous mobile emotion detection studies show that users emotional states[5,12,17,18,19] and personalities[4] are recognized from nonverbal interaction on mobile devices. Although those methods are helpful, except [12], the analyses are unable to provide a general user independent subjectivity detection model, which may be due to focusing on one aspect of nonverbal physical interaction. Besides, they don't take into account the change in user subjectivity based on event-by-event change[4,5,12,17,18,19]. Also, some of those methods are evaluated with limited numbers of user participation[18].

This study aims to recognize how the viewers perceive an eventual scene on TV from their non-verbal communication on mobile second screens. It reflects the two certain attributes of embodied interaction[8]: physical/tangible contact with a mobile device and social computing of a mobile experience. A user study is performed to understand viewers' engagement with live events on TV. Event predictability[11] is later added as one dimension of Core Affect[24] and it indicates to what extent sequences of events in videos are predictable for a viewer[11]. 19 viewers are invited to the lab. 14 instances from different TV content types are extracted and presented to them on TV-like screen and they are asked to create a tweet and then report their emotional states for each video after they viewed them. Custom Twitter based social media app collects touch and inertial sensors' data of which features are extracted to model their physical interaction with mobile screens. Viewers self-reported the predictability ratings via a slider with 9 scales of which later are divided equally into three levels indicating whether viewers describe events in videos as unpredictable, medium or predictable. Bayesian networking classifier is created to recognize the three predictability labels from features described in physical interaction model. The study results show that the predictability labels are recognized with 85.7% average accuracy.

RELATED WORK

This study synthesizes knowledge from three disciplines to propose a new method for sensing event predictability dimension of Core Affect to describe user emotional state: Second Screen TV viewing user experience, affective science and mobile affective computing.

Viewing TV with Second Screens

Second screens are used either to view and interact with TV content via applications[2] or socially connect with wide viewers community on social media while viewing TV[21,30] at the same time.

This study adopts second style of Social TV viewing model[3], where a viewer texts about her/his TV viewing experience via a mobile second screen app to share it synchronous with virtual community of other viewers on social media. Twitter's open network structure enables its users to diffuse their opinions via weak ties. Users' motivation to share their experiences on social media is to feel connected to a larger community with common interest[7,21,30] and simply micro-blogging their experience with no particular audience in mind[7,20,30], but for those viewers who are interested in the topic by using hashtags[30][20]. Certain events within the program have caused them to tweet and tweets include comments on story and characters' quotes[21].

Affective Science

User subjectivity is named as sentiment, mood, emotion, affect, etc. and although they are different, it is hard to distinguish one another. If, for instance, emotion is selected, most researchers still don't agree upon how to describe emotion[9,24] and how to distinguish emotion types from each other. Therefore, the present study is grounded on present findings of Affective Science researches.

User Emotional Experience/Episode

Humans tag their emotional episode with some labels as a result of self categorization of her/his personal state based on interaction with environment[24] (Happiness, sadness, anger, fear, disgust, surprise, and neutral). Those labels become emotion description given at Basic Emotions Theory[9]. However, they represent meta-level emotional experience as humans divide their affective experience to communicate them. Based on psychological construction model of human emotion[24], users' emotional episode is formed following those steps: affective quality of a stimulus cause change in core affect (neurophysiological state[24]) and user feels it through its dimensional attributes (arousal, valence, dominance and recently added event predictability[11]). Then, user attributes the feeling to an event and appraises the event based on factors[24] of its relevance, implication, user's potential to deal with it and (personal, social) norms. Therefore, It provides a good start point to investigate emotion hierarchy in accordance with Affective science research studies.

Describing User Emotions

Emotion is described either based on its types[9] or its dimensions Emotion types used in the study are happiness, sadness, anger, fear, surprise, disgust, and neutral. Emotion dimensions[24] are arousal, valence, dominance, and (event) predictability[11]. The valence scale ranges from feeling unpleasant to pleasant. The arousal scale ranges from feeling passive to active. The dominance scale ranges from feeling in-control to without-control. Event predictability[11] describes to what extent the sequences of events in the videos are predictable to a mobile user. To have control on human emotions, video[26] was previously used stimulus to elicit their emotions. In this study, 14 videos exemplifying different TV content are selected considering their potential of emotional influence on viewers.

Embodied Interaction with Mobile Devices

Interaction with computing devices evolves electrical interaction to symbolic, textual, and graphical form of interaction, and now tangible and social interactions[8]. The last two interactions indicates physicality and contextual meaning assigned to an embodiment of user ideas into real life settings[8]. This study explores embodiment of user emotions in the form of mobile device usage behavior to communicate views related to live events on TV.

Mobile users communicate their intentions via several body cues (posture, movement) to control and command the device. Some of those movements have special meanings mobile devices can sense those gestures (i.e. touch gesture). Recent studies show that mobile users communicated their emotions and personalities not only via touch gesture[12][5,17], but also in various nonverbal bodily forms, such as through use of mobile device[4,19] and its software features[18] for social communication purposes, and device motions[5]. This paper aims to combine all those bits of embodied interaction behavior into a single eventual user experience and to recognize user emotion and emotion dimensions from their embodied interaction with mobile device. Mobile device usage encompasses control of device and commanding the device by body expressions. Bodily expressions are less studied in literature to recognize people's emotions[13]. Discrete gesture types are studied in the context of acting performance and results show that body can be a good modality for emotion recognition[13,29]. Many of the researches in the field demonstrate that rather than use of gesture specific features, emotion dynamic features, general descriptive features to generate gestures, and exploring temporal phases of gestures improve affect recognition performance[13].

USER STUDY

Mobile emotion experiment is a detailed study of user non-acted experience (second screen TV viewing) in controlled lab settings. It has two main design goals: First, to create new methods to recognize several dimensions of user emotions and personalities. Second, to design new interaction methods benefitting from newly proposed methods to improve mobile interaction. As the study is large in scale, only the parts related to detection of self-reported predictability ratings from user physical interaction with a mobile device is reported in the paper.

Experiment Procedure
The participants are recruited through an electronic bulletin board, where participants choose studies by reading title, goals and brief introduction of the tasks in the experiments. The study took place in a lab environment and participants gained course credits for their participation. The experiment has three steps following each other: filling out pre-experiment questionnaire, user tasks completion and filling out post-experiment questionnaire. The experiment with its three steps took around 50 minutes. Pre-experiment questionnaire explores user demographics, and their mobile and social media experiences, which are reported in the "Subjects" section below. Post experiment questionnaire investigates users' concern on videos and design of an affective tool.

Participants are informed about their rights, the goals of the experiment and the user tasks at least four times through the bulletin board, verbal introduction when they first came to lab, on the consent form and when they entered into task room where they will perform assigned user tasks. After they signed consent form and invited to the room, their task for each of the videos, meaning of emotion dimensions that they will report are explained verbally and through instructions on the screen, and through a full live demonstration by the experimenter including steps of the user task for each assigned video. After live demonstration, participants are asked whether they had understood user task for each video. After getting of their confirmation, the experiment has been started. In order to encourage viewers to report their emotional states, Users are on their own in the task room as suggested in [26] and they wear headphone to have optimal flow[6] with event sequences in video, to increase their engagement with videos, and to remove any contextual noise. Viewers were sitting during the experiment, as typing while walking will introduce extra errors to the experience[23]. They viewed videos in random order. Participants follow the described steps for each of videos in the experiment. Before two user tasks, they take 30 seconds break to reduce the effect of previous video on their subjectivity.

Twitter Based Custom Mobile Social Media Application
Mobile device used in the study is iPhone 4 and it samples inertial sensors' (accelerometer, gyroscope) readings at 100 Hz. Application is programmed in Objective C and Twitter API's released by Twitter. Each participant will read instructions on the screen, and then they will view video at full screen mode. After viewing the video, they will take mobile phone located on a desk, and type their personal

Emotional Meta Experience	Stimulus Film and Video Source
Happiness	The Lottery Ticket, Laughing Baby Ripping Paper
Sadness	Titanic, Requiem for a Dream
Disgust	Ear Worm, Manager of a sport Team
Anger	The Out of Towners, Five Easy Pieces
Fear	The Day After Tomorrow, Aftershock: Earthquake in New York
Surprise	Inception, Wayne's World 2
Neutral	You've Got Mail, The Terminal

Table 1: 14 TV contents selected for various Social TV viewing experience based on meta-level user emotions

view about events within videos. Application starts collecting sensors' data when the user starts typing and ends when s/he presses "finished button" on the screen (Figure 1a and 1b). Then, the user reports his/her ratings for several aspects of their emotional states (see Figure 1c). Finally, the user presses on "Send button" (Figure 1d) to post message on anonymous and private Twitter profile and leave the phone back on the desk.

User emotion types are selected by choosing one face image representing 7 different emotional states. Emotion dimensions (arousal, valence, dominance and event predictability) are reported via horizontal slider (see Figure 1c) with 9 discrete levels ranging from unpredictable to predictable on its left and right ends. Later reported 9 discrete levels are converted into three predictability labels by equally dividing the 9 levels into three groups namely, unpredictable, medium and predictable. For instance, if a user moves the bar on horizontal slider to its first, second or third position on the left (see Figure 1c), then it corresponds to that user decides that the event sequences in a viewed video is unpredictable for her/him.

TV Contents as Affective Stimulus
Each two of 14 video clips (see Table 1) are selected for viewers to experience one of 7 emotional experiences. The video clips exemplify some instances from TV programs (11 movie scenes, 1 sports scene, 2 reality show scenes (unscripted situations and unknown participants)). All video clips were found through video sharing web sites (i.e. YouTube, Vimeo). The videos seem like that they are cut from original films uploaded and they are good in audio and video qualities.

Videos are selected with an emphasis on events, story and the expressive capability of the videos, as users should evaluate the event within the video to create a response through the provided second screen app. Some videos were further processed in order to provide considering discrete single event to the viewers. Depending on the event type,

length of the videos varies: shortest video is about 20 seconds and longest one is about 120 seconds. The average length of stimuli set is about 90 seconds.

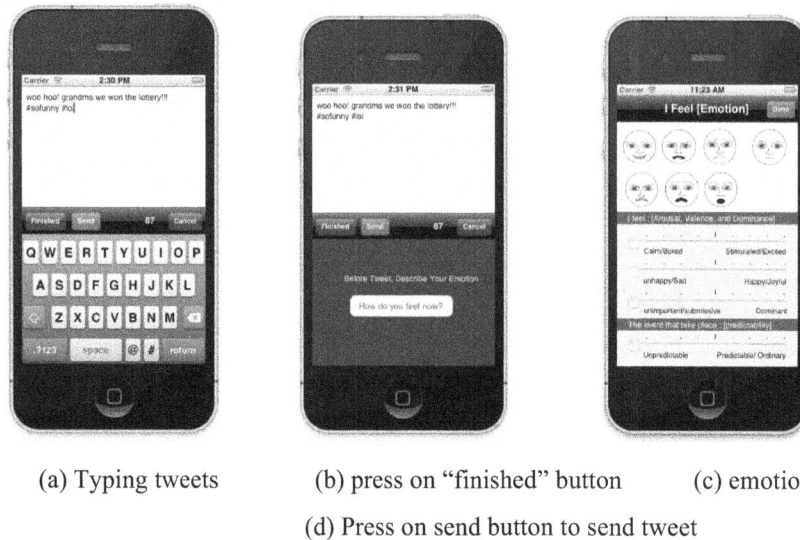

(a) Typing tweets   (b) press on "finished" button   (c) emotion reporting interface

(d) Press on send button to send tweet

Figure 1: The steps of second screen app usage to share TV viewing experience on social media (Twitter)

Subjects

20 undergraduates participated in the experiment and gained course credits for their participation to the study. 14 of subjects are female and the rest 6 subjects are male. All of the subjects were older than 18 years. Users have experience in two fields: mobile phone usage, and video and film viewing. Social TV viewers with second screens are desired participant of the experiment, however as it is newly emerging experience, mobile users with TV viewing experiences are recruited for the experiment. All participants have at least 5 years of mobile phone usage experience. More than half of the participants have exchange 50 messages on a typical day and use Twitter for social interaction purposes. Lastly, more than half of the participants watch TV around 2 hours on a typical day. They prefer to watch TV episodes and movies on TV. 14 of the subjects reported that they like to send tweets or (SMS) messages to their friends about what they watch and the messages includes contents related to taking attention of their social connections, and emotional and opinion messages about the TV contents.

MODELING USER PHYSICAL INTERACTION WITH MOBILE DEVICE

A mobile user communicates her/his intention via several body cues (posture, movement, gesture) to control and command the device. However mobile devices can only sense some physical aspects of user interaction, such as touch and its variations on mobile device[16]. As the previous studies showed promising results about investigation of nonverbal aspects of mobile device, a user physical interaction model is proposed, which explores nonverbal aspect of a social communication message composed with touch gestures and meta-level

communicating movements/gestures that a user is creating dynamically to express her/his intention nonverbally. The contents of textual messages were out of the scope of the study and they are not analyzed at all, because the study only looks for ways to model user physical interaction based on physical body/hand controlled device movements.

Basic Challenges of Creating a User Physical Interaction Model

Using body cues as a single non-verbal communication medium for all interactional needs over mobile phones cause overload on the medium and the underlying communication becomes more complex than ever before. Besides, users' physical behavior is dynamic in nature and they create new behavioral expression based on environmental conditions rather than applying previously recorded behavioral responses[24]. To propose a user independent model that has generalization capability over multi users, Users body cues (movement/gesture, posture) should be explored along the whole nonverbal psychical expression in response to an eventual video during textual content creation on mobile devices. Body expressions are less studied modality to recognize human emotions[13] and current state of art in the field is about exploration of discrete body gestures[13], not of whole communication of nonverbal affective messages.

Meta Analysis of Behavioral Response

Model creation is started with division of user behavioral response into two main parts (instrumental action and expression) in the psychological construction model of emotion[24]. It is equivalent to composing a sentence with words composed by letters. Expression represents variations in the whole affective message whereas instrumental action implies intent to do something and step forward[24]. Variety in expression can be better explored frequency domain analysis of device motion signals, and time domain analysis of the signals will be helpful to explore some visual changes in the instrumental action.

Communication Gestures

A new nonverbal communication language emerges from embodied mobile interaction and social communication. Generally, they can be communication gestures/movements. When using a mobile phone, users decode the attributes of their speech and looks for ways to encode them with non-verbal device usage gestures. Touch gesture defined on mobile phones are created for nonverbal communication purpose[13]. Another example to communication gesture some of paralinguistic features of a speech is encoded via word lengthening phenomenon, such as in typing the word cool as Coooollll![1]. In a user independent physical interaction model, it is hard to identify who created a communication gesture, when it is generated, how long does it take and how many touch gestures are used to create the communication gesture. Therefore, rather than dynamically seeking where a non-verbal gesture starts and ends, a common communication gesture composed of n touch gestures and its temporal phases are defined below. The whole expression is summarized through computation of standard deviation and mean of all communication gestures along their temporal phases.

Communication Gesture Definition by Touch Size

Considering applicability of emotion recognition from typing on PC keyboards[10], following method is proposed. Two types of communication gesture are defined: One includes two consecutive touch gestures. Other includes three consecutive touches. One whole physical interaction may have one or more communication gestures that include two and three touch gestures. Four different types of temporal phases are identified on a communication gesture. They are duration of each touch gesture, overall communication gesture duration, duration from start of first touch gesture to start of next touch gesture and from stop of first touch gesture to stop of next touch gesture. Based on temporal phases definition, communication gesture with two touches has 5 temporal phases and the other has 8 temporal phases.

Bodily Expression Features

The modeling problem now becomes proposing a model to recognize user affects from body gestures. Based on strong supports in recognition of affect from discrete gestures[13,29], following features explaining qualitative aspects of device movement are selected:

- Amount of movement: It represents how much displacement occurs during the movement.

- Energy/power: How much the user is passive or active during the device usage period

- Smoothness/Jerkiness: Jerkiness is third derivative of the displacement.

- Emotion Dynamics: Behavioral expressions are created at the time when needed and users have their own style to produce a behavioral response. The literature suggests that discrete body based gestures can better recognized with extraction of emotion dynamics features.

- Entropy: It represents how much information a communication gesture conveys during physical interaction.

- Relative Amount of Applied Force: The feature corresponds to the displacement when the force is applied and it is relatively measured based on change at movement signals[15] when the touch gesture is applied.

FEATURE EXTRACTION

From the collected sensors' data, following low-level kinematics features are computed: 3 dimensions of linear acceleration, of angular velocity (yaw, pitch, roll) and of earth gravity. The only feature computed for earth gravity is spectral centroid of the gravity. All features given below are computed through both movement signals. Feature set should be rich enough, as nonverbal expression of emotions is creative combinations of behaviors based on assessment of individual's current state[24]. Feature calculation is performed with Matlab R2011a running on Mac OSX.

Computation of Amount of Movement

Time Domain Features

Absolute value of the signals, difference in device movement and correlation within 3 dimensions of motion signals and inter-correlation between movement signals are computed. Difference in device movement is computed by getting first order and second order difference, mean and zero cross, Interquantile range of motion signals. Inter-correlation motion signals are computed by getting angle between two movement signals, pairwise correlation of 3 axes of the two signals and their rate of changes.

Frequency Domain Features

Absolute values of Fourier transform, cepstrum. logfft and Mel-frequency cepstrum transforms are computed to substitute the amount of movement on the domain.

Computation of Smoothness/Jerkiness

On time domain, smoothness is computed through getting absolute gradient of linear acceleration. When it is applied on angular velocity and it provides acceleration on 3 angular dimensions. On frequency domain, smoothness is explored through computation of spectral flatness by dividing geometric mean of the spectrum to arithmetic mean.

Emotion Dynamic Features

Common Dynamic Features

Along time series, gesture duration, number of local maximum and minimum, min, max, central moments (mean, variance, skewness, kurtosis, higher moment), standard deviation, root mean square, matrix norms[22] (1-norm, Frobenius norm, infinity norm, squared l2 norm) are calculated. Along frequency series, number of local max, local minimum, variance, skewness, kurtosis, higher moment, root mean square, and standard deviation are calculated.

Spectrum Dynamic Features

- Band Analysis: Fourier spectrum of the movement signals are divided into five equal bands and named as low, low-medium, medium, medium-high and high frequency bands. Fourier transforms are computed along the bands to observe the effect of band-based change on improving the recognition performance.

- Power Spectrum Dynamic Features: A couple of features descriptive for power spectrum dynamics are computed: bandwidth, spectral centroid, spectral roll-off frequency, area under power curve, and flux of power spectrum (first order difference in the spectrum).

Removing Individual Idiosyncrasies from Features

In order to provide person independent recognition, individual idiosyncrasies are subtracted from the device usage model for each user through the normalization with minmax method. In this method, minimum value of a feature is subtracted from it and the value is divided into a value, which is calculated by subtracting of minimum feature from maximum of feature. With this method, a feature's value for each user is spread to [0,1] range.

Reducing Dimensionality of the Features

Feature selection filter independent from the classifier is applied to find best informative feature set for the same task. The applied feature selection filter is correlation-based feature subset selection method[14] with best first search method that are implemented in Weka, a machine learning code library maintained by University of Waikato. The method is based on the idea that good feature sets should have features highly correlated with output class and yet uncorrelated with each other. Before applying the method, features should have nominal values. Unsupervised discretization filter on Weka is used before the data feed into Bayesian Network classifier.

CLASSIFICATION

The application is build via Twitter API's provided by Twitter. However, from time to time, without any specific reason application stops sending tweets to Twitter. Due to that challenge, some of the data is excluded from the study. Distribution of remaining data along predictability labels is given at Table 2. The number samples exemplifying unpredictable labels is high in total data counts.

Total	Unpredictable	Medium	Predictable
265	116	89	60

Table 2: Distribution of collected data along the event predictability labels

Bayesian theory is a probabilistic model that implicitly assumes significance of priors on posteriors' performance. Mobile device usage is a developmental skill. Each of previous mobile experience will inform a user's learning process and it results in change in users mobile device usage behavior. Due that reason, supervised Bayesian Networking classifier implemented in Weka is selected to recognize the predictability labels from user physical interaction with mobile device. Classifier input is features described in user physical interaction model and its output is predictability labels self-reported by viewers to rate how much the sequences of events in the video are predictable for the viewers.

Applying Wrapping Filter to Remove Features Unrelated to the Classifier

Wrapper approach with information gain attribute in Weka is used to maximize the performance of Bayesian network classifier. Features in the set is ranked according to how much information they gain, starting from lowest ranked features, one feature at a time has been removed from the list to improve the Bayesian Networking classifier performance with less features.

Evaluation

As the size of data set is limited, to evaluate the performance of the classifier, 10 fold cross validation method already implemented in Weka tool, the standard practice in such conditions, is used. Any data collected for classification purposes is first divided into 10 equal folds to decide data sets for training and testing the model and each time, a different fold is removed for testing the model, which is trained with the 9 remaining folds of the data. By this method, all data would be used to test the model's recognition performance and the performance of the model is an average of those 10 different testing results. Accuracy performance rates (true positive, false positive), F-measure, and kappa statistics are reported showing the performance of the model for recognition of user predictability ratings. F measure is computed by dividing multiplication of precision and recall values of classifier performance to addition of those two values. Kappa value can be between 0 (chance agreement between users) and 1 (perfect agreement)[10]. If kappa statistics is larger than 0.4, it will be accepted that the classification rate is true reflection of the model.

RESULTS

Table 3 shows weighted average results of the classification. 85.7% of user predictability ratings are correctly recognized from the user reports. The kappa value for the classifier is 0.77, meaning that the classification rate

	TP	FP	F measure
Unpredictable	0.879	0.114	0.868
Medium	0.865	0.068	0.865
Predictable	0.8	0.044	0.821
Average	0.857	0.083	0.856

Table 3:Bayesian Networking classifier performance for recognition of event predictability labels (TP: True Positive, FP: False positive)

truly reflects the model. True positive rates and F measure values along the three levels are 80% or more and false positive rates are between 4% and 11%, which demonstrate that the model performs well not only average performance but also recognition of class levels.

Selected Features
The study acknowledges previous affective bodily recognition results by showing effectiveness of emotion dynamic features, general descriptive features to generate communication gestures, and exploring temporal phases of those gestures improve affect recognition performance[13,29]. Final feature set includes 65 features. Half of the features are describe angular changes during the experience and the other half describes linear acceleration. The distribution of features along three dimensions (x, y, z) is equal for the dimensions. The most descriptive non-verbal communication gesture size is 3. Weighted numbers of features are resulted from band-based dynamics of frequency domain features. Some information about features in final set is given below:

- The amount of movement: relative absolute force, absolute values of fft and cepstrum coefficients, difference in time series movement (Interquantile range, zero cross and mean cross, and rate of change between linear and angular movement), correlation (within the signal dimensions, and between the two signal dimensions)

- Energy, power, entropy

- Common dynamic features (min, number of local minimums, kurtosis, standard deviation, mean, higher moment, skewness, variance) and Spectrum dynamics of energy, entropy, power and area under power curve and power spectrum dynamics of area under curve and spectral roll-off frequency.

DISCUSSION
The results show that during a second screen TV viewing experience, how a viewer perceives an eventual scene on TV can be recognized from her/his nonverbal physical interaction with a mobile second screen social media application. Significance of event predictability detection and opportunities for future work are discussed.

Event Predictability
Detection of how much a live event is predictable for a viewer is important as that information can give better reasoning whether the content is interesting for a viewer. For instance, if content is predictable for a viewer, then s/he feel bored and look for finding enjoying activity. Implementation of this method in second screens might be useful in Social TV system design to improve personal experiences, community scale experiences. Viewers could know what program or a certain event just takes place that other viewers are excited by and can switch to the channel the content is broadcasted. Directors/producers of TV channels could create contents satisfying viewers' expectations and advertisers' could take better decisions to place commercials into time slot where more people enjoy with the content. They will be willing to pay more if they know how viewers perceive live events on TV in real time.

Conclusion and Opportunities for Future Work
The present study explores event predictability dimension of Core Affect influencing details of user personal emotional episodes/experiences. TV contents are selected based on meta-level emotional experiences and there are many other emotional experiences that should be explored to have idea how viewers behave in those emotional states. However, TV content selection is really a challenging task when considered possible diversity in user emotional experiences. As a future work opportunity, researchers may look for other video clips to study more diverse set of emotional states. The main challenge of the study is dynamic nature of nonverbal behavior generation not only across mobile users with different backgrounds but also across usage of mobile device by same user. The literature mentions that behavioral expressions are creative combinations of behaviors in individuals' repertoire based on task requirements, environment conditions, biological states and some other conditions. One way to overcome the challenge may be improving the physical interaction model in order to meet behavioral differences in those conditions not addressed in the paper. The next step of this study is to create rich user experiences via composition of novel eventual scenes with audio, pictures and stories. By this way, it is aimed to create stories required for recognition of mobile users' subjectivity by their use of mobile devices.

ACKNOWLEDGEMENTS
Author's study is granted by National Ministry of Education, Republic of Turkey. I would like to thank Prof. Julie Dickerson and Prof. Veronica Dark for providing me opportunity to study the present topic and . I would like to thank reviewers who provided improvements for the paper.

REFERENCES
1.Brody, S. and Diakopoulos, N. Cooooooooooooooooolllllllllllll!!!!!!!!!!!!!!: using word lengthening to detect sentiment in microblogs. In *Proc. EMNLP '11*, ACL(2011), 562–570.

2. Cesar, P., Bulterman, D.C. a., Jansen, J., Geerts, D., Knoche, H., and Seager, W. Fragment, tag, enrich, and send. *ACM TOMCCAP*, 5, 3 (2009), 1–27.

3. Cesar, P. and Geerts, D. Understanding Social TV: a survey. In *Proc. NEM Summit 2011*, (2011), 94–99.

4. Chittaranjan, G., Blom, J., and Gatica-Perez, D. Who's Who with Big-Five: Analyzing and Classifying Personality Traits with Smartphones. In *Proc. ISWC 2011*, IEEE (2011), 29–36.

5. Coutrix, C. and Mandran, N. Identifying emotions expressed by mobile users through 2D surface and 3D motion gestures. In *Proc. Ubicomp 2012*, ACM Press(2012), 311–320.

6. Czikszentmihalyi, M. F*low: The Psychology of Optimal Experience*. Harper and Row, 1990.

7. Doughty, M., Rowland, D., and Lawson, S. Who is on your sofa?: TV audience communities and second screening social networks. In *Proc. EuroITV 2012*, ACM (2012), 79–86.

8. Dourish, P. *A History of Interaction*. In Where the Action Is: The Foundations of Embodied Interaction. The MIT Press, London, England, 2004, 1–23.

9. Ekman, P. *Basic emotions*. Handbook of Cognition and Emotion. John Wiley & Sons, Ltd., Sussex, U.K, 2005.

10. Epp, C., Lippold, M., and Mandryk, R.L. Identifying Emotional States using Keystroke Dynamics. In *Proc. of CHI 2011*, ACM Press (2011), 715–724.

11. Fontaine, J, Scherer, K.R., Roesch, E.B., and Ellsworth, P.C. The World of Emotions Is Not Two Dimensional. *Psychological Science* 18, 12 (2007), 1050–1057.

12. Gao, Y., Bianchi-Berthouze, N., and Meng, H. What does touch tell us about emotions in touchscreen-based gameplay? *ACM TOCHI*, 19, 4 (2012), 31.

13. Gunes, H., Shan, C., Chen, S., and Tian, Y. *Bodily Expression For Automatic Affect Recognition*, Advances in Emotion Recognition. Wiley-Blackwell, 2012, 1–31.

14. Hall, M.A. *Correlation-based Feature Selection for Machine Learning*. 1999.

15. Heo, S. and Lee, G. Forcetap: extending the input vocabulary of mobile touch screens by adding tap gestures. In *Proc. Mobile HCI*, ACM (2011), 113–122.

16. Hinckley, K. and Wigdor, D. *Input technologies and techniques*. The Human-Computer Interaction Handbook CRC Press, USA, 2012, 95–132.

17. Kim, H. and Choi, Y.S. Exploring Emotional Preference for Smartphone. In *Proc. IEEE CCNC 2012*, IEEE (2012), 245–249.

18. Lee, H., Choi, Y.S., Lee, S., and Park, I.P. Towards Unobtrusive Emotion Recognition for Affective Social Communication. In *Proc. IEEE CCNC 2012*, IEEE(2012), 276–280.

19. Likamwa, R., Liu, Y., Lane, N.D., and Zhong, L. MoodScope : Building a Mood Sensor from Smartphone Usage Patterns. In *Proc. MobiSys'13*, (2013).

20. Marwick, a. E. and Boyd, D. I tweet honestly, I tweet passionately: Twitter users, context collapse, and the imagined audience. *New Media & Society* 13, 1 (2010), 114–133.

21. McPherson, K., Huotari, K., Cheng, F.Y.-S., Humphrey, D., Cheshire, C., and Brooks, A.L. Glitter: a mixed-methods study of twitter use during glee broadcasts. In *Proc. CSCW 2012*, ACM (2012), 167–170.

22. Miluzzo, E., Varshavsky, A., Balakrishnan, S., and Choudhury, R.R. Tapprints: your finger taps have fingerprints. In *Proc. MobiSys 2012,* ACM (2012), 323–336.

23. Nicolau, H. and Jorge, J. Touch typing using thumbs: understanding the effect of mobility and hand posture. In *Proc. CHI 2012*, ACM(2012), 2683–2686.

24. Russell, J.A. Core Affect and the Psychological Construction of Emotion. *Psychological Review* 110, 1 (2003), 145–172.

25. Sahami Shirazi, A., Rohs, M., Schleicher, R., Kratz, S., Müller, A., and Schmidt, A. Real-time nonverbal opinion sharing through mobile phones during sports events. In *Proc. CHI 2012,* ACM Press (2011), 307–310.

26. Soleymani, M. and Lichtenauer, J. A multimodal database for affect recognition and implicit tagging. *IEEE Transactions on Affective Computing* 3, 1 (2012), 42–55.

27. Spangler, T. TV Viewers Aren't Thrilled with Second-Screen Synchronized Content, Study Finds. 2014. http://variety.com/2014/digital/news/tv-viewers-arent-thrilled-with-second-screen-synchronized-content-study-finds-1201040757/.

28. Spangler, T. Yahoo Is Shutting Down TV App IntoNow - But the Second Screen Isn't Dead Yet. 2014. http://variety.com/2014/digital/news/yahoo-is-shutting-down-tv-app-intonow-but-the-second-screen-isnt-dead-yet-1201075160/.

29. Wallbott, H.G. Bodily expression of emotion. European *journal of social psychology* 28, (1998), 879–896.

30. Wohn, D.Y. and Na, E.-K. Tweeting about TV: Sharing television viewing experiences via social media message streams. *First Monday* 16, (2011), 1–13.

31. Yew, J., Arbor, A., Shamma, D.A., and Churchill, E.F. Knowing Funny : Genre Perception and Categorization in Social Video Sharing. In *Proc. CHI 2011*, ACM Press (2011), 297–306.

32. Zhao, S., Zhong, L., Wickramasuriya, J., and Vasudevan, V. Analyzing Twitter for Social TV: Sentiment Extraction for Sports. In *Proc. EuroITV 2011*, (2011), 1–8.

Parasocial Relationship via Reality TV and Social Media: Its Implications for Celebrity Endorsement

Siyoung Chung
Singapore Management University
50 Stamford Road Singapore 178899
sychung@smu.edu.sg

Hichang Cho
National University of Singapore
10 Kent Ridge Crescent, Singapore 119260
cnmch@nus.edu.sg

ABSTRACT

The purpose of this study was to explore the ways in which audiences build parasocial relationships with media characters via reality TV and social media, and its implications for celebrity endorsement and purchase intentions. Using an online survey, this study collected 401 responses from the Korean Wave fans in Singapore. The results showed that reality TV viewing and SNS use to interact with media characters were positively associated with parasocial relationships between media characters and viewers. Parasocial relationships, in turn, were positively associated with the viewers' perception of endorser and brand credibility, and purchase intention of the brand endorsed by favorite media characters. The results also indicated that self-disclosure played an important role in forming parasocial relationships and in mediating the effectiveness of celebrity endorsement. This study specifies the links between an emerging media genre, a communication technology, and audiences' interaction with the mediated world.

Author Keywords

Reality TV, Social Media, Parasocial Relationship, Celebrity Endorsement, Credibility, Purchase Intention.

ACM Classification Keywords

J.4 [**Social and Behavioral Sciences**]: Psychology

INTRODUCTION

Recently, there have been two interesting media phenomena that change the way people interact with their favorite media characters. Reality TV and social media have enabled TV audience to relate to celebrities in a highly intimate and personal way. They have also narrowed the distance between the audience and celebrities and altered the role of audiences from spectators and admirers to active participants in media experience and friends of celebrities.

With *Big Brother*, *Survivor*, and other shows in the early 2000s being early pioneers, the phenomenon of reality TV quickly made its way into homes of TV audiences. Reality

TV shows have, in general, "the voyeuristic focus on unguarded, unscripted, and intimate experiences of other people, whether ordinary people or celebrities, from unseen, unacknowledged vantage points" [1, p.7]. While some express concerns about the exhibitionism and voyeurism nature of reality TV [2], viewers welcome reality TV because it is more realistic and engaging than conventional programs, and reality TV shows are more popular than ever [3].

Social networking sites (SNSs), such as Facebook and Twitter, are also changing the dynamics of the audience-media character relationship. In the past, such a relationship was uninteractive, unreciprocal, and highly controlled by media characters or celebrity management companies. Interaction with audience was limited and carefully planned for publicity and promotion. However, SNSs have changed this one-sided relationship to a more interactive and reciprocal one. On SNSs, media characters willingly share seemingly personal information with the audience. In response, audiences 'follow' their favorite celebrities 24/7, peeking into their private lives and getting to know them up close and personal. Using SNSs, viewers can now feel intimately connected to media characters and believe they know the celebrities personally. This type of relationship that people make with celebrities or media characters is called a parasocial relationship [4].

Despite the popularity of reality TV shows and the unprecedentedly rapid adoption of SNSs, surprisingly little is known as to whether or how this changing media environment affects parasocial relationships. Previous research on parasocial relationships was studied in a scripted, non-interactive media setting. Therefore, it is plausible to assume that the process and outcome of parasocial relationships in this new media environment may be qualitatively different. Furthermore, it would be interesting to explore what economic impacts these new media phenomena have, particularly on celebrity endorsement. Since celebrity endorsement is considered as an effective tool in marketing, the interplay among reality TV, SNSs, and celebrity endorsement must be of great interest to researchers and marketers.

In specific, this paper seeks to investigate 1) the ways in which SNSs and reality TV are linked to parasocial relationships between media personality and audiences and 2) the extent to which parasocial relationships are related to the effectiveness of a media personality as a brand endorser.

To address these research topics we used empirical data from an online survey of 401 fans of the Korean Wave (*Hallyu*) in Singapore. This study presents the results of our hypothesis testing using structural equation modeling (SEM), and concludes with a discussion of the findings and implications for future research and practice.

LITERATURE REVIEW

Definition of Parasocial Relationship

Parasocial relationship is a "simulacrum of conversational give and take" [4, p.215] between an audience and a media character which is created due to the mode of direct address, personal, and private conversational style of the media character. Horton and Whol argued that using a direct and personal conversation style media characters, "personae", can create powerful intimacy with television viewers. At the opposite site, through repeated viewing, media viewers would feel this bond of intimacy with the media characters and engage in more "ritualistic viewing" of episodes and develop loyalty toward the media characters [5]. Parasocial relationships resemble interpersonal, face-to-face relationships among people, yet they are typically one-sided and unreciprocal as media characters would neither know the existence of nor have the obligation to maintain such a relationship with media viewers [6,7].

Parasocial relationships start when the audience think media characters *as if they were in the circles of their peers* [4]. Rubin and McHugh [8] found that this anticipated friendship was a more important factor in developing a parasocial relationship than physical attraction. Through repeated viewing and interpretation of media characters' performance, audiences think that they "know" media characters like they know their close friends. Knowledge about the media characters, including their style, personality, preferences, and personal life, is accumulated, and interpretation and understanding of meanings of characters' behaviors (on stage) become more accurate. Viewers think that they really "understand" the media characters.

Intimacy is frequently mentioned and emphasized by Horton and Wohl. They suggested that media characters, through "undisturbed" intimacy, can create such an "influential" and "satisfying" relationship with the audience that the audience wishes to receive advice from the media characters and buy the products that the media characters recommend. Just as people rely on close others for important information, advice, and approval for various behavioral decisions [9], audiences in a parasocial relationship with media characters often seek important and useful information from media characters [10,11,12]. This implies that media characters who have successfully established a strong parasocial relationship with audiences can become effective brand endorsers.

Reality Television

Reality Television is defined as "programs that film real people as they live out events in their lives, contrived or otherwise, as they occur" [13]. It provides unscripted, unrehearsed actions and interactions among participants. Reality TV has enjoyed highest ratings among other TV genres since its arrival. Ordinary people who appeared on reality TV shows have gained instant, though may be temporal, popularity. Reality TV shows hosting stars are also popular (e.g., *The Simple Life, The Osbournes, Newlyweds: Nick and Jessica,* etc.), and they provide media characters with an opportunity to rebrand personalities and propel careers. For example, T.I. a rapper, who is infamous for his violence and crime, shows his unknown fatherly side in a reality TV show called *T.I. & Tiny: The Family Hustle* and Tia and Tamara are enjoying their second peak in their entertainment career after a long pause thanks to the success of *Tia & Tamara*.

Perceived Reality in Television

Numerous studies have reported that the realistically perceived television content has an effect on beliefs and attitudes of viewers [14,15,16]. Busselle and Greenberg [17] stated that individuals who judge television as more realistic are more likely to be influenced by that content. Perceived reality is the success factor of reality TV programs. Papacharissi and Mendelson [18] found that the majority of reality TV viewers perceived the interactions on the shows as real. Other studies reported that the perceived reality of the reality shows was the number one reason for viewing [19,20]. The widely accepted format of reality TV shows is a narrative or conversational style and close surveillance on characters. In this setting, the cast on the shows is made to show unrehearsed, impromptu, and seemingly honest reactions and behaviors in front of cameras. Smart camera techniques such as close up shots and deep focus, selective editing (i.e., cherry-picking scenes, frankenbiting), and frequent interviews with the characters also enhance reality and make the audience feel as though they are watching real life events and real characters. Hence, we predicted the following:

> H1: Reality TV Viewing and perceived TV reality are positively associated.

Perceived reality in television content has been reported to influence parasocial relationship. Horton and Wohl [4] argued that when media characters seem "real," rapport between the characters and audience is easily created. They also suggested that when a TV character acts in a "vivid and arresting way" (p. 215), viewers feel that these remote and hard-to-reach stars are closer as if they were acquaintances or friends. Parasocial interaction is more likely to occur when media characters use a conversational style, inviting responses from audience members [21,22]. Rubin, Perse, and Power [21] reported that perceived realism of media characters was important for forming a parasocial relationship. Hence, we predicted the following:

H2: Perceived reality of television is positively associated with parasocial relationship.

The prospect of connecting to and engaging in conversation with famous people is exciting for audiences. As media characters appear more realistic and down-to-earth, audiences would feel that these stars are more approachable and thus, would be more motivated to contact them directly. Leet, Becker, and Giles [23] found that desire for seeking information (often personal) about celebrities and opportunity for face-to-face meetings or friendship were top motivations to contact celebrities. To contact and communicate with media characters, viewers these days use SNSs because finding and contacting media characters are easier with SNSs than with fan mails or phone calls. Hence, we predicted the following:

H3: Perceived TV reality and SNS use are positively associated.

Social Networking Sites (SNSs)

Celebrities these days use various SNSs such as Facebook and Twitter to engage in a constant conversation with their fans. For example, Snoop Dogg tweeted to his fans to "keep pimpn" and Mariah Carey sent direct messages to her fans using Twitter. Celebrities like Lady Gaga, Katy Perry, and Justin Bieber have more than 60 million fans following them on Twitter or Facebook. Celebrities use SNSs to keep their fans updated with upcoming events such as concerts and movie premiers, to write about personal projects, and to promote charity events. But the most obvious reason for using SNSs is to create a sense of closeness and connectedness with their fans by disclosing their thoughts and emotions. The use of first-person voice, highly opinionated statements on controversial topics, photos taken by celebrities themselves, 'insider' information such as backstage happenings or feuds between other celebrities, and spelling and grammatical errors in messages make SNS messages from celebrities feel personal, intimate, and inviting [24], thus "eras[ing] for the moment the line which separates persona and spectator" [4, p.218].

SNSs are particularly effective in fostering parasocial relationship in many ways. First, using SNSs, audiences can engage in real conversations with their favorite celebrities. People can direct their messages to celebrities using @reply on Twitter or write on the celebrities' Facebook walls and celebrities reply to their fans [24]. Communication via SNSs tends to be frequent and ongoing. This constant communication helps enhancing the feeling of intimacy and bonding, thus deepening the parasocial relationship. More importantly, SNS messages are often self-disclosing and confessional. Horton and Wohl [4] argued that media characters who are "personally and privately" conversing with the audience make the audience more response anticipated, and thus, can create parasocial relationships easily. This "strategically managed self-disclosure"[24] can create "digital intimacy' [25] and may actually provide the audience with the possibility of a substantial and meaningful interactions with celebrities whom the audience cannot meet in person. As information about the media characters increases and uncertainty about them decreases, audiences would feel that they understand the celebrities. As a result, the parasocial relationship with the media characters will deepen. Hence, we predicted the following:

H4: Fans' SNS use and parasocial relationship are positively associated.

Endorser Credibility, Brand credibility, and Purchase Intention

To assess the degree to which parasocial relationships via reality TV and SNS use have a commercial impact, this study explored celebrity endorsement. Celebrity endorsement is considered an effective way to gain attention from and maintaining relationships with consumers. About 20% of U.S. advertisements feature celebrities and this figure is much higher in other countries, such as India (24%) and Taiwan (45%) [26]. Celebrity endorsement is believed to increase attention to advertisements, product recall purchase intention, and brand loyalty [27,28,29,30,31]

A review of relevant literature revealed that one of the most important factors for the effectiveness of endorser is credibility [32]. Expertise and trustworthiness are two major components of credibility. Expertise is defined as the extent to which the endorser is perceived as a valid source of information about the product, and it refers to the knowledge, experience, and skills possessed by the endorser [33]. Trustworthiness refers to the endorser's honesty, believability, and integrity [34]. When consumers evaluate the objectiveness of the endorser to present the information highly, the endorser will be viewed as trustworthy and can be a highly credible source [35].

Marketers always try to capitalize on celebrities who have a high level of persuasive power. It is plausible to think that fans that are in a personal relationship with their favorite celebrities are more likely to think that the celebrities are credible. A high level of intimacy, friendship, and understanding fans have acquired through the parasocial relationship would make the celebrities' claims more appear credible and believable. Therefore, our hypothesis is posited as follows:

H5: Parasocial relationship is positively associated with endorser credibility.

Similarly to endorser credibility, brand credibility refers to the willingness of firms to deliver what they claim (trustworthiness) and the ability to deliver what they promised (expertise) [36]. Brand credibility can be created and shaped by cumulative impact of all previous marketing strategies such as advertising and promotions [37]. Therefore, source appeals in advertisements are expected to have an influence on the perception of brand. Highly credible endorsers are able to transfer their credibility to the brands they endorse [38]. Therefore, the hypothesis is posited as follows:

H6: Endorser credibility and brand credibility are positively associated.

Evidences about the effects of brand credibility have been accumulated in marketing literature. Erdem and Swait [36] suggested that brand credibility increases perceived quality of brand and decreases perceived risk and information costs. Consumers can trust on a credible brand to deliver what it claims to do. When consumers believe that a brand is credible, they repeatedly purchase it, and are even willing to pay higher price for credible brands [39,40]. Hence, Hypothesis 7 is posited as follows:

H7: Brand credibility and purchase intention are positively associated.

METHOD

Procedure

An online survey instrument was used to collect data from adult fans (above 18 years old) of the Korean Wave in Singapore. The Korean wave or *Hallyu* refers to the popularity of South Korean culture including music, drama, and movies. Currently it is the most popular pop culture in Asia including Singapore. This study was conducted in Singapore because advertisements endorsed by Korean celebrities are not as widespread in Singapore as in Korea and thus prior exposures to advertisements featuring Korean celebrities were minimal. Respondents were recruited through popular Korean Wave fan sites in Singapore (i.e., soompi.com, sgkwave.com, sgforum.com, etc.), Facebook, Twitter, and word-of-mouth. At the beginning of the survey, respondents were asked to choose one favorite Korean media character. Respondents answered a set of survey questions about the media character whom they chose. After that, they were shown a mock-up advertisement featuring the media character of their choice, and answered questions assessing endorser and brand credibility and purchase intention. A total of 138 mock-up advertisements featuring different celebrities were created for this study. To avoid the effects from the existing brand knowledge or brand loyalty, the mock-up advertisement featured a fictitious juice brand. The survey took about 10-20 minutes to complete. At the end of the survey, respondents were offered a 10-dollar voucher.

Sample

One hundred and forty of the 541 survey responses returned were incomplete, leaving a sample of 401 completed surveys. Of the sample respondents, 83.0% (N=333) were female and 16.9% (N=68) were male. The majority belonged to the age group of 21-24 (63.4%), followed by 18-20 (18.9%) and 25-29 (11.2%), and the rest were 30 years older (6.5%). Most respondents were Chinese (86%), followed by Malay (6.4%) and Indians (1.5%), and the rest were other Southeast Asians (4.7%). Given the fact that the Korean Wave is especially popular among young female audiences and the major ethnic group in Singapore is

Chinese, this demographic profile of the sample is considered representative of the target population.

Measurements

A total of 95 questions were created on matters including key variables and demographics. Most survey items were adapted from pre-validated research work to increase the construct validity. Seven-point Likert scales were used to measure parasocial relationship and purchase intention, and five-point Likert scales for perceived TV reality, SNS use, reality TV viewing, endorser credibility, and brand credibility.

Parasocial relationship: This scale was adopted from the previous studies [11,12,41], with some items created based on the original definition and description of parasocial relationship by Horton and Wohl [4]. A total of 12 items were employed to assess four sub-constructs of parasocial relationship; namely, friendship, self-disclosure, understanding, and identification. An explorative factor analysis (EFA) with Varimax rotation revealed that understanding and identification can be merged into a single factor (labeled as "understanding"). As such, the concept of parasocial relationship was measured by 3 distinctive factors which included <u>perceived friendship</u> (e.g., *"If he/she were not celebrities, we would be good friends")*, <u>self-disclosure</u> *(e.g., "He/she reveals himself/herself")*, and <u>understanding</u> *(e.g., "When he/she behaves in a certain way, I know the reasons why").*

SNS use: Two-item scale was employed to assess how frequently people use SNSs to follow, or engage in conversation with their favorite celebrity. Based on the popularity and penetration rates, Facebook and Twitter were chosen for this survey.

Reality TV viewing: Respondents were asked to indicate how frequently they watch Korean reality TV shows by selecting their viewing frequency from "never" to "always" for 21 Korean reality TV shows that were available via network TV, cable TV, or the Internet (i.e., streaming videos or peer-to-peer file sharing sites) at the time of the survey.

Perceived TV reality: This variable measured how realistic and true-to-life viewers perceive the depictions of reality TV shows to be. The Perceived Realism Scale was adapted to the context of reality TV [11,12]. A five-item scale was employed in the present study, measuring perceived TV realism (e.g., *"In general, these [reality] TV shows present things as they really are in life"*).

Endorser credibility: This variable was measured with a scale developed by Ohanian [32]. Respondents were presented with a mock-up advertisement featuring their selected celebrity and asked to indicate how they felt about the celebrity in the advertisement. Six items were presented in a 5-item semantic differential scale measuring *expert, knowledgeable, qualified, honest, reliable* and *trustworthy*.

	Alpha	AVE	√(AVE)	1	2	3	4	5	6	7	8	9
1. Reality TV viewing	.899	n/a	n/a	-								
2. Perceived TV Reality	.831	.510	.714	.143	-							
3. SNS use	.799	n/a	n/a	.296	.198	-						
4. Self-disclosure	.893	.740	.860	.227	.373	.305	-					
5. Friendship	.928	.541	.735	.197	.243	.251	.541	-				
6. Understanding	.934	.684	.827	.302	.287	.415	.612	.572	-			
7. Endorser Credibility	.942	.763	.874	.147	.340	.143	.447	.340	.351	-		
8. Brand Credibility	.887	.623	.790	.145	.293	.143	.372	.329	.374	.547	-	
9. Purchase Intention	.741	.565	.751	.128	.271	.179	.360	.338	.332	.442	.481	-

Table 1. Evaluation of the Measurement Model

Brand credibility: This variable was measured with the scale developed by Erdem and Swait [36] with two items removed due to the length of the survey. The measure included 5 items such as *"This brand has the ability to deliver what it promises"* and *"This brand has a name you can trust."*

Purchase intention: Respondents were asked how likely they would consider purchasing the product featured in the advertisement in the future. This is a 3-item measure and used a 7-point Likert scale ranging from *very unlikely* to *very likely* (e.g., *"How likely is it that you consider purchasing the product shown in the advertisement above?"*).

RESULTS

We examined the measurement model, the structure of the research model, and each hypothesized path using structural equation modeling (SEM). We used AMOS 21, which allows researchers to perform path-analytic modeling with latent variables. Figure 1 shows the research model and the results of SEM analyses. As Figure 1 shows, all factors in the model were latent variables except for two media use factors. Specifically, reality TV viewing and SNS use were treated as a composite variable since the number of items employed to assess those two factors were either too large (21 items for Reality TV Viewing) or small (2 items for SNS use), which is inappropriate to create a latent variable [42]. Note that we allowed covariance between three subordinate constructs of parasocial relationship. Though the results of EFA indicated the distinctiveness of three parasocial relationship factors, they referred to the same higher-order construct (i.e., parasocial relationship). Also, preliminary analyses showed that the overall model fit was significantly better when three parasocial relationship factors were treated as separate but positively correlated variables ($\chi^2(642) = 1330.244, p < .001$) than being uncorrelated ones ($\chi^2(645) = 1566.725\ p < .001; \chi^2 diff\ (3) = 236.481, p < .001$).

First, we evaluated the validity of the measured constructs by conducting a confirmatory factor analysis (CFA). The results are presented in Table 1. As shown, all latent variables had good convergent validity (AVE > .50,

Cronbach's $\alpha > .70$) and good discriminant validity (square root of AVE larger than the factor correlation).

Second, we evaluated the research model's goodness-of-fit. The results showed that the chi-square statistics were significant for the research model ($\chi^2 (642) = 1330.244, p < .001$), indicating that the fit of the data to the hypothesized model was not entirely adequate. However, the appropriateness of the chi-square test for assessing the overall model fit has been routinely questioned owing to its sensitivity to sample size and model complexity [43]. As such, alternative model fit indices have been proposed (e.g., RMSEA, CFI, TLI) to test a model's approximate fit [43]. For our model, these indices revealed an acceptable approximate fit for the research model: *RMSEA = .052, CFI = .938, IFI = .939, TLI = .933*, and a ratio of chi-square to degrees of freedom $\chi^2/df = 2.07$.

The final step in the model estimation was to examine the significance of each hypothesized path. As Figure 1 shows, all the paths in the research model were significant at either the .001 or .05 level. More specifically, reality TV viewing had a positive association with perceived TV reality ($\beta = .172, p < .001$), which, in turn, had a positive relationship with all subordinate factors of parasocial relationship such as self-disclosure ($\beta = .400, p < .001$), friendship ($\beta = .270, p < .001$), and understanding ($\beta = .257, p < .001$). Hence, H1 and H2 were supported. Perceived TV reality was positively associated with SNS use ($\beta = .230, p < .001$), which in turn had a positive relationship with self-disclosure ($\beta = .232, p < .001$), friendship ($\beta = .224, p < .001$), and understanding ($\beta = .378, p < .001$). Hence, the results supported H3 and H4. Parasocial relationship had a positive relationship with endorser credibility to the extent that self-disclosure ($\beta = .354, p < .001$) and friendship ($\beta = .169, p < .05$) were positively associated with endorser credibility. However, another parasocial relationship factor, understanding, was not significantly associated with endorser credibility ($\beta = .020, p = .787$). Hence, H5 was partially supported. Finally, endorser credibility had a positive association with brand credibility ($\beta = .499, p < .001$), which, in turn, had a positive relationship with purchase intention ($\beta = .446, p < .001$). Hence, H6 and H7 were supported.

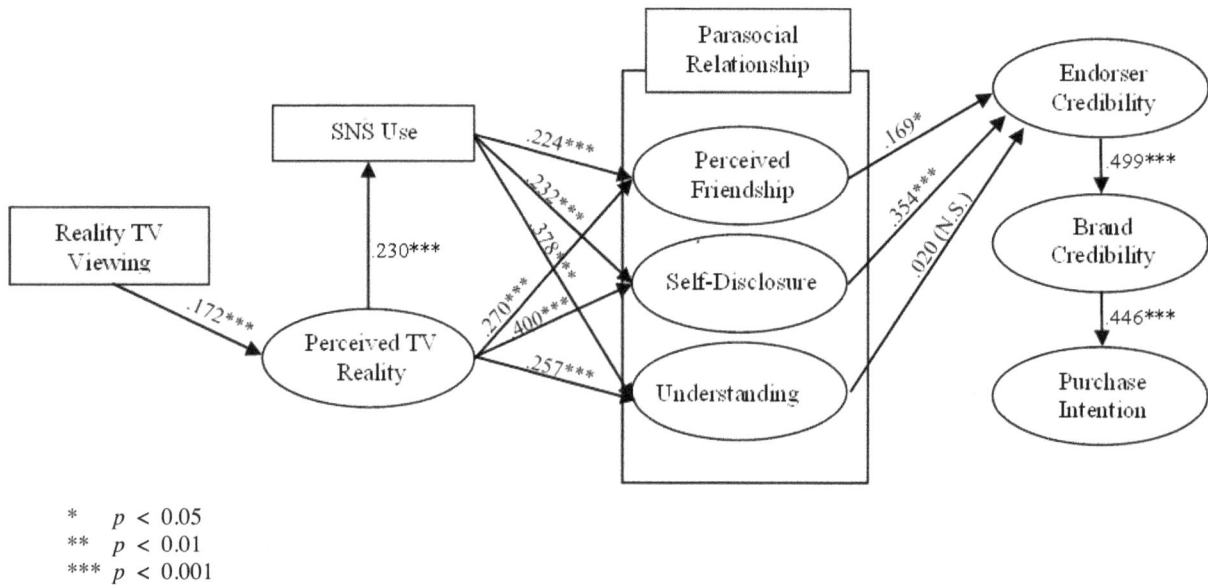

* $p < 0.05$
** $p < 0.01$
*** $p < 0.001$

Note: For visual clarity, covariances among the sub-factors of parasocial relationship are omitted in this diagram

Figure 1. Results of SEM Analysis

Overall, the results supported our research model in that reality TV viewing and SNS use led to higher levels of parasocial relationship. Increased parasocial relationship had a significant economic value to the extent that it led to higher levels of endorser credibility, which, in turn, had a positive association with purchase intention via brand credibility. Implications of the results for research and practice are discussed below.

DISCUSSION

Overall, the findings show that reality TV leads to people's perception that media characters are more real and approachable, which helps breaking the wall between the media characters and viewers. This motivates people to use more SNSs to connect with favorite TV characters, leading to strengthened parasocial relationships with them. More specifically, viewers believe that TV personae whom they watch on reality TV shows and they communicate with on SNSs are more personal, friendly, and understandable. The findings also show that this emerging form of media experience has a substantial economic impact and practical implications in that parasocial relationship has a positive association with celebrity endorsement. The multifaceted implications of the findings for research and practice are discussed as follows.

First, the findings extend our knowledge about the process and outcomes of viewers' bonding with media characters. Though claims about rapidly changing media environments are abundant, many of them have yet to be examined empirically. The present study tested empirically the implications of emerging media technologies (SNSs) and TV genre (reality TV) for a specific dimension of media experience, parasocial relationship, and specified its relationship with celebrity endorsement.

Second, this study contributes to media studies by (a) providing a more thoroughly defined conceptual and operational definition of parasocial relationship; and (b) specifying its relationship with other theoretical concepts such as perceived TV reality, media use, and celebrity endorsement. Though self-disclosure was often discussed in the original work of parasocial relationship by Horton and Wohl [4], it has rarely been incorporated in the measurement models and empirical tests of parasocial relationship. The findings reveal that self-disclosure is a central element of parasocial relationships and further show that it is not only a distinct subordinate factor of parasocial relationships but also has a significant relationship with media consumption behavior and a perception about celebrities as brand endorsers. It is worthwhile to note that both perceived TV reality and SNS use had a stronger association with self-disclosure than with the other two types of parasocial relationship such as friendship and understanding. Similarly, self-disclosure had the strongest association with endorser credibility among the three parasocial relationship sub-concepts. We suggest that future studies of parasocial relationship or celebrity endorsement should incorporate the concept of self-disclosure in order to a reveal more complete and precise picture of the way in which the audience engage with media characters and its implications in modern media environments.

Third, the findings show that reality TV and SNS use have positive associations with parasocial relationship and celebrity endorsement. Consistent with previous research [14,15,16,17], more realistic and interactive media characters can effectively form valuable relationships with viewers. This has important implications for content production and celebrity management. Producers and broadcast companies should endeavor to make reality TV shows more realistic, true-to-life, and without distortion or dramatization. This principle of honest depictions of characters and events can be applied to other TV formats such as talk shows and news programs. Likewise, media characters should understand the changed expectations and norms of communication with the audience. Instead of using SNSs for promotion of a personal brand and publicity, they should maintain intimacy, honesty, and interactivity in their communication with viewers.

LIMITATION AND DIRECTIONS FOR FUTURE RESEARCH

Some research limitations of this study are worth noting. First of all, this study employed a voluntary response sample of media viewers who identified themselves as fans of a media character. Voluntary response samples tend to oversample people who have strong opinions and particular attitudes, thus they may not be representative of the study population. Additionally, the present study is limited in that data were gathered using an online survey. Although our study represents a sufficient sample size, the external validity of online samples remains a problem. Since there are no central registries of fans to create a reliable sampling frame, this limitation might be unavoidable. However, findings of the present study should be further validated by research employing various sampling strategies and frames. Second, this study was conducted in Singapore because we wanted to avoid the effects of overexposure to celebrity endorsements. Therefore, the generalization of findings from this study may be limited to Singaporean population. Nonetheless, given that the Korean Wave is a transnational socio-cultural phenomenon, similar findings can be expected from other study settings where the popularity of Korean celebrities is high. However, future studies may be conducted in other countries for empirical validation of the findings of the present study. Finally, the study is based on cross-sectional data. Though we employed an SEM technique, a causal modeling approach, the findings are based on correlational analyses, making it difficult to establish causality. Also, the significant associations between variables observed in this study can be attributable to common-method bias, since all variables in this study were measured using a single source [44]. Hence, we suggest that future studies should employ different research designs, such as a longitudinal study and experimental research, or a multi-method approach in order to further validate the findings of this study.

CONCLUSION

Our media environment is rapidly changing in the direction where the distinction between mediated and non-mediated worlds becomes blurry, and the roles and effects of media characters and fans are switched and expanded. As such parasocial relationships will become more central to the audience' interaction with media characters. With more revolutionary changes in media technologies and genres coming to our way, scholars and practitioners should make continous efforts in predicting and controlling the influence of television in our lives.

ACKNOWLEDGMENTS

We would like to thank the anonymous reviewers for their valuable comments and suggestions to improve the quality of the paper. As well, we gratefully acknowledge the research grant (C207/MSS12B010) from the Office of Research, Singapore Management University.

REFERENCES

1. Beck, D., Hellmueller, L.C., and Aeschbacher, N. Factual Entertainment and Reality TV. *Communication Research Trends*, *31*, 2 (2012), 4-27.
2. Reiss, S. and Wiltz, J. (2004). Why people watch reality TV. *Media Psychology*, *6*, 4 (2004), 363-378.
3. Papacharissi, Z. and Mendelson, A.L. An exploratory study of reality appeal: Uses and gratifications of reality TV shows. *Journal of Broadcasting & Electronic Media*, *51*, 2 (2007), 355-370.
4. Horton, D. and Wohl, R. R. Mass communication and para-social interaction: Observations on intimacy at a distance. *Psychiatry*, *19*, 3 (1956), 215-229.
5. Ballentine, P.W. and Martin, A.S. Forming Parasocial Relationships in Online Communities. *Advances in Consumer Research*, 32 (2004), 197-201.
6. Borchers, T.A. *Persuasion in the Media Age*. Boston: McGraw Hill, 2002.
7. Nacos, B.L. Terrorism as breaking news: Attack on America. *Political Science Quarterly, 118*, 1 (2003), 23-31.
8. Rubin, R. B. and McHugh, M. P. Development of parasocial interaction relationships. *Journal of Broadcasting and Electronic Media, 31* (1987), 279–292.
9. Ajzen, I. and Fishbein, M. *Understanding Attitudes and Predicting Social Behavior*. Englewood Cliffs, NJ: Prentice-Hall, 1980.
10. Boon, S.D. and Lomore, C.D. Admirer☐celebrity relationships among young adults. *Human Communication Research*, *27*, 3 (2001), 432-465.
11. Perse, E.M. Involvement with local television news cognitive and emotional dimensions. *Human Communication Research*, *16*, 4 (1990), 556-581.
12. Rubin, A.M., and Perse, E.M. Audience activity and soap opera involvement a uses and effects investigation. *Human Communication Research*, *14*, 2 (1987), 246-268.
13. Nabi, R.L., Biely, E.N., Morgan, S.J., and Stitt, C.R. Reality-based television programming and the psychology of its appeal. *Media Psychology*, *5, 4* (2003), 303-330.
14. Atkin, C.K. Effects of realistic TV violence vs. fictional violence on aggression. *Journalism Quarterly, 60* (1983), 615-621.

15. Perse, E.M. Soap opera viewing patterns of college students and cultivation. *Journal of Broadcasting & Electronic Media, 30* (1986), 175-193.

16. Weaver, J. and Wakshlag, J. Perceived vulnerability to crime, criminal victimization experience, and television viewing. *Journal of Broadcasting & Electronic Media, 30,* 2 (1986), 141-158.

17. Busselle, R.W. and Greenberg, B.S. The nature of television realism judgments: A reevaluation of their conceptualization and measurement. *Mass Communication & Society, 3,* 2-3 (2000), 249-268.

18. Papacharissi, Z., and Mendelson, A.L. An exploratory study of reality appeal: Uses and gratifications of reality TV shows. *Journal of Broadcasting & Electronic Media, 51,* 2 (2007), 355-370.

19. Barton, K. M. Reality television programming and diverging gratifications: The influence of content on gratifications obtained. *Journal of Broadcasting & Electronic Media, 53,* 3 (2009), 460-476.

20. Ebersole, S. and Woods, R. Motivations for viewing reality television: A uses and gratifications analysis. *Southwestern Mass Communication Journal, 23,* 3(1) (2007), 23-42.

21. Rubin, A.M., Perse, E.M. and Powell, R.A. Loneliness, parasocial interaction, and local television news viewing. *Human Communication Research, 12* (1985), 155–80.

22. Stefanone, M., Lackaff, D., and Rosen, D. The relationship between traditional mass media and "social media": Reality television as a model for social network site behavior. *Journal of Broadcasting & Electronic Media. 54,* 3 (2010), 508-525.

23. Leets, L., de Becker, G., and Giles, H. Fans: Exploring expressed motivations for contacting celebrities. *Journal of Language and Social Psychology,* 14, 1-2 (1995), 102-123.

24. Marwick, A. and boyd, d. To see and be seen: Celebrity practice on Twitter. *Convergence: The International Journal of Research into New Media Technologies, 17,* 2 (2011), 139-158.

25. Thompson, C. Brave new world of digital intimacy. The New York Times, (2008). Retrieved January 29, 2014, from The New York Times, http://www.nytimes.com/2008/09/07/magazine/07awareness-t.html?pagewanted=all&_r=0.

26. Solomon, M.R. *Consumer Behavior: Buying, Having, and Being,* Upper Saddle River, NJ: Pearson Education, Inc. Prentice Hall, 2006.

27. Lafferty, B.A., Goldsmith, R.E., and Newell, S.J. The dual credibility model: The influence of corporate and endorser credibility on attitudes and purchase intentions. *Journal of Marketing Theory and Practice, 10,* 3 (2002), 1-13.

28. Buttle, J.E., Raymond, H., and Danziger. S. The advantage of a famous face: Particularly rapid configural visual processing. *International Journal of Psychology, 35,* 3-4 (2000), 1296-1306.

29. Atkin, C. and Block, M. Effectiveness of celebrity endorsers. *Journal of Advertising Research, 2* (1983), 57-61.

30. Friedman, H. H. and Friedman, L. Endorser effectiveness by product type. *Journal of Advertising Research, 19,* 5 (1979), 63-71.

31. Ohanian, R. The impact of celebrity spokespersons' perceived image on consumers' intention to purchase. *Journal of Advertising Research, 31,* 1 (1991), 46 -54.

32. Ohanian, R. Construction and validation of a scale to measure celebrity endorsers' perceived expertise, trustworthiness, and attractiveness. *Journal of Advertising, 19,* 3 (1990), 39-52.

33. Hovland, C. I. and Weiss, W. The influence of source credibility on communication effectiveness. *Public Opinion Quarterly, 15* (1951), 635-650.

34. Erdogan, B. Z. Celebrity endorsement: A literature review. *Journal of Marketing Management, 15,* 4 (1999), 291-314.

35. Seno, D. and Lukas, B.A. The equity effect of product endorsement by celebrities - A conceptual framework from a co-branding perspective. *European Journal of Marketing, 41,* 1-2 (2007), 121-134.

36. Erdem, T. and Swait, J. Brand credibility, brand consideration, and choice. *The Journal of Consumer Research, 31,* 1 (2004), 191-198.

37. Baek, T.H. and King, K. W. Exploring the consequences of brand credibility in services. *Journal of Services Marketing,* 25, 4 (2011), 260-272.

38. Spry, A., Pappu, R., and Cornwell, T.B. Celebrity endorsement, brand credibility and brand equity. *European Journal of Marketing 45,* 6 (2009), 882-909.

39. Kemp, E. and Bui, M. Healthy brands: Establishing brand credibility, commitment and connection among consumers. *Journal of Consumer Marketing, 28,* 6 (2011), 429-437.

40. Netemeyer, R., Krishnan, B., Pullig, C., Wang, G., Yagci, M., Dean, D., Ricks, J., and Wirth, F. Developing and validating measures of facets of customer-based brand equity. *Journal of Business Research, 57,* 2 (2004), 209-224.

41. Auter, P.J., and Palmgreen, P. Development and validation of a parasocial interaction measure: The Audience-Persona Interaction scale. *Communication Research Reports, 17* (2000), 79-89.

42. Hoyle, R. H. *Structural equation modeling for social and personality psychology*. SAGE Publications Ltd., 2011.

43. Bollen, K.A., and Long, J.S. *Testing structural equation models*. Newbury Park, CA: Sage, 1993.

44. Podsakoff, P. M., MacKenzie, S. B., Lee, J. Y., and Podsakoff, N. P. Common method biases in behavioral research: a critical review of the literature and recommended remedies. *Journal of Applied Psychology, 88,* 5 (2003), 879-903.

Disinhibited Abuse of Othered Communities by Second-Screening Audiences

Mark Doughty, Shaun Lawson,
Conor Linehan, Duncan Rowland
University of Lincoln,
Lincoln, UK.
mdoughty@lincoln.ac.uk

Lucy Bennett
Independent Researcher
Cardiff, UK.
bennettlucyk@gmail.com

ABSTRACT

Second-screening and live-tweeting alongside broadcast television generates new concerns with respect to online abuse. We present an investigation into the nature of Twitter-facilitated second-screening posts relating to *Thelma's Gypsy Girls*, one of a series of controversial documentary programmes portraying the Irish Traveller community that have recently been aired by the UK public-service television broadcaster Channel 4. Sentiment analysis highlighted the general negativity of these posts whilst a detailed thematic inquiry revealed the often abusive and aggressive messages aimed directly at the community and individuals portrayed in the broadcast material. We discuss why users might be susceptible to exhibiting these behaviours, and the implications for the broadcast industry, and social TV designers and developers.

Author Keywords

Television; Social TV; Social Media; Live-tweeting; Online Disinhibition; Second Screening; Abuse.

ACM Classification Keywords

H.5.m. Information interfaces and presentation (e.g., HCI): Miscellaneous.

INTRODUCTION

The viewing of broadcast television has always given rise to the concept of 'backchannel' communications [1]. Traditionally this has, perhaps, has taken the form of sharing private comments about a broadcast show with partners and family, while watching together in the living room, or discussing the show the following day with work colleagues or friends. In each of these instances, we are naturally drawn into the sharing of our opinions regarding the media we are co-consuming as well as the characters and individuals portrayed in that media. The deliberate activity of simultaneously watching a broadcast television show whilst engaging in *online* discussion about its content, variously known as 'co-viewing' [10], 'second-screening

[11], or 'live-tweeting' [23], is a widespread and rapidly increasing phenomenon. Broadly positioned within the more established research field of social TV [8, 12], this still-emergent model of socially-experienced television incorporates the use of a 'second screen' through which an individual can interact with other viewers, who together comprise a wider, distributed co-interested audience. Online second-screen activity therefore expands television-related discussion far beyond co-located family, friends and colleagues into a much wider, networked group, public, or audience.

The current predominant, user-driven, approach to second-screening can be considered a *loosely-coupled* model of interaction as it is enabled by general-purpose social media platforms such as Twitter [23]. In this model, any shared statements (e.g. tweets), any interactions between viewers (e.g. re-tweets, (RTs) and replies), and any client software itself (e.g. the Twitter app on a tablet device) are independent of the broadcast content, and of the control of the broadcaster. In the case of Twitter, live ad-hoc online audiences form through the shared and negotiated use of #hashtags. Using Twitter's search function to stream tweets containing the hashtag #Sherlock, for instance, allows easy, and instantaneous, access to live discussion about a particular broadcast TV show, generated by an ad hoc group of Twitter users who do not need to be connected through previously established 'follower' networks (see [6] for discussion). Of course, not all tweets about a broadcast will contain the same, consistent, hashtag; some tweets will contain alternative hashtags, such as the name of the TV Channel (e.g. #BBC1), whilst others may not contain a hashtag at all. The use of hashtags however offers enormous power and flexibility to the user; moreover, the experiences that they facilitate remain independent of broadcasters' control.

Second-screen experiences can also be facilitated by bespoke 'companion apps' that deliver additional digital content and filtered social media streams to a second-screen device. This, more *tightly coupled*, model of second-screening allows broadcasters to stage-manage the user experience and is increasingly being pursued by that industry. However the orchestrated use of #hashtags by broadcasters is also becoming apparent. A case of this has arisen around the controversial documentary programme

Benefits Street recently aired by the British public-service television broadcaster Channel 4 where it has been alleged[1] that viewers were deliberately reminded of the relevant hashtag *(#BenefitsStreet)* at carefully planned moments within each episode in order to intensify online discussion and, perhaps, arouse further controversy.

The broadcast of *Benefits Street* has provoked intense UK media discussion, and criticism, primarily because of the nature of its portrayal of a particular community whose lives, allegedly funded by state-benefits, have been placed in public view on prime-time, free-to-air television. Observations of second-screen discussions on Twitter using *#BenefitsStreet*, have also highlighted the particularly high levels of antipathy, anger and abuse directed at the community, and individuals, portrayed within the programme[2]. Such discussion is reflective of recent instances in the UK where discriminatory, abusive and emotionally harmful tweets, which clearly refer to a specific individual or group/community, have received high-profile media attention, resulting, in some cases, in criminal prosecutions[3]. Despite the obvious public nature of the Twitter timeline, and the clear possibility that the owner of any Twitter account can be identified and, potentially, prosecuted, the online abuse of individuals and groups/communities remains an everyday occurrence[4]. In response to this, Guitton [14] recently called for a concerted research effort to understand the 'dark side of social media' and poses questions including: "Why do individuals display such aggressive behaviors toward people they don't know via social media?" and "Why do temporary communities emerge to systematically attack and harass those who appear as ''weaker'' on social media?".

We believe that second-screening and live-tweeting alongside broadcast television represents a particularly problematic area with respect to abuse and social media. Broadcasters increasingly rely on "reality" TV to garner audience share; these productions often emphasize how individuals, groups and communities can be extraordinary but negatively different [28] to general society. This

---

[1] As discussed in "Benefits Street – poverty porn, or just the latest target for pent-up British fury?" Article in *The Guardian* (12 Jan 2014) http://www.theguardian.com/commentisfree/2014/jan/12/benefits-street-poverty-porn-british-fury

[2] See "Benefits Street Twitter reactions: The angry, the idiotic and the defensive" Article in The Independent (8 Jan 2014) http://www.independent.co.uk/arts-entertainment/tv/features/benefits-street-twitter-reactions-the-angry-the-idiotic-and-the-defensive-9046806.html

[3] For instance "Twitter 'trolls' Isabella Sorley and John Nimmo jailed for abusing feminist campaigner Caroline Criado-Perez" Article in the Independent (24 January 2014) http://www.independent.co.uk/news/uk/crime/twitter-trolls-isabella-sorley-and-john-nimmo-jailed-for-abusing-feminist-campaigner-caroline-criadoperez-9083829.html

[4] For instance: "Sky Sports condemns 'unacceptable and offensive abuse' of Beth Tweddle" Article in The Guardian (21 Jan 2014) http://www.theguardian.com/sport/2014/jan/21/sky-sports-abuse-beth-tweddle

othering [21] is not only evident in many broadcast productions but also anecdotally continues in the parallel and subsequent online discussion by second-screen audiences. This raises very broad questions around whether social media is being used, unwittingly or otherwise, to amplify, exaggerate, legitimize, or else facilitate the othering or marginalization of groups or communities. Additionally therefore, what is the effect of this second-screening abuse in offline settings and society in the large, and what are the implications of this phenomenon for the broadcast and social TV industries? For the TVX community there are initial questions around whether there is indeed clear empirical evidence for such abuse and, if so (to return to Guitton's questions), why do people feel that they are able to post such abuse with impunity in online settings? Deeper understanding of these issues would allow for subsequent informed debate around the larger societal issues and industry implications.

The work presented in this paper focuses upon an analysis of the posts generated by second-screening viewers of *Thelma's Gypsy Girls*, one of a series of broadcast documentaries portraying the Irish traveller community in the UK and also recently aired by Channel 4. Like *Benefits Street*, this series of programmes has also provoked intense media discussion and observations of othering have been made of the second-screen discussions [28]. We investigate the extent to which the second-screening posts around *Thelma's Gypsy Girls* exhibit positive or negative sentiment, and, through a qualitative analysis, determine the themes present in the posts. Our discussion then focuses on possible explanations for the negative and abusive posting that we found and, in particular, whether there was evidence of online disinhibition [24] being displayed. Finally, we discuss the implications of this second-screening behaviour for the TVX research community and the broadcast industry.

BACKGROUND

For the purposes of this study it is useful to define what constitutes abuse when considering online interactions. Abuse and threats of violence are a criminal act, whether these are made in face to face (F2F) or online settings. Jay and Janschewitz [16] propose that offensive language consists of vulgar, pornographic and hateful terms. If this offensive language is directed at an individual, group or culture through an online interaction then we consider this an abusive communication. Cyber-bullying [19, 29] is also a relevant term within this context. Constituting the writing and posting of electronic messages to facilitate deliberate harassment or threat to another individual or group, it is an important aspect of the behaviour to consider when reviewing the implications for the work presented here. Thus offensive text aimed at an individual, ethnic or minority group, whether or not within the intention of the writer to offend is classed as abusive and harmful.

Explanations for Online Abuse

A common, broad, finding of computer-mediated communication is that users can behave differently or say things online which they would not usually say in F2F settings. This phenomenon, known as the online disinhibition effect [24, 18], is understood to be as a result of the less socially-constraining nature of online communications [7] possibly resulting from the asynchronous or anonymous characteristics therein. The nature of online disinhibition can be described [18] as behaviour which is characterized by an apparent reduction in concerns for self-presentation and the judgment of others. Online disinhibition can manifest itself in different forms relating to what Suler [24] calls 'benign' factors such as self disclosure, involving fears, wishes and emotions, as well as more 'toxic' factors such as rude language, anger, hatred and threats. Both positive and benign disinhibition can be observed in Twitter communications [9].

One negative dimension of online disinhibition is the concept of 'flaming' [25]. While Kiesler, as cited by Joinson [18], categorizes flaming as messages including impolite statements, swearing, exclamations or the use of superlatives, O'Sullivan and Flanagin [25] highlight the problem of the contextual ambiguity of flame messages and the difficulty in interpreting them when viewed from one of the three perspectives of sender, receiver and third party observer. However, while these ambiguities are present in Twitter, the contextualising of a posting to a particular individual, group or topic using hashtag classifiers and user names can potentially reduce contextual ambiguity and result in more targeted and clearly abusive messages.

Thelma's Gypsy Girls

The documentary series *Thelma's Gypsy Girls* forms the focus of the second-screening activity investigated in this paper. It is a sequel to a previous documentary series *Big Fat Gypsy Weddings*; both series were produced by Firecracker Films and broadcast in the UK by Channel 4. Each series has caused controversy due to their alleged negative depiction of the Irish Traveller community [28]. *Thelma's Gypsy Girls* follows the activities of a group of young teenage women from this community as they undertake an apprenticeship with a specialist dressmaker (the eponymous "Thelma"). Viewing figures for *Thelma's Gypsy Girls* averaged two million viewers per episode [2] which placed it consistently in top three shows viewed on Channel 4 during its run from 8th July to 12th August 2012.

DATA COLLECTION

Using the public Twitter stream API, we gathered 1,382 tweets from 839 unique users that contained the hashtag *#ThelmasGypsyGirls* on 22nd July 2012 between 21:00GMT and 22:00GMT: the broadcast time for episode three of the show during its original run. The broadcaster, Channel 4, publicized this hashtag on screen before, and periodically during, the show. It is self-evident that there will have been tweets posted about the show which did not contain this hashtag; however by using this tag, we can be very certain that the poster was intending the tweet to be about the show. Retweeted messages (or simply retweets, RTs) potentially indicate the existence of conversation [4], community structure [11], and affirmations of sentiment; in this study we were *primarily* interested in original, unique posts and the individuals' motivations for making those posts. Therefore the 207 RT messages in the dataset were set aside for separate analysis, leaving a main corpus of 1175 tweet messages. There were no incidences of tweets in a language other than English that required removal prior to analysis.

In order to determine how different our *Thelma's Gypsy Girls* corpus was from messages otherwise posted commonly on Twitter, a sample of random tweets was gathered using the public stream API. By collecting the messages at approximately the same time as the broadcast, and filtering the sample to remove non English tweets and RTs, a corpus of 7,902 *general tweets* was obtained. In order to compare like sample sizes, every 6th tweet was removed from this sample of random tweets to create a final general sample of 1,317 tweets.

Corpus	Negative Sentiment Mean (Standard Deviation)	Positive Sentiment Mean (Standard Deviation)
#ThelmasGypsy Girls (n=1175)	-1.65(1.05)	1.51(0.73)
General tweets (n=1317)	-1.23(0.66)	1.52(0.68)
#ThelmasGypsy Girls (RTs) (n=207)	-1.98(1.12)	1.38(0.63)

Table 1. Comparison of sentiment strengths across different tweet corpuses.

SENTIMENT ANALYSIS

A sentiment analysis of the collected tweets was undertaken to make a judgment on the degree of positive or negative opinion, or attitude, encoded in the tweet posts about *Thelma's Gypsy Girls*. Sentiment analysis is the computational treatment of opinion, sentiment and subjectivity in texts and encompasses many foci of study; however, for the purposes this work, we were interested in assessing the sentiment polarity of the text. Any written text may contain a mix of positive, negative or neutral sentiment, and there may also be differing strengths of the sentiment expressed [26]. The levels of sentiment in Twitter postings should not be exaggerated in their importance [27]; nevertheless, the levels investigated in this study provide a useful initial context.

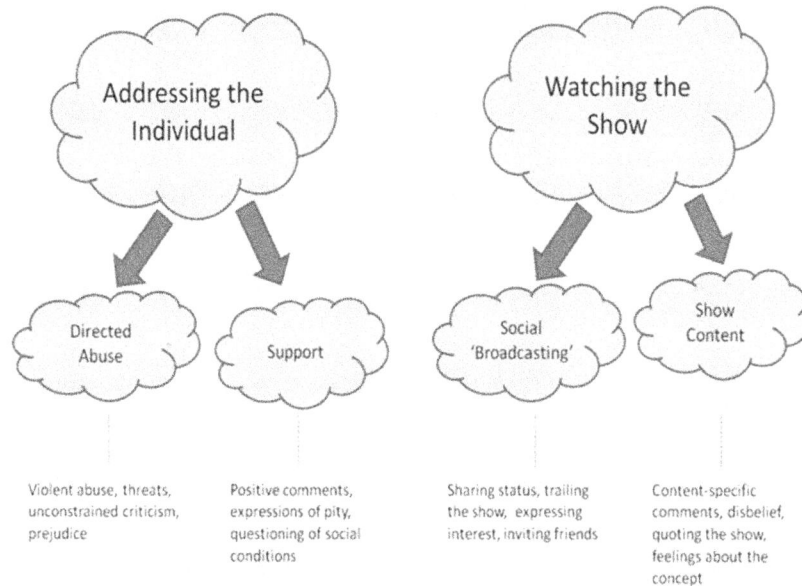

Figure 1: Thematic structure of the tweets tagged with *#ThelmasGypsyGirls*

The SentiStrength application [26] was used to perform an assessment of the sentiment polarity of the tweet messages gathered with the *#ThelmasGypsyGirls* hashtag and also the corpus of general tweets. The figures in Table 1 represent an *average* sentiment level for each dimension for each tweet corpus. They suggest that the second-screen posts on Twitter that were tagged with *#ThelmasGypsyGirls* and posted during the broadcast of *Thelma's Gypsy Girls* contained notably more negative language, and therefore more negative sentiment, than a sample of general tweets. Additionally, the retweeted *#ThelmasGypsyGirls* posts also reveal an even higher negative and lower positive sentiment than the main *#ThelmasGypsyGirls* corpus; this further suggests that second-screen viewers were agreeing with negative messages and were willing to reiterate this sentiment publicly.

SentiStrength estimates the strength of positive and negative sentiment in short texts, and has been shown to have human levels of accuracy for short social web texts [26]. Two sentiment strengths are reported for each message: from -1 to -5, or from 'not negative' to 'extremely negative', and from 1 to 5, or from 'not positive' to 'extremely positive'. The ratings for sentiment are derived by comparing the text to a dictionary or positive and negative terms. Refinement of the score is made by detecting mis-spellings and 'booster' or 'negating' terms. For example, '*Love #thelmasgypsygirls the insight into the Travellers lives is an eye opener!*' returns a score of (3, -1), indicating a strong positive sentiment and no negative results, while the message '*These girls are f****** idiots #thelmasgypsygirls*' (profanity censorship is added here) returns a result of (1, -5) indicating no positive, but extremely negative sentiment.

Each corpus of tweets was analyzed and overall levels of sentiment were determined. Compared to the general tweet messages, the messages containing *#ThelmasGypsyGirls* were reported to have higher levels of negative sentiment and lower levels of positive sentiment as shown in Table 1. The negative dimension of the sentiment analysis was significantly higher than that of the general tweets (t = 11.53, p<0.01) indicating that the negativity measured in the *#ThelmasGypsyGirls* tweets was higher than that shown in the sample of general tweets. The positive dimension showed no significant difference between the two (t=-0.42, p>0.1). In addition, the 207 RT messages which were set aside from the main corpus were also assessed for sentiment strength. By assessing the whole of this group and including the duplicates which are formed when a message is retweeted more than once, an indication of the retweeted sentiment was determined (also shown, in bottom row, in Table 1).

The reasons for the predominantly negative tweet messages are, of course, not able to be determined from this analysis alone. By undertaking a thematic analysis of the tweet messages a better understanding of the context and subjectivity of the content can be reached, rather than the context-limited, quantitative approach of the sentiment analysis.

THEMATIC ANALYSIS

The approach to the thematic analysis [13] used in this study was an inductive, data-driven method as described by Boyatzis [3] and deployed previously for tweet text analysis by other authors e.g. [14]. The analysis was initiated by taking a split of half (group A, n=586) of the 1175 *#ThelmasGypsyGirls* tweet messages and reading them all individually. Category codes which described the content and/or sentiment of the tweet message were recorded by the researcher as the reading took place. The codes were further refined through rereading and a final list of 32 category codes were identified. Following this process, the second half (group B, n=557) of the tweet messages were allocated to three researchers who used the 32 category codes to categorize each of the tweet messages in this sample.

All of the group B tweets were read by the three researchers and a consensus was reached on the assignment of the category codes. By cross-referencing the category codes with the tweet texts, overall themes were identified. From the analysis and consideration of the data, four first order themes were identified which were collected together into two second order themes. These two themes, "Addressing the Individual" (263/557 tweets, 47.2%) and "Watching the Show" (248/557 tweets, 44.5%) formed the root of the majority of the tweet texts observed. The remainder of the tweet messages (46/557 tweets, 8.3%) was ambiguous and was not assigned to these categories. The relationship of these higher order themes with the first order themes is shown in Figure 1 and discussed below.

Addressing the Individual
This second order theme reveals of much of the intent and directed comments of the second-screen audience. With its decomposition into two opposing first order themes of *directed abuse* (210/263 tweets, 79.8%) and *support* (53/263 tweets, 20.2%), the content of the tweets reflect people's reactions to the broadcast as it aired. Tweets coded in this theme specifically mentioned the tweeters own reaction to, and feelings about, the subjects of the show, along with wishes, demands for action and threats. Each of the first order themes are discussed below and typical tweet message contents are used for illustration. For the purposes of privacy, no actual names, user names or unique Twitter ID's are included, whilst insulting or offensive words are removed.

Directed Abuse
This theme was very evident; it was a repetitive theme in the dataset with 210 out of 557 tweets being attributed to this category (37.7% of the total). The tweets coded in this theme typically contained abusive language directed at the girls in the show and, in the main, expressed a Twitter user's dislike for the person or their actions, for example *"They've all got bad attitudes #thelmasgypsygirls"* or *"These Traveller girls are so violent it makes me sick!",* *"These Gypsy girls are nuttas!,"* *"These girls wanna act tough and gain respect for themselves but they are so immature it's unreal."* Many also contained direct threats or wishes of violence: *"I want to f****** slap these stupid f****** girls,"* *"WOW some of these girls need a slap to knock them into the real world,"* *"Pretty sure a swift tap with a baseball bat would sort them out ... I'm offering...".* Some of the messages were graphic in nature and represent a seemingly disproportionate reaction to broadcast content: *"I'd kill the girls on #thelmasgypsygirls,"* *"I just feel like*

*killing ***".* What was evident was the graphic and seemingly un-self-regulated nature of many such messages, as well as how many of them include a "lol" or "haha", indicating laughter *"Lol 19 years old n dnt know ur ABC,"* *"LOOOL these girls are getting upset over the word Virgin and they behave like animals".* Many of the messages in this theme were, in fact, quite clearly offensive, and inappropriate for publication, even with censorship applied to the offensive terms used. Many of the tweets contained terms which revealed a hatred and dislike of both the girls featured in the broadcast, and the Traveller culture more broadly.

Support
In contrast to the directed abuse theme, many contributors to the Twitter stream exhibited support and empathy for the show's participants with 53 out of 557 tweets being credited to this group (9.5% of the total). This was seen in different ways – whether it was an expression of pity or regret: *"Really really can't stand the fact those girls cannot read or write",* *"Really angers me that those girls are deprived of an education,"* *"Sooo sad that a 17 year old couldn't even recognise all the letters of the alphabet,"* or whether it was a positive observation: *"I would love to be one of #ThelmasGypsyGirls omg",* *"Just want to hug lilly-anne on #thelmasgypsygirls!!".* The theme suggests that viewers may have been surprised to learn of some of the customs and practices of a different culture, and such messages of support may have been a reaction to that. Indeed, a number of tweets (8 of 557) specifically expressed positive sentiments about Traveller culture, *"I wanna be a gypsy,"* *"i shud have been a gypsy then again amount of times i move i may aswell be,"* *"I'd love to be a Traveller for a day,"* *"really don't see what everyone has against gypsy's."*

Watching the show
The tweets coded in this theme were about the interaction of the second-screening viewer with the television show itself, and with fellow second screening audience members. This is encapsulated in the two supporting first order themes of *social broadcasting* (68/248 tweets, 27.4%) and *show content* (180/248 tweets, 72.6%).

Social Broadcasting
This theme (12.2% of the total) became evident through the observation of tweet messages which were intended for other second-screening viewers or users. Those other users in this context could be friends or followers of the originator, or, more generally, anyone who was monitoring the Twitter stream which was 'tuned' to display tweets with the #ThelmasGypsyGirls hashtag. By updating personal status to friends, or by microblogging a desire to watch the show, the social aspects of using Twitter as a second-screen application were employed. Some typical tweet messages in this theme were: *"Giving #thelmasgypsygirls a go tonight. Looks quite amusing!"* and *"Time for Thelma and the girls #ThelmasGypsyGirls".* In some cases the show

was included as a context to other activity which was separate to viewing the show, such as: "*Js Had A Nice Shower Now Watching #ThelmasGypsyGirls :P!*". It was interesting to note how there was very little negativity expressed in these tweets; many in fact were positive and upbeat in their content, indicating that viewers were pleased to be watching or about to watch the show and were keen to share this on the public timeline.

Show Content

The Show Content theme (32.3% of the total) was comprised of messages which discussed and commented on what was happening in the show. However, unlike tweets coded as "addressing the individual," they do not specifically mention the tweeters own reactions, wishes and threats. *"Bridget needs to win this! She's like the only getting involved! It's like being in high school all over again,"* "*its all kicking off on #thelmasgypsygirls*" "*The Travellers are fighting cos she deleted her off bbm.*" In many cases, these messages were questions; viewers questioned the content of the show and wanted clarification or seemed to be initiating conversation relating to some of the issues raised: "*Could they not let Shannon work for free or something? #ThelmasGypsyGirls*". The questions frequently expressed disbelief or surprise for many incidents that occurred during the documentary: "*How can a wedding dress weigh more than my actual being?! #ThelmasGypsyGirls*" and "*They seriously can't even tell the f****** time? #ThelmasGypsyGirls*".

DISCUSSION

Whilst our thematic analysis did reveal themes that were positive towards the documentary, it also highlighted a strong theme of directed abuse. Moreover, our sentiment analysis indicated that tweets tagged with *#ThelmasGypsyGirls* were significantly more negative in their content than a sample of random tweet messages captured at the same time, and furthermore, that retweeted messages exhibited an even higher negative sentiment. It would seem clear that, for this broadcast episode of the documentary at least, Guitton's framing of an emergent 'dark side of social media' [14] holds true. Specifically, the tweets we analysed displayed elements of aggressive behaviour on the part of the tweeters directed toward people they did not know. Further, it appeared that an ad hoc group was formed during the broadcast that attacked a group who appeared different or weaker. The questions for discussion are why might this be happening, and what are the implications?

Why do individuals take part in the abuse?

Suler [24] suggests that, when interacting in online contexts, people often display less inhibition and apprehension over breaking social norms than they would in other contexts. This leads to people engaging in behaviour that they would otherwise deem unacceptable, a phenomenon that Suler refers to as the "online disinhibition effect." Suler suggests that the lack of overt social cues in

this environment, such as direct feedback from either the wider community or the person or group being targeted allow people to feel that they are engaging in a "hit and run" type of interaction, with little consequence for either themselves or the target of their behaviour. The immediacy of Twitter posting, coupled with the fact that it is unmoderated, makes live-tweeting and second-screening susceptible to such a type of disinhibited behaviour. This disinhibition can manifest itself as abusive or offensive tweet messages directed at members of a particular show, the makers of that show, or other viewers. As has been seen in this research and other popular recent second-screen events (such as the *Benefits Street* TV show in the UK), Twitter users can amplify (or misunderstand) the sentiments of the show and demonstrate disinhibited behaviour through their postings.

Wider concerns: Othering and fear

Broadcast television produces controversial and challenging content [17] in an effort to 'stimulate' the viewer. In the case of documentaries such as *Thelma's Gypsy Girls*, the deliberate systematic and repeated highlighting of Travellers' cultural differences [20] seems provide this challenge and stimulation. Of course, promoting large-scale constructive debate around cross-cultural and societal issues can be useful, particularly when the public do not readily engage in such debate. However, broadcast material also has the potential to promote increased stereotyping, or othering, by the television audience of a particular group depicted in that broadcast. Although Said [22] argues that the practice of othering, and the continuous interpretation and reinterpretation of 'difference', is an essential mechanism for the construction of cultural and societal identity, the term is more typically deployed in contexts where the 'other' are negatively perceived, stigmatised, excluded, marginalised and discriminated against. These contexts range from the existentialist philosophy of de Beauvoir's *Second Sex*, which designated the Other as female, through to the casual everyday othering of any group or community, including ethnic minorities, immigrants, religious groups, asylum seekers, those on benefits, single parents, sex-offenders, political extremists and bankers. Whereas research in media communications has investigated the role of traditional media in influencing attitudes and behaviours, there are unanswered questions around the role of digital services, and social media in particular, in the facilitation and mediation of the othering of groups or communities. For example, the disinhibited nature of social media communication may facilitate the amplification and normalization of cultural stereotyping in wider society, detrimentally impacting upon social cohesion and wellbeing.

boyd [5] has recently drawn attention to the role that digital media and online activities can have in propagating *cultures of fear*. Whilst she does not explicitly use the term othering, she highlights the fact that "we fear the things – and people -- that we do not understand far more than the things we do, even if the latter are much more risky". More importantly, she points to the change, and potential disruption, that social media brings to the propagation of fear and that "hysteria isn't necessarily from on high, but, rather, all around us." In other words, no longer is fear (or hysteria) delivered solely in a top down manner, e.g. from government and the mainstream media, instead it is present in the user-generated social data streams that we absorb from our encounters with the web, and in particular from social platforms such as Twitter, Facebook, and YouTube. A concrete example of this appears to be the very material that is posted during second-screen discussions of *Thelma's Gypsy Girls*. boyd's statement that 'technology allows us to see people who are different than us, the very people we are likely to fear' [5] goes some way towards explaining why people make abusive and offensive statements while second-screening.

Implications for broadcasters and for Social TV

TV shows such as *Thelma's Gypsy Girls* are carefully planned, edited and positioned to highlight the perceived differences between an audience and the Othered group depicted in the programme. Broadcasters create these programmes in the full knowledge that they will create a great deal of social media interest and discussion. Indeed, it is common practice to show Twitter hashtags on-screen during broadcast. However, as demonstrated by the data set analysed here, online discussion can often display anti-social characteristics which are apparently facilitated by the disinhibited nature of social media communication. The abusive messages identified in this paper are an unwanted side effect of a second-screening activity. While the enriching and enhancing qualities of second-screen discussions have been noted [10], the unregulated and unmoderated nature of a Twitter stream permits the posting of material which would be unacceptable and, in many cases, illegal, if spoken in public or printed for publication.

The implications for television broadcasters and social TV application developers seem clear: the way that people engage in second-screen activities around programming must be carefully designed and promoted in order to discourage abusive, anti-social and illegal behaviour. This task becomes easier the more tightly coupled the social TV application and the broadcast become. Dedicated second-screening applications or social TV screen overlay systems, such as the *4Now*[5] app, have the ability to monitor and filter the message streams that they display, while more loosely coupled systems, such as Twitter, afford less opportunity to do so. In addition, perhaps new applications can be developed with the intention of undermining the online

disinhibition effect, such as removing the likelihood of anonymous messages.

Broadcasters should also consider how they publicise a Twitter hashtag as the 'preferred' tag for the second-screen discussion. The publication of a hashtag on-screen encourages discussion of that programme on Twitter. However, the conversation is not then controlled or moderated by the broadcaster. Broadcasters must consider whether they are, in any way, responsible for reactions to their programming on social media sites. If broadcasters were seen as encouraging the abuseive posts identified here, they may be open to future criticism by the public, advertisers and regulatory bodies.

CONCLUSION

This paper contributes to the understanding of how users engage in second-screen discussion whilst viewing broadcast television. We present an investigation into the nature of Twitter-facilitated second-screening posts relating to Thelma's Gypsy Girls, one of a series of controversial documentary programmes portraying the Irish Traveller community that have recently been aired by the UK public-service television broadcaster Channel 4. Sentiment analysis highlighted the general negativity of these posts whilst a detailed thematic inquiry revealed the often abusive and aggressive messages aimed directly at the community and individuals portrayed in the broadcast material. We suggest that second-screening and live-tweeting alongside broadcast television generates new concerns about online abuse. Specifically, the nature of social media interactions, being asynchronous, anonymous, and lacking in direct feedback, lowers people's inhibitions about engaging in abusive and anti-social behaviour. We argue that this disinhibited behaviour, when directed towards characters on a TV programme, particularly where those characters are portrayed as different to the social norms of the audience, can facilitate stereotyping, othering and prejudice in wider society. Television broadcasters and social TV application developers have a responsibility to be aware of these dangers and to act so as to minimize the impact upon social cohesion and wellbeing.

REFERENCES

1. Atkinson, C. *The Backchannel: How Audiences Are Using Twitter and Social Media and Changing Presentations Forever*, New Riders, 2010.

2. Broadcasters' Audience Research Board, (2012) http://www.barb.co.uk/

3. Boyatzis, R., *Transforming Qualitative Information: Thematic Analysis and Code Development*, Sage Publications, 1998.

4. boyd, d., Lotan, G., Tweet, Tweet, Retweet: Conversational Aspects of Retweeting on Twitter, *43rd Hawaii International Conference on System Sciences* (HICSS), 5-8 January, 2010.

---

[5] See "Channel 4 second-screen app *4Now* to allow real-time viewer interaction" Article in The Guardian (5 June 2013) "http://www.theguardian.com/media/2013/jun/05/channel-4-second-screen-app-4now"

5. boyd, d., The Power of Fear in Networked Publics. *SXSW*. Austin, Texas, March 10, 2012.

6. Bruns, A., Burgess, J., (2011) *The use of Twitter hashtags in the formation of ad hoc publics*. In 6th European Consortium for Political Research General Conference, 25 - 27 August 2011, University of Iceland, Reykjavik

7. Caspi, A., Gorsky, P., Online Deception: prevalence, motivation and emotion, *CyberPsychology & Behavior*. February 2006, 9(1): 54-59.

8. Cesar, P., Bulterman, D., Jansen, A., Usages of the Secondary Screen in an interactive television environment: Control, enrich, share and transfer television content, Changing Television Environments, *Lecture Notes in Computer Science*, 2008, Volume 5066/2008, 168-177.

9. Chen, L., & Chen, T. L. (2012). Use of Twitter for formative evaluation: Reflections on trainer and trainees' experiences. *British Journal of Educational Technology*, *43*(2), E49-E52.

10. Doughty, M., Lawson, S., Rowland, D., Co-viewing live TV with digital backchannel streams, *EuroITV '11 Proc. 9th international interactive conf. on Interactive Television* Pages 141-144 ACM New York, NY, USA.

11. Doughty, M., Rowland, D., Lawson, S. (2012). Who is on your sofa?: TV audience communities and second screening social networks. In Proceedings of the 10th European conference on Interactive tv and video (EuroiTV '12). (pp. 79-86) ACM, New York, NY, USA.

12. Evangelia Mantzari, George Lekakos, and Adam Vrechopoulos. 2008. Social TV: introducing virtual socialization in the TV experience. *In Proc. of the 1st International Conference on Designing Interactive User Experiences for TV and Video*, 2008.

13. Fereday, J., Muir-Cochrane, E., Demonstrating Rigor Using Thematic Analysis: A Hybrid Approach of Inductive and Deductive Coding and Theme Development, *Int. J. of Qualitative Methods*, 5(1), 2006.

14. Guitton M.J. (2014) The importance of studying the dark side of social networks. *Computers in Human Behavior* 31 (2014) 355.

15. Jamison-Powell, S., Linehan, C., Daley, L., Garbett, A., Lawson, S. 2012. "I can't get no sleep": discussing #insomnia on twitter. *In Proc. 2012 ACM annual conference on Human Factors in Computing Systems* (CHI 2012). ACM, New York, NY, USA, 1501-1510.

16. Jay, T., & Janschewitz, K. (2008). The pragmatics of swearing. *J. of Politeness Research. Language, Behaviour, Culture*, 4(2), 267-288.

17. Jensen, T, Ringrose, J., Feminist Media Studies (2013): Sluts that Choose Vs Doormat Gypsies: Exploring the Affect in the Postfeminist, Visual Moral Economy of *My Big Fat Gypsy Wedding, Feminist Media Studies*

18. Joinson, A., Disinhibition and the Internet, in *Psychology and the Internet: Intrapersonal, Interpersonal, and Transpersonal Implications*, ed. Gackenbach, J., 2007, Elsevier Press, Burlington, MA.

19. Kowalski, R., Limber, S., Agatston, P., *Cyberbullying: Bullying in the Digital Age*, 2nd ed. John Wiley & Sons, 2012.

20. Richardson, J. & O'Neill, R., 'Stamp on the Camps': the social construction of Gypsies and Travellers in media and political debate, in *Gypsies and Travellers: Empowerment and Inclusion in British Society, eds. Richardson, J. & Ryder, A.,* The Policy Press, 2012.

21. Riggins, S. H. (1997). The rhetoric of othering. The language and politics of exclusion: Others in discourse, 1-30.

22. Said, E. (1978). *Orientalism* (New York. Pantheon, 6, 14-27.

23. Schirra, S, Sun, H., & Bentley, F. (2014) Together Alone: Motivations for Live-Tweeting a Television Series, to appear in Proc CHI 2014. ACM Press.

24. Suler., J., The Online Disinhibition Effect, *CyberPsychology & Behavior*. June 2004, 7(3): 321-326.

25. O'Sullivan, P., Flanagin, A., Reconceptualizing 'flaming' and other problematic messages, *New Media & Society* March 2003 vol. 5 no. 1 69-94

26. Thelwall, M., Buckley, K., Paltoglou, G., Cai, D., Kappas., A., Sentiment strength detection in short informal text, *J. American Society for Information Science and Technology* 61(12) 2010, 2544–2558

27. Thelwall, M., Buckley, K., Paltoglou, G., Sentiment in Twitter events, *J. American Society for Information Science and Technology*, 62(2), 2011, 406–418.

28. Tremlett, A., (2013) Demotic or demonic? Race, class and gender in 'Gypsy' reality TV. to appear in The Sociological Review.

29. Vandebosch, H., & Van Cleemput, K. (2009). Cyberbullying among youngsters: Profiles of bullies and victims. *New Media & Society*, *11*(8), 1349-137

TV Discovery & Enjoy: a New Approach to Help Users Finding the Right TV Program to Watch

Jorge Abreu
University of Aveiro
3810 – 193 Aveiro
Portugal
jfa@ua.pt

Pedro Almeida
University of Aveiro
3810 – 193 Aveiro
Portugal
almeida@ua.pt

Bruno Teles
University of Aveiro
3810 – 193 Aveiro
Portugal
bmteles@ua.pt

ABSTRACT

This paper presents the development and evaluation cycle of an interactive television (iTV) prototype that aims to improve the way users discover and select their TV content, bearing in mind the cognitive model that the viewer typically uses in mindless zapping situations.

The development of the iTV application was supported by a study of the habits and behaviours of TV viewers (namely the ones related to the referred cognitive process), followed by the specification of its conceptual model and features, interface mock-ups and its integration in the filtering engine of the iTV application. Additionally, an indexing and cataloging system interconnected with the filtering engine was designed. The developed prototype was evaluated by a group of users, with the results revealing to be very positive, both in in what relates with the interest on the application and its usability. In parallel to the development of the iTV application, a tablet version was conceptualized and evaluated with the aim of studying the suitability of the extension of the same conceptual model to a secondary screen approach.

Author Keywords

Interactive television; EPG; prototype; usability tests; interaction; IPTV.

ACM Classification Keywords

H.5.2. Information interfaces and presentation (e.g., HCI): User Interfaces.

INTRODUCTION

The current landscape of the television ecosystem has been facing significant changes in the media used for watching TV namely regarding the features offered by TV operators and also the multiplicity of live or on demand content available. In addition to this increased offer, Digital TV operators have also invested in providing time shift content. Video-on-demand (VoD) systems and time shifted TV

(based in cloud storing from the last 7 days or more) provide increasing options for viewers when they sit in front of the TV with no clear idea of what to see. It is precisely in these situations, rather frequent, that the user engages in an activity here referred as *mindless zapping* and for which the developed application (TDE - TV Discovery and Enjoy) provides an alternative approach to the Electronic Program Guide (EPG), helping the viewer find a suitable program to watch.

All these technological developments have contributed to a change in the ways and habits of watching TV. According to a Nielsen study [26] which focused on the 2nd quarter of 2013 in the U.S., traditional TV viewing has been losing spectators. However monthly viewing time has increased when compared with the same period of 2012. In what relates with time shifted TV, there has been an increase both in terms of users (almost 15 % more between 2012 and 2013), as in the level of monthly consumption (with a slight increase). Another study, carried by Digitalsmiths, supports the idea of a decrease of traditional TV viewing time, considering that between the 1st and 3rd quarter of 2013 [9], the number of viewers that stated to watch TV more than 3 hours a day decreased by almost 10%. In the specific Portuguese context a decrease in the TV consumption is not noticeable. Actually between 2011 and 2012, daily television viewing time among users of pay TV increased by almost 2 minutes [20]. In parallel various features and applications available in the set-top boxes (STBs) have also been more popular (except for VoD and pause TV) particularly automatic recordings (time shift), TV guide and the restart TV features with an increase respectively of about 5%, 8% and 10% between March and September 2013 [3]. In the opposite direction to this slight broadcast TV decrease, we can find the on-demand content solutions, including the ones based in OTT (over-the-top), like Netflix [19], Hulu [16] or Roku [24]. These services have been gaining more and more users internationally and are available either through STBs or media-centers, smart TV applications, PC and mobile devices, making these providers, in many cases, like regular TV operators.

The growth of OTT solutions is also supported by the spread of mobile devices at home, which has traditionally been "inhabited" only by televisions. Actually, smartphones and tablets are increasingly used as devices for watching video. In the first half of 2013 the amount of videos watched increased by 41% in smartphones and 59% in tablets [22]. Despite most of these videos are on demand videos, live content is getting more and more attention [22]. Mobile devices are not only used by OTT services, actually the TV operators are also developing applications that allow its customers to watch live and on demand content (e.g. BBC iPlayer [4] or TWC TV [27]). In addition, these applications provide enhanced information like synopsis, casting details, trailers, among others. All this contributes for more flexible viewing schedules [10]. Given this situation, the current business models and the new viewing habits, broadcasters have the need to innovate and adapt, in particular, trying to keep current viewers that are specially interested in watching movies, series, documentaries and other content without having to follow a linear program grid [10] helping them to find the right content for each viewing context (people with whom they are sharing the screen, time available and even the emotions they are seeking from the program to watch). However, if the viewer relies in the current EPG to search the right content for his specific context, he will find that the current models provided by TV operators, are not efficient. The Digitalsmiths report [9], of the 3rd quarter of 2013, shows that 36.8% of viewers find it difficult to find something they can see on TV and 88.9% have the feeling of always seeing the same channels (more 4.1% than in Q1 of 2013). As a consequence the willingness to get personalized recommendations has been increasing (6.3% more when the 1st and 3rd quarter of 2013 are compared).

The academic community has tried, over the past few years, to contribute to reverse this trend by developing EPG prototypes that can, on the one hand, explore new graphic and interaction models and, on the other hand, combine innovative features to support the viewer finding more easily what he wants to see (examples include Unified EPG [21], iEPG [14] or PINGO [8]). It is also for this challenge that the TV Discovery and Enjoy application tries to be helpful, since it presents itself as an alternative EPG to solve some of these problems by displaying content regardless of its origin and taking in consideration the preferences and context of each user.

After this brief introduction, this paper is structured in the following sections. In the state of the art services and applications that relate with this research both in terms of its features and its interaction models are described. After this, the features of the TV Discovery and Enjoy application are presented and its development process is explained. The "Evaluation of the Prototype" section includes an explanation on the methods and procedures involved in the various evaluation phases, followed by the results and data analysis. Finally, in the last section, a tablet-oriented model developed as a spin-off of the TDE results is presented.

STATE OF THE ART
The evolution of electronic program guides (EPGs),

developed for the STBs of the TV operators has witness a low level of innovation when compared with the advances that have occurred on other equipment also used to watch TV (e.g. Smart TV's, new generation video game consoles or mobile devices). This may be due to the fact that STBs are, in general, more closed platforms, with restricted hardware, and, therefore, limited upon their exploitation by researchers, designers and developers. Despite this, several companies and research groups have focused their concerns on trying to offer a better service to viewers, in what relates with the easiness of navigation and discovery of content.

When considering TV recommendation systems (with a scope in line with the goals of this research), many research projects have been developed over the past few years. In 2007 the "AIMED" system [15], which uses as indicators for recommendations information based in the activities, interests, mood, experience and demographics, was created. It is a hybrid recommendation system as it combines two different techniques: content-based recommendation (based on the user's television footprint) and collaborative recommendation (based on the tastes of users with similar profile) [2]. In addition, the AIMED system stores the viewing behaviours of each user (e.g. channel, time and length of viewing session), comparing it with the different moods of users (manually inputted via a remote control which includes 3 coloured buttons: "Happy", "Bored" and "Unhappy") [15]. The "Sybil Recommender System", an experimental prototype for the web, funded by BBC Research & Development, introduces a model for the evaluation and recommendation of TV programs. The system displays a set of recommendations that can be filtered by gender (e.g. children, comedy or drama). For that, users drag and drop the recommendations to "Like" or "Dislike" boxes. Each time content is drawn into one of the boxes, the list is updated with new content, increasingly closer to the tastes of the user [5]. The Fraunhofer FOKUS has also introduced an application for the recommendation of TV content called "TV Predictor". This system analyses the viewing habits and the evaluations of users to determine, among other things, channels, genres, directors or favourite actors, as well as preferred viewing times [11].

Considering work related with interface and interaction paradigms one can highlight the "iEPG" research project. It provides a nonlinear way to search for content in the DVR, through an endless web alike representation. This prototype converts the stored content into a diagram consisting of a central node to which various items are attached radially (e.g. if the central node is a film, the peripheral items may be actors or directors). By selecting one of these items it becomes the primary node surrounded by other items [14]. The "iFanzy" research project introduces an EPG with TV, web and mobile versions. Through the creation and management of profiles, each user is granted with a personalized EPG, taking into account the viewing habits and content reviews. The colour is used to differentiate TV programs according to the suitability to the user profile [6].

For industry born projects, one can highlight two proposals: the "Freetime" launched by Freesat with a creative and unusual EPG interface. It also includes a "Showcase" which provides viewers with recommendations of what to see in that evening and programs that were already broadcasted, however classified as not to miss [12]. A second interface proposal worth to be highlighted is the one based in "snowflake". This system, developed by NDS, includes a modern and minimalist interface. The menus are simple (with basic text information and flat white images). The only colour elements are in the channel PIP [18].

Considering the tools that support the discovery of content on Smart TVs it is important to highlight the F7000 series from Samsung. One of its main features is the "S Recommendation" which allows users, among other things, to search by voice, categories of specific programs (e.g. "What's good on tonight" or "Find us a romantic comedy"). This search can return unified results both from broadcasters and online streaming services. It is also important to highlight the "On TV" area, displaying a large PIP of the main channel, the live programs at the moment and programs that are coming next [25]. This approach to search, independent on the source of the content, is also available in other systems, like Google TV. After inputting keywords the user gets a list of results that can be filtered by Live TV, TV & Movies, Youtube or Web [13].

The Portuguese TV Operators

Regarding the Portuguese context, Pay-Tv operators have also been upgrading their services with discovery and content recommendation features. The MEO service allows its users to find TV content, either Live or time shifted, through textual search. It also includes a filtering method by category, genre or data [23]. The ZON Iris service also includes a search feature which uses as keywords the names of programs, actors or directors. The user can also search by setting different filters, such as the day, channel, category and genre. It also allows reviewing content with that information being used to provide recommendations according to the preferences of each user [29]. Finally, the "My Zapping" Vodafone system provides recommendations based on favourite programs for a certain time of the day. This way, users can watch up to 6 PIPs of recommended programs. In addition Vodafone "My Zapping" users can browse the most viewed TV programs by genre [28].

In this context TDE aims to contribute to this field, including the discovery and visualization, on the same screen, of TV programs from different sources and the possibility of filtering the content through various criteria, some of which are not available from most TV operators, as the audience and the mood/emotion.

THE TV DISCOVERY AND ENJOY APPLICATION

Considering the framework described in the previous section, the main goal of this research was to develop an application to support the viewers in a contextualized

discovery of TV content from all available TV channels, automatic recordings by the operator (cloud storage) and from existing VoD movies catalogue of an IPTV operator. Thus, the prototype allows users to filter TV content from the various sources mentioned by setting 5 criteria (see next section): *Category* (movies, series ...), *Genre* (drama, comedy ...), *Program Duration, Mood* (emotion conveyed - amusement, fear ...) and *Audience* (family, children ...). The prototype was developed with the support of an IPTV operator (MEO) which provided its development platform (Microsoft Mediaroom - Presentation Framework) allowing the researchers to work on the STB, ensuring access to some of the operator services, and also allowing to carry an evaluation in a commercial platform close to real uses and users. This application tries to support the situations when the users don't know in advance what to see on TV. Therefore, when the user engages in a "mindless zapping" activity, a background algorithm detects it and shows an OSD notification telling the user that he can call the application via the blue button (a shortcut key dedicated to this application on the remote control) (see Figure 1).

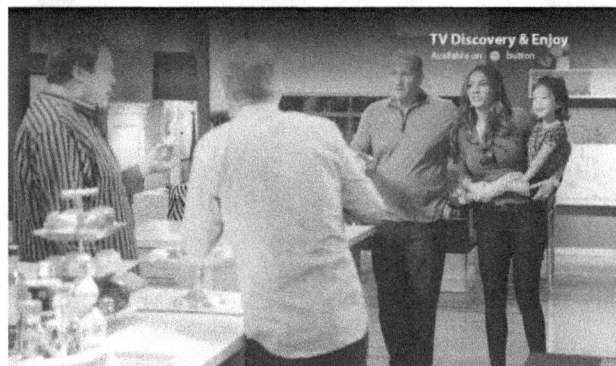

Figure 1. Notification suggesting the application

When the application is open the user is faced with an interface showing the 5 referred filtering criteria on the right and, in the left, within a vertical carrousel, the programs that match the defined criteria (see Figure 2).

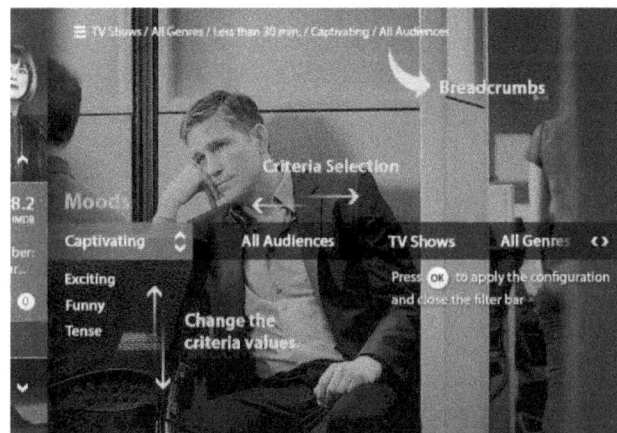

Figure 2. The right section of the TV application

The navigation between the criteria and in each of its values is done with the arrow keys in the remote control. The chosen criteria are always visible through a breadcrumb at the top of the screen. After closing the filters bar (using the "OK" button in the remote), the user is able to see and navigate in all the results (see Figure 3). The contents list is sorted by relevance to the chosen criteria. Per content (program) the following information is provided: length, synopsis, source (TV channel or VoD), broadcast schedule and rating (from IMDB). The navigation through the list is done by the "up" and "down" arrow keys.

Figure 3. The left section of the TV application

Users can also rate programs with "likes" or "dislikes" using the keys "9" and "0". This review is stored and analysed by the system to be able to be used in future recommendations. At any time the viewer can start the chosen program by pressing the "OK" button.

DEVELOPMENT OF THE TV APLICATION

The development of the application described in the previous section was supported by an online survey targeted at gathering information about TV habits and the cognitive process related with viewer's activity of deciding what to watch on TV when he sits in front of the TV having no specific idea of what to see. The survey was available for about 3 months and reached 550 responses. The results were extremely important for the development of the application since it helped in defining the basic concepts and features to include, in particular in the choice of the filtering criteria to be provided by TDE, allowing to map the related cognitive process. In this sense, it was asked to the respondents of the questionnaire which were the most important criteria when deciding what to see on TV. They were then asked to order the chosen criteria in accordance with the given relevance for each respondent. Through the survey analysis it was determined that the television genre was clearly the most preferred option (criteria), followed by the mood/conveyed emotion and, finally, the audience and the time available, these ones with close values [1]. After the analysis of the online survey, the functional requirements of the application were defined, taking into account technological restrictions imposed by an

implementation in commercial STBs, as well as the time limitations inherent to the research project. The interface design and the interaction model development followed.

The process involved the specification of different interaction models for the application. This was made through the use of interactive mock-ups followed by a team validation and the selection of the chosen model. It was then implemented, designed and integrated as the final interface. In parallel to this design process, a cataloguing and indexing of TV content tool was developed. This tool was then interconnected with the filtering engine. The development of this system revealed to be crucial since there were serious limitations on the metadata, associated with TV content, provided by the operator. The solution included the integration of metadata gathered in specialized TV programs cataloguing web portals. IMDB was used as a source of information about the genres of television programs and its rating. On the other hand, the Jinni platform [17] was useful as it provided the necessary information for the audience and mood criteria. This was a crucial phase of the project since this system allowed the classification of all the TV programs according to the identified criteria, with a reasonable matching between the user's expectations and the suggested results.

Finally, the last step of the development phase of TDE comprised the implementation of the interface in the STB application and the interconnection of the filtering engine to the developed cataloguing system.

EVALUATION OF THE PROTOTYPE

The last stage of the project consisted of the evaluation of the prototype aiming to: validate the suitability of the developed functional solutions to the results of the preliminary survey (on the TV consumption habits and related cognitive processes); clarify questions that arose after the survey analysis and during the development process; evaluate the application usability in what concerns with its graphical and interaction components; determine the suitability of the number of recommended content and the real interest on the different criteria; gather some opinions related to the user experience and the general interest towards the use of the application. The research team chose to carry a lab evaluation, which allowed assessing, in a controlled environment and with the direct support of the researchers in all the stages of the evaluation, all the prototype features and particularities. The lab sessions were carried for 4 days and took place in the CETAC.MEDIA lab, in the room Social iTV which was prepared to recreate a friendly atmosphere, in some way similar to what you'll find in a living room with some sofas and a TV (see Figure 4).

To select the sample of evaluators a priority was given to people that had already participated in the first survey and that had showed willingness to collaborate on future initiatives [1]. The remaining members of the sample were people who voluntarily decided to participate because they felt curious or interested in the project or were chosen by convenience (mainly students and staff).

Figure 4. The evaluation room

In the beginning of each evaluation session the participants were contextualized about the research goals and got a brief introduction about the application. Then, participants were asked to interact freely with TDE, so that they could have a hands-on perception of the features and its usefulness. Later, in order to track usability issues, they were asked to perform a set of tasks that included finding and playing content with different criteria: *"series / funny"* and *"movies / crime / captivating / more than 60 minutes / for men"*. Participants were asked, following the thinking aloud protocol, to express their difficulties and doubts at any time. Along with a script to declare the tasks to perform the researchers used and an observation table in which all the actions and verbal and nonverbal behaviours of the participants were registered. The sessions were also video and audio recorded. This allowed to carefully review and analyse each of the sessions, as well as to determine the average time that each participant took to perform the tasks. At the beginning and after interacting with the TV application, the participants were asked to answer a questionnaire. The first one was designed to gather answers to demographic questions (gender, age) and to questions regarding the frequency and uses of media devices and the second, information on the experience of using TDE. The section related with usability issues was based on the typology of questions of the SUS questionnaire [7].

RESULTS AND DATA ANALYSIS

Sample Characterization

The sample consisted of 20 participants, of whom 55% were aged between 22 and 26 years and 50% were male. The most represented professional sectors were related to the areas of Research and Development (30%) and Multimedia (20%). Regarding the educational qualification, 8 participants were graduated, 6 had PhDs, 5 had masters and 1 a post-graduation. The fact that the sample targets young people with higher education and access to technology allowed the researchers to evaluate the application in a segment of the population that potentially represents a worst case scenario, considering that they have an higher percentage of time shifted TV consumption and are using other media devices in substitution of regular TV.

Regarding employment status, participants were mostly students (50%) or working-students (20%). Of the respondents, 85% reported living with other adults, 10% reported living alone and only 5% reported living with adults and children. Regarding TV consumption habits, participants referred an increase of the viewing time at the end of the day, both on weekdays or weekends. Considering the use of the services offered by TV providers (EPG, DVR, automatic recordings, VoD and text search) their frequency of use was low. Nevertheless, despite the overall low use of these features, EPG and Recordings (DVR and automatic) were the preferred ones.

Results from the evaluation sessions

The post-test questionnaire results were analysed considering two groups of 10 evaluators each, structured taking into account the average weekly viewing frequency of each evaluator. Throughout the questionnaire, respondents were able to evaluate the application according to the: interface aesthetic, usability, amount of information visible in different areas, interest in the filtering criteria and overall interest in the application. Throughout this analysis, the group with lower TV consumption (1 to 3 hours a week) will be named **LC**, leaving the remaining group (4 to 7,5 hours a week) with the designation **HC**.

Considering the evaluation of the TDE interface in what relates with its graphical component, both groups granted (on a Lickert scale) the best score to the "organization of the areas of information" (40% of the **HC** group and 50% of the **LC** group qualified it as "Very Good") and to the "Graphical aesthetic" (50% of the **HC** group and 50% of the **LC** group qualified it as "Very Good").

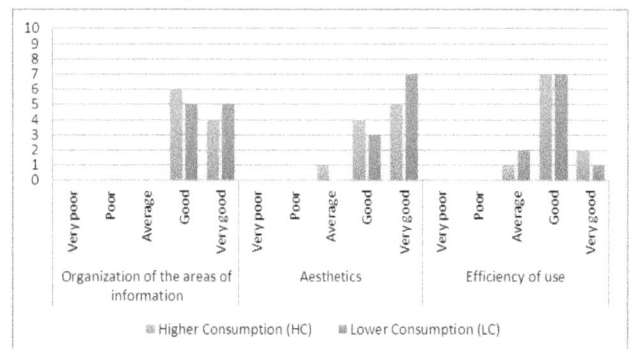

Graphic 1. UI – organization, aesthetics and global efficiency

The last parameter of the interface is related to the overall efficiency ("ease of navigation"). In this case, the results were less optimistic, but still highly positive, since 70% of both groups chose the "good" option (see Graphic 1).

Concerning the interaction actions and patterns (Graphic 2) the *navigation between recommended programs* and the *definition of the criteria* were the features that had better appreciation by the users of both groups, since all answers focused on the two higher levels of the scale.

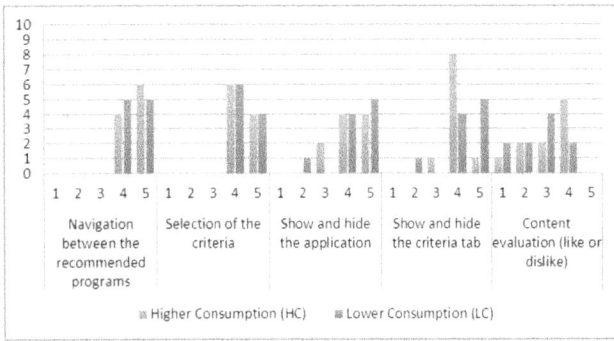

Graphic 2. UI – interaction actions

The actions of *show/hide the application* and *show/hide the filter bar*, despite a positive appreciation, were considered less functional for a small number of respondents, 10 % of the **HC** group with "Partially functional" in both features, whereas in the **LC** group, 1 opted for the middle level of the scale about the *filter bar* and 2 filled with level 3 the task of *show/hide the application*. The less appreciated action by both groups was the *evaluation of the programs*, collecting 30% below the middle level of the scale, by the **HC** group, and 40% from the **LC** group.

When asked about the suitability of the number of recommendations simultaneously visible on the screen, the vast majority of respondents from both groups felt that the current number (3) was correct (80% of the **HC** group and 90% of the **LC** group). Only 1 respondent from the **HC** group wanted to see a smaller amount of recommendations. Regarding the level of information for each program, respondents from the **LC** group showed greater willingness to view more information (30%). The vast majority of the **HC** group felt that the existing information was suitable (90%).

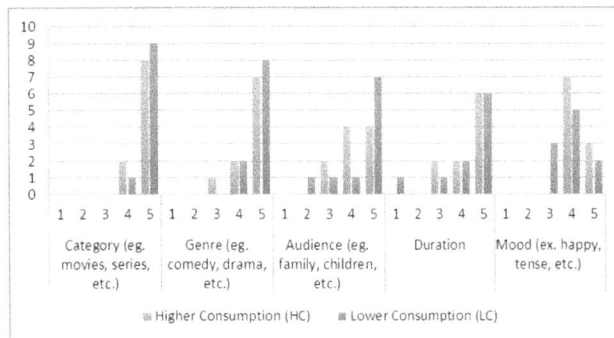

Graphic 3. Interest in the criteria for filtering TV programs

As regards to the level of interest in the content filtering criteria (Graphic 3), *Format* and *Gender* were clearly the favourites in both groups, but more preferably for participants with lower TV consumption (**LC**). For the remaining criteria, the interest of the **HC** group was focused on *Duration*, *Mood*, and finally *Audience*. The order of the **LC** respondents is different, since they chose as the 3rd most interesting criterion the *Audience*, followed by *Duration*, and lastly *Mood*.

When asked to demonstrate the accordance with 7 statements about the user experience, the vast majority of the evaluators in both groups demonstrated agreement or complete agreement. When looking for the evaluations that could reflect potential problems, one can highlight that in the **HC** group 20% disagree (and 10% strongly disagree) that *The application has sufficient mechanisms to allow me undo, if I make a mistake* and 20% neither agree or disagree with the statement *I always knew where I was in the application*. Regarding the **LC** group, the most dissonant statements were *My actions in the remote matched what happened on the screen* (10% disagree and 20% neither agree or disagree) and *The visual aids are appropriate* (10% neither agree or disagree) (see Graphic 4 and 5).

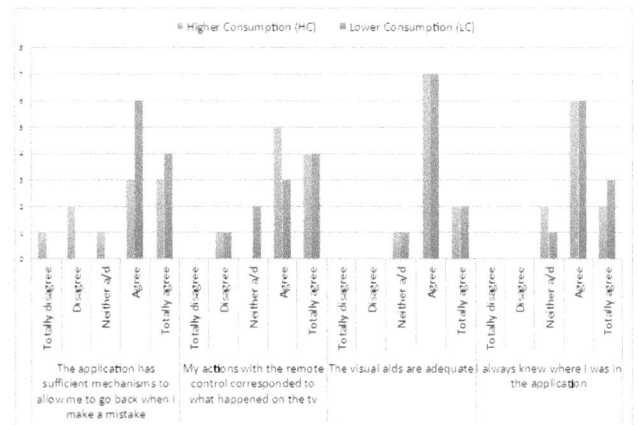

Graphic 4. Level of agreement with the statements – ½

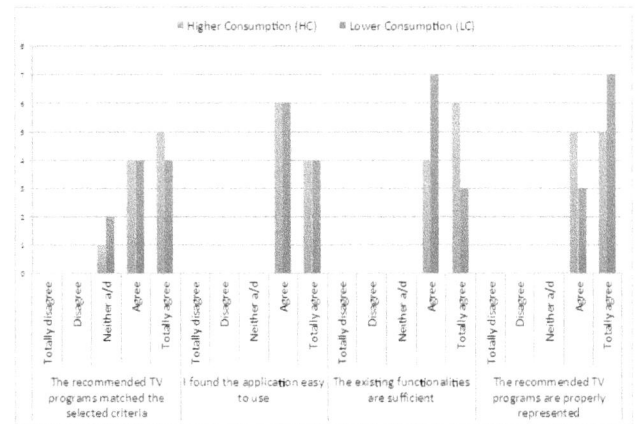

Graphic 5. Level of agreement with the statements – 2/2

The last question asked participants about the level of interest in the application. 70% of the group with higher TV consumption said to have much interest and the remaining 30% were interested. The results of the **LC** group are similar but slightly more positive, since 80% of respondents considered that it would be very interesting and 20% interesting to have TDE in their homes.

CONCEPTUALIZATION OF THE TABLET APPLICATION
This research project also envisioned the conceptualization of a tablet application that could offer a more interactive

and dynamic way of discovering TV content as compared with the TV app and, at the same, could offer the ability to choose what to see in a second screen approach. In this sense, the features to include in such an application were conceptualized, an interface based prototype for it was drawn and an evaluation with target users was made.

Figure 5. Interface of the main screen of the tablet application

Some of the features introduced in the prototype (see Figure 5) were: a spatial representation of the recommended content based on the criteria previously defined by the user; presentation of detailed information about each program (e.g. synopsis, credits, trailer, among others); programs evaluation; a favorite list; connection with social networks, and; statistics about the user's TV consumption habits. To ensure some interactivity and to attempt to simulate the interaction model of the tablet application, an agile prototype was developed. The assessment of this conceptual model is here brieffly described since it allows informing about the potential of such type of application. The assessment of the app was performed just after the evaluation of the TV application and the results were very positive. Considering the organization of information and the level of aesthetic of the interface, all these aspects were considered by the evaluators as "good" or "very good". Considering the level of interest in the proposed features, almost all were considered as "interesting" or "very interesting". In addition to the overall high level of interest in all the features one can highlight: the discovery model offered by the various criteria; the spatial representation of programs, and; the ability to have access to detailed program information. Less appreciated, but still with positive assessment among evaluators, was the social networks sharing features. Finally, when asked about the overall interest in the application, 85% of respondents were "very interested". The questionnaire was also used to try to understand how the next version of the application could be improved. In this sense, some features were rated as the most interesting, including: *notifications for when a program of your preference is near to start* and *TV program recommendations based on references on social networks.*

CONCLUSIONS

The results of this study, despite the limitation imposed by the small number of participants who evaluated the TDE application help us to identify that the conceptual model of the proposed application which maps the cognitive processes of users when they try to find something on TV, has a very interesting potential, especially as an alternative to the traditional model of EPGs (grid based). Moreover, this research allowed the implementation of the conceptual model into an IPTV fully functional prototype which obtained an overall positive evaluation, both in terms of its usability and in terms of the adequacy of the number and quality of the proposed content, considering the criteria that participants decide to choose. However, with regard to the preference for each of the available filtering criteria, it was found that the less desirable criteria for the **HC** group was the *Audience* and for the **LC** group the *Mood*. In the remaining analysis, differentiated between evaluators with higher and lower television consumption there were no other significant differences. It should be noted also, that the suitability of the proposed contents, related with the evaluators chosen criteria had a very positive result. This shows that the system developed for the enrichment of television content with meta-information required for the filtering engine is an interesting approach for automated cataloguing of various TV programs of an iTV operator. From the operator perspective there was also a business interest on this application due to its potential to increase the VoD consumption, since the recommended programs in TDE are from unified sources, including premium content. Additionally, this research helped to create the foundations for the development of a tablet application that, within the same conceptual model, will be enriched with a set of additional features that potentially will make the task of discovering content even more in harmony with the name of this application, TV Discovery and Enjoy.

ACKNOWLEDGMENTS
Our thanks to PT Inovação for the financial support granted to this study.

REFERENCES

1. Abreu J.F., Almeida, P., Teles, B. & Reis, M. (2013). Viewer behaviors and practices in the (new) Television Environment. In *Proceedings of the 11th European conference on Interactive TV and video (EuroITV '13).* ACM, New York, NY, USA, 5-12.

2. Adomavicius, G., & Tuzhilin, A. (2005). Toward the Next Generation of Recommender Systems: A Survey of the State-of-the-Art and Possible Extensions. *IEEE Trans. on Knowl. and Data Eng., 17(6), 734–749.*

3. Anacom. (n.d.). Serviço de Televisão por Subscrição - 3o trimestre 2013. Retrieved January 27, 2014, from http://www.anacom.pt/streaming/STVS_3T2013.pdf?contentId=1181617&field=ATTACHED_FILE

4. BBC. (2011). BBC iPlayer. *Apple Store*. Retrieved January 27, 2014, from https://itunes.apple.com/gb/app/bbc-iplayer/id416580485?mt=8

5. BBC Research & Development. (2012). *Sibyl Recommender System*. Retrieved December 26, 2013, from http://sibyl.prototyping.bbc.co.uk/

6. Bellekens, P., Kerckhove, G. Van, & Kaptein, A. (2009). iFanzy - A Ubiquitous Approach Towards a Personalized EPG. In *Networked Television: Adjunct proceedings of EuroITV 2009* (pp. 130–131). University of Leuven.

7. Brooke, J. (1996). "SUS: a "quick and dirty" usability scale". In P. W. Jordan, B. Thomas, B. A. Weerdmeester, & A. L. McClelland. *Usability Evaluation in Industry*. London: Taylor and Francis.

8. Concolato, C. (2009). Generation, Streaming and Presentation of Electronic Program Guide. In *Networked Television: Adjunct proceedings of EuroITV 2009* (pp. 46–49). University of Leuven.

9. Digitalsmiths. (2013). *Q3 2013 Video Discovery Trends Report: Consumer Behavior Across Pay-TV, VOD, OTT, Connected Devices and Next-Gen Features*. Retrieved December 26, 2013, from http://www.digitalsmiths.com/downloads/Digitalsmiths_Q3_2013_Video_Discovery_Trends_Report.pdf

10. Ericsson ConsumerLab. (2013). *TV and Media: Identifying the needs of tomorrow's video consumers*. Retrieved December 26, 2013, from http://www.ericsson.com/res/docs/2013/consumerlab/tv-and-media-consumerlab2013.pdf

11. Krauss, C., George, L., & Arbanowski, S. (2013). TV predictor: personalized program recommendations to be displayed on SmartTVs. In *Proceedings of the 2nd International Workshop on Big Data, Streams and Heterogeneous Source Mining: Algorithms, Systems, Programming Models and Applications* (BigMine '13). ACM, New York, NY, USA, 63-70.

12. Freesat. (2012). *Freetime from Freesat. Catch up on the past seven days of TV and watch On Demand, subscription free*. Retrieved December 26, 2013, from http://www.google.com/tv/

13. Google. (n.d.). *Google TV*. Retrieved December 26, 2013, from http://www.freesat.co.uk/freetime/

14. Harrison, C., Amento, B., & Stead, L. (2008). iEPG: An Ego-Centric Electronic Program Guide and Recommendation Interface.

15. Hsu, S., Wen, M.-H., Lin, H.-C., Lee, C.-C., & Lee, C.-H. (2007). AIMED- A Personalized TV Recommendation System. In *P. Cesar, K. Chorianopoulos, & J. Jensen (Eds.), Interactive TV: a Shared Experience (Vol. 4471, pp. 166–174)*. Springer Berlin / Heidelberg

16. Hulu. (n.d.). *Watch TV. Watch Movies. | Online | Free | Hulu*. Retrieved December 27, 2013, from http://www.hulu.com/

17. Jinni. (n.d.). Jinni. Retrieved January 28, 2014, from http://www.jinni.com/

18. NDS. (n.d.). *NDS EPGs & User Interface Services*. Retrieved December 27, 2013, from http://nds-snowflake.com

19. Netflix. (n.d.). *Netflix - Watch TV Shows Online, Watch Movies Online*. Retrieved December 26, 2013, from https://signup.netflix.com/global

20. Obercom. (2012). *Anuário da Comunicação 2011-2012*. Retrieved January 27, 2014, from http://www.obercom.pt/client/?newsId=28&fileName=Anuario2012.pdf

21. Obrist, M., Moser, C., Tscheligi, M., Alliez, D., Desmoulins, C., Teresa, H., & Miletich, S. M. (2009). Connecting TV & PC : An In-Situ Field Evaluation of an Unified Electronic Program Guide Concept. In *EuroITV '09 Proceedings of the seventh european conference on European interactive television conference*.

22. Ooyala. (2013). *Ooyala Global Video Index Q2 2013*. Retrieved December 26, 2013, from http://go.ooyala.com/rs/OOYALA/images/Ooyala-Global-Video-Index-Q2-2013.pdf

23. PT Comunicações. (n.d.). *MEO Fibra e MEO ADSL - Funcionalidades - Experiência TV - TV - MEO*. Retrieved January 28, 2014, from http://www.meo.pt/tv/experiencia-tv/funcionalidades/fibra-adsl

24. Roku. (n.d.). *Roku Streaming Player*. Retrieved December 27, 2013, from http://www.roku.com/

25. Samsung. (2013). *Samsung Smart TV 2013 with Smart Interaction*. Retrieved December 26, 2013, from http://www.samsung.com/us/2013-smart-tv

26. The Nielsen Company. (2013). *Q2 2013 Cross-Platform Report: Viewing On Demand*. Retrieved December 26, 2013, from http://www.nielsen.com/content/dam/corporate/us/en/reports-downloads/2013%20Reports/Q2-2013-Cross-Platform-Report.pdf

27. Time Warner Cable. (2011). *TWC TV*. Retrieved December 26, 2013, from https://itunes.apple.com/us/app/twc-tv/id420455839?mt=8

28. Vodafone. (n.d.). *My Zapping - Vodafone Tv Net Voz*. Retrieved December 26, 2013, from http://www.vodafone.pt/main/Particulares/tv-net-voz/IPTV/ServicosInteractivos/my-zapping.htm

29. ZON Multimedia. (n.d.). *IRIS - A melhor experiência TV do mundo | Residencial*. Retrieved December 26, 2013, from http://www.zon.pt/tv/iris/vantagens1/Pages/default.asp

MyChannel: Exploring City-Based Multimedia News Presentations on the Living Room TV

Frank Bentley, Karolina Buchner, Joseph 'Jofish' Kaye
Yahoo Labs
Sunnyvale, CA USA
{fbentley, karolina, jofish}@yahoo-inc.com

ABSTRACT

We see the television as a primary device to connect viewers with the information and people that matter most in their lives. Televisions, as central places where the family gathers, provide a unique location to elevate news and social updates that can connect family and friends across a distance. Through creating the MyChannel service, a TV-based personalized news program, we have explored the types of content that work best in this format. We have also gained a detailed understanding of how television content can inspire feelings of connection and communication with friends and family at a distance through an 8-day in-home field evaluation. We describe the system and findings from our studies and close with a discussion on the future of personalized television news.

Author Keywords

Television; News; Multimedia; Field Study; Design.

ACM Classification Keywords

H.5.m. Information interfaces and presentation (e.g., HCI): Miscellaneous. H.5.1 Multimedia Information Systems: Evaluation/methodology

INTRODUCTION

The traditional nightly television news broadcast has been losing viewership in the US and throughout the world. US evening news viewership on the major networks is down from 42.3 million viewers in 1980 to 15.6 million viewers in 2012. [9] The idea of a 30-minute program that contains a generic view of the news fit for everyone in the country seems outdated to those who have grown up with millions of articles at their fingertips on the Internet, tailored to their specific interests and viewpoints. While some viewers have moved to cable news for news-based entertainment, many cable networks aim to provide more entertainment than actual news facts and tend not to follow the format of the summary broadcast.

In contrast to television news, reading an online news story or watching a short video news clip is quite different from the rich, long-format multimedia presentation of a TV news broadcast. Much online news resembles a traditional print style of delivery with relatively long articles that go in depth into particular stories. They require a great deal of time and attention to sort through to find stories of interest and then to read each story. This is a very different way of experiencing the news compared to a traditional lean-back TV news program. However, the detailed personalization provided by today's online news platforms has the potential to transform a traditional television news experience and to show more content that is relevant to the people, places, and issues that matter to the viewer.

We are exploring the design space of a highly personalized lean-back news experience, consumed daily on the living room television. Through this work, we have built and evaluated a series of prototypes that select and present a variety of Internet-sourced news content to viewers on their home television sets.

We started this work with a set of research questions related to creating a lean-back, personalized news experience on the television: How can a television-based news experience foster feelings of connection and communication with friends and family who live at a distance? How does viewing social and local content on the television change the way that content is perceived? What is the best way to structure and present local and social news for a television-based presentation?

In order to answer these questions, we iteratively constructed a functional prototype, interleaving two user studies as we designed and developed the system. Our final study consisted of an 8-day field evaluation with our system running on participants' living room televisions. We will show the benefits and drawbacks of using the cities where users have many friends as a basis for content personalization as well as discuss findings on how a personalized news system on a television fits into daily life and inspires communication with remote friends and family.

RELATED WORK

There are several domains of research that are relevant as background for our work. Content personalization, most commonly found in online news and social websites, automatically-generated multimedia, and television-based interfaces for news are all related to our efforts.

TVX '14, June 25 - 27, 2014, Newcastle Upon Tyne, United Kingdom
Copyright 2014 ACM 978-1-4503-2838-8/14/06...$15.00.
http://dx.doi.org/10.1145/2602299.2602302

For many years, researchers and corporations have created a variety of systems that personalize news feeds. The Freshman Fishwrap project at MIT [5] balanced personalized and popular content as well as included news and weather from a user's home town. In MyInfo, Zimmerman et al [16] created a television-based system that presented personalized news based on an explicit user profile. However this work does not appear to have been evaluated in use.

Others have explored ways to personalize online news based on user modeling [3], information novelty [8], click behavior [11], and collaborative filtering [7]. These techniques form the backbone of today's online news platforms, however have not been widely explored in the context of television news.

Nadamoto and Tanaka [12] developed the first PC-based system that created news broadcasts from Internet content. Nichols and Hammond [14] created the News at Seven system in 2009 that also presented news content using avatars. Viewed on the desktop web, yet inspired by television news broadcasts, this is the closest vision to our current system. Many of the dialog generation techniques we used in our work, such as varied transitions and alternating between male and female voices was inspired by this system's attention to standard news production practices.

Allen et al. [1] explored automatically generating sports stories from game statistics, including creating specific "angles" to use for presenting content. Concepts such as looking for shutouts or other types of "interesting" games led to us create a variety of different templates for presenting sports results. These techniques are also used by the company Narrative Science to automatically identify and generate a variety of written news stories.

Commercially, platforms are now available to receive a variety of news content directly on the television. Platforms such as Yahoo's Smart TV or Roku enable a variety of news content to be viewed on a television set. However, the experience of viewing this content is quite different from the lean-back style of watching a news program or other television content. Typically, users need to actively navigate applications to select stories to read or short video news clips to watch. Every minute or two some action is required which runs counter to the sit-back-and-watch experience of interacting with television.

Cornejo et al. [6] studied the use of physical devices in the living room that displayed Facebook content from family members who live in other cities. They found that this object created impromptu family gatherings around the device to view and discuss posts. We were interested in this idea of the family gathering around a central device in the living room to view social content from contacts at a distance in addition to more traditional news sources.

Missing from this work is a system that can be used in the home and that creates highly personalized news programs for each user based on the important places in their lives. Particularly, we were interested in how such a system would be used in daily life, something that the previous work did not address.

CONTENT EXPLORATION

In order to better understand the types of content that we should select and present, we began with a small prototype and in-lab user study to explore both content ranking and presentation style before building a system for in-home use.

Selecting Content

Early on, we had the idea that using the cities where the user has many friends as a way to personalize content might select interesting and relevant content that can inspire communication with friends and family who live at a distance. This was one of the main content selection techniques that we wanted to test before building out the full system.

For this initial study, we built a simple web application that allowed a user to authorize our system to access their Facebook friends list and news feed. We found the top three cities where they had the most friends, and then used these cities to find a variety of content. We accessed weather information for each of these top cities, including any severe weather alerts. We then found the results of any professional sporting events in those cities in the past day. We queried the Yahoo Local News API to find the top ten news stories for each of these cities and the Facebook News Feed API to find posts and photos from friends in these cities.

Typically, this process generated between 60-100 items per user. We printed each item on a sheet of paper for users to filter and order as they wished as described below.

Initial Study

We recruited six diverse participants (3 male, aged 20s-40s) for a quick in-lab study to understand preferences in selecting and presenting content. This was intended as an early stage design research study to help us focus our design efforts.

At the start of the interview, the participant authorized our system to access their Facebook information. While the system ran and a team member printed out the stack of content, we conducted a short interview about current online and offline news practices to better understand how the participant currently accessed news and other online information.

We then presented the user with the stack of content items along with a set of blank pages for new items they wished to add. We asked them to imagine that they were watching a short news presentation on their TV and to select and order the content that they would like to see presented to them. Throughout the process, they were asked to think aloud so that we could understand their motivations for including or discarding a particular piece of content.

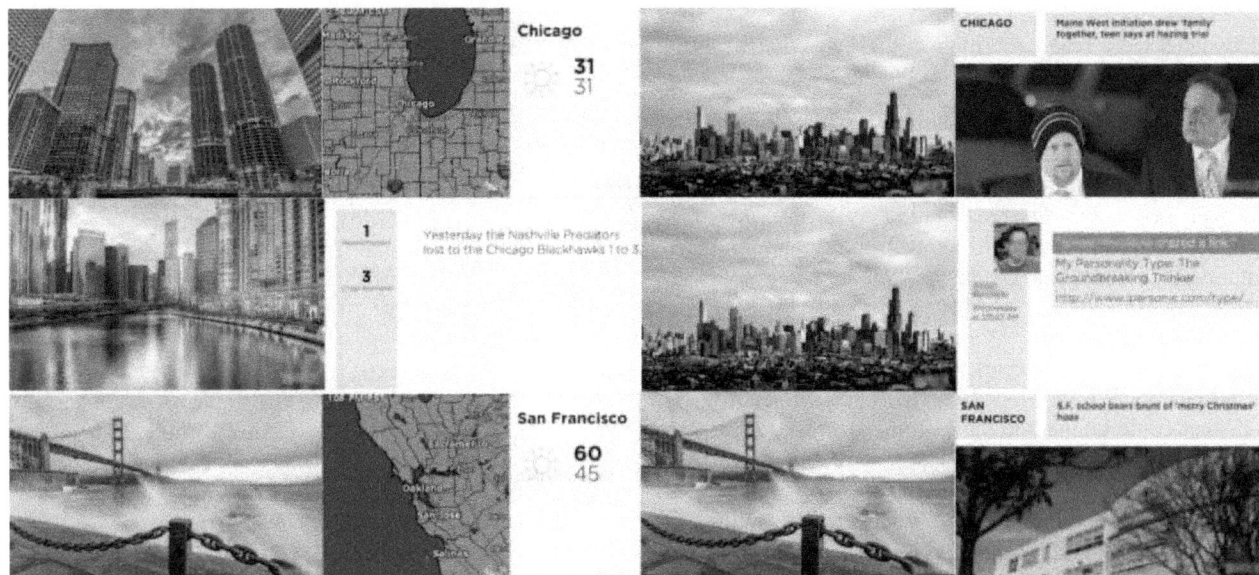

Figure 1: Sample screens from a MyChannel presentation. News, Weather, Sports and social information are presented for each city, with photos of each city from Flickr used for visual transitions between content types.

Finally, we asked the participant to act out their presentations, so that we could better understand the amount of information that they wanted read for particular items, in addition to allowing us to be inspired by novel presentation styles that we might not have considered.

Findings

This quick study showed us that there was promise in our technique for selecting news and other content based on Facebook friend locations, extending Chesnais' inclusion of hometown in Fishwrap [5]. Participants regularly spoke of being interested in the news stories that we selected, and at times found interesting personal connections, such as a flood in an apartment building where close friends lived.

We also learned that about two news stories per city works well, as to give a bit of diversity of topics covered, as well as to fit in the time allotted. This study also showed us the importance of the social information. All participants included some of the social content, especially photos posted from friends in the cities that we selected.

Four participants organized their content by city. For example, they started with Boston and included news, weather, sports, and social information for Boston, and then went on to New York. However, other participants ordered the content by type, putting all of the news together and all of the social updates together. The ordering and presentation of content remained an open question that we would address again in the longer field study.

THE MYCHANNEL SYSTEM

Taking into account the findings from our initial in-lab study, we created a functional system for use in the home. MyChannel is implemented as a server that generates HTML5 presentations which can be viewed on a variety of devices. For this study, we were particularly interested in its presentation on a television and created an application that would run on a Google Chromecast plugged into a participant's television that was activated through a single click on a mobile phone app.

Content

Based on findings from our initial study, we decided to use the three cities where the user has the most Facebook friends as the main filter for selecting content. We kept the news, sports, weather, and social content that we used in the initial study and developed content ranking algorithms that aligned to our users' preferences.

For news, we chose the "biggest" two stories in the region. We determined this by the number of sources that reported on the story. For Facebook content, we prioritized photos over status updates. We also added birthdays of friends and friends who are traveling as introductory content items before beginning the city-based content display.

We then worked out presentations for each of the content items. We had to decide what to display on the screen as well as what to speak out loud and how to say it to present each item. We utilized a text-to-speech system for the audio portion of the presentation and adopted a fairly traditional news broadcast style for presentation with key transitions selected randomly from templates (e.g. "And now for Boston's news" or "Turning to Boston weather").

For news articles, we read a 2-3 sentence summary of the story created using the Summly API. For weather, we read the high temperature and weather condition, along with any severe weather alerts for that city. Sports scores were read mentioning each team and their score and using sports vernacular such as "shut out" or "blow out" when appropriate.

Social updates were read as written in the Facebook news feed.

Once we had selected the content and the presentation for each item, we had several options for arranging the content for presentation. In the study described below, we experimented with seven different presentation styles in order to better understand the ordering of content and the length of presentation that works best for this new medium.

Display on the Television
We used the Google Chromecast to display the presentation on the television. We developed custom apps for Android and iOS that could connect to the Chromecast and start the presentation with one click. The Chromecast device then connected to our server and rendered the HTML5 presentation for that user on the television. Some screen captures from a typical presentation can be seen in Figure 1. An example of the audio of the presentation follows:

Welcome to your daily [update]. Here are today's stories picked for you!

Starting with Chicago weather. It's much colder than average today in Chicago with a low of 4.

And now, Chicago's news.

Dennis Rodman's global "worming" with Kim Jong-un is bad news. Team Worm will play against some North Korean players on Kim's 31st birthday Wednesday, and one wonders if those North Korean athletes will be shot or eaten by dogs if they lose.

Dressed like pint-sized Eskimos, kids returned to McPherson Elementary School Wednesday morning, delighted to see their friends & their parents equally thrilled to get the little ones out of the house. "It's been crazy just keeping the kids busy" said parent Kendra Reilly, dropping off Zoe, 5, and Gavin, 3. After two days off school because of the extreme cold, Chicago Public Schools students headed back to class, but the extra play time was no freebie. Students will be required to make up the days later this year, CPS spokeswoman Keiana Barrett said.

And now for the Chicago sports scores. Yesterday the Chicago Bulls beat the Phoenix Suns 92 to 87.

Looking at Chicago social news.

[David] posted "Let the Andrew Bynum era in Chicago BEGIN.... And END!!!"

[Jane] is traveling to Bellevue, Washington.

[Alice] posted a link. "If L.E. has a long lost daughter... she's staring in the puppy bowl: Puppy Bowl X, Meet the Starting Lineup"

Turning to weather for Boston. Today will be nice and sunny with a high of 22 degrees.

Looking at Boston news.

WESTPORT, Mass. The wife of the hunter who survived falling into the frigid Westport River, an accident that claimed the lives of his two friends, says the men were experienced outdoorsmen who'd hunted in similar conditions before. Dr. Gregg Angell of Westport was the lone survivor after the small skiff capsized Tuesday morning. His wife, Lorraine Lubiejewski, tells WJAR-TV that although the weather was "cold and nasty," the friends were used to it.

More than one-third of health care spending in Massachusetts is wasteful, squandered on unnecessary hospital readmissions and emergency room visits, according to detailed new report released today. The study from the Health Policy Commission, a state watchdog group charged with monitoring health care costs in Massachusetts, also found that preventable

infections acquired in health care settings cost - 10 million to 18 million a year. Massachusetts spends more per capita on health care than any other state, and health care costs here have grown faster than the national average. The Health Policy Commission will discuss the findings of its report at a meeting today.

And now for the Boston sports scores. Yesterday the Anaheim Ducks beat the Boston Bruins 5 to 2. Yesterday the Denver Nuggets beat the Boston Celtics 129 to 98.

And now, San Francisco's weather. It will be mostly cloudy with a high of 58 degrees.

Looking at San Francisco news.

The case of Jahi McMath, the 13-year-old girl who was declared brain-dead after a tonsillectomy at Children's Hospital Oakland, is now the centerpiece of a political fundraising effort aimed at lifting California's $250,000 cap for pain and suffering awards in medical malpractice cases. Consumer Watchdog, a Southern California nonprofit that has teamed up with the state's trial lawyers on a proposed November ballot initiative to lift the limit, just sent out a mailer to supporters saying, "Hospitals like Children's actually have an incentive to let children like Jahi die." If children who are victims of medical negligence live, hospitals are on the hook for medical bills for life, which could be millions," the letter says. The letter from Consumer Watchdog President Jamie Court asks for "whatever tax-deductible contribution you can make" to help with its "patient safety work" and to qualify the initiative to raise the malpractice limit.

A pedestrian was struck and killed by a car Tuesday evening while running across busy Van Ness Avenue in San Francisco, police said - the latest in a string of severe pedestrian accidents in the city since New Year's Eve. The most recent death happened shortly after 6 p.m. when the pedestrian sprinted across Van Ness heading east near Grove Street, said Officer Albie Esparza, a police spokesman. The victim, a 38-year-old man, had been embroiled in a verbal altercation just before running into traffic, Esparza said, and made it across six of the street's seven lanes before being hit. "There was apparently no negligence on the part of the driver, since the traffic was flowing at the time," Esparza said.

And now for the San Francisco social news.

[Erin] posted: "Everyone takes care of each other here in the city... And so many smiles and dogs ... Can't believe it's the start if a second quarter, I feel like I just got here. One of my last days of freedom, eating at one of my favorites."

[Jack] posted a photo. "It's nice to finally be able to talk about what I have been working on."

And that's all for today!

FIELD STUDY
After creating a functional system, we were interested in exploring how the system would be used in daily life and particularly in understanding the experience of watching this presentation in the living room on a television. We designed an eight-day field study to explore the system's use.

Methods and Recruiting
We recruited seven diverse users from the greater San Francisco Bay Area for our study. We utilized a database of external participants and sent an email to this list with a recruiting screener. From the people who replied, we selected a set of seven people with varying age (20s-50s), occupations, gender (3 female), and socio-economic status. Occupations included, for example, a copy editor, marketing professional, stay-at-home mom, and nurse, and represented varying family situations. Some participants lived

with partners and/or children while others lived alone or with relatives. We were particularly interested in understanding if watching the presentation would become a "family event."

The initial in-home visit consisted of a 15-20 minute initial interview covering participant's existing media behaviors. We asked about specific ways that they currently viewed content such as news, weather, sports, and social information. We then installed the Chromecast on their television and our app on their phone, and asked participants to authorize our system to access their Facebook data. We demonstrated the functioning of the system and left instructions for calling into our voicemail system each day after watching the presentation.

For the next eight days, participants watched the presentation at least once per day and called us after viewing it. They were asked to leave a voicemail detailing what they liked or didn't like about that day's presentation as well as anything else that they would like to tell us. Each day, they viewed a slightly different presentation style. These consisted of:

Day 1: System as-is (3 cities, 2 news stories per city – as in the text example above)

Day 2: With one news story per city (instead of 2)

Day 3: With 30-second video news clips instead of text-to-speech for news (where available)

Day 4: Ordering by type instead of city (all of the weather, then news, then sports, then social)

Day 5: Just the user's local city (based on the user's Facebook profile city) and no friend-based cities

Day 6: No social news (just weather, news, and sports arranged by city)

Day 7: Human voiceovers instead of text-to-speech (content generated the same as day 1)

Day 8: System as-is (same as day 1)

After the eight days, we conducted a final interview where we asked participants to expand on details from the voicemail entries and asked follow up questions on system use in general including questions on any social communication that was inspired by use of the system.

Participants were compensated for their time with a $100 American Express Gift Card and were given the Chromecast ($35 value).

Findings

Initial interviews, the voicemail diaries, and final interviews were transcribed by an external service and analyzed in a grounded theory-based affinity analysis. The items for analysis were exact quotes from our users and we had 407 items in total. Themes were identified inductively to arrive at the topics that will be discussed below.

Context of Use

We were particularly interested in how viewing this presentation would fit into people's lives. When would they watch it? Would it become a family event? The only instruction we gave to participants was that we would like them to watch it at least once per day. The rest was up to them.

Three participants made the system a part of their morning routine. They played it in the background as they ate breakfast or got ready in the morning, similar to how they used to turn on the morning news. Chuck[1] told us that "instead of getting up in the morning and going onto the Internet and looking up the weather, looking up the, you know, social media, some of those things can be just read to me while I'm getting dressed or something. That's really nice." Mark also played the presentation in the morning and said that it would "inform things I would do for the day or perhaps news articles I would want to look into further."

The remaining 5 participants watched the presentation in the evening, often with other family members present in the room. Chuck and Lisa both watched it with their spouses in the evenings. Lisa: "My husband watched a few of them with me and we conversed on the topics … some of them were interesting and we caught up a little bit about it."

For participants in long-term relationships, we observed that the couple felt connected to many of the same places as they might have moved together over the years, and one partner's family is now a core part of the other's life. While future work could make presentations that encompass multiple individuals' networks and cities, we observed that the whole family often enjoyed the updates based on just one person's data, due to shared family history.

Because the presentation was being shown on a large screen in the living room, at times visitors saw the content being displayed. For Mark, this turned into an interesting exchange where a social update from a mutual friend was being shown while another friend who was visiting walked through the living room. He was asked, "Is that [Jane] on the television?" Content that appears on the television is elevated to a very special status just because of its presence on this central, family device.

Viewing on the TV Makes it More Interesting

Participants described the experience of "watching" news and social updates on their living room television. One area of discussion was around how the television demands attention in a way that computer screen full of links or posts does not. Mark told us that he "was intrigued" by a story about the mayor of SF that he wouldn't have read otherwise. "I think it's just because you're overloaded with so much media that with it present right there on the TV, it engaged me, because it had my attention."

---

[1] All participant names are pseudonyms.

Participants also spoke about the feelings evoked from having news and social updates presented on the TV. Lisa felt that having Internet content read aloud on the TV brought about "almost the feeling of nostalgia. Or not quite the same, obviously, but just the feeling of someone else reading to you as a kid. It was always cooler when someone else read things to you." Ian felt that using the system "was fairly old school. Like back in the day when everyone had a TV and you would turn on a TV in the morning." For both of these participants, having content read aloud on the TV brought about feelings that didn't arise in their standard habits of viewing Internet news and social updates on the web or in a mostly text-based mobile app.

The system also helped users to feel more connected to their friends that were shown on the TV. Participants felt like social updates were being "announced" – something much more formal than just seeing a list of updates in a feed on a computer or phone. Lisa: "To have someone read to you is just a different experience that brought a new light to my friends' news. Just hearing that being announced I don't know, it just made it a little different and made it a little nostalgic, a little fun. I like that … It almost makes you feel associated with the places that are far away. It is … like someone was telling me about them. It's different than just scrolling through and everything, especially when it's centralized to certain locations."

Mark spoke about the personal engagement that was created by using the television as the interface: "There is something personal about them showing up on your TV in your living room, versus on your computer or the phone … It was really engaging, it felt like that person was sort of sending me a private message."

Overall, the qualities of the TV only showing one content item at a time, thus demanding that some level of attention be paid to each item, as well as the reading/ "announcing" of each item contributed a much more intimate interaction with this content compared to traditional web or mobile-based interfaces.

Sharing with Others
Overall, participants reported ten specific instances where information learned in the system was shared with friends and family. After seeing a story about the Whitey Bulger trial, Ian "mentioned it to my coworkers just because it's an interesting Boston thing. One of my other coworkers lived in Boston for a while."

Chuck saw a news story about an upcoming concert near his sister's very rural town in the South and told us that he was going to tell her about it. To him, it was special that this event was coming to such a rural location.

Daniel liked seeing the sports scores for his hometown, as they provided conversation topics for talking to his dad who still lives in Philadelphia. "I think he always wanted me to be a big sports guy but I should be able to talk about it be-

cause he's really into the specifics … It's good to have something to talk about."

Lisa liked seeing the weather where her family was located: "Southern California is having more rain than us this year somehow. Just seeing what they're going through and then I can reach out to them. I have my sisters down there. I have aunts and I have grandparents. So just something that I can have a common ground and talk to them about."

When spouses or other housemates were not watching the presentation with the participant, often details from the content were shared with them at a later time. Lisa talked about some of the sports stories with her husband as well as a story about soldiers at a military base near some of their friends in San Diego preparing for Thanksgiving. Content in the MyChannel system, because it was related to the places where close friends and family lived, became a spark for conversation.

In this way, our system demonstrated a form of ramping communication [15] similar to that seen by Harboe et al. in their work on Social Television [10] where content in the interface inspired additional social interactions.

Use of Friend Cities
Using the top cities from participants' social network worked well to identify content that they would find interesting. Hearing news about a place where a friend lived inspired communication and helped people to feel more connected to the places where their friends/family lived.

Lisa spoke about feeling connected to a place where she used to live and still has many friends: "It was nice to see everybody down there because it brings the feeling of when I was down there, and I absolutely wouldn't have minded more of that either, of hearing people's stories from centralized places." Having all of the content for a city aggregated together, on the days when we presented content by city instead of by type, helped participants to feel connected to those places.

However, the Facebook-derived cities were not always perfect. Chuck told us that he "would have liked to have seen more in the locations that I like, like I was raised in Virginia Beach." Even though he was raised there, he did not have a lot of friends that have remained, yet this location was still important to him.

Another important location to include is a person's local city. Two participants did not have a large number of local friends and thus missed out on important and relevant local news and weather. Mark liked the day that we showed local content and "found those things actually kind of interesting. The local news, the weather, that actually was a lot more interesting to me when it was there on the TV. It was sort of like I was watching the news."

However, all participants mentioned missing the other cities on the day when we only showed local content. Balancing cities where people have a large number of friends with their hometown and current city seems to be the best balance to select the most relevant content.

Selecting and Presenting Content
We had started this project assuming that it would be difficult to command a user's attention for more than 2-3 minutes. We knew that our production quality would not be on par with traditional news and assumed it would be best to keep things short, as is common for web-based videos. However, our participants, who often sat in front of the television for hours at a time, discussed wanting longer presentations. Perhaps this should not have been surprising to us, given TV's history of being a platform for long-form content, but we were encouraged that many participants spoke of wanting more.

When selecting user-generated or social content, it's important to consider the environment where the program will be viewed. One social update contained quite a long list of swear words from one of our participant's friends and she commented that it would not be appropriate if her small children would be watching it with them.

One participant, Daniel, explicitly discussed liking when a longer summary was produced for news items. The Summly tool produces 2-3 sentence summaries, however at times longer, more complex sentences are produced, leading to more words being used to describe a news story. He told us "It was nice to see stories - quite a few stories, actually - that had a rather long reading of them … They read just a few sentences, while sometimes it goes up to a minute being read. That's great! I like that."

Ian and Chuck spoke of wanting more detailed weather information including hourly forecasts and longer-range forecasts. Daniel and Lisa spoke of wanting a diversity of news content – both positive and negative stories from the cities that we selected. While selecting the "top" two stories based on the number of sources that published articles about them worked well, often this accentuated negative stories such as murders and robberies. These participants reported wanting more "positive" and uplifting stories. Lisa especially enjoyed a news story about a local Turkey Trot in San Jose saying, "It was nice to see more of a cultural, fun, upbeat news as opposed to everyday mundane stuff." Understanding positive and negative aspects of stories is important in creating a balanced and entertaining newscast.

Other issues arose over clustering cities together. During a pilot, we discovered that the presentation is not very interesting if many of your friends live in nearby suburbs. For example, weather and news for three adjacent suburbs of San Francisco is not likely to provide an interesting diversity of content. We decided to just pick the one city with the most friends per state, but this also led to issues (e.g. with friends in Los Angeles and San Francisco, both in the state of California yet located hundreds of miles apart). Ideally, it seems best to cluster friends per metropolitan area, but then

it is also important not to lose the specific suburbs when selecting news so as not to miss an important local story in a town where friends/family live. Also, cities on the border of two states will often have the same top news stories, and some level of de-duplication is necessary.

A final issue that arose in content presentation was the quality of the voice that we picked for our text-to-speech engine. Following findings from previous work, we had selected both a male and female voice and alternated between them. We chose a British accent for the male voice as previous research had shown this to be more acceptable, as listeners assume that mispronunciations or stutters are due to differences in language [13]. However, it was the male voice which participants found a bit difficult to understand. The day when we provided human voiceovers was appreciated by most participants, showing that more natural voices make a difference. However, it is interesting to us that not all participants were able to distinguish between the computer-generated voices and human voices.

DISCUSSION
This study has allowed us to see the rich potential for presenting personalized news and social content on the television. We began with an assumption that many of the news stories that people find engaging are those that have a connection to people and places that they care about. By elevating social connections to the primary means of personalization, we have created a new type of news program that is centered on places that matter in the lives of our participants and the people who live in these places. This hyper-personalized and socially embedded program generated feelings of connection with these places and inspired communication with friends and relatives who live at a distance. We find this to be more engaging than traditional topic-based personalization, given the increased opportunities for social interaction about the content and the feelings of nostalgia and connection to remote places that are evoked.

The act of "presenting" the content turned out to be quite important to the experience our users felt when viewing the presentation. Having a human-sounding voice read news stories and social updates on the living room television set added an importance to the information that was different from what is felt when visually reading news stories or social updates on other devices.

By conducting a field evaluation of this system, we were able to learn much more about how this type of presentation is used in daily life, including the sharing of information with others and increased feelings of connection to the places discussed in the presentation. This goes beyond existing research that has often focused on the technical aspects of selecting content or rendering it on the television.

We see an opportunity to combine this attention-commanding presentation on the television with second-screen interactions that can contain expanded and related content. Being able to get the full text of a news story or related Wikipedia pages on the second screen, similar to Basapur et al.'s work on Parallel Feeds [3], can create the ability to get more detail than what can be spoken in a few sentences on the television presentation. Second screens could also more easily provide the ability to share content or start conversations with friends and family who are in the locations where the news is occurring, encouraging the "ramping communication" [10] that we observed occurring organically in our field evaluation, This can lead to even more conversations with friends and family at a distance.

Beyond television-based presentations, we see the potential for city-based explorations of news and social content as a new way to display and navigate content that is important to people on a variety of devices.

CONCLUSION

We have presented the MyChannel system, a television-based presentation of personalized news and social updates based on selecting content from cities where the user has many friends. Through a field evaluation of this system, we have learned how the system integrates into daily life and provides viewers with topics to inspire future communication with friends and family at a distance.

While this system serves as an initial demonstration of the potential of this type of presentation, much work still needs to be done in creating programs with the production value of a traditional television news show. Using better voices, aggregating content by metropolitan area, and incorporating more professionally produced video content can help to create an even more engaging experience. Utilizing second screens to provide additional content beyond what can be presented on the television is another area to pursue.

We believe that the television is the next frontier for creating personalized, entertaining experiences that can connect viewers to the places and people that matter most in their lives. Through future iterations, we hope to study use over longer durations as well as explore additional ways to integrate best practices from television production to create engaging presentations of Internet-based content.

ACKNOWLEDGMENTS
We would like to thank our participants from both studies as well as the feedback of colleagues from around Yahoo for their insights on this work.

REFERENCES
1. Nicholas D. Allen, John R. Templon, Patrick Summerhays McNally, Larry Birnbaum, Kristian Hammond. 2010. StatsMonkey: A Data-Driven Sports Narrative Writer. AIII Fall Symposium 2010.

2. Basapur, S., Novak, A., Harboe, G., Vuong, V., Mandalia, H., and Metcalf, C. (2011) Field trial of a dual device user experience for itv. In Proc. EuroITV'11

3. Daniel Billsus and Michael J. Pazzani. 2000. User Modeling for Adaptive News Access. *User Modeling and User-Adapted Interaction* 10, 2-3, 147-180.

4. Birnbaum, L.; Hammond, K.; Allen, N. D; Templon, J. R; McNally, P. S. 2010. "*StatsMonkey: A Data-Driven Sports Narrative Writer*", 2010 AAAI Fall Symposium Series.

5. Chesnais, P.R.; Mucklo, M.J.; Sheena, J.A., "The Fishwrap personalized news system," *Community Networking, 1995. Proceedings of the Second International Workshop on Integrated Multimedia Services to the Home*, vol., no., pp.275,282.

6. Cornejo, R., Tentori, M., and Favela, J. (in press) "Enriching in-person encounters through social media: A study on family connectedness for the elderly". International Journal of Human-Computer Studies

7. Abhinandan S. Das, Mayur Datar, Ashutosh Garg, and Shyam Rajaram. 2007. Google news personalization: scalable online collaborative filtering. Proc. WWW '07.

8. Evgeniy Gabrilovich, Susan Dumais, and Eric Horvitz. 2004. Newsjunkie: providing personalized newsfeeds via analysis of information novelty. In Proc WWW '04.

9. Emily Guskin, Mark Jurkowitz and Amy Mitchell. The State of News Media: 2013. Network: By the Numbers. http://stateofthemedia.org/2013/network-news-a-year-of-change-and-challenge-at-nbc/network-by-the-numbers/

10. Gunnar Harboe, Crysta J. Metcalf, Frank Bentley, Joe Tullio, Noel Massey, and Guy Romano. 2008. Ambient social tv: drawing people into a shared experience. In Proc CHI '08.

11. Jiahui Liu, Peter Dolan, and Elin Rønby Pedersen. 2010. Personalized news recommendation based on click behavior. In Proc IUI '10.

12. Akiyo Nadamoto and Katsumi Tanaka. 2005. Complementing your TV-viewing by web content automatically-transformed into TV-program-type content. In *Proc Multimedia '05*

13. Nathan Nichols. 2010. Machine-Generated Content: Creating Compelling New Content from Existing Online Sources. PhD Thesis. Northwestern University.

14. Nathan Nichols & Kristian Hammond. 2009. Machine-Generated Multimedia Content. Second International Conference on Advances in Computer-Human Interactions.

15. Rhodes, B. and Maes, P. (2000) Just-in-time information retrieval agents. IBM Systems Journal 39(3–4).

16. Zimmerman, J.; Dimitrova, N.; Agnihotri, L.; Janevski, A.; and Nikolovska, L., "Interface Design for MyInfo: A Personal News Demonstrator Combining Web and TV Content" (2003). HCII. Paper 237.

Design and Evaluation of a Children's Tablet Video Application

David J. Wheatley

Rovi Corporation, UX Research & Innovation,

10 N. Martingale Rd. Ste. 610, Schaumburg, Illinois 60173 USA

david.wheatley@rovicorp.com

+1 847 762 5861

ABSTRACT

Video consumption is moving from the TV to other, portable wireless platforms and from linear to on-demand viewing. This paper describes a series of user experience studies carried out to define the end user requirements for a targeted (1-10 yrs) children's tablet video application. Other studies (not reported here) were also carried out to define parents' needs for parental control functionality. The process consisted of three phases. Phase 1 consisted of an online survey of parents to understand children's current viewing patterns and behaviors. This data, and secondary research, was then used to develop some initial design concepts for the application, and some key design and interaction elements were evaluated with children using paper & card mock-ups in phase 2. Children also evaluated an early application prototype in this second phase. Results suggested that three different levels of interface complexity would likely be necessary for the target age range. The third phase consisted of field trials of 3 prototype interfaces carried out with 25 children in 11 families. A primary objective of the field trials was to evaluate any impact on individual and family viewing patterns and behaviors. Results indicated that interface preferences broadly aligned with the expected age targets, and other major benefits of the application included the strong feelings of ownership, control and independence engendered in children which reduced the need for parental monitoring and direct involvement in content selection and device control. This paper focuses on the iterative design process and the impact of the application on content selection and control.

Author Keywords

User experience; TV and video viewing; user interaction design; children's TV viewing; field trials; parental control.

ACM Classification Keywords

H.5.2 [**User Interfaces**]: Evaluation/methodology, user centered design; H.3.7 [**Digital Libraries**]: User Issues.

INTRODUCTION

TV viewing has changed substantially in recent years and the indications are that it will change even more dramatically over the next few. The domestic TV experience no longer consists of family co-viewing of a single screen in a fixed location in the shared space of the living room, but is transitioning to new platforms and in new locations. There are two major factors contributing to this change. The first is the move to IP delivery systems and on-demand streaming services; the second is the use of many other hardware platforms for content consumption, particularly tablets and smartphones. As a result of this, the way we choose what we watch has changed, and there are many more choices regarding where, when and on what device we watch TV and video content. This has opened the door to the possibility of more niche-focused mobile video applications targeted at specific viewers and at specific markets or content types. Children are growing up with these mobile devices and technologies, adopting them seamlessly and accepting them as an integral part of their everyday lives. The concept of a tablet application specifically for children to choose and watch video and TV shows would likely find a broad and accepting market, especially if parental control and content filtering capabilities were appropriately integrated. This paper describes a series of user studies carried out to inform and evaluate the design of a companion second screen video application for access to a curated video on demand (VOD) library of children's video content.

BACKGROUND

Whether it is regarded as good or bad, children watch a lot of television and video, and the amount of time they spend viewing continues to increase, fueled in large part by the greatly increased number of content sources and the flexibility and mobility of viewing platforms mentioned above. A 2003 telephone survey of more than 1000 parents in the USA [11] found that 74% of children had watched TV before the age of 2 years and 43% of those under 2 yrs watched TV every day. Those under 6 yrs of age spent about 2 hrs/day with screen media with 62% using the remote control themselves to change channels. In contrast, in a 2007 study [16], 90% of parents reported that their children under the age of 2 watch some form of media every day and by 3 yrs of age, almost one-third have a TV in their own bedroom. More recently (2012), data from Nielsen, reported in Gerbrandt [7], indicated that traditional TV viewing has increased to about 3.55 hours (hrs)/day for ages 2-11 and that, with the addition of time-shifted and online viewing, the total now averages 3.77 hrs/day. Children's TV and video viewing is clearly continuing to increase. However, even these figures may still underestimate the extent of children's exposure to TV/video content since (on average) the TV is on approximately 6 hrs/day in US homes and 39% of families have the TV on constantly [13]. Furthermore, there are now many other platforms available for video consumption and tablets in particular are now being widely used in schools with more than 600 US school districts having iPad programs [8]. This is in addition to their use at home. A 2013 report [2] indicates that in the past two years, there has been a five-fold increase in tablet ownership in the US among families with children aged 8 and under, and that 72% of children aged 8 and under, and 38% of those under 2 have used a mobile device (such as a tablet or smartphone) for some type of media activity [2]. Children are also accessing video content in different ways; 45% of children aged 5-15 in the UK are now (2013 data) using devices other than the TV to watch video content; an increase of 11% from the previous year, with 15% of them watching TV programs on tablets [10]. In fact, this survey concluded that younger children (5-7 yrs) were 5 times more likely to mostly use a tablet than in 2012 (19% vs 4% in 2012).

Though time-shifting is an increasing trend, in homes with DVR capability 87% of children's TV viewing was still "live" linear broadcast, with only 13% of viewing being time-shifted. Younger children (4-9 yrs), who broadly correspond to the target age range of the application described here, were somewhat less likely (11%) to time-shift their viewing compared with older children (10-15 yrs), who time-shifted 15% of the time [10].

It must be considered that an application for children will not necessarily be subject to the same design principles and interaction patterns that would be appropriate for an "adult" application; child users are likely to have different mental models, different values and will clearly be looking for a quite different user experience. It is also necessary to take account of wide variations in, and the different stages of cognitive and physical/motor development. This paper describes a number of user experience studies that were carried out in three phases to evaluate some potential functions, interface designs, and interaction elements of a tablet application which was to be used by children between the ages of 1 and 10 yrs old.

USER EXPERIENCE STUDIES

There are two key stakeholders representing the end users of such an application, hence the user experience studies followed two distinct tracks. The first category of user was the parent, and studies (reported elsewhere) were undertaken to establish parental attitudes and current approaches to limiting or controlling their children's TV and video viewing, and how this control might be implemented within a mobile tablet application. This data was used to help define the parental control functionality. The second category of user is the children who would be using the application and it is these studies which are described in the current paper. It must be noted that children were not involved in the studies which were focused on parental control, but were involved in both the functional evaluation and field trial phases described in the current paper. The benefits and challenges of involving children in the development process have been well documented by Druin, who segmented this into the four main roles of user, tester, informant and design partner [3]. For this project, a mixed methods approach was used supporting an iterative design process with end users (children) directly involved in most, but not all, of the research phases.

In the first phase, an online survey of parents was carried out to establish children's current behavior patterns with regard to TV viewing and the use of other devices for games and TV/video viewing. This included the devices that their children used in the home and in what locations, how frequently they were used and what they were used for, both as a primary and a second screen interaction, while watching the TV. This data was used to generate a number of design concepts for the tablet interaction, some elements of which were explored in more depth with children using paper prototypes and mock-ups in the second phase. In the third phase, a prototype application with 3 different interfaces was built and evaluated over a 7-day period in field trials with 25 children between the ages of 2-10 yrs.

PHASE 1; ONLINE SURVEY

Firstly, an online survey of parents was carried out to confirm the extent of tablet and mobile device use among children and to get a more in-depth understanding of children's viewing behaviors, such as how, when and with whom they generally watched TV and video content and how this was chosen. The survey was completed by 497 parents ranging in age from 19 to 65+. The vast majority of these (89.9%) being within the 25 to 54 yrs age range, 70.4% were female and 29.6% male. The following data is based on the reported patterns and behaviors of at least 1,148 children under the age of 12.

One part of the survey set out to establish the extent to which children currently had and used tablets and mobile devices, and they regularly used a wide range of fixed and mobile connected devices; 81.7% had a games console, 63.6% a mobile gaming device, 63.4% had a smartphone and 50.7% had tablets while 35.2% had a Kindle (see Figure 1). There was therefore a wide range of platforms available for video consumption.

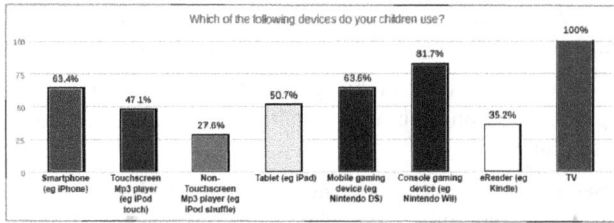

Figure 1: Children's Use of Connected/Unconnected Devices

Mobile devices (e.g. smartphone, tablet, mp3 player, eReader or handheld gaming devices) were frequently and regularly used by children under 12 yrs, with 61.3% using these 1 to 6 times per day and 20.6% 10 times or more per day. Subsequent questions set out to determine in more detail the functions or activities for which these were mostly used. The highest level of usage was for games (90.5%), followed by music (67.1%) and video (64.7%) as shown in Figure 2.

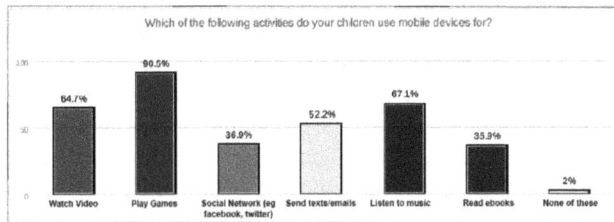

Figure 2: Children's Activities using Mobile Devices

It was clear that many used mobile devices to watch video, some very heavily, with 47.4% watching video either every time or most of the time that they used a mobile device with only 3.7% of children never watching video on a mobile device. This would indicate that, despite their relatively small screens, tablets, smartphones and other mobile devices have already been readily accepted as video viewing platforms, raising the question of whether portability and/or mobility are key attributes which offset any potential drawbacks of the smaller screen size. This certainly seems to be the case, since 79.1% have used a mobile device to watch video when traveling in the car, 72.9% in their bedrooms and 44.2% when out and about, such as at the grocery store, medical office, etc. (Figure 3). This reflects the value of video on mobile devices to keep children amused and help prevent boredom in such physically constrained situations. Even so, 91.3% also watched video on a mobile device when in the same location as the fixed family TV, indicating that there is user value within the home as well as the value provided by mobility outside of the home environment.

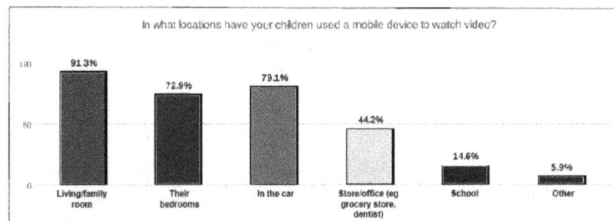

Figure 3: Locations where Children use Mobile Devices

Part of the online survey was structured to determine if and how content selection and device control varied with the age of the child. The most significant age related change was found to be in the decision about what to watch. For children under the age of 2, this was almost entirely the parent's decision, with 86.9% of parents deciding 50% of the time or more. Above the age of 2, the extent of parental decision-making fell significantly but then remained more or less constant, with about 38% of parents deciding 50% of the time or more (Figure 4).

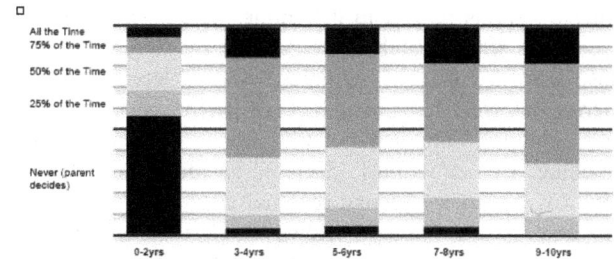

Figure 4: Content Choice by Child's Age

Respondents were also asked how much time their children spent watching TV or video in each viewing session (on average). The results indicated very conclusively that as children get older, their viewing sessions got longer and they watched more long form content, such as movies. As can be seen in Figure 5, those under 2 yrs very often watched for less than 15 min at a time. Longer viewing sessions of more than an hour at a time accounted for only 13.2% of viewing at the age of 2, increasing in an approximately linear manner to more than half of viewing sessions by the age of 9-10 yrs.

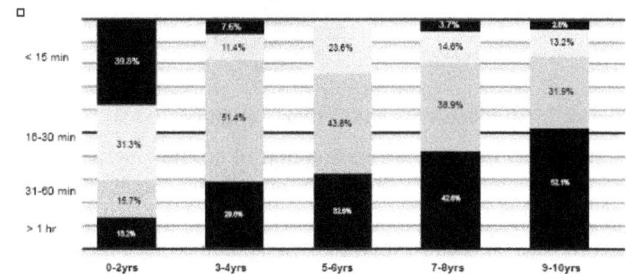

Figure 5: Viewing Session Length by Child's Age

This age related increase in length of viewing session seems to reflect an increasing span of attention as a child gets older; this might also suggest that the frequency of channel changing might also change with age. In fact this was found to be the case, with younger children (ages 2-6) tending to stay on the same channel when watching TV and watch whatever is on next, rather than making a conscious choice about what specific content to watch next (Figure 6). This suggests a kind of "viewing inertia" which may be due to younger children having less ability to operate the remote control.

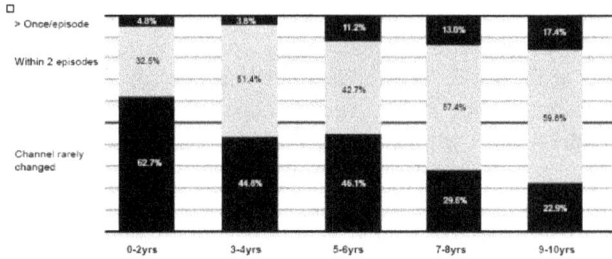

Figure 6: Frequency of Channel Changes by Child's Age

Other questions helped to determine the extent of second screen use while watching content on the TV, and what those second screen activities were. Second screen interactions were high, with 82% of parents reporting that their children interacted with second screens while watching TV sometimes (52.7%), or most of the time (29.2%); 7.5% used second screens "every time the TV is on" and 10.6% "rarely". However, this second screen activity rarely had any connection with what was being watched concurrently on the TV (see Figure 7). Results indicated that children were "most often"; playing games (54.6%), sending texts/emails (21.7%), or social networking (8.9%). Watching video was stated as the primary second screen activity by only 6.8% of respondents, however it is not known whether this would likely be related in any way to the primary TV screen content.

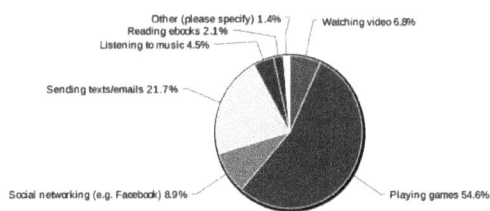

Figure 7: Children's Second Screen Activities

A final area of exploration was that of co-viewing and how frequently siblings "watched TV and videos together". This would clearly be a relevant factor given the smaller tablet screen size and the individual personalization capabilities that were to be explored in the later studies. Results indicated that siblings mostly watched together, with 39% watching together always or most of the time and 37.6% sometimes watching together. 17.7% rarely or never watched together and 5.6% were single child household to which this question did not apply.

The key conclusions from the online survey, which helped to guide the application conceptualization, were as follows:,

• Tablets and mobile devices are already widely owned, used and accepted by children.

• They are frequently used for watching video, despite the smaller screens.

• For children under the age of 2, the parent mostly chooses the content and this is rarely long form content.

• The relevance of, and need for long form content increases in direct correlation with children's age

• Though wireless mobility is valuable, there is also significant "non-mobile", portable use within the home environment.

• Second screen use while the TV is on, is very prevalent, but rarely has any direct connection with what is being watched on the TV.

• Children rarely watch video alone: 39% of the time they watch with siblings and only 6% of them never watch with a sibling.

PHASE 2; CONCEPT EVALUATIONS

Based on the phase 1 online survey, initial design concepts were developed for the tablet application and two rounds of concept evaluation were carried out in phase 2, each with 15 children in the age range of 3-12 yrs, (8F, 7M, mean 8yr 2mo). Each of the two sessions lasted about one hour and took place at the Rovi offices, in the Chicago area. In the first of these observational studies, children interacted with a number of paper/card mock-ups, representing or simulating various functional elements of the tablet interaction. In the second round of evaluation, the same 15 children interacted with an initial prototype of the application within which three different types of interface were embodied. To ensure that the video content was relevant, parents were asked about their children's favorite shows, and these were pre-loaded onto the tablets prior to the sessions. Children were given each prototype for 15 minutes and were taken through a sequence of interaction flows such as selecting and watching a video, using the trick play controls and looking for specific content. Children were observed for their reactions and any difficulties or hesitancy in using the different interfaces, and interface preferences were determined by a combination of direct questioning and subjective assessment of the level of engagement with the prototypes. In both of these studies, siblings participated together and parents were not present unless it was essential in order for the child to be at ease.

Functional Evaluations

There were five design aspects of the initial concept which were considered to be important to the overall value and usefulness of the application. These five functional elements were evaluated in the first study and explored different approaches to personalization of the application and different visual presentations of box art.

One approach to personalization was the creation of a personal avatar by taking and inserting a head and shoulders photo, taken using the tablet's built-in camera. The study found that this was not a viable approach, since most children had great difficulty capturing a suitable image due to the iPad camera lens being greatly offset from the screen. The second personalization approach evaluated was the creation of a character from three separate body components and then placing that character within an environment or background (see Figure 8). It was surprising perhaps that the majority of children, when creating characters from parts, tended to build rational, coherent characters and to set them within appropriate backgrounds. This suggested that there was little benefit in adding complexity to the interface by providing four variable components and that a single character/background combination would likely be sufficient.

Figure 8: Character & Background Selections for Theme

A third activity evaluated different ways of selecting the theme components using different interaction approaches. In the first of these, separate hardcopy elements were placed on a background to create the theme, the second used rotating "wheels" and the third used sliding windows (see Figure 9). There was an overall preference for the sliding window approach and furthermore, since the application was to be used on a tablet, a horizontal swiping interaction was felt to be more natural and intuitive than a rotating action; hence this approach was chosen for the final prototype.

A fourth design element used mock-ups to ascertain whether there was any influence of image size (box art) on content selection. Children were presented with three show images of equal (medium) size and asked to choose which one they would like to watch.

Later, after completing a number of other activities they were asked to choose again, only this time the image they chose initially was smaller than the others. 67% made the same choice and were not influenced by the larger image size of the alternative shows, 14% switched to a larger image and 19% to a smaller image. It was therefore concluded that it was the content that was important and not the size of the box art.

A fifth evaluation focused on the importance of including a show character within the box art image and whether this had any influence on content selection. In this part of the study, children were shown a screenshot from a show and asked to identify the show by selecting from six alternative images, which included both character imagery and box art, which in some cases also comprised the show title. In 30 trials, 77% identified the show by matching to the box art rather than to the character.

Select & Place Theme Objects

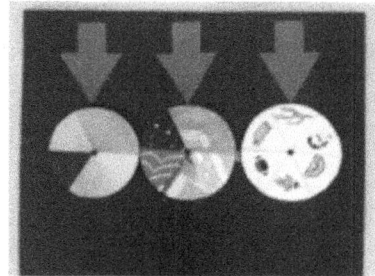

Rotate to Select Theme Objects

Slide Window to Select Theme Object

Figure 9: Theme Element Selection Methods

It was therefore concluded that box art was an effective way to reliably identify video content. This was an important finding from a business perspective since there are licensing and cost implications of using character imagery.

Interaction Evaluation

A second study was carried out in phase 2 with the same 15 children, to evaluate several different forms of device interaction and to determine whether engagement might be enhanced by providing a more game-like and more interactive approach to finding and selecting video content. Children's responses to five different physical interactions were observed using existing, commercially available tablet games or applications. These presented a variety of different screen interactions including "digging" to find an object, turning sections of an image to line them up and create a coherent whole image, tilting the tablet to align objects, mixing (dragging) and matching (dropping) objects and hiding/finding objects. It was a little surprising perhaps that older children in particular perceived video watching (passive) and games (active) as distinctly separate experiences and that watching video was still the primary objective of the current tablet interaction. This suggested that providing additional game-like interactivity would be appropriate only to the middle age range. An early application prototype was also evaluated with children in this phase to better understand the forms of physical interaction with the tablet that might be appropriate for different age ranges.

PHASE 3; APPLICATION FIELD TRIALS

The findings from phase 2 suggested that a single design solution would not be appropriate for the target user age range of 1 to 10 yrs and that different levels of interaction and content options would be needed. It is not within the scope of this paper to summarise the extensive literature relating to child development however, it was hypothesized that three different interfaces might be sufficient to address the differing needs of the different age groups. Key elements and differences between these interfaces were as follows;

	1-3 yrs	4-6 yrs	7-10 yrs
Interaction	Very simple	More playful	More "adult"
Trick play	Play/pause	Play/pause + scrubber	Play/pause + scrubber
Media content	Short form	Short form	Short & long form
Content choice	Limited (4), single items	Broader (10), episode structure	Wide (18+), episode structure
Personalisation	No	Yes	No

Three interface prototypes were designed and implemented on an iPad Mini. A basic UI was designed for those under 2 yrs, consisting of four content choices and limited trick-play functionality. The show images were large and covered most of the screen area to make them easy to select. There was also the ability to "swipe" a show image off the screen for it to be replaced by a new content item. A slightly more complex UI was designed for the 3-5 yr age range, consisting of 10 content choices. This also had more animation and interactivity. Opening the application and selecting the name bar would result in a set of 10 content choices "falling down" from the top of the screen. A more extensive UI was designed for the 7-10 yr age range consisting of 18 or more content choices which was structured in "scrollable" horizontal rows and similar to the design approach used by many current online video streaming services. The home screens for these three interfaces are shown in Figure 10. Though several studies had been carried out with children to iterate the application design, these were not designed to help understand how it would be assimilated and used on a longer term basis, in the home environment and any impact on viewing behaviors and patterns both at the individual and the family group levels.

Home screen for ages 1-3

Home screen for ages 4-6

Home screen for ages 7-10

Figure 10: Home Screens for the Three User Interfaces

These three age-targeted interface prototypes were built and field-tested with 11 families and a total of 25 children who ranged in age from 2 to 10 yrs (10M, 15F). Families were recruited from the local Chicago area in order to minimise travel logistics and scheduling issues, since interviews were carried out in the participants home and a focus group discussion also held in the Rovi offices. Logistics needed to take account of the limitations of both parents work hours and children's school hours and families were compensated for their participation in the field trials. The approach of this study included evaluation of children's viewing behaviors and parent attitudes before and after using the prototypes for a 7-day period. To do this, parents completed a "baseline diary" prior to the evaluation period, documenting 7 days of typical TV/video viewing and subsequently completed a similar diary during the 7-day prototype evaluation period. This included such data as what was watched, when, where, on what device and with whom. Parents also completed a ratings based questionnaire to assess their expectations prior to the evaluation and a similar "post-evaluation" questionnaire afterwards to identify any changes in opinion, primarily to assess parents' desires and expectations for such an application and whether those expectations were met. More detailed qualitative feedback was obtained via individual interviews conducted with parents and children together, which was followed by a focus group discussion held with parents only. The individual feedback discussions used a semi-structured questionnaire approach and were carried out in the family home so that child feedback could be obtained in a relaxed and familiar environment. The focus group discussion was held in the office environment in order that parents could discuss issues openly and without the distraction of children. Clickstream data, including user ID, content ID, content rejections, date/time, theme selections and other user activities was also collected via the participants Wi-Fi and internet connection and used to supplement or confirm the diary data.

The prototypes were very well received by both parents and children, and the most important value/benefit of the concept was reported to be that it provided young children with an unexpectedly high degree of independence, ownership and control, releasing parents from the necessity to constantly choose content and control the TV. This enabled parents to have more free time to get things done and, since the content was also curated and approved, it greatly reduced the degree of parental monitoring that was required. Enabling children to watch their content on the iPad, also freed up the primary TV for the parents to watch (beneficial even in household with multiple TVs) because the children could still be in the same room. As one participant characterized this;

".... What turned out to be so nice was that we could watch what we wanted to watch on TV, and they were in the room with us. I thought we were going to lose that family time, and not sit in the same room, but we were able to watch....the news and we would all be on the couch together, typically we wouldn't get to watch the news"

It was also found that it also reduced sibling conflict in some instances, since one child could use the iPad while the other watched the TV. As such, the application was regarded as a valuable *supplement* to the family TV and not as a replacement for it. Parents additionally felt that their children were more focused and engaged when using the iPad prototype than when watching the primary TV and despite the small screen, often watched together. One participant felt that this was primarily due to their directly interacting with the smaller device;

"He's very focused on it, he would not be this focused on the TV, they get bored with the TV. A lot of times the TV is on in the background and none of them are really watching it but because (the iPad) *is little and they are changing things all the time, they are very engaged with it"*

The interfaces were all found to be very easy to use and children's preferences broadly followed the expected target age range for each, except that the 0-3 yr age range interface was also liked and used by 4 and 5 yr olds. There were no password barriers to using the access points set up for each child in the household, and these were explored by the children, but they almost invariably gravitated back to using their own log-in because it enabled access to "their"

content in "their" space and this sense of ownership was very highly valued. In fact the named log-in panel implemented in the prototypes was perceived by some children to be a personal entry point, not unlike a nameplate on their bedroom door. For these reasons, parents did not feel any pressing need for a passcode or other barriers to prevent one child from accessing a sibling's content, despite their rating of this as a necessary function in the pre-study expectations questionnaire. Personalisation of the application using themes was not used extensively; qualitative feedback suggests that this was due to the limited options provided in the prototype rather than a fundamental lack of value in this capability. More options, including downloadable and/or show-related themes might add value, which may also provide a means to monetize the application.

Portability around the home was highly valued but mobility outside of the home was greatly missed and was judged to be essential. This was not surprising, but emerged as an issue since wireless streaming of video to the tablet was not possible with the prototype due to content licensing issues.

Some changes to the UI design were indicated by the study, including the provision of an on-screen audio volume control in addition to the tablets control buttons, indication that a show had been watched, title search capability (7-9 interface), and elimination of a "hidden" back button (0-3 interface). The objective of this was to keep younger children "contained" within their own content area and make it harder for them to go back to the log-in screen and access sibling's content. However, it was found that this simply caused confusion and frustration at first – until the button was found – and at which point it ceased to serve any useful function.

CONCLUSIONS

The prototype evaluation confirmed that the concept had considerable value to both children and parents but that some of the key values and benefits might not have been obvious or predictable. There was considerable research and iterative development of the user interface with children, and this proved to be very easy to use, with only a small number of design improvements indicated. However, it was the broader impact on family viewing behaviors and interactions which were of the most interest and benefit.

Perhaps the most significant finding regarding younger children's attitude to the video application was the extent to which they perceived the named log-in as a personal portal to their own content and their own "space." This imparted such a strong sense of ownership that the need for password protection to prevent siblings accessing each other's video content was considered to be largely unnecessary. This perception of ownership of their own space was still strong even though the same pool of video content was often available to all siblings. One slightly surprising finding was that siblings co-viewing behaviors were largely unchanged despite the relatively small screen size, though this co-viewing did create some initial conflicts over physical control of the device and choice of what to watch in some cases, children mostly co-operated in sharing access and using each other's log in, or took turns in using the application and watching alone. Interestingly these were usually resolved within a few days, often without parental involvement.

This sense of "ownership," coupled with the ease of use of the interfaces, created an independence that benefited parents considerably. Firstly it freed them up from the need for constant content monitoring and device control. Secondly, coupled with the portability around the home, it also freed up the primary TV for parents own use.

Finally, though it was expected that mobility outside of the home (using the cellular network) would be a key benefit, the value of portability within the home (using the Wi-Fi network) was perhaps underestimated and there were definite benefits in the ability to watch video anywhere within the home and the immediate vicinity.

ACKNOWLEDGEMENTS

The author would like to thank Mycal Elliott and Justin Wear for carrying out the initial studies, and Bill Korbecki, Jon Arme and Amanda Mallardo for building the application prototype and managing the clickstream data collection.

REFERENCES

1. American Academy of Pediatrics (2013) *"Children, Adolescents, and the Media"* Pediatrics; originally pub. Online Oct 28 2013; DOI: 10.1542/peds.2013-2656.
   http://pediatrics.aappublications.org/content/early/2013/10/24/peds.2013-2656

2. Common Sense Media (2013) *"Zero to Eight – Children's Media Use in America 2013"* Fall 2013

3. Druin A. (2002) *"The Role of Children in the Design of New Technology".* Behavior and Information Technology, 21(1) 1-25.

4. Druin A. (2009) *"Mobile Technology for Children",* ISBN; 978-0-12-374900-0 Morgan Kaufman, Apr 2009.

5. Evans C.A, Jordan A.B., Horner J. (2011) *"Only Two Hours? A Qualitative Study of The Challenges Parents Perceive in Restricting Child Television Time"* Journal of Family Issues Sept 2011, Vol 32 No 9, pp 1223-1244.

6. Falloon G. (2013) *"Young Students using iPads: App design and Content Influences on their Learning Pathways"* Computers & Education Vol 68, Oct 2013, pp 505-521.

7. Gerbrandt L. (2012) *"Over-the-Top Video in 2012: Trends and Technologies to Watch"* GigaOm Pro, June 2012.

8. Koebler J. (2011) *"More High Schools Implement iPad Programs"* US News, Sept 7 2011 at;
   http://www.usnews.com/education/blogs/high-school-notes/2011/09/07/more-high-schools-implement-ipad-programs

9. Ludwig S. (2011) *"Netflix now Testing Awesomely Easy Interface Targeted at Kids"* VB Media, Aug 12 2011 at: http://venturebeat.com/2011/08/12/netflix-now-testing-awesomely-easy-interface-targeted-at-kids/

10. Ofcom (2013) *"Children and Parents: Media Use and Attitudes Report"* Independent Regulator and Competitive Authority for the UK Communications Industries, Oct 2013.

11. Rideout V.J. Vandewater E.A. & Wartella E.A. (2003) *"Zero to Six; Electronic Media in the Lives of Infants, Toddlers and Preschoolers"* Kaiser Family Foundation, Fall 2003.

12. Taveras E.M., Hohman K.H., Price S., Gortmaker S.L. & Sonneville K. (2009) *"Televisions in the Bedrooms of Racial/Ethnic Minority Children; How Did They Get There and How Do We Get Them Out?"* Journal of Clinical Pediatrics, Sept 2009, Vol 48, No 7, pp 715-719.

13. Vandewater E.A., Bickham D.S., Lee J.H., Cummings H.M., Wartella E.A., & Rideout V.J., (2005) *"When the Television is Always On, Heavy Television Exposure and Young Children's Development"* American Behavioral Scientist, Jan 2005 Vol 48, No. 5, pp 562-577.

14. Vandewater E.A., Park S.E., Huang X., Wartella E.A. (2005) *"No: You Can't Watch That – Parental Rules and Young Children's Media Use"* American Behavioral Scientist, 2005, Vol 48, No 5 pp 608-623.

15. Wright J.C., Huston A.C., Vandewater E.A., Bickham D.S., Scantlin R.S., Kotler J.A., Caplovitz A.G., Lee J.H., Hofferth S. & Finkelstein J. (2001) *"American Children's Use of Electronic Media in 1997: A National Survey"* Journal of Applied Developmental Psychology, Vol 22, pp 31-47.

16. Zimmerman F.J., Christakis D.A. & Meltzoff A.N. (2007) *"Television and DVD/Video Viewing in Children Younger Than 2 Years"* Arch. Pediatr. Adolesc Med, 2007; 161(5): 473-479

Mirror, Mirror, On The Wall:
Collaborative Screen-Mirroring for Small Groups

Mark McGill[†]
m.mcgill.1@research.gla.ac.uk

John Williamson[‡]
jhw@dcs.gla.ac.uk

Stephen A. Brewster[†]
stephen.brewster@glasgow.ac.uk

[†] Glasgow Interactive Systems Group [‡] Inference, Dynamics and Interaction Group
School of Computing Science, University of Glasgow, Glasgow, G12 8QQ, UK

ABSTRACT

Screen mirroring has been available to consumers for some time, however if every mobile device in the room supports screen mirroring to the main display (e.g. a shared TV), this necessitates a mechanism for managing its use. As such, this paper investigates allowing users in small intimacy groups (friends, family etc.) to self-manage mirrored use of the display, through passing/taking/requesting the display from whomever is currently mirroring to it. We examine the collaborative benefits this scheme could provide for the home, compared to existing multi-device use and existing screen mirroring implementations. Results indicate shared screen mirroring improves perceived collaboration, decreases dominance, preserves independence and has a positive effect on a group's activity awareness.

Author Keywords

Screen mirroring; multi-user; single display;

ACM Classification Keywords

H.5.m. Information Interfaces and Presentation (e.g. HCI): Miscellaneous

INTRODUCTION

Consumer screen mirroring technology has grown in popularity in recent years, with either Apple's Airplay[1] or Miracast[2] available in most new mobile devices, allowing the mirroring of screen content, as well as driving entirely separate presentations. Additionally, devices capable of displaying this mirrored content are ubiquitous (be it TVs, HDMI dongles such as Chromecast or software servers such as Reflector[3]), whilst projects such as Android Transporter[4] have demonstrated the capability for real-time device-to-device mirroring.

Given that, in the near future, every device in a living space might well support the sharing of device content through mirroring, the issue of who gets to mirror their content, and

---

[1] http://www.apple.com/airplay/

[2] http://www.wi-fi.org/wi-fi-certified-miracast

[3] http://www.airsquirrels.com/reflector/

[4] http://esrlabs.com/android-transporter/

when, will become more pressing. For example, groups of friends and family sharing a display may be unable to adequately self-organise their usage of this mirroring functionality across their personal devices.

In this paper, we study a range of mirroring strategies that groups can use to share and self-mediate use of a receiving display across multiple screen mirroring devices, examining both potential sharing behaviours, and the effect sharing the display has on intra-group collaboration, and activity/artefact awareness.

RELATED WORK

Screen mirroring (also screen {sharing, casting, annexing}) is not a new concept, having first been demonstrated by Doug Englebart in 1968 [4] as a tool for remote collaboration. This concept has been elaborated upon in recent years: Greenberg *et al.* [16] utilized distributed screen-sharing to facilitate artifact awareness (awareness of documents and tools others are using) in groups, whilst XICE [3] proposed a toolkit for display annexation.

Commercial applications of screen mirroring have seen increasing popularity in recent years, however their adoption has not been universal, despite the ubiquity of mobile devices supporting the feature. A recent NPD survey [12] of smartphone users found a 40% awareness of the existence of screen-mirroring capabilities, with only 7% having ever used such features. Of these individuals, 75% had used this capability for mirroring videos, whilst approximately 50% had mirrored photos. Indeed the study stated that:

> "Bringing sharing experiences to a larger consumer base will require simplifying hardware requirements [and] amplifying the value of being able to share content across screens"

Collaborative Browsing In The Home

A notable absence from discussion in the NPD second-screening report was that of collaborative browsing, an activity known to occur frequently in the home. In 2009 Morris *et al.* [2] found that, of the co-located searches that occurred in the home, 58% were informational searches, with the majority of searches being spontaneous (70.6%) and lasting only a few minutes (64.7%), occurring in pairs (70.6%) or groups of three or four family members or friends (29.4%). Most searches were conducted using a single, shared machine (laptop/desktop) (76.5%).

A 2013 update [9] to their research found that the majority of smartphone users (92.8%) used their phones to engage in co-located collaborative searches with several people simultaneously, with these events occurring on a frequent basis (38.9% doing so at least once per day, and 65.6% at least a few times per week).

There have been a number of studies looking at the facilitation of collaborative web browsing, for example Schmid *et al.* [13] recently explored multi-device collaborative search using a shared display, however this required intercepting requests using a forward proxy, raising potential privacy concerns. PlayByPlay [21] implemented collaborative web browsing across both desktop and mobile devices, using saved IM sessions as a means for managing search activity across clients, whilst CoSearch [1] enabled co-located collaborative web search using a shared PC, showing that this preserved communication and collaboration.

Single/Multi-display Groupware

In collaborative terms, screen sharing has largely been supplanted by Single-Display Groupware (SDG, supporting collaboration between users that are physically close via a shared display) and Multi-Display Groupware (MDG, supporting collaboration using multiple displays). Within SDG, work has centered around shared displays or tabletops facilitating multiple users, for example via multi-touch [10].

MDG has extended these concepts, allowing for flexible combinations of displays, for example supporting personal and shared workspaces [20], shared workspaces and public displays [11] and other such permutations of personal/private/shared workspaces [17].

Of note within this field is the effect of having personal workspaces with shared displays, versus one single shared display. SDG configurations have been shown to provide more awareness, whilst personal displays have been found to offer "sheltered" and potentially personalized workspaces with less visual distraction, with the end result of better supporting individual cognition [19].

Awareness

Awareness within collaborative systems is a key issue and has been studied for many years, with a variety of definitions [5]. For the purposes of this paper, the most relevant interpretations are those of Greenberg *et al.* [6], and Schmidt [14].

Greenberg *et al.* [6] discussed the concept of workspace awareness ("one persons understanding of another person's interaction with a shared workspace") [16], specifically artefact ("what objects are they working on") and action ("what are they doing") [6, 5] awareness. Schmidt [14] referred to awareness in terms of actors; actors both monitor activities, and display activities perceived as relevant to their colleagues. The effect of this is improved situation awareness, which in turn allows for more effective collaboration. [6]

Awareness is a necessary trait for effective collaboration; in the home, this activity awareness is typically achieved through a shared focal point (e.g. TV/laptop/tablet/phone as seen in the collaborative browsing studies mentioned previously), however there is no catch-all solution that both

facilitates independence and provides activity awareness to whomever else is in the room.

Overview

Whilst technologies such as second screening and social TV have seen considerable research, the interaction between those in the room has perhaps been underinvestigated. Collaborative behaviour in the home is well understood, but systems designed to support this collaboration, in a manner that utilizes the technology typically available (mobile devices, a large shared TV) and is appropriate for the home context (relying on simple interfaces and established behaviours to provide activity awareness) have yet to be examined fully.

STUDY

Whilst there has been growth in screen-mirroring technology, specifically in consumer devices, multi-user use is often poorly facilitated, for example with users having to disconnect from the display to allow another user to mirror his or her device, a potentially laborious procedure to repeat.

To address this issue we set out to examine the merits of facilitating shared use of the receiving TV (given the possibility that every device in the room supports mirroring, and that the TV is typically the best display in the room and as such provides a shared focal point that should be opened up to social use). We chose to study this within the confines of small group collaboration, in order to provide a realistic task with which to motivate usage (e.g. a small group of friends or family sharing use of a TV in a living room). Additionally, we wanted to examine the effect screen mirroring had on artefact/activity awareness within the group, which in turn influences a groups ability to collaborate effectively.

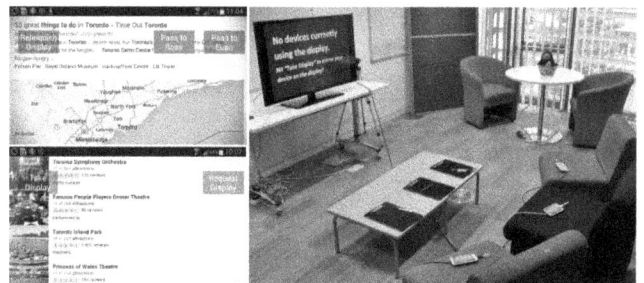

Figure 1. Left: client UI (top is current "owner" of the TV, bottom is another participant). The coloured glow around the edges was unique to each device, whilst overlayed semi-transparent buttons enabled management of the shared mirroring TV. Right: Living-room-like space used for conducting study, with 3 phones (one per participant) wired up to our mirroring system.

Control Scheme: Possession of the Display

For the purposes of this study, we treated the display as a commodity that was owned by whomever was currently mirroring to it, partially influenced by previous work on sharing behaviour [8]. As such, if a user owned the display, he/she could relinquish it, or pass it to individuals that requested its use. Similarly, if a user did not possess the display, he/she could request or take it using buttons overlayed on the screen of the client device.

This control scheme satisfied a number of concerns. Firstly, there was the issue of privacy: a user must actively participate (i.e. request or take the display) in order to end up having their content mirrored to the shared display. If they no longer wished to be mirrored, they could simply relinquish the display. Secondly, we wished to examine how users would choose to manage this resource: would they see taking the display as socially acceptable, given the task is about collaboration? Or would they prefer to use a request-pass mechanism for managing display usage, a potentially more socially acceptable.

Collaborative Task

Whilst there are a number of potential use cases for shared screen-mirroring, we decided to validate its use through the potential for aiding small group collaboration in the home, evaluated via a collaborative browsing task. This allowed us to rely on previous work regarding metrics for how well groups felt they collaborated (for example using questions from Websurface [18] and Mobisurf [15]). Additionally we chose to examine how the shared screen-mirroring display affected visual attention and awareness of others activity, whilst presenting users with a typical and realistic scenario that occurs in home environments among small groups.

Our collaborative search task was a variant of the travel search task derived from Morris *et al.* [9] in other studies previously [18, 15]. Participants were given 15 minutes to plan a trip to a given city (New York, London, Sydney) and pick tourist attractions/shows to see as a group. These cities were chosen due to their abundance of potential attractions and associated English-language materials online. Participants were free to browse using their devices however they saw fit in relation to the task. This task was ecologically valid, having been shown to be conducted in the home previously, with additional validity derived from the use of consumer mobile devices and the freedom given to participants to use these devices naturally.

Participants

Six groups of three participants took part (male=13, female=5, age MEDIAN=22.2, SD=2.81), recruited in groups, on the basis that group members knew each other (being friends/family/colleagues). Additionally, participants were required to be regular users of mobile web browsers.

Experimental Design

Three conditions were examined: 1. mobile devices with no screen-mirroring (as a control; this is analogous to the situation where people use phones to collaborate over an activity); 2. mobile devices with one device permanently mirrored (representative of existing consumer screen-mirroring where unpairing/pairing devices is a costly process); and 3. mobile devices with shared screen-mirroring (use of the TV screen could be passed/taken/relinquished/requested). A split-screen approach was also considered, however ruled out on the grounds of scalability (splitting the screen does not scale well with multiple users).

The study was carried out within subjects; conditions were counterbalanced, with task cities assigned such that each condition had each city twice across the course of the study. For the permanent mirror condition, the groups were asked to volunteer a member to control the mirrored device.

Participants were seated in a sociopetal arrangement around a table, approximately 2 meters from the shared display, and approximately 30cm from each other (see Figure 1). This proximity was chosen both because of its realism (individuals sitting close together on a couch in a living room) and so that participants would have the opportunity to share what was on the screens of their devices directly by showing them to each other, in order to fully examine whether participants would use the shared display, or instead prefer physically sharing device views.

This study was designed to feature a high degree of internal and ecological validity (e.g. utilizing ecologically valid devices, in social groups representative of those found in the home, conducting a task previously found to be conducted in the home).

Implementation

Participants used Android smartphones to control the system and share content, one per participant. These devices were mirrored onto a 46inch HDTV. Mirroring was accomplished via Mobile HD-Link (MHL) cables and an HDMI switch controlled via serial port, with each device attached via an MHL cable to the switch. This was chosen over wireless display technology so as to avoid any issues with bandwidth constraints/contention, transmission issues, or performance. The cables were 3m long and not rigid, thus participants had a good degree of movement/flexibility.

Control of who currently owned the display was managed using controls overlayed on all applications within Android (see Figure 1). These controls could be moved via a long-press if they were preventing access to a particular UI element, however they could not be hidden, so as to ensure participants would not forget about the functionality. Button presses were relayed to a server controlling the HDMI switch, which in turn changed which device was currently being displayed. The switching delay was approximately 2.2 seconds, during which a black screen was shown. Additionally, when the display was relinquished entirely (i.e. no client owned the display) a screen was shown indicating that clients could mirror to the display by hitting the "take display" button.

HYPOTHESES AND METRICS

We hypothesized that the shared display would have an effect on visual attention (attending significantly to the shared display), activity awareness (the extent to which participants were aware of each other's activity), and perceived collaboration within the group, with participants using the shared display and it's capability to be passed and taken to share views instead of co-viewing using the mobile devices.

In order to test these hypothesis, we recorded and analysed video footage of each participant, coding timestamps regarding which display the participant was looking at, if any. These timestamps were then parsed to form a viewing array which categorised which display each participant was looking at in

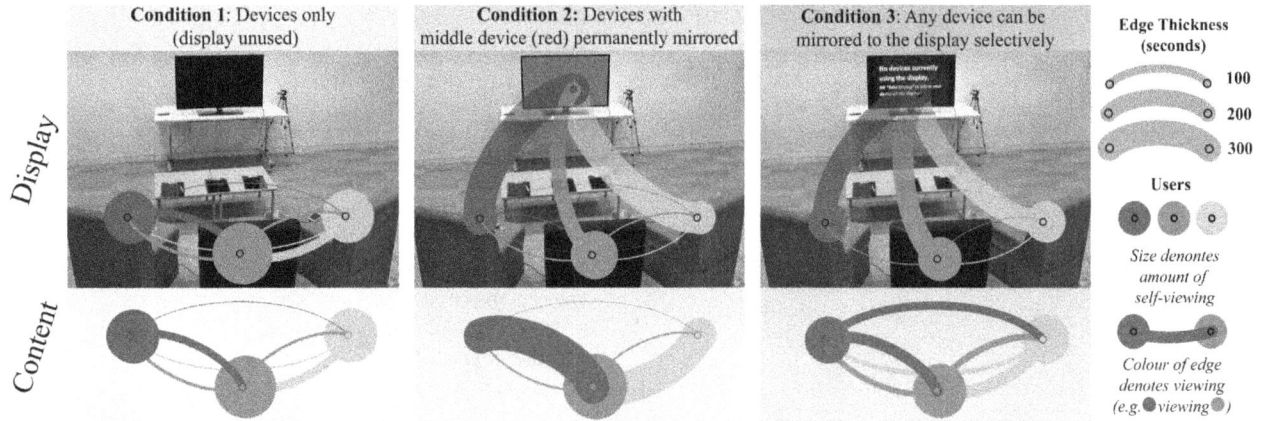

Figure 2. Mean cumulative viewing of displays (top) and user content (bottom). Each colour denotes a participant, with edge weight representing the cumulative amount of time spent looking at the node they are directed to. Top shows cumulative viewing time of the displays present (TV, and three mobile devices, one per participant), whilst bottom shows cumulative viewing of user content (presented either on the display, or on the owners device).

100ms intervals, from which mean viewing and Gini coefficients (as a measure of equity of the viewing distribution[20]; 1 denotes maximum inequality, 0 maximum equality) were calculated.

Viewing logs were generated manually by watching each participant in real time (11 hours footage in total), pressing assigned keys which coded the video log on the basis of which physical display users were attending to. These logs were then combined with logs regarding what content was mirrored, and parsed to extract cumulative viewing and co-viewing data. Footage was captured by a HD video camera placed at seated head height of participants, next to the display such that we could identify whether participants were looking at the display, their devices, or the devices of others in their group. Participants were seated and lit such that these shifts in viewing could be easily discerned by the experimenter *post hoc*.

Additionally, post-condition questionnaires were delivered including NASA TLX [7], and applicable questions derived from previous collaborative browsing studies [18, 15, 10] (7-point Likert-type) asking users about awareness and how effectively they felt they collaborated.

RESULTS

Unless otherwise stated, a repeated measures ANOVA (conducted using linear mixed-effects model fit by maximum likelihood (*lme()* in R)) was performed with a *post hoc* pairwise Tukey's test for each question/data set. p values less than 0.05 are statistically significant.

Cumulative Viewing

Figure 2 shows the cumulative viewing of both the available displays (4 in total, the 3 phones and the TV), and user activity (denoted by seating position), whilst Table 1 shows the mean cumulative viewing of a participants activity, broken down by seat and condition, excluding self-viewing (e.g. the left participant looking at the left phone display) in order to show the amount that the content on a display was shared with others.

Condition 1 can be seen as being somewhat insular: the outermost participants exhibit limited viewing of the central users

	Mean (SD) Cumulative Viewing (in seconds)		
Participant (by seat)	Condition 1	Condition 2	Condition 3
Left	45.9 (31.9)	25.5 (22.8)	194.2 (135.4)
Middle	221.2 (224.4)	884.0 (534.4)	314.8 (174.7)
Right	65.7 (71.7)	27.6 (43.3)	141.6 (55.0)

Table 1. Mean (SD) cumulative content viewed by others (excluding self-viewing) in seconds across groups, by participant position (e.g. in condition 1, the activity of the participant sitting left was viewed for an average of 45.9 seconds total by the other participants).

activity, and little viewing of each others activity, whilst the central user has a limited awareness of the outer user's activity.

With the introduction of the shared display in Conditions 2 and 3, the viewing patterns change significantly, with the shared display offering a focal point for the group. Condition 2 shows a notable disparity in terms of equity of activity viewing; the mirrored user's content dominates the viewing of the group. Condition 3 exhibits greater equity in that respect, with users viewing each others content more than in any previous condition.

	Gini Coefficient of $3 * 3$ cumulative viewing matrix by group, excluding self-viewing (diagonal) RM-Anova: $\chi^2(2) = 16.3, p < 0.01$			
Condition	Mean Gini Coefficient (SD)	1	2	3
1	0.432 (0.153)	–	$p < 0.05$	$p = 0.11$
2	0.611 (0.115)	–	–	$p < 0.01$
3	0.298 (0.0605)	–	–	–

Table 2. Mean Gini coefficients across conditions, calculated from each $3 * 3$ $Left, Center, Right * viewed Left, Center, Right$ matrix of cumulative viewing, with results of *post hoc* pairwise Tukey's test.

This is confirmed in Table 2, where the equity of distribution of viewing is significantly different between Condition 2 and Conditions 1 and 3 (however not between conditions 1 and 3, predominantly because the Gini coefficient does not take into account the magnitude of viewing).

Cumulative Co-viewing

Two and three person co-viewing denotes any instant of time where two or three users were looking at the same

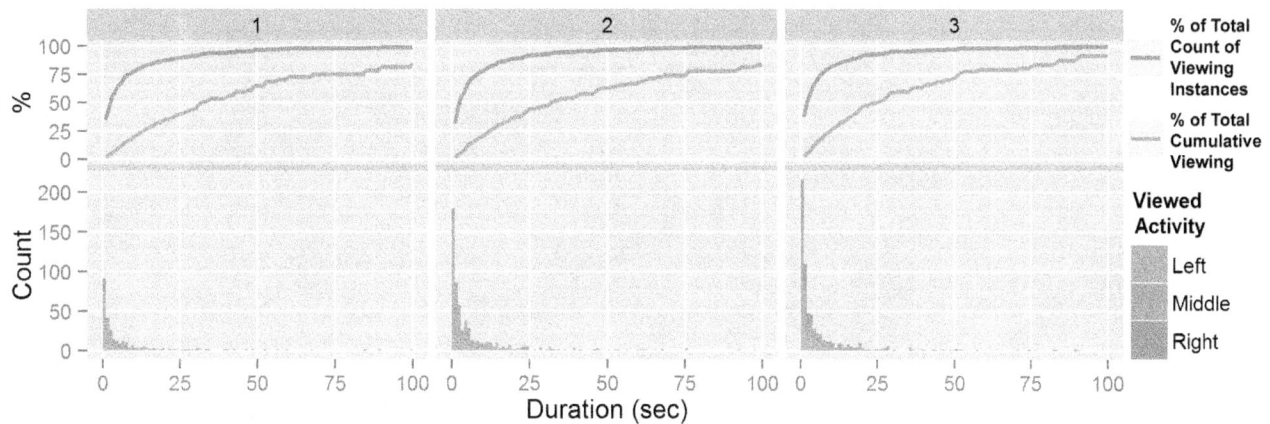

Figure 3. Graph of individual viewing behaviour across all participants (excluding self-viewing). Bottom: Histogram presents 1 second sized bins counting number of instances of viewing of a given duration. Top: Graph presenting percentage of overall cumulative viewing and percentage of overall number of viewing instances.

content/activity (with the subset of two person co-viewing within three person co-viewing excluded from two person co-viewing statistics).

Two Person Co-viewing			
	Mean (SD) Cumulative Viewing (in seconds)		
Participant (by seat)	Condition 1	Condition 2	Condition 3
Left	28.6 (23.8)	18.8 (18.5)	81.3 (74.3)
Middle	109.4 (83.1)	227.8 (68.1)	113.4 (24.3)
Right	22.6 (21.2)	21.4 (35.5)	70.1 (17.6)
Three Person Co-viewing			
Left	5.32 (5.88)	1.17 (1.34)	53.3 (34.59)
Middle	51.87 (74.0)	312.67 (269.94)	92.78 (97.91)
Right	18.75 (27.04)	0.97 (2.37)	32.5 (19.17)

Table 3. Mean (SD) cumulative content viewed in seconds across conditions, by participant position, across both two and three person co-viewing.

Table 3 illustrates the equity of distribution of two and three person co-viewing across conditions: conditions 1 and 2 feature dominance by the middle participant in terms of activity coviewed, in contrast to condition 3 where, again, a more equitable distribution of viewing across different participant's activity is demonstrated.

Gini Coefficient of Two Person Co-viewing RM-Anova: $\chi^2(2) = 18.36, p < 0.01$				
Condition	Mean Gini Coefficient (SD)	1	2	3
1	0.367 (0.077)	–	$p < 0.05$	$p < 0.05$
2	0.55 (0.139)	–	–	$p < 0.01$
3	0.209 (0.118)	–	–	–
Gini Coefficient of Three Person Co-viewing RM-Anova: $\chi^2(2) = 10.25, p < 0.01$				
1	0.469 (0.175)	–	$p = 0.223$	$p = 0.191$
2	0.605 (0.14)	–	–	$p < 0.01$
3	0.327 (0.1)	–	–	–

Table 4. Mean Gini coefficients by two and three person co-viewing, calculated from each $3 * 1$ $viewedLeft, Center, Right$ matrix of cumulative viewing, with results of *post hoc* pairwise Tukey's test.

Table 4 confirms this view, with condition 3 exhibiting the lowest mean Gini coefficients, in contrast to condition 2 which features the highest mean Gini coefficients, an indicator of the bias toward viewing the middle participants content. Indeed the draw of viewing the shared display is such that it draws the focus of the other participants from their own devices, such that they view the central participant's activity far more than they chose to do so in condition 1.

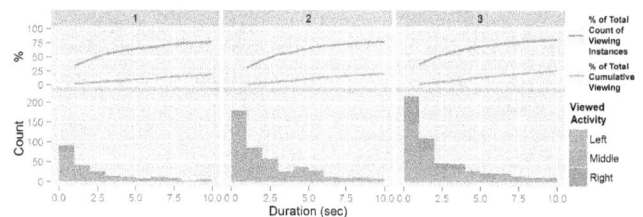

Figure 4. Graph of individual viewing behaviour across all participants (excluding self-viewing), focussing on viewing instances between 0-10 seconds. Bottom: Histogram presents 1 second sized bins counting number of instances of viewing of a given duration. Top: Graph presenting percentage of overall cumulative viewing and percentage of overall number of viewing instances.

Viewing Behaviour

We further analysed the viewing data collected by looking at time series histograms of viewing instances (using 1 second sized bins) in order to determine how participants gained awareness.

Figure 3 shows the viewing of each individual's content broken down by length of view; over all three conditions, ~75% of the total instances of viewing lasted between 0-6 seconds, however this typically only constituted ~20% of the overall viewing.

Figure 4 shows a zoomed in view of Figure 3, constrained to viewing instances lasting between 0-10 seconds. Of particular note here is the viewing distribution exhibited: Condition 1 and 2 show similar distributions, with the difference that Condition 2 is ~100% longer at each viewing interval.

Condition 3 shows a similar viewing distribution to condition 2 (with a heavy right skew toward the 0-2 second bins), however a greater proportion of the left and right participants activity is now apparent.

	Condition				Wilcoxon
Question	1	2	3	Friedman Test	Post-hoc ($p < 0.05$)
WS-1: We were able to collaborate effectively	3.94 (1.55)	4.28 (1.23)	5.17 (0.924)	$\chi^2(2) = 8.03, p < 0.05$	3-1, 3-2
WS-2: We were able to work independently to complete the task	4.89 (1.08)	3.33 (1.37)	4.78 (1.22)	$\chi^2(2) = 12.7, p < 0.01$	3-2, 2-1
WS-3: It was easy to discuss the information we found	4.06 (1.63)	4.72 (1.18)	5.39 (0.85)	$\chi^2(2) = 11.6, p < 0.01$	3-1
WS-4: We were able to work together to complete the task	4.67 (1.08)	4.72 (1.23)	5.33 (1.08)	$p = 0.053$	NA
WS-5: I was able to actively participate in completing the task	4.72 (1.27)	4.67 (1.37)	5.44 (0.984)	$\chi^2(2) = 6, p < 0.05$	None
MO-1: How well did the system support collaboration?	2.83 (1.82)	3.67 (1.71)	5 (1.08)	$\chi^2(2) = 11.5, p < 0.01$	3-1, 3-2
MO-2: How well did the system support you to share particular information with a particular user in the group?	3.11 (2.05)	3.28 (1.87)	4.83 (1.29)	$\chi^2(2) = 8.03, p < 0.05$	3-1, 3-2
MO-3: How well did the system support you to share particular information with everyone in the group?	2.17 (2.18)	3.94 (1.98)	5.17 (1.04)	$\chi^2(2) = 16, p < 0.01$	2-1, 3-1
MO-4: How well did the system support you to see/review what the other users were talking about?	2.89 (1.97)	3.39 (1.69)	5.22 (1.06)	$\chi^2(2) = 12, p < 0.01$	3-1, 3-2
WE-1: I was aware of what other users were doing	2.83 (1.54)	3.39 (1.61)	4.78 (1.31)	$\chi^2(2) = 14.7, p < 0.01$	3-1

Table 5. Questions derived from previous studies. WS: WebSurface[18], MO: Mobisurf[15], WE: WeSearch[10]. Questions were 7-point Likert scale (results range from 0-6, higher is better). Means with standard deviations are presented across conditions. A Friedman test was conducted with *post hoc* Bonferroni corrected Wilcoxon tests.

Co-viewing Behaviour

The distributions of two and three person co-viewing behaviour (see Figures 5 and 6) exhibit many of the same traits as previously discussed, for example the heavy right-skewed distribution, and the majority of the viewing instances lasting between 0-6 seconds in length.

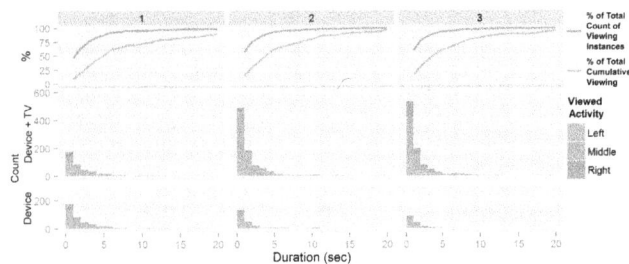

Figure 5. Graph of two person co-viewing behaviour across all participants. Middle: Histogram presents 1 second sized bins counting number of instances of viewing of a given duration, involving mixed-mode viewing (i.e. a combination of TV/device). Top: Graph presenting percentage of overall cumulative viewing and percentage of overall number of viewing instances. Bottom: Histogram of viewing excluding TV.

Of note within these Figures is the extent to which co-viewing occurred using the devices (infrequently), or using a combination of device and shared display (frequently), as an indicator of how often pairs or tuples of participants shared the common focal point of a device.

Whilst two and three person co-viewing still utilized devices as shared screens in conditions 2 and 3, the occurrence of this behaviour decreased significantly, with the majority of co-viewing involving a combination of device and shared display. This transition toward heavy use of the shared display illustrates its potential usefulness above and beyond device based sharing.

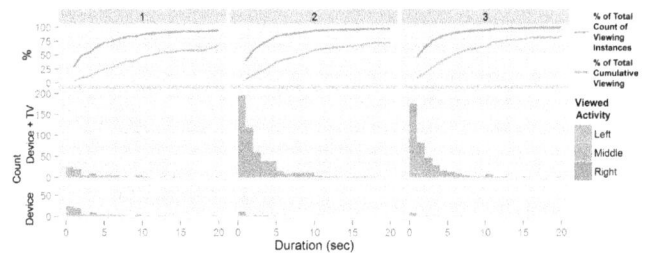

Figure 6. Graph of three person co-viewing behaviour across all participants. Middle: Histogram presents 1 second sized bins counting number of instances of viewing of a given duration, involving mixed-mode viewing (i.e. a combination of TV/device). Top: Graph presenting percentage of overall cumulative viewing and percentage of overall number of viewing instances. Bottom: Histogram of viewing excluding TV.

Indeed, three person co-viewing was barely prevalent in Condition 1, however this behaviour was clearly facilitated well by the shared display, hence the orders-of-magnitude increase in three person co-viewing when the shared display was introduced in Conditions 2 and 3.

Questionnaire

Our post-condition questionnaires (see Table 5) revealed some of the consequences of both providing a mirrored display, and facilitating shared-mirroring.

In terms of perceived collaboration, users responded positively to the shared screen mirroring, with statistically better ratings in response to WS-1 and MO-1 with respect to condition 3. Indeed WE-1 indicated why this was so, with users reporting a significant different in terms of awareness of what others were doing, indicating awareness was improved by the shared screen mirroring system.

Of note was the response to **"We were able to work independently to complete the task"** with condition 2 found to be significantly different (for the worse) than both condition 1 and 3, suggesting that the fixed screen dominance actually compromised independence within the group.

There was also a presentational aspect to the system, with the responses to MO-4 suggesting users took control of the display in order to present information to the group and aid in discussion.

Controls for Managing Mirrored Display
We additionally examined participant usage of the control scheme for our shared screen mirroring system. From table 6 we can see that taking the display from whomever currently possessed it was the prevalent means of display management, in contrast to the request-pass mechanism implemented (which required not one action (pressing the take button), but two actions across two users (pressing the request button and waiting for the receiver) in order to transfer the display).

	Request	Pass	Take	Relinquish
Total Occurrences	18	17	59	13
Mean Acceptability (SD)	4.72 (1.36)		4.83 (1.34)	NA

Table 6. Usage of display management controls provided in condition 3. Acceptability ranged from 0 (lowest) to 6 (highest) on a 7-point Likert scale. N.B. One participant was omitted as an outlier for having a request count more than two standard deviations from the mean.

Whilst participants reported feeling adequately notified when someone requested the display (MD:4.5, SD:1.38), one participant's results was omitted due to a large amount of requests made in a short period, potentially indicating issues with such mechanisms if the requester feels that the owner of the display has not been adequately notified, or has been ignored.

DISCUSSION
Our analyses show that in introducing a mirrored display that does not support flexibly changing the content or activity mirrored to it, there are a number of effects on collaboration, in terms of compromising the independence of collaborators and compromising a group's ability to be aware of each members activity.

Our proposed shared screen mirroring solution allows for the independence that users found when using only mobile devices for collaboration, whilst significantly improving group awareness of individual's activity.

Equity of Awareness and Independence
Our analysis of the cumulative group viewing suggests that the primary factor inhibiting the viewing of others content is the accessibility of that view; in the device-only condition, viewing (and co-viewing) were dominated by the central participant, whose device was most easily accessible to the other group members.

This poses a problem, in that there are a subset of group users that are essentially cut off from observing each other. The

central user, whose view is most accessible, contributes disproportionately to the collaborative experience.

Given that our experimental seating arrangement was designed to be accessible and sociopetal, it could be expected that these issues would be exacerbated in a real-world living room environment, where the seating arrangements are less accessible, and potentially dispersed over a greater area. Thus the large TV display provides obvious benefits regarding being able to make whomever is in the room aware of your activity, in a way that does not disrupt their current ongoing device activity in the room.

Indeed this is where it would be expected that current screen-mirroring technology would provide an ideal means toward facilitating better awareness of activity. However, our results show that this is not the case; in utilizing a screen-mirroring solution that does not facilitate multi-user management of the shared display (Condition 2) we are limited to only one user (whomever has paired to the screen-mirroring device) having the ability to reach the group.

This compromises collaboration by undermining the independence of the other users: the shared display, and by extension the user's activity that is mirrored to that display, is viewed to the extent that said user essentially leads the collaborative task. There may be cases where this is beneficial, however in this study this was not the case. The reasons for this are that in this condition, there still exist the dual problems of there being a subset of group users that are essentially cut off from observing each other, and the central user contributing disproportionately to the collaborative experience.

We posit that these problems can be addressed by exposing a simple set of functionality for enabling flexible use of the mirroring display. Our shared screen mirroring system (Condition 3) has been shown to improve perceived collaboration, as well as providing an equity of awareness which allows every user to potentially contribute and present to the group as a whole, and allows users to retain their independence.

Self-Management of the Display: Taking is Sharing
Our system enabled a basic set of functionality for transferring and relinquishing use of the display: request-pass, take, and relinquish; of these, participants showed a strong inclination toward taking the display, both in terms of frequency of use, and self-rated acceptability.

In opening the display up to be managed by members of the group, this allowed users to work fluidly together, using their social capabilities to determine the acceptability of taking the display (in order to present their own activity or content to the group) at any given moment.

Shared Focus of Attention
Utilizing the shared display additionally provided a shared focal point for the group; incidence of two and three person co-viewing increased dramatically in the shared display conditions, providing users with a shared reference point which we believe aided in the communication and discussion necessary for effective collaboration. Indeed, this represents an

additional benefit regarding utilizing the display over, for example, tablet or mobile devices for providing awareness, as the shared display typically provides a reference point accessible to anyone in the room.

Use Cases

We foresee that facilitating shared screen mirroring behaviours might have an impact on other kinds of collaboration than have been considered here. For example tasks where multiple parties must come to some kind of consensus (e.g. planning where to go to eat, what to watch in an evening etc.), or indeed any task involving flexible sharing of user activity or media content (e.g. presenting a video to the group, at which point a friend seamlessly takes the display to show a follow up video/app/website) would be likely to benefit from having the capability to use the nearest TV for flexibly mirroring content.

Limitations and Future Work

Further work will be required in order to establish external validity and user appropriation of shared mirroring TVs in the home. We anticipate that different social groups and contexts will result in markedly different behaviours and uses as users begin to explore the sharing capability these displays would enable. Additionally, we wish to explore the capability for sub-dividing the screen to allow multi-user mirroring, and the extent that this might potentially compromise use of the shared display (through the increased visual load, decreased area for representing mirrored content, and the loss of a single shared focal point).

CONCLUSIONS

Current screen mirroring technology, where a single device/user is paired with a TV, can aid collaboration in groups. However there are negative side effects, specifically with respect to group awareness being dominated by the activity of the mirrored user, leading to the compromise of independence within the group.

Our shared screen mirroring system significantly improves a small group's ability to collaborate, by enabling device users to pass/take/relinquish the display as required. Through a basic set of behaviours for managing use of the display, our shared screen mirroring system was shown to better facilitate collaboration and content sharing in small groups, resulting in greater equity of participation and awareness of others' activity. In opening the display up to the group, this allows fringe members to more actively participate, sharing content with members they were unlikely to share with previously.

We suggest that shared screen mirroring, and the controls we have presented in this paper, represent a viable extension to existing screen mirroring technologies that could be readily implemented, within the Miracast standard for example, thus enabling new sharing behaviours and interactions and lending further value to screen mirroring in the home.

ACKNOWLEDGMENTS

We would like to thank Bang & Olufsen and the EPSRC for funding this work.

REFERENCES

1. Amershi, S., and Morris, M. R. CoSearch. In *Proc. CHI 2008*, ACM Press (2008), 1647–1656.

2. Amershi, S., and Morris, M. R. Co-located collaborative web search: understanding status quo practices. In *Proc. CHI EA 2009*, ACM Press (2009), 1657–1660.

3. Arthur, R., et al. XICE windowing toolkit. *ACM TOCHI 18*, 3 (2011), 1–46.

4. Engelbart, D., and English, W. A research center for augmenting human intellect. *FJCC* (1968).

5. Gross, T., et al. User-Centered Awareness in CSCW-Systems. *International Journal of Human-Computer Interaction 18*, 3 (2005), 323–360.

6. Gutwin, C., and Greenberg, S. A Descriptive Framework of Workspace Awareness for Real-Time Groupware. *CSCW 11*, 3 (2002), 411–446.

7. Hart, S., and Staveland, L. Development of NASA-TLX (Task Load Index). In *Human mental workload* (1988).

8. Mentis, H. M., et al. Taking as an act of sharing. In *Proc. CSCW 2012*, ACM Press (Feb. 2012), 1091–1100.

9. Morris, M. R. Collaborative search revisited. In *Proc. CSCW 2013*, ACM Press (2013), 1181–1192.

10. Morris, M. R., Lombardo, J., and Wigdor, D. WeSearch. In *Proc. CSCW 2010*, ACM Press (2010), 401–410.

11. Nacenta, M. A., et al. The LunchTable. In *Proc. PerDis 2012*, ACM Press (2012), 1–6.

12. NPD. Inception of Screen Sharing. `https://www.npd.com/`, 2013.

13. Schmid, O., et al. Collaborative web browsing. In *Proc. EICS 2012*, ACM Press (2012), 141–150.

14. Schmidt, K. The Problem with 'Awareness'. *CSCW 11*, 3 (2002), 285–298.

15. Seifert, J., et al. MobiSurf. In *Proc. ITS 2012*, ACM Press (2012), 51–60.

16. Tee, K., Greenberg, S., and Gutwin, C. Artifact awareness through screen sharing for distributed groups. *International Journal of Human-Computer Studies 67*, 9 (2009), 677–702.

17. Terrenghi, L., et al. A taxonomy for and analysis of multi-person-display ecosystems. In *Personal and Ubiquitous Computing*, no. 8 (2009), 583–598.

18. Tuddenham, P., et al. WebSurface. In *Proc. ITS 2009*, ACM Press (2009), 181–188.

19. Wallace, J. R., et al. Investigating teamwork and taskwork in single- and multi-display groupware systems. In *Personal and Ubiquitous Computing*, no. 8 (2009), 569–581.

20. Wallace, J. R., et al. Collaborative sensemaking on a digital tabletop and personal tablets. In *Proc. CHI 2013*, ACM Press (2013), 3345–3354.

21. Wiltse, H., and Nichols, J. PlayByPlay. In *Proc. CHI 2009*, ACM Press (2009), 1781–1790.

In Front of and Behind the Second Screen:
Viewer and Producer Perspectives on a Companion App

David Geerts, Rinze Leenheer, Dirk De Grooff
CUO | Social Spaces, iMinds / KU Leuven
Parkstraat 45 Bus 3605, 3000 Leuven, Belgium
firstname.lastname@soc.kuleuven.be

Susanne Heijstraten, Joost Negenman
Nederlandse Publieke Omroep (NPO)
Sumatralaan 45, PB 26444, 1202JJ Hilversum
firstname.lastname@omroep.nl

ABSTRACT
The growing success of tablets and smartphones has shifted the focus of the interactive TV industry to the introduction of second screen applications. One example is second screen companion apps that offer extra information about a television program, often synchronized with what happens on screen. In this paper, we investigate a second screen companion app, from the perspective of the viewers and producers of such apps. Based on observations and interviews with viewers and producers, and actual usage data of a companion app from Google Analytics, we present several insights and recommendations for how to design companion apps related to ease of use, timing, social interaction, attention and added value.

Author Keywords
Interactive TV; Second Screen; User Experience; Producers

ACM Classification Keywords
H5.1 [Information Interfaces and presentation]: Multimedia information systems – audio, video; H5.m [Information Interfaces and presentation (e.g., HCI)]: Miscellaneous

INTRODUCTION
The growing success of tablets and smartphones has dramatically changed the approach to interactive television, in research as well as in practice. Whereas the main focus used to be on how to add interactive features to the main television set [7], this has shifted to interacting with television programs using tablets and smartphones as second screen devices [2]. Accordingly, research topics are changing from how to deal with screen real estate or appropriate input devices to trying out which concepts are most suited for the second screen [1] and how this distracts from the first screen [6]. The television industry has quickly realized the potential of the second screen as well, and many television shows now come with companion apps that offer extra information about a television program, often synchronized with what happens on screen [9]. However, little is known yet about what works and what doesn't work when using and producing second screen companion apps.

In this paper, we investigate a second screen companion app, from the perspective of the viewers as well as from producers of such apps. We do not only study how viewers experience second screen companion apps, and how they could be improved, but also reflect on the issues that producers face during the development and deployment of these apps. With this, we hope to provide a more complete picture of how to design and implement successful second screen companion applications.

RELATED WORK
Even before the advent of powerful tablet computers and smartphones, the use of a secondary device while watching television has been studied. One of the earliest explorations into the combination of a second device and TV studied the use of a PDA for a real-estate prototype which allowed the user to browse and select information on the PDA, while watching pictures, videos and detailed maps on the TV screen [10]. The study resulted in several design guidelines, some of which are still very relevant today, such as "combine devices so that the ensemble provides more than each independent device". More recently, Cesar et al. [2] discussed four types of activity that could be supported by second screens in conjunction with TV: control, enrich, share and transfer TV content. As they consider control as the ability to select and preview personal content, e.g. for showing enhanced information, this is the model that the companion app in our study fits in.

Since smartphones and tablets have been introduced, second screen applications have been created or studied for different types of activities such as electronic programing guides (EPGs) [4], Social TV [8] or more recently as companion apps for television programs. Murray et al. [9] created Story-Map, a synchronized iPad app for long form TV narratives with multiple characters and story arcs to support orientation in the fictional world, offer reminders of story developments and enable review of key scenes. Many broadcasters have experimented with similar companion apps alongside TV shows. Basapur et al. [1] developed and evaluated a companion app that provides synchronized content updates around TV shows, generated by the viewer's social circle. Their results show that participants felt better connected to the TV show and their social life around TV content was enriched. However, they also felt distracted from the TV show sometimes. One of the main questions when introducing a second screen alongside television is indeed how much this will distract from the main television screen. Some studies actually try to measure how much viewers are distracted. Holmes et al. [6] found in an eye tracking study with a synchronized tablet app that 63% of gaze time went to TV, 30% to the tablet and 7% off screen. Even when there was no interactive push or ad content on the TV, considerable gaze time went to the tablet screen.

While the user experience of interactive TV in general and second screen applications in specific has already been studied quite often, the view of iTV professionals is less explored. A search for professional perspectives on interactive television reveals several approaches. van Dijk & de Vos [12] did a worldwide survey of 74 corporate ITV experts about interactivity, interactive TV and the future of television, looking for suitable business models. They discovered differences in views from TV producers versus Internet producers, where the former had a more passive view on interactivity than the latter. Cauberghe & De Pelsmacker [3] performed a survey in two waves among Belgian advertising professionals about their knowledge, perceptions and intentions toward iTV as a marketing communication tool, before and after the introduction of iTV. Their results show limited knowledge and low perception of effectiveness of advertising using iTV. Ursu et al. [11] looked at broadcasters' support for interactive narrative development by studying BBC's commissioning documents and experiments from other broadcasters and created an authoring tool for interactive narratives taking producer's considerations into account. In the existing literature however, little could be found on the issues producers face when designing and developing second screen applications. Nevertheless, the complex ecosystem of television broadcasting, both technologically and economically, has consequences for how second screen applications can be designed, and also impacts the user experience. In this paper we therefore not only provide the perspective of who's in front of the second screen, but also the producer's perspective, behind the second screen.

METHODOLOGY
We combine data from three sources in order to get a full picture of how second screen companion apps are being produced and experienced, and to explore the relationship between end-user requirements and the requirements from a producer's perspective. First, we conducted interviews with six second screen producers in Belgium and The Netherlands about their view on creating second screen applications. Second, we video recorded five couples while they were using a second screen app during a television show ("De Ridder"), and interviewed them about their experience afterwards. Finally, we had access to Google Analytics data from the second screen companion app we studied, which allowed us to get the actual usage data before, during and after the show was broadcast.

Producer interviews
For interviewing producers we used semi-structured interviews at their work location. Audio recordings were made of all the interviews, which were fully transcribed for further analysis. The initial, open, questions were aimed at understanding what the users' jobs entailed, which activities they do related to interactive TV (including second screen applications), which tools they use, and what the challenges and opportunities are they face in this context. As the interview progressed, the interviewer would ask clarifying questions on specific projects, unique for each of the interviewees. The interviews lasted about one hour each.

Participants
We interviewed six producers, whom we coded with letters A to E. As one interview was done with two persons at once, we coded them as B1 and B2. Four of the producers work as head of new media at different broadcasters within the Dutch public broadcaster NPO: three from TV (coded as B1, B2 and C) and one from radio (D), which also has an online video stream that is sometimes featured on the main broadcast channels. Two were heads of technology companies that are dedicated to developing second screen applications for broadcasters, one in Belgium (A), who produced the companion app used in this study, and one in The Netherlands (E). The participants had between 2 and 10 years of experience in working with interactive TV.

Viewer observations
To get a detailed picture of how viewers experience second screen companion apps in a social context, we recruited five couples and observed them in their own home environment while they were watching a television show and using a second screen application that was specifically developed for that show. The interviews and observations took place in the second half of the TV series season.

A camera was placed in their home before the day of the show, so no researcher had to be present during the actual broadcast. This was done to minimize the intrusion for the participants and to have them watch as naturally as possible (a similar approach has been used in [5]). For the same reason, the participants were instructed to watch the show and use the second screen application as they would normally do. We placed the camera in an angle that would give the best view of the users, their devices and their immediate surroundings. See **Figure 1** for an impression of the observation setup. One or two days after the show the researcher returned to collect the footage and watch the recording together with the participant(s) using event-triggered retrospective think aloud. This means that when specific events took place in the recording, such as interaction with the second screen device or social interaction between the participants, the researcher asked if the participants could clarify what they were doing and why. This in-depth interview lasted about two hours per couple.

Figure 1: Camera view from one of the observations.

The show that was selected is a drama series about a young prosecutor called "De Ridder", which ran from 13 October 2013 to 5 January 2014. This show was selected because it was a highly anticipated and well-watched show (over 1.2 million viewers) and it prominently featured a newly developed second screen experience. The second screen application is an HTML5 based website which can be accessed on any device with an Internet connection (e.g. laptop, tablet, smartphone), without installing anything or creating an account. It features a timeline that shows content related to the television show as the program progresses, synchronized with the activities on the main television screen. An animated slider on top of the screen visually shows when the next update is scheduled. The content updates could be quotes from the show, polls which users can respond to, information about specific terms used in the show, maps of the location of characters which the users can interact with, etc. All types of content can be 'liked' in the application or shared via Facebook or Twitter. **Figure 2** shows a screenshot of the app.

Figure 2: Screenshot of the "De Ridder" app

Participants
Because the goal was to observe viewers in their natural environment while watching as they always do, participants had to be regular viewers of "De Ridder" and already be users of the second screen application while watching the show. Participants were selected by placing recruitment messages on Twitter, Facebook and the research and

innovation page of the website of the broadcaster of the show, Vlaamse Radio- en Televisieomroeporganisatie (VRT).

We selected five households based on availability and household composition. We chose to recruit couples, as part of our focus was on social interaction between couples while watching TV with a second screen, but also to have a more homogenous set of participants. Participants (n=10) were therefore all couples (5 male, 5 female, average age 33.6, sd = 4.98), some of whom with young children who were not old enough to watch the show with their parents. All couples were regular viewers of "De Ridder" and all of them consistently watched the show with a second screen on a laptop or a tablet.

Data analysis
The data gathered from the producer interviews as well as viewer interviews and observations, were processed by the authors in two separate workshops. All data was transcribed and gathered in one document per interview/observation. These documents were used as the basis for the workshop. During the workshop the researchers singled out all relevant quotes and observations from the data and turned them into snippets (individual notes). These snippets were then grouped according to their content. The emerging groups were given a name, which resulted in a number of categories. When all snippets were allotted to a category the categories were reviewed and an appropriate main/sub category structure was created.

RESULTS
The producer interviews, viewer observations and actual usage data revealed interesting insights into how second screen applications are produced and consumed, which we will present in five distinct categories: ease of use, timing, social interaction, attention and added value.

Ease of Use
Not surprisingly, ease of use and usability are an important concern of viewers. As this is a requirement for most apps, we will not go into much detail for this topic. One thing however that was very clear from our interviews and crucial for getting viewers to use second screen companion apps, is a low threshold to start using an application. Accounts for instance are a big inconvenience and enough to scare people away.

"An account would be a threshold. What is keeping me a little from using the app of [a polling show] is that you have to create an account or a profile first" (Couple 3)

The producers we interviewed also emphasized that a second screen companion app should be simple on a discovery and accessibility level so the user does not have to put in an effort to start his interactive TV experience.

"It just shouldn't cost too much effort, if people need to install a different app for each program, that's a hassle.

What users really want is a single app with which you could follow all the second screen shows of a broadcaster." (B2)

Timing

Timing is a crucial issue in the world of television broadcasting. While most programming is scheduled at a specific time, and broadcasters expect viewers to sit in front of their television screens at that time, the advent of digital recorders has made it easier than ever to 'time-shift' and watch a program at another time – sometimes even before it is scheduled. The introduction of second screen companion apps adds another layer of complexity, as many of them require synchronising the content of the app with the content on the TV screen. To further complicate matters, companion apps can also be used without watching the television show, e.g. to revisit content between two shows, although that often diminishes the value of the companion app. In our interviews and observations, we could distinguish three types of timing issues that impact the use of second screen companion apps: synchronisation between the app and the TV show during the broadcast; delayed viewing or time-shifting; and reviewing content.

Live synchronisation

As described earlier, the 'De Ridder' app is being synchronised with the live broadcast of the television program, and updates appear on the second screen at the same time as something relevant happens on the main television screens. Our participants appreciated it a lot when an update was well synchronized with the show:

"If [the main character] receives a text message on the show, you can immediately see its contents on the second screen. That's a well thought out feature." (Couple 4)

In other cases, where content was not well synchronized, viewers are easily annoyed. We observed that when a poll came up too late for Couple 1 and the answer to the question was already given on the show, this reduced the value of participating in the poll for them.

Our interviews with producers show that synchronization is not an easy matter in practice. Even though new technologies are being developed, synchronising first and second screen is still done by hand by some broadcasters. All our producers indicated the need for an easy but accurate way of synchronizing content.

"Better synchronisation would make our life easier. What is available now is insufficient. For instance we believe watermarking is still in its infant stage. Especially considering the UX. If you have to sync for 6-10 seconds that is really too long and it also drops out often, so that technology just isn't good enough yet according to us." (A)

Delayed viewing

Many participants expressed that they watch most programs delayed through digital recordings. For some couples, this meant that they watched the program on a different day.

Others watched with a small delay, not to skip advertising (as it is aired by a public broadcaster) but because of personal scheduling issues. The 'De Ridder' app has to be used live for the updates to automatically appear synchronised with the show. Our participants expressed that they would prefer if they could also use the companion app in a synchronized way with delayed viewings.

"A disadvantage is that you only get the 'live experience' when you watch the show live. If you record it you lose the synchronicity." (Couple 1)

On the other hand, they also indicated that they do not consider the synchronized experience important enough to watch it live so they can use the companion app. This means that a good companion app should also have a synchronized experience with delayed viewing.

Our producers are aware of this, and any technical issues with synchronization set aside, realize that a big challenge for them is to offer an on-demand experience that feels no different than a live experience. However, broadcasters are still interested in enticing people to watch live TV (which can be attractive for commercial purposes), and propose to add attractive interactive components to live broadcasts, in order to increase the attractiveness of live viewing.

Interestingly, the data from Google Analytics shows that most viewers use the app during the period of the live broadcast (see **Figure 3**). The rest of the week there is barely any activity in the app, so it is clear that the interest of viewers using the app – whether for delayed viewing while using the app or reviewing the content (see further) – is not sustained over a longer period. After 15th December, this pattern changes, and for three weeks the amount of users on Sunday are significantly less and more people use the app in between two broadcasts. As this period more or less coincides with the Christmas holidays, this could mean people had more free time during the week and thus watched the episodes delayed, or that the content of the app was being reviewed more often in between.

Reviewing second screen content

Another behaviour related to timing is reviewing content of the app, either while the broadcast is still running, where viewers can 'break' the automatically updated timeline temporarily to scroll back to previously pushed content, or in between two broadcasts as the content remains accessible on the timeline and can be reviewed manually at any given time. Our participants liked the fact that the updates are 'permanent' and can be looked up at any time during the show.

"Sometimes I return to the info updates. You can expand them, so sometimes I go back and look at those when it slows down." (Couple 2)

However, they usually do not look at the updates after the show has ended. The updates 'live' for them as long as the show lasts, often just until the credits have run.

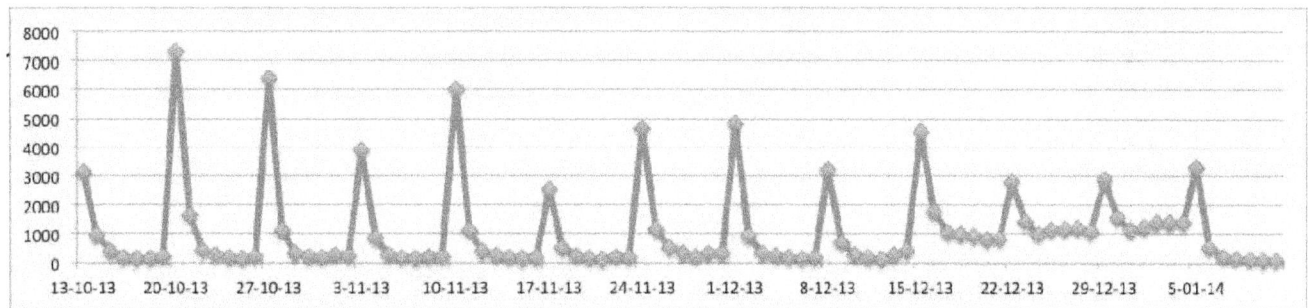

Figure 3: Number of users (y-axis) per day (x-axis) for the "De Ridder" companion app (full season)

"[The video] might be something we'd watch back after the show. But we didn't because you don't think about it anymore. If we would we might have watched it."(Couple 5)

Our producers would like the second screen to become a more permanent experience, with updates that can be revisited between airings of episodes from the show. However, they are aware that now this is rarely the case.

"If you also have a presence before and after the show, you will be more in the picture. If you are only 'there' once a week, it will be more difficult for people to find you again and for you to pull them back in again. But for now people don't 'find' the second screen outside of the show's broadcasts." (B2)

The data from Google Analytics supports the results from our interviews that the content of the second screen companion app is rarely revisited between two episodes. As discussed earlier, the only exception is the Christmas holidays, which shows higher activity between two episodes, but it's unclear if this is because of delayed viewing or because people review the content in the app.

Social interaction
Watching television is often done in a social context, and viewers interact with each other while watching television. Using a second screen companion app could affect the social interaction patterns of users, so we were interested to observe and discuss interaction occurring between the people watching the show in the same room as well as the interaction with remote viewers, be it through the companion app itself or via Facebook or Twitter.

Interaction in the living room
For some couples the updates on the second screen often lead to a comment or discussion. Especially the polls lead to brief conversations.

"It absolutely increases the amount of social interaction. Like with the polls, I always communicate them to [my wife] as well as the percentages after voting. Or like with the information updates or that map which we discussed briefly." (Couple 1)

For many of our participants, the app provided a conversation starter. In the household of Couple 2 for

example, an info update on a court term used in the show leads to a discussion, as do most polls and info updates.

Our producers see opportunities in the way the different devices (first and second screen) are used to accommodate this interaction. The first screen could be used as aggregator for e.g. poll or quiz results, showing joint results from either the household or the public as a whole. The second screen could be used for personal interaction with content (e.g. answering polls), and allows individual activity such as voting or social interaction with the outside world.

"What you miss with just a first screen is the interaction together. But you can solve this by using your phone as a sort of interactive remote with four buttons and everybody can join in on the main screen" (B1)

Remote interaction
The app for "De Ridder" has integrated features to share each update through Twitter or Facebook. However, the participants we interviewed didn't find this a very appealing feature, or at least not one they would readily use.

M: "The sharing or like features are not something we would quickly use. For actualities this might be the case or with [a comedy drama] because the updates there are very funny sometimes." (Couple 5)

Our participants mentioned that when Twitter or Facebook are used during TV watching, the conversations usually do not relate to the show. An exception seems to be news and actualities when they sometimes share opinions. The value of share features seems to very much depend on the content of the show and the updates, and the types of updates in the "De Ridder" app were not considered 'shareable'.

Some of the producers mentioned that social media is very important to stay in touch with their viewers and they use it to display viewers' comments on the main screen or in the app. Other apps (like the "De Ridder" app) offer the possibility to share updates through Twitter or Facebook without showing them directly in the app. Although for broadcasters it is a way to keep connected with their viewers, our participants did not see the value for sharing the content in this specific app.

The data from Google Analytics supports our participants' behaviour and shows that on average 188 items per show were shared (106 via Facebook and 82 via Twitter) on an average of 7529 users per show. So maximum 2,5% of viewers share items, most likely even less assuming that some people share multiple items. It is clear that just introducing a sharing option is not a guarantee for successful social media interaction.

Attention
One of the most discussed aspects of using a second screen application while watching television is how much attention it draws away from the television screen. We observed and talked with our participants about how they experienced the attention they had to pay to the second screen companion app, if they also used other apps on their second screen, and how they managed a good balance between being engaged through or distracted by the second screen companion app.

Attention to second screen companion app
As the second screen companion app presents regular updates, it needs to draw attention to these updates so viewers know when to look at it. Every participant appreciated the timer that indicates when the next update is going to be shown. There is also a sound to call attention to the app if there is an update but most of the participants had the sound of their device switched off. The advantage of the timer is that people know how long it will take before the next update will come and can plan accordingly. One participant even waited before checking on her child that was calling her because an update was very close, and only went there after the update appeared. Most participants glanced regularly at the second screen to check how far the time indicator is to the next update. Another interesting observation was the fact that people were starting to use events on the show as triggers to look for updates on the app. If a character on the show gets a text message or a phone call, the app usually gives an update with the contents of the text message or an indication of who is calling. Some participants started to look immediately at the app when a character received a text message and were even slightly disappointed when there was no accompanying update on the app. In all of those instances, the participants did not use the timer indication for checking if there was a new update.

"You heard the text message on the TV and it showed up on the second screen, it's a reflex. If the cell phone goes off on TV, you can see what the message is." (Couple 4)

Attention to other second screen applications
Our participants used their second screen also for other activities, and not just for consulting the companion app. Usually, one partner of the couple was holding or controlling the second screen device. From the participants that were holding the second screen device, most switched from the "De Ridder" app to a different application (e.g. Facebook or e-mail) on occasion. The reason they gave for this was usually a mutual slowdown in both the show itself

and the updates in the app. The following quote shows that this does have some side effects.

"If there's nothing happening for a while I tend to switch to something else. You might miss some updates then, because you don't switch back to the app in time." (Couple 5)

There are also participants that mentioned they are more engaged with the show thanks to the second screen companion app because they would be tempted to use apps like Facebook, Twitter or email otherwise.

Similarly, our producers believe that a good second screen experience can actually increase the attention of viewers for the show on TV, because the second screen is relevant to the content of the show and viewers will be less prone to watch unrelated content on their second screen device.

"If you offer a good second screen app with a TV show and you can engage viewers through this second screen, you will end up with a more attentive TV viewer." (E)

However, not all program makers share this vision, as they are worried that people will focus too much on the second screen and lose focus for the first.

Distraction vs. Engagement
The main focus of all our participants was still on the program itself and they apply a form of self-regulation in order not to get distracted. When they know a certain update has so much content that it would distract them, they tend to skip that update or just glance over it. A special case is that some updates on the second screen were videos, which leads to a conflict in type of content.

"I didn't open the [movie update] because then you would be watching two videos at the same time. If we'd want to watch these videos, you should actually stop the episode. What would be nice, if you click the video on the second screen, the show on TV would be paused." (Couple 5)

What people do not like is being taken out of the app, as it does not just distracts them, but also breaks their experience.

"We once clicked through for the interactive map, but then you break out of the app. That is a pity and then you're messing with the tablet. [...] In the end I think the overview map is sufficient to situate where it is." (Couple 5)

Our producers are very conscious about the delicate balance between the first and the second screen, especially as program makers do not want their audience to get distracted on purpose. Moreover, as not everyone uses the second screen application, the companion app should not be essential to enjoy the TV program. The general consensus was that a good dialogue between program makers and app developers is crucial to maintain this balance.

"The problem is that many program makers say the group of second screen users is only a small percentage of our viewers and won't change their show just for them." (B1)

Added Value

As a last result, we discuss the added value that the second screen companion app brings to the viewing experience. As the app we used for our study presents specific types of content, we discuss for each of the main types how users perceive their added value, and try to draw more general conclusions from this. The types of updates that are provided throughout the app are character quotes, polls, diegetic content and non-diegetic content.

Character quotes

Character quotes are updates that show quotes made by the characters on the program accompanied by a picture of that character. The consensus among all participants is that, although these updates don't bother them, they also bring very little added value. Only very funny quotes are sometimes appreciated.

"Quotes don't have a lot of added value for us. Maybe if they would be really funny." (Couple 5)

Although presenting quotes from the characters is specific to this show, more generally it shows that people expect their content to give something extra and not just repeat something literally from the television show.

Polls

Polls present the viewer with a question directly related to what happens on the program, and ask the viewers to select from two possible answers. The questions can relate to an action that will occur in the program immediately after the poll (e.g. "Will the car start?") or they can be asking for an opinion (e.g. "Is the sentence these characters received fair?"). The polls cause mixed reactions. Some participants thought the questions were mostly uninteresting, while for others they lead to a short debate nearly every time. In some cases, the polls ask questions about the choices characters should make, but which are quite obvious.

"Of course she will continue, that's the whole show. I click yes anyway but I don't really find it interesting" (Couple 3)

Some participants even felt that giving their opinion on the polls doesn't matter, as it does not influence how the program continues.

Diegetic Content

Diegetic content are updates that originate from characters or events in the program, like text messages that you can hear characters receive and respond to, but that don't get their content shown on TV. It also includes pictures from legal files, characters' Facebook status updates or (fake) newspaper articles about the events in the show. This type of updates is in general very much appreciated by the participants.

"What I really enjoyed were the updates with text messages or telephone messages of the characters. Those are interesting because you get to know a bit more than just from the TV." (Couple 5)

What seems to be appreciated most by the participants is the content and information they receive which they would not have had if they only watched the show.

Non-diegetic content

Non-diegetic content refers to updates that provide information that relates to the show but doesn't originate from the characters themselves. In "De Ridder", these are often explanations of legal terms, information on music played, or updates with maps from the locations that are visited in the show. These updates are appreciated a lot by the participants as well, if they are not too long. Information updates for example usually have a short description of a term and a foldout with more elaborate information.

"With information updates it depends on the content. If we don't know the term, it is interesting and we will at least read the 'basic part'. It is a good feature in any case." (M, Couple 5)

Some participants also mentioned that they would not mind even more information that isn't directly story related, like information on actors. A recurring discussion between many of the couples would be about an actors name or where they had seen him/her before.

DISCUSSION AND CONCLUSION

As second screen apps – and companion apps in specific – are becoming mainstream, we can gradually get more insights into what works and what does not work in practice. The results from our study indicate several aspects that need attention when developing such apps, and that can guide their development. We therefore present in this section some lessons learned and implications for design.

Discoverability is an important concern of people creating the second screen applications. If the app is not well announced on screen, people will not know it is there. The next step is providing a very low threshold for accessing the app, without barriers such as downloads, installations or registration, in order to reach a sufficient number of users to make the app deployment financially viable. Moreover, second screen companion apps should also take into account changing habits surrounding television watching, such as delayed viewing, and not only offer synchronized experiences in a live situation but also when watching delayed. This conflicts with the wish from most broadcasters to keep their audience watching live, but it's a reality that cannot be ignored either. A compromise could be to add extra interactivity during a live broadcast, but still offer a (reduced) synchronized experience when watching delayed. Both broadcasters and app developers are interested in keeping the audience engaged with the content spanning multiple episodes or between broadcasts, but our results show that for this the app should offer added value beyond the actual show.

The app used in our study stimulated social interaction in the living room, by offering polls or other types of information that served as conversation starters. This area of research is still underexplored, although it holds a lot of potential to create social TV applications that do not just focus on interaction with the outside world via social media, but also with the people you are watching TV with. Standards such as HbbTV make it possible to join results from several second screens in one room (or even beyond) and provide them as grouped personalized information on the main screen. This could stimulate social interaction in the living room even further. From our results it is clear however that just introducing social media features is not sufficient to make people share, the content itself has to be shareable as well, i.e. be relevant enough for people that are not watching the show themselves.

The most crucial aspect of developing second screen applications is finding the right balance between engagement and distraction. A companion app, especially in the context of TV fiction, should engage viewers with the show and not distract them so they cannot follow the plot anymore. Content updates should not be too long, videos are not useful as they cannot be watched at the same time and are not revisited, and viewers should not have reason to break out of the app. As the second screen device itself offers other opportunities for distraction as well, the companion app updates should be closely matched with the pacing of the show itself.

Finally, we looked at which types of content viewers find most interesting and adding value to their experience. Updates that literally repeat what happens on-screen are quickly dismissed, while extra information (diegetic and non-diegetic) that offers something extra is much appreciated. Polls that are relevant to the show and are not too obvious are also appreciated, and as an extra benefit stimulate social interaction in the living room (see above).

To conclude, we have offered more insight into how viewers are experiencing second screen companion apps, and contrasted this with the perspective of producers of such applications and actual usage data. Our study shows that second screen companion apps for fiction shows hold promise, but that there are several design choices that can make or break their success. In future work we will design a new second screen companion app based on these recommendations, and validate this in large field trials.

ACKNOWLEDGMENTS

The research leading to these results was carried out in the TV-Ring project (EC grant agreement ICT PSP-325209).

REFERENCES

1. Basapur, S., Mandalia, H., Chaysinh, S., Lee, Y., Venkitaraman, N., & Metcalf, C. (2012). FANFEEDS: Evaluation of Socially Generated Information Feed on Second Screen As a TV Show Companion. In *Proc. of the 10th European Conf. on Interactive TV and Video* (pp. 87–96). New York, NY, USA: ACM.

2. Cesar, P., Bulterman, D. C., & Jansen, A. J. (2008). Usages of the Secondary Screen in an Interactive Television Environment: Control, Enrich, Share, and Transfer Television Content. In *Proc. of the 6th European Conf. on Changing Television Environments* (pp. 168–177). Berlin, Heidelberg: Springer-Verlag.

3. Cauberghe, V., & De Pelsmacker, P. (2006). Opportunities and thresholds of advertising on interactive digital TV: a view from advertising professionals. *Journal of Interactive Advertising*, 7(1), 21–37.

4. Cruickshank, L., Tsekleves, E., Whitham, R., & Hill, A. (2007). Making Interactive TV Easier To Use: Interface Design For A Second Screen Approach. *The Design Journal*, 10(3).

5. Darnell, M. J. (2007). How Do People Really Interact with TV?: Naturalistic Observations of Digital TV and Digital Video Recorder Users. *Comput. Entertain.*, 5(2).

6. Holmes, M. E., Josephson, S., & Carney, R. E. (2012). Visual Attention to Television Programs with a Second-screen Application. In *Proc. of the Symposium on Eye Tracking Research and Applications* (pp. 397–400). New York, NY, USA: ACM.

7. Jensen, J. F. (2005). Interactive Television: New Genres, New Format, New Content. In *Proceedings of the Second Australasian Conference on Interactive Entertainment* (pp. 89–96). Sydney, Australia, Australia: Creativity & Cognition Studios Press.

8. Lochrie, M., & Coulton, P. (2012). Sharing the Viewing Experience Through Second Screens. In *Proceedings of the 10th European Conference on Interactive TV and Video* (pp. 199–202). New York, NY, USA: ACM.

9. Murray, J., Goldenberg, S., Agarwal, K., Chakravorty, T., Cutrell, J., Doris-Down, A., & Kothandaraman, H. (2012). Story-map: iPad Companion for Long Form TV Narratives. In *Proc. of the 10th European Conf. on Interactive TV and Video* (pp. 223–226). New York, NY, USA: ACM.

10. Robertson, S., Wharton, C., Ashworth, C., & Franzke, M. (1996). Dual Device User Interface Design: PDAs and Interactive Television. In *Proceedings of the SIGCHI Conference on Human Factors in Computing Systems* (pp. 79–86). New York, NY, USA: ACM.

11. Ursu, M. F., Thomas, M., Kegel, I., Williams, D., Tuomola, M., Lindstedt, I., & Hall, N. (2008). Interactive TV Narratives: Opportunities, Progress, and Challenges. *ACM Trans. Multimedia Comput. Commun. Appl.*, 4(4), 25:1–25:39.

12. van Dijk, J. A. G. M., & de Vos, L. (2001). Searching for the Holy Grail Images of Interactive Television. *New Media & Society*, 3(4), 443–465.

Many-Screen Viewing: Evaluating an Olympics Companion Application

Edward Anstead[1]   Steve Benford[1]   Robert J. Houghton[2]

[1.]Mixed Reality Lab, [2.] Human Factors Research Group,
University of Nottingham, Nottingham, UK.
{firstName.lastName} @nottingham.ac.uk

ABSTRACT

The trend of users integrating second screen behaviours in their viewing habits, and practitioners' interest in designing systems to support them has evolved a strong research agenda. In this paper we extend these ideas to explore many-screen interaction, investigating how users, gathered around the television with multiple second screen devices, share, control and coordinate their interactions. We report on a formative evaluation into behaviours with a many-screen prototype app for watching sport programming. The Olympics Second Screen application allows users to watch, share and control highlight programmes in a collocated group. We discuss our findings through recommendations to designers and HCI practitioners. Our results suggest the importance of supporting parallel viewing between collocated viewers, and sharing and queuing of programming between devices. Additionally, results highlight the significance of the television in a viewing ecology, and user awareness of control and interaction.

Author Keywords

Second Screen; Multiscreen; iTV; User Experience

ACM Classification Keywords

H.5.m. Information interfaces and presentation (e.g., HCI): Miscellaneous.

INTRODUCTION

There is a growing trend for employing multiple screens for television viewing, augmenting the traditional TV screen with tablets and phones. This movement has been identified by a range of authors from academia [9] and industry [28], who have variously attempted to rationalise these new multiscreen viewing behaviours, revealing how they empower the user to "control, transfer, enrich, and share" [8] television viewing.

Much of this work has focused on the ad-hoc use of second screens by viewers [14,18] as they engage in media 'stacking' and 'meshing' [25]. Other work has focused on the explicit design of second screen companion applications that bring

additional interactive functionality to television programmes, for example content to deepen a viewer's knowledge of characters [21], supplementary web media about the themes, topics or the actors in a programme [1], enabling viewers to share opinions and judgements through social media [2], and to access Electronic Programme Guides (EPGs) [10].

Other studies have investigated sports programming and the interplay between user-generated content, professional broadcasting and the experience of being at an event [12, 5]. Significantly, CoStream@home [12] shared user-generated video of an event and spectators' reactions between viewers at home and spectators in the stadium. Home users interacted with a second screen display merging this content with professional video. The authors present a technical implementation and a research agenda that includes embedding these interactions into the social setting of viewing.

This research has been mirrored by developments in the broadcast industry where a growing number of second screen applications are being commercially deployed (e.g., In the UK 'The Million Pound Drop' [15] and 'Antiques Roadshow' [3] in the UK both offer apps that allow viewers to play along). In spite of this wealth of technical implementation and user experience research, little has been reported about how we might understand and design for situations in which groups of viewers gather around a television and interact with multiple second screens. These we refer to as many-screen applications. How might such groups coordinate their viewing and interactions when using multiple second screen devices? How will this impact on their social interaction, and what kinds of shared companion apps might be appropriate? We therefore present a formative user study to reveal the design issues that arise when complex ecologies of devices are used for many-screen television viewing. We describe the design of a prototype 'Olympics' application that allowed collocated viewers to follow multiple simultaneous channels of sports events and associated statistics, switching them between different devices and backwards and forwards in time. We present the results of a study in which users were observed interacting with first one, then two, and then three companion devices. We conclude with a series of recommendations for the design of many-screen viewing applications.

STUDY DESIGN

Our study was designed to collect formative user observations and opinion on the impact of a many-screen application on collective viewing of sports programming. Through both industry engagement and the development process, 3 specific research objectives came into focus that have guided our discussion and conclusions. Firstly, *(1)* how might programming and supplementary media be shared between a group of collocated viewers on a collection of devices, *(2)* how do collocated viewers consume a schedule of television programming and associated many-screen content across an ecology of devices that changes size, and *(3)* how does the many-screen approach alter the viewing experience, beyond dual screen and more traditional viewing practices?

To answer these questions, we first constructed a prototype sports companion app as described below. We then studied this app being used by groups of three viewers at a time, who were given increased access to display devices. We recorded user interactions on video and interviewed them as a group afterwards to discuss their experiences. We conducted these formative investigations in a laboratory setting, which permitted the close observation of user activities and allowed for the study to be constrained to the precise behaviours of our interests, specifically the introduction of additional screens during the study period and the availability of content.

Industry Engagement

The study was developed during a period of immersion within a corporate setting in order to foreground industry relevance. The BBC's R&D lab was approached due to their extensive experience within the multiscreen context. Over recent years they had deployed several multiscreen applications, maintained a research interest in their development, and were keen to prototype and investigate the potential of second screen technology, especially for use in sports broadcasting. Academic literature also supports sport as a salient genre for the development and user acceptability of second screen programming[16]. The development process was informed through a series of formal discussions with both sports producers and software developers. The purpose of these discussions was (a) to highlight and respond to the issues surrounding second screen systems and (b) to establish relationships that would allow for an on-going, iterative design process.

Prior to our engagement with the BBC they had received critical acclaim for their broadcasting of the 2012 Olympic Games and were keen to build on these achievements. At peak times during the Olympiad they broadcasted 26 simultaneous video feeds. We took this as an opportunity to engage with the possibilities around a multisport tournament, where the action unfolds concurrently across a number of different events. We therefore built an application that would allow for the watching of highlights of the Olympic games across a number of devices, while also supporting additional statistics synchronised with the video programming.

Application design

The prototype Olympics Second screen system is comprised of three separate applications that communicate with each

other: a television that can display a single video stream; a remote control app for switching the television channel; and a second screen app that runs on a tablet and that can simultaneously display other video streams and/or associated statistics. In the study, the television application was deployed through a desktop PC (also running the server) connected to a large flat screen, while the remote was deployed to a smartphone and the second screen app to a 9-inch tablet.

To allow for rapid prototyping, each of these components was built using HTML5 web standards, communicating through a server that delivered the video and supplementary content, keeping the components in sync with each other.

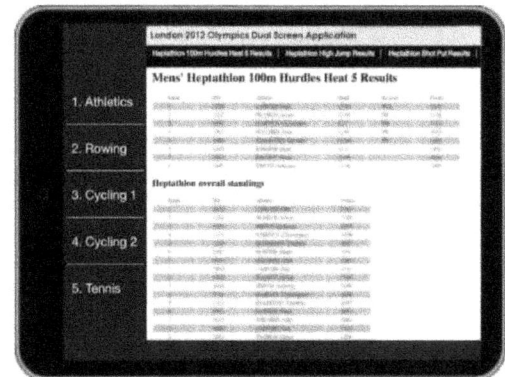

Figure 1: Olympics Tablet Application

Our study applications provided the following functionality:

'Broadcast' a schedule of television programming: The application recreated the effect of a broadcast so that programmes of highlights were only available to users to select and watch at specific times. Each channel therefore had a 'live playhead'. Unlike a regular playhead, which increases with user progress through a video. The live playhead charts time passing, again allowing for a replication of a live broadcast. If the user selected to watch a particular channel, the video would start playing from the live playhead.

Control the television from a second screen and remote application: Both the remote and second screen applications could control the television. Both devices allowed the user to pause, rewind and fast-forward the video. Fast-forwarding was only an available option however when the user had rewound the programme, as would be expected from a PVR on a live television broadcast. The second screen application offered a richer selection of control options for selecting a programme than the remote, which only allowed users to watch programmes from the live playhead. On the tablet application, users could select between watching a programme from the start, resuming where they were last watching (on either the second screen or the television) or from the live playhead.

Augment video programmes with statistics and other relevant information: Each of the available programmes of highlights had an associated feed of statistical updates about the events in the video. These updates were available to users on the second screen app and were only available after the event had been watched on the television or the tablet.

Video could be played on the second screen application and the television: In addition to the second screen application being used to view statistics and control the television, users were able to watch the video content directly on the device.

Multiple second screen applications could be connected to the television: The system was designed so that any number of second screen application instances could be connected to the television. In the user trial discussed here, users had access to between 1 and 3 second screen applications at a time.

Application Content

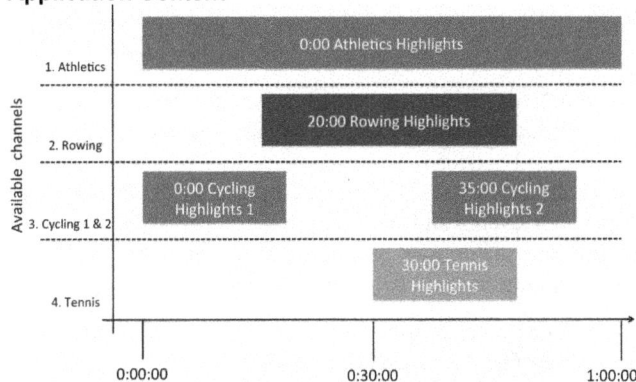

Figure 2: Application Trial Programme Schedule

For our study, we constructed 5 channels of content, Athletics, Rowing, Cycling 1 and 2, and Tennis. Each of these feeds consisted of edited video highlights from the London 2012 Olympics along with an associated statistics feed, which contained a series of updates on events results and additional stories about the video feed. For the purposes of our study, this content was scheduled to generate a 'golden hour', where the most exciting moments would coincide across different channels, requiring our viewers to make decision about which to watch and how best to employ their various second screen devices. Our study was conducted approximately one year after the games, and while we were therefore unable to encapsulate the excitement of witnessing the games live, our study schedule allowed for the replication of a highlights broadcast. Many of the study participants relished the opportunity to revisit the events and to see moments that they had missed during the Olympiad. The programming was also scheduled to play out during the trial so not all of the channels were available at the same time, as shown in Figure 2. Finally, the application would not allow viewers to fast-forward beyond the current 'live' playhead as this schedule unfolded.

STUDY PROCEDURE

At the start of the trial, the workings of the application were explained to the participants and they had the opportunity to ask questions about its functionality. While the researcher prepared the application the participants were asked to discuss, with the help of the programme schedule, how they would make use of the time they had to watch, stating

preferences and organising content between devices. Participants were then asked to watch Olympic Highlights for approximately 50 minutes, attempting to watch as much content as they could in the time. At the start of the trial period participants had access to a single tablet, the television and remote control. An extra tablet was given to the participants to use 20 minutes into the trial and then another tablet at 35 minutes. We also provided a pair of headphones with each tablet, although it wasn't indicated when or whether participants should use them. We video taped our participants using one camera located below the television set pointing back at them and another behind them looking over their shoulders, to maximise coverage of their activities, providing us with views of their interactions with each other and also with the various tablets.

At the end of the study period participants were asked to complete a short semi-structured interview, explaining their experiences with the application. Questions centred on user opinion of the application, how they managed the content across the devices and what they believed to be the effect of adding additional tablets during the trial.

The assembled data was analysed thematically. Coding key moments of interaction, collaboration and user error from the trial video recordings. Additionally, user opinion and reflections were codified from the interview data. These nodes were subsequently ordered into high-level categories. In the following section we report on the key themes that emerged from this analysis.

RESULTS

30 participants, 16 male and 14 female, completed the study. We recruited participants in groups of three, who knew one another well and watched TV together. Three groups were comprised of work colleagues (groups 1, 2 and 9), a further three groups of students (6, 8 and 10) and 4 groups of friends (3, 4, 5 and 7). All participants were aged between 16 and 65 and experienced with smart devices. We asked users to talk about their experiences of second screening. In all groups at least 2 participants responded that they used their devices while watching, to augment viewing, by playing along or looking up further information. However, only 2 participants had used dedicated second screen applications.

We begin by summarising their general opinions about the application before focusing in greater detail on how users organised their local ecology of devices, how they shared devices and how they used them to control the content.

General opinions
General responses to the application were broadly favourable from the large majority (27) of participants who could see it being embedded in their television viewing practices when watching the Olympics or indeed, when viewing in general. Several responded that they could imagine using the application in a family situation where they were balancing viewing tensions between them. For example S102 (study

group 10 participant 2) describes how she could imagine using the tablet to watch the gymnastics allowing S101 the television for watching athletics. S31 and S21 highlighted how the application's stats feature could be part of a more social experience.

S21 "The TV is inherently social. Everyone sits down together the bits of the application that go with that are being able to look up stats and negotiating what goes on the main screen."

Three of the participants offered negative opinions. Two were reticent to engage with the multiple features of the application, describing a desire to just watch television without interference from the tablet:

S91:"television would be the main focus [...] If I was with other people. Say in your living room watching something. My principle concern would not to look like I was distancing myself from them by bringing that out [point to tablet.] Unless we had said 'ooh about such and such, lets look it up'".

A further participant criticised the inability of the application to capture the wealth of information about events above those offered by services on the open Web.

Broadly speaking, other participants were more positive. Nine stated that they found the statistics feature to be a welcome addition to the Olympics experience, offering more depth than the TV programme alone could provide, reinforcing findings from earlier studies, such as of Basapur *et al.*'s companion device [1]. Positive opinions were also shared on the application's ability to offer the individual user more freedom in viewing within the group, such as being able to control the television from each device and watch what they wanted on the tablet. In the following sections, we look beyond this initial feedback to describe participant behaviour and opinions central to the research objectives on many-screen television watching.

Ecology size, sociality and the arrangement of devices
As the trial progressed and the number of tablets available to participants increased, the configurations employed and the sociality of users changed. 8 groups of participants responded positively to the increase in the number of tablets, stating a preference for the individual experience, the freedom of making their own selection, and a sense that they weren't keeping others away from a limited resource.

S12: "At the start with the iPad I shared out info which people asked for or I found interesting, when more came in I hogged the one tablet"
S13: "In real life you would always want your own iPad you wouldn't want to be sharing it"

As well as highlighting a preference for having more tablets available, this quote is also indicative of behavioural differences between users sharing a tablet and having one each. When the participants only had access to one tablet, we observed a number of sharing practices where the group decided who would use the tablet, and they would be called

upon by others to relay additional information about what they were watching as a group on the television (we discuss this in greater depth in the section titled Focus and sharing). As the number of tablets increased this sociality was observed to decrease; in instances where all three participants were using a tablet to either watch video or reading statistics, they appeared to be more isolated from each other.

One user felt that the social situation in which they were watching would influence how available tablets would be utilised. This suggested that limited access to tablets could spark sibling disputes, as they fought over getting to use the tablet, and social situations where the sharing of information between friends would be used to spark discussion and debate.

S53: "If you had the one tablet and you were siblings that you would probably fight over it [...] but if you were mates"

Additionally, when faced with a single tablet, participants were forced to more carefully consider how the devices were distributed between them and which devices the content was played on. Group members stated preferences for particular sports or events and the group tried to accommodate these while organising who was going to use the tablet and what was playing on the television.

S31: "if we start by somebody watching cycling on the tablet and two of us watch athletics on there."[...]
S33: "can I have the tablet?"

The role of the television
For many users the TVs role in the ecology was as the 'big screen', the preferred focal point for viewing, if it could be negotiated between users. When important events such as the men's 100m final were coming up, users would switch from watching on the tablet to the TV if they could.

S13 (watching on the tablet): "The men's 100m is coming up"
S11 (Holding the remote): "let me know if you want it on the big screen"

This interchange was typical of discussions around the men's 100m final, often seen as the most prestigious event of summer Olympic games. It is worthy of note that all our study groups watched this event on the television during the evaluation.

Headphones and sound
where both devices where generating sound, participants had issues with sound overload when trying to watch video simultaneously on the television and on the tablet. 7 of the 10 study groups experienced this issue. Different strategies were however adopted to rectify the problem. Group 2, for example, attempted to balance sound across each device so that the tablets were loud enough to hear, but did not disrupt the television. However this approach was quickly dismissed and headphones were used. Alternately, groups 9 and 10 turned the volume down on the tablets and used them just as visual video displays, relying on the on-screen graphics for contextual information. In all other instances however groups

opted to use the headphones that were provided to watch the video feeds on the tablets.

S41: "It's a bit much if you've got more than one thing going on at once. But the other time using headphones made it feel a bit more asocial than otherwise."

Users wrestled with the sociality of wearing headphones while watching together in a group and our results show a distinct dichotomy. Some felt that the wearing of headphones, so as not to disturb the viewing of others, was the socially responsible action. Five other participants however felt that by isolating themselves from the rest of the group wearing headphones was an antisocial act; one that took them away from communal viewing on the television. 4 users were observed trying to rectify these social issues by wearing the headphones so a can covered one ear only and the other was able to hear the TV and conversations of the other viewers.

Focus and Sharing
We now consider some of the ways in which our participants shared their tablets.

Requesting and showing
We observed two ways in which statistical content available on the tablet was shared between users. The first of these was by request; when a user, who wasn't using a tablet at the time, would ask another user to answer a question for them about what they had seen on TV or to add credence to the discussion the group were having about the events or results.

S103: "so did she win it or not."
S102: "get some stats up"
S101: [looks at the stats feed on their tablet] "she came second [...] they got the same time [...] oh you get get the photo finish."

The second mode of sharing was when a user would see something of interest on the tablet and pass it on to the others. This was also used as a method of scheduling, determining what content to play next on the television or other tablets. Although our application didn't have EPG features, we observed several examples where users would engage in a dialogue about what one another were watching on the tablets, and the availability of channels, when making decisions about what to watch next and how to balance the available content between the devices.

S42: "oh I think this might be it. Yes this is it [men's 100 metres]"
S41: "you want to get it on [the television]"

We recorded a number of ways in which this content was shared between those participants with a tablet and those without; most obvious of those was verbal communication. Other practices were however employed, which maybe of more interest to designers, as participants made use of these personal devices in a much more public way. Frequently, participants would lean in to see what was on another tablet or the tablet would be held out and turned round so that other

participants could see what was on it. We observed this particularly with graphical content on the tablet. Where a photo finish, an image of an athlete or video clip couldn't be fully conferred to the others through explanation.

S23: It looks like a mug shot or something. [S21 leans over to see tablet]
S22: Is that the tennis things
S23: No [shows tablet to S22]

Using the tablet to queue up content for the big screen
Group 10 exhibited a distinctive and especially structured approach towards using tablets in relation to the television, by using the tablet as a preview screen for queuing up what they wanted to see next on the television. While one channel was playing on the TV, the group would have another running on the tablet, which they would keep an eye on from the location of the coffee table. When an upcoming event of interest was spied on the tablet. it would be paused. When the event on the TV was finished, the channel playing on the tablet would be resumed on the television at the same point as it had been paused on the tablet. The channel that had been playing on the TV was then resumed on the tablet and the process would repeat, hopping between the two channels. When an additional tablet was made available to the group, this was used as a further preview screen.

Watching alone
Although sharing was common, it was not always the case as tablets allowed for an individual to be able to watch their choice of video content while the rest of the group watched another channel on the television. This functionality was used by at least 1 participant in 9 of the study groups, at some point in their collective viewing.

Content control
Both the remote control and each tablet offered a mechanism for controlling the television channel and the playhead in the video stream. During interview S72 referred to this as "a bombardment of controlling the same thing in many different ways". During our study this led to users from 5 groups being unable to identify who was making changes to the state of the content on the television. For example, if a user was interacting with the tablet and another made a change to the television station they would become concerned that they had inadvertently changed the TV station by mistake.

S82: Oh what's happened there was that me
S81: Was that you. Did you do that [S83 nods]
S82: Ok just making sure that wasn't me

While mistaken actions and confusion between control mechanisms was characteristic of several groups' experiences, some used this for mischievous ends. S83 for example subjected his colleagues to multiple renditions of 'god save the queen', strategically rewinding so that the medal ceremony looped repeatedly. This was compounded as other members of the group realised that removing the remote control from the offending participant didn't stop their behaviour, as they could use the tablet in the same way. S23 and S22 referred to this as S21 "Still having the power" despite them having removed the remote from his reach. During the interview S13 talks about how he could see the applications and the multiple points of control as being the "source of fights" with friends while watching, suggesting also that the amount of simultaneous choice leads to everyone having to make compromises about what and when they watch certain events.

Liveness

The application allowed participants to pause, rewind, fast-forward and play TV channels independently on different devices. This led to users from half (5) of our groups having issues with comprehension both when they were watching live and when they were watching 'replayed' (somewhere behind the live playhead) events. Part of the problem was the lack of visible representation of where they were in each video, as the application didn't offer visibility of the video playhead, relative to the live playhead, or of overall progress through the programme. This also led to confusion as to whether the fast forward functionality was available. We observed 7 groups try to fast-forward beyond the live playhead in an attempt to skip past programming that they were not interested in, unaware that they were already watching live.

This confusion around liveness and a lack of its visibility were especially apparent when a viewer switched the television to a channel that another was already watching on the tablet, where either of these devices was not watching at the live playhead. This could cause the especially painful problem of 'spoilers', in which one device would prematurely reveal the result of an event that was being watched on another device. For example while watching the athletics on their tablet, participant S82 rewound to get back to the start of an event. Sometime later, their colleague S81 changed the TV channel to the athletics as well, but in 'live mode'. As a result, S82 got to see the result of the event too early. Group 7 experienced similar problems where the television channel was changed while S71 was watching the same channel, leading to the exclamation "they are happening at the same time but different times".

DISCUSSION

We organise our discussions around five key implications for the designers of many-screen television applications, grounded in our findings on the nature of watching television across a number of devices. We draw upon literature from iTV, mobile television and broader HCI fields to substantiate our proposals. We also suggest several avenues our findings suggest for future research in this field.

1. Support parallel viewing: At first glance, the desire to concurrently view a programme on a personal device *and* a television, whilst collocated with other viewers, seems an unlikely use case. However, the majority of the participants in our evaluation responded positively to this functionality and could envisage usage scenarios where this style of interaction

was a welcome addition to their television viewing experience. This finding is supported by D'heer *et al.* [13], who allowed users to consume their personal viewing choices alone, while still being a part of the living room family dynamic.

As was seen in our evaluation, the watching of video on the television, simultaneously with other devices, raises issues with the delivery of audio. Previous work in the mobile television field has reported a user dislike for wearing headphones while watching the TV [7,20]. Whilst it wasn't many of our users' first choice, headphones quickly became the chosen option. However, users did try and utilise the headphones in ways that allowed them to remain a part of the wider sociality of the experience, with some users abandoning headphones altogether and watching the video feeds on the tablet without any sound. Users who adopted this behaviour found it to be an acceptable way to watch sport programming, relying instead upon on-screen graphics.

Not only did supporting parallel viewing afford viewers opportunities for agency in what they were watching, potentially balancing domestic tensions, but it also provided a unique method of television scheduling. We discuss the consequence of this in the next implication.

2. Support Scheduling, Queuing and Sharing: Unlike other studies into EPGs, which provide mechanisms by which users could see what events and programming were about to start [10], the Olympics application did not offer this feature. Instead, users engaged with content on the tablet, through both the video and statistical feeds, utilising the range of control mechanisms on the tablet and remote applications to ensure that the most exiting content was shared on the television for all to watch and enjoy.

Complex viewing behaviours, most notably that of queuing, were enabled by the applications 'resume' feature, allowing the user to resume playback from the tablet on the TV, and from the TV on the tablet. This feature was particularly important in allowing users the freedom to schedule their viewing across the feeds, ensuring they saw as many key events as possible. However, users suggested the option to play content on the TV or the tablet from the start of an event, offering a potentially more elegant solution. In light of this, we would recommend in building-in a resume playback function between devices, or a mechanism by which viewers could skip to key moments of the action. This feature offers the desirable opportunity to allow users to perform ad-hoc scheduling of content as the situation unfolds. Subsequently we see opportunities that build on this functionality, especially in relation to complex sequencing of sports events observed in our participant groups such as groups 10, who queued up the next event on the tablet before switching the television to it at the next opportune moment. In this context interactive mechanisms would allow users to collaboratively generate playlists of events and content they wish to see.

Our ecology of tablets was "fluidly" coupled. This, in theory, allowed users to make use of as many as they desired. Our evaluation suggests a relationship between the availability of tablets and sociality. Where viewers were sharing the tablet between them there was an enhanced sense of sociality, more sharing and discussions. Therefore, restricting the number of tablets that can be used in a given situation may allow designers the opportunity to play with the social dynamics of the viewing groups. Terrenghi, *et al.* [27] summarise that an understanding of the scale of a display ecosystem can be helpful in establishing the design space. Our finding mirrors this idea, suggesting that being able to tailor the ecology to specific numbers of devices may be helpful in informing the design of effective socially grounded systems.

3.Maintain User Awareness and Respect the Big Screen: Users struggled to understand which of them was controlling the TV when presented with a range of devices, all of which were capable of making these changes. In preceding HCI literature on awareness, Bier & Freeman [6] suggest the concept of per-user feedback, highlighting the user making changes on the communal display groupware device. Projecting which user or device initiated an action on the television is a potential solution to this problem. However this raises further design issues and opportunities. We witnessed 'bad behaviour' by several participants, exerting too much control on the television and our participants observed that this might arise in 'real life' situations, such as squabbling children. Future work could look at design solutions that mitigate this kind of conduct and better democratise viewing between the group members.

The television has long since been considered as a cornerstone of domestic life and plays a key role in the social environment that surrounds it. Not only does its physical presence in a room play a part in the home but also the content that is broadcast through it [26]. Silverstone's descriptions of the TV in the domestic environment describe it as a slowly evolving landscape. While a minority of our participants responded negatively to the intrusion of the tablet application into their television watching practice, this was not a view shared by all. For many though, more ready to accept the opportunities of many-screen viewing, the television was still principle within the hierarchy of viewing devices that users interacted with. The big screen was always the preferred place to watch the most significant events and exciting moments.

4.Acknowledge Liveness and the Impact of Spoilers: We observed users struggling to establish a sense of whether they were watching live or whether they were watching from an earlier location in the video programme. As discussed in the previous discussion point, these issues might be ameliorated by improved feedback to the user, informing them whether they are watching live and any impact this has on fast-forward functionality. Issues of liveness led to instances where viewers were potentially seeing spoilers on the television of events they had yet to see on the tablet. The impact of spoilers has been considered, given the distribution of PVR systems and social media services [22,23]. Our findings suggest that spoilers can come from other places, for example where multiple users are simultaneously watching the same programme, at different points in the narrative, on different devices. Designers of many-screen apps could use a number of strategies to reduce the possibilities of users seeing spoilers, either by blocking future content on the television until all users have caught up, or by providing adequate warning to viewers of potential spoilers.

5.Recognise the Complexity of Gesture and Attention: O'Hara *et al.* [24] reflect on the complex uses of personal mobile devices and their utilisation with video, in the home. They found that often the experience of watching is not limited to the individual user, but is shared in complex ways. We witnessed participants behaving similarly, both with video content and the statistical feeds in the application. They would shift focus and move in closer to see the relatively small screen, or it would be held aloft by users to show others what they were seeing, diverting attention away from the television.

This has implications for technologies that try to track the viewer's gaze. Prior work in the television literature has focused on attention as an important factor in measuring the impact of programming and advertising. Often these investigations have used gaze tracking as their principle methodology (see [17] for an overview). More recently, gaze detection has been employed in multi-feed sports broadcasting on a single screen [11] and second screen systems [19]. Looking towards the deployment of many-screen television systems, this line of inquiry is evidently a useful direction and one that we are confident will continue. However, we also saw that sharing of content and focus on devices was embedded within the complex social setting of viewing. In applications that make use of complex vision systems to obtain interaction from the user, such as those proposed by Dezfuli *et al.* [12], the system will be required to untangle the mix of social queues and gestures, involving the smart devices and those which are intended to address the ecology and instigate action [4]. The design opportunities for fostering these systems will come from a deeper understanding of the way content is shared between users and attention and gesture are directed at different devices within a local ecology.

CONCLUSION

We have detailed and discussed the findings of a formative user study into the implications of many-display devices on second screen television viewing. In preparation for our study we developed the Olympics second screen app. The application allowed viewers to revisit highlights of the 2012 Games across a range of devices. Our findings lead to five implications for designers and practitioners involved in the development of these systems, which came to the fore through our work. We observed a number of ways in which sharing of content was enabled through the use of multiple devices. This led to a recommendation to support viewers in queuing up content on a tablet before then 'pushing' it to the big screen of the television for communal watching. Parallel viewing was observed to be a further way in which users enriched the experience of watching together. Enabling viewers to watch alone and have agency over the second screen device, even in the collocated environment, was positively received, in certain social settings. These practices however resulted in challenges to users' understanding of liveness. They struggled to maintain comprehension as to the point they were watching in the broadcast across several devices, between multiple participants. These behaviours therefore highlight the importance of on screen viewer feedback in reducing user confusion and avoiding the possibility of spoilers.

ACKNOWLEDGMENTS

We would like to thank all the study participants and our industry collaborators at BBC R&D North Lab. The first author is supported by RCUK (Grant No. EP/G037574/1)

REFERENCES

1. Basapur, S., Harboe, G., Mandalia, H., Novak, A., Van Vuong, and Metcalf, C. Field trial of a dual device user experience for iTV. In *Proc. EuroITV'11*, ACM Press (2011), 127-136.

2. Basapur, S., Mandalia, H., Chaysinh, S., Lee, Y., Venkitaraman, N., and Metcalf, C. FANFEEDS: evaluation of socially generated information feed on second screen as a TV show companion. In *Proc. EuroiTV'12,* ACM Press (2012), 87-96.

3. BBC, Antiques Roadshow App. http://www.bbc.co.uk/programmes/b006mj2y/features/play-along-app.

4. Bellotti, V., Back, M., Edwards, W.K., Grinter, R.E., Henderson, A., and Lopes, C. Making sense of sensing systems: five questions for designers and researchers. In *Proc. CHI'02*, ACM Press (2002), 415-422.

5. Bentley, F.R., and Groble M. TuVista: meeting the multimedia needs of mobile sports fans. In *Proc MM '09*, ACM Press (2009), 471-480

6. Bier, E.A. and Freeman, S. MMM: A user interface architecture for shared editors on a single screen. In *Proc. UIST'91*, ACM Press (1991), 79-86.

7. Buchinger, S., Kriglstein, S., and Hlavacs, H. A comprehensive view on user studies: survey and open issues for mobile TV. *In Proc. EuroITV'09*, ACM Press (2009), 179-188.

8. Cesar, P., Bulterman, D.C., and Jansen, A.J. Usages of the secondary screen in an interactive television environment: control, enrich, share, and transfer television content. In Proc. *EUROITV'08*, Springer-Verlag (2008), 168–177.

9. Courtois, C. and D'heer, E. Second screen applications and tablet users: constellation, awareness, experience, and interest. In *Proc. EuroiTV'12,* ACM Press (2012), 153-156.

10. Cruickshank, L., Tsekleves, E., Whitham, R., Hill, A., and Kondo, K. Making interactive TV easier to use: Interface design for a second screen approach. The Design Journal 10, 3 (2007), 41–53.

11. Cummins, R.G., Tirumala, L.N., and Lellis, J.M. Viewer Attention to ESPN's Mosaic Screen: An Eye-Tracking Investigation. Journal of Sports Media 6, 1 (2011), 23–54.

12. Dezfuli, N., Günther, S., Khalilbeigi, M., Mühlhäuser, M., and Huber J. CoStream@Home: connected live event experiences. In *Proc.* SAM '13, ACM Press (2013), 33-36.

13. D'heer, E., Courtois, C., and Paulussen, S. Everyday life in (front of) the screen: the consumption of multiple screen technologies in the living room context. In *Proc. EuroiTV'12*, ACM Press (2012), 195-198.

14. Doughty, M., Rowland, D., and Lawson, S. Who is on your sofa?: TV audience communities and second screening social networks. In *Proc. EuroiTV'12*, ACM Press (2012), 79-86.

15. Endemol, Be A Contestant The Million Pound Drop. https://www.themillionpounddrop.com/be-a-contestant/.

16. Geerts, D., Cesar, P., and Bulterman, D. The implications of program genres for the design of social television systems. In *Proc. UXTV'08,* ACM Press (2008), 71-80.

17. Hawkins, R.P., Pingree, S., Hitchon, J.B., et al. What Holds Attention to Television? Strategic Inertia of Looks at Content Boundaries. Communication Research 29, 1 (2002), 3–30.

18. Hess, J., Ley, B., Ogonowski, C., Wan, L., and Wulf, V. Jumping between devices and services: towards an integrated concept for social TV. *In Proc. EuroITV'11*, ACM Press (2011), 11-20.

19. Holmes, M.E., Josephson, S., and Carney, R.E. Visual attention to television programs with a second-screen application. In *Proc ETRA'12*, ACM Press (2012), 397–400.

20. Miyauchi, K., Sugahara, T., and Oda, H. Relax or Study?: A Qualitative User Study on the Usage of Mobile TV and Video. In Changing Television Environments. In *Proc. EUROITV'08*, Springer-Verlag (2008), 128–132.

21. Murray, J., Goldenberg, S., Agarwal, K., et al. Story-map: iPad companion for long form TV narratives. In *Proc. EuroiTV'12*, ACM Press (2012), 223-226.

22. Nakamura, S. and Komatsu, T. Study of information clouding methods to prevent spoilers of sports match. In *Proc. AVI'12*, ACM Press (2012), 661-664.

23. Nakamura, S. and Tanaka, K. Temporal filtering system to reduce the risk of spoiling a user's enjoyment. In *Proc. IUI'07*, ACM Press (2007), 345-348.

24. O'Hara, K., Mitchell, A.S., and Vorbau, A. Consuming video on mobile devices. In *Proc. CHI'07*, ACM Press (2007), 857-866.

25. OfCom. *Attitudes to Broadcast Media 2012*. 2013.

26. Silverstone, R. Television And Everyday Life. Routledge, 2004.

27. Terrenghi, L., Quigley, A., and Dix, A. A taxonomy for and analysis of multi-person-display ecosystems. Personal and Ubiquitous Computing 13, 8 (2009).

28. UM. *Little Book of Curiosity Screen Time*. UM, 2012.

Visual Attention Measures for Multi-Screen TV

Radu-Daniel Vatavu
University Stefan cel Mare of Suceava
Suceava 720229, Romania
vatavu@eed.usv.ro

Matei Mancaş
University of Mons
20, Place du Parc, 7000 Mons, Belgium
matei.mancas@umons.ac.be

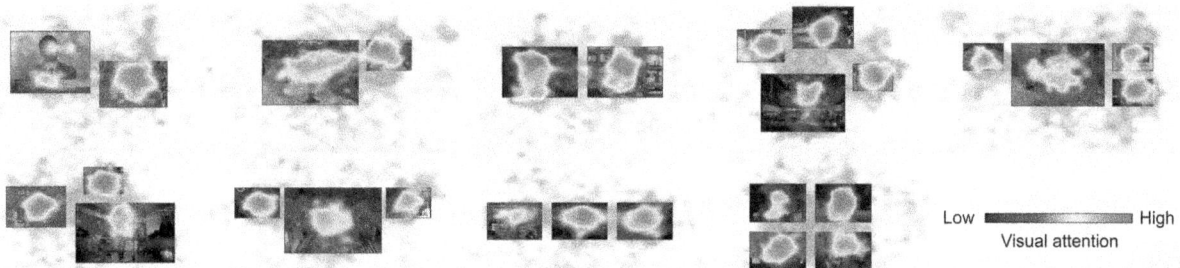

Figure 1. Visual attention heat maps for all nine multi-screen TV layouts evaluated in this study.

ABSTRACT

We introduce a set of nine measures to characterize viewers' visual attention patterns for multi-screen TV. We apply our measures during an experiment involving nine screen layouts with two, three, and four TV screens, for which we report new findings on visual attention. For example, we found that viewers need an average discovery time up to 4.5 seconds to visually fixate four screens, and their perceptions of how long they watched each screen are substantially accurate, *i.e.*, we report Pearson correlations up to .892 with measured eye tracking data. We hope our set of new measures (and the companion toolkit to compute them automatically) will benefit the community as a first step toward understanding visual attention for emerging multi-screen TV applications.

Author Keywords

Visual attention; interactive TV; multi-screen TV; multi-display; eye gaze; eye tracking; measures; evaluation; TLX.

ACM Classification Keywords

H.5.1 Multimedia Information Systems: Evaluation / methodology; Video. H.5.2 User Interfaces: Evaluation / methodology.

INTRODUCTION

Multi-screen systems that customize visual output to more than one screen are able to deliver more content and more control as well as new ways to enrich, share, and transfer content [2]. Due to such particular attractiveness, the multi-screen scenario has been investigated by the HCI community in terms of technical design [20,25] and performance

evaluation [7,16,17,22]. In the context of the interactive TV, today's common implementation of the multi-screen concept is the secondary screen, with tablets used in conjunction with the TV set [2,4]. In a larger context, Vatavu and Mancaş referred to multi-screen TV systems as "TV potpourris", as they represent hybrids of screens with different form factors, layouts, and broadcasted programs and genres [24].

However, beside obvious advantages, more screens also demand higher cognitive load for viewers to understand what they watch, and increased visual attention distributed across displays. Therefore, it is likely for multi-screen TV to increase viewers' visual and cognitive attention load up to the point where the TV experience is no longer pleasant. Unfortunately, such important aspects have not been thoroughly addressed by the TV community up to now. In fact, in a recent work investigating visual attention in multi-display interfaces, Rashid et al. note that "further research is needed to investigate the influence of different categories of content coordination on attention switching and task performance" [17] (p. 4). In this work, we make one step further toward understanding viewers' visual attention patterns for multi-screen TV and, in doing so, we provide the community with a set of general and reusable measures to characterize visual attention for these scenarios.

Our contributions are as follows: (1) we introduce a set of measures that we compute from eye tracking data to characterize viewers' visual attention patterns for multi-screen TV; (2) we use these measures to report new findings on visual attention, such as viewers' subjectively-perceived watching time per screen is substantially accurate; and (3) we provide a toolkit to compute our measures automatically. In the end, we hope this work will benefit researchers and practitioners of the interactive TV community who will employ our measures to further investigate viewers' visual attention behavior for emerging multi-screen TV applications.

RELATED WORK

The simplest form to emulate a multi-screen environment is to define individual screens as part of a video projection, with all screens controlled by the same computer [25]. Alternatively, physical screens can be put together to create multi-screen environments by using platforms that control the distribution of content. Phone as a Pixel is one such platform that can scale up to hundreds of displays [20].

More screens deliver more content and offer more control to viewers. Conversely, they may also have side effects on visual attention and task performance. In this section, we review previous work that showed interest in visual attention in general, but also in conjunction with the TV set.

Multi-screen environments and task performance

Multi-screen environments have been investigated in terms of attention demands [16,17] and their effects on task performance [7,22]. For example, Rashid et al. [16] explored the cost of switching attention between the small display of a mobile device and a large screen, and reported decreased user performance because of the adaptation mechanisms that occur when shifting eye gaze between the two screens. Tan and Czerwinski [22] addressed the effect of visual separation between displays and physical discontinuities, such as monitor bezels. They found that discontinuities do not affect users' performance, but displaying content on screens positioned at different depths has small yet detrimental effects on task performance. Forlines et al. [7] observed participants performing worse during a visual search task when the information was displayed at different rotation angles on four vertical screens than when presented on a single screen. The authors of that study concluded that scanning of multiple views added to the length of the task, but not to its accuracy.

Visual attention

Attention is the cognitive process to selectively interpret information subsets while ignoring others, *i.e.*, to selectively focus on solely one aspect of the environment [1] (p. 519). By definition, attention allows people to focus on a single task at one given time. Sohlberg and Mateer [21] identified five levels of attention, which are focused, sustained, selective, alternating, and divided attention.

Visual attention has been modeled by cognitive psychologists with the spotlight [5] and zoom-lens models [6]. The spotlight model describes attention in terms of focus (*i.e.*, the region from which information is extracted and processed at high resolution), fringe (*i.e.*, the low-resolution extraction of information at the boundaries of the focus region), and margin (the cut-off of the visual attention area). The zoom-lens model [6] upgraded the spotlight model by making it adaptable in size, and thus explained the trade-off in efficiency of processing visual information, *e.g.*, larger the focus, slower the processing will be.

Researchers have also modeled the way the brain attends to stimuli and processes information in what is known as bottom-up and top-down processing [23]. For example, some stimuli attract attention because of their stringent nature (*e.g.*, a quick motion or a telephone ring), which makes our brain process information at a preconscious level. On the other hand, top-down processing represents the act of individuals controlling their attention toward achieving a specific goal. Finally, attention is known to be overt (*i.e.*, when eye gaze attends to some region in space) and covert (mental focus can shift without necessarily moving the eyes) [14]. Overt attention is sequential by using eye saccades (*e.g.*, ballistic movements) and fixations (*e.g.*, the eye gaze stops at some spatio-temporal stable area). In contrast, covert attention can process several stimuli in parallel. Humans are known to be able to simultaneously attend to 7 ± 2 stimuli at once [13].

Visual attention and TV

Researchers have found that individual looks at the TV vary in length and people develop different watching strategies to follow content on TV. For example, people may look at the TV only at the right times, just enough to be aware of what is happening, while being engaged in some other activity. When investigating such phenomena, Geerts et al. [9] found that the genre of TV content correlates with how much people talk during watching TV, and that the plot structure influences talking during social television watching. Such findings reveal the importance of top-down attention during the everyday TV watching experience.

Surprisingly, most TV looks are very short, *e.g.*, 2 seconds, and can be described as mere glances [10]. This fact can be characterized with the "hazard look" function that gives the probability that looks persisting a given length will terminate in the next half second. Once a look begins, it is likely to terminate in the first second, with a hazard peak at 1−1.5 seconds. Hawkins et al. [10] investigated this phenomenon and identified monitoring looks less than 1.5 seconds, orienting looks up to 5 seconds, engaged looks between 6 and 15 seconds, and staring after 15 seconds.

To characterize visual attention, researchers have employed eye tracking devices that accurately follow viewers' eye gaze. For example, Kallenbach et al. [12] used an eye tracker and found that text displayed on TV affects the patterns of visual attention, memory, and cognitive workload more than simple pictorial information does. Holmes et al. [11] examined the visual attention of people watching TV in a secondary-screen scenario and reported that 30% of the attention was allocated to the tablet. In a multi-screen sports study, Cummins et al. [3] found visual attention to vary function of screen size, game play (*i.e.*, action), and repeated exposure. They also reported that viewers had to adopt screen watching strategies to cope with the many pictures displayed simultaneously. Finally, Rashid et al. [17] identified five factors that affect visual attention patterns for multi-display user interfaces, namely display contiguity, angular coverage, content coordination, input directness, and input-display correspondence.

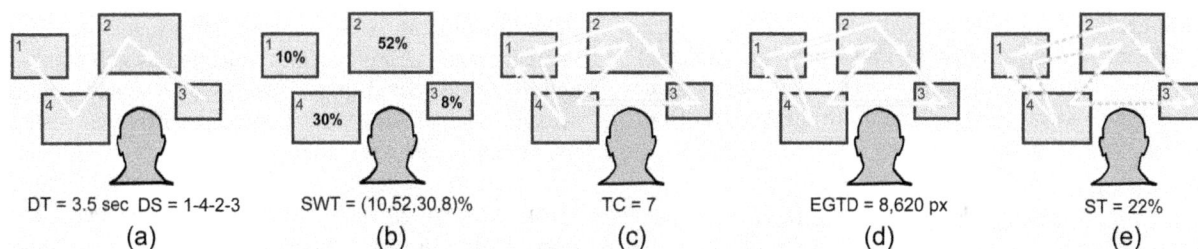

Figure 2. Illustrations of our six *objective* visual attention measures.

VISUAL ATTENTION MEASURES

By following the results of previous work in terms of experimental findings and modeling of visual attention, we define six *objective* measures to characterize viewers' visual attention behavior in the context of multi-screen TV:

1. **Discovery Time (DT)** is defined as the time required for the viewer to make a pass over all TV screens so that each screen has been fixated visually at least once (Figure 2a). DT is the minimum time imperative to understand what is happening on all screens in order to inform what to watch. The discovery time may depend on several factors, such as the number of screens, their layout and form factors, and displayed content.

2. **Discovery Sequence (DS)** is defined as the sequence of screens that was traversed by the viewer's eye gaze during the discovery time (Figure 2a).

3. **Screen Watching Time (SWT)** is the percentage of visual attention devoted by viewers to each TV screen during the monitoring time interval. For example, the SWT distribution for a 3-screen layout may be uniform, with ≈33% of time devoted to each screen, but it may also be non-uniform, with one screen capturing the viewer's visual attention more, such as 60%, 40%, and 10%. SWT may depend on the form factors, screen layout, and the content displayed by the screens, *e.g.*, the larger the screen or more attractive its content, more time will likely be devoted to consume that content. SWT can also be visualized as heat maps (see Figure 1).

4. **Transition Count (TC)** is defined as the number of eye gaze transitions between consecutively fixated TV screens that occurred during the monitoring time interval (Figure 2c). Larger TC values reflect more distributed attention, but may also show design flaws in the layout.

5. **Eye Gaze Travel Distance (EGTD)** represents the total distance travelled by the viewer's eye gaze during the monitoring time interval, expressed in the units reported by the eye tracking equipment, such as pixels (Figure 2d). Different EGTD values may reflect different visual attention patterns, different preferences for some channels over time, and they may possibly correlate with watching fatigue. Real-world distance units, such as centimeters, should be used when measuring EGTD for screens with different pixel pitch densities.

6. **Switch Time (ST)** is defined as the percentage of time during which eye gaze travels between screens (Figure 2e). Large ST values may show flaws in layout design,

e.g., larger the ST value, further apart the screens are located one from the other in that particular layout.

We introduce these six new measures to characterize viewers' TV watching behavior in more nuanced ways, not easily accessible with generic eye gaze heat maps and scan paths. For example, heat maps (as those shown in Figure 1) are generally used to describe the spatial distribution of eye gaze, which is useful for investigating specific elements that attract attention *within* the same screen. However, our SWT measure reflects viewers' allocated watching time for the entire screen with one single value integrating the heat map spatially-distributed data, while TC and ST characterize attention switch *between* screens. Also, DT and DS are computed on top of the scan path to reflect viewers' specific behavior occurring at specific moments, *e.g.*, during discovery of TV content to inform what to watch. Our measures are also flexible in terms of the units of measurement, a choice that we ultimately leave to the practitioner to make. For example, EGTD may be expressed in screen coordinates, such as pixels, or using real-world distance units, such as centimeters or inches. SWT and ST (and also PSWT introduced below) are expressed in this work using percentages that normalize these measures with respect to the entire monitoring time interval of the experiment. However, they could also be expressed using actual time units, *e.g.* seconds or minutes, should the practitioners employing them would actually need precise time values of their viewers' TV watching behavior.

We also define and employ three *subjective* measures:

1. **Perceived Screen Watching Time (PSWT)** is defined as the percentage of the visual attention devoted to each screen during the monitoring interval, as it was perceived by viewers themselves. We show later how subjective PSWT correlates with measured SWT.

2. **Perceived Comfort (PC)** is a subjective assessment of how comfortable the TV layout was for the viewer to watch. PC is measured on a 5-point Likert scale, from 1 to 5: very uncomfortable, uncomfortable, neutral, comfortable, and very comfortable.

3. **Content Understandability (CU)** represents the capacity of the viewers to understand content delivered by the multiple screens of some layout. CU is assessed by asking viewers questions about the content they just watched, and is measured as the percentage of correct answers. For example, in our experiment we asked one question of moderate difficulty for each TV screen.

EXPERIMENT

We conducted an experiment to understand the effect of multiple TV screens on visual attention and to validate our new visual attention measures. To inform the design of our experiment, we first ran a preliminary study.

Preliminary study

Previous work showed that the number of screens, their form factors, and displayed content affect viewers' visual attention patterns. Therefore, we ran a preliminary experiment to inform on the upper limit of the number of TV screens that can be followed comfortably at the same time. Four participants were presented with five TV layouts composed of 2, 4, 6, 9, and 12 screens of equal size arranged in matrix-like configurations. To prevent participants from visually privileging some screens over the others, all the screens displayed non-overlapping sequences extracted from the same movie scene. All video sequences had one minute in length. The audio was turned off. Each participant watched the movies separately (there was no social TV watching).

We found participants generally looking in the center of the matrix layouts trying to cover most of the information within their visual field. While the eye repartition remained well distributed in the case of two and four screens, the central screens took more importance and peripheral screens tended to be ignored for layouts with more than four screens, which confirms the spotlight model [5] for our specific matrix-like screen layouts. Also, participants witnessed that more than two/three screens was too much to follow because they were trying to make sense of the various sequences of the same movie, *i.e.*, putting the pieces together. However, they were interested in multiple screens that would convey *complementary* information to a single, main screen. Therefore, findings revealed that the concept of a primary screen with an easily-identifiable form factor (*i.e.*, larger than all the other screens) is important to understand the layout. These preliminary findings informed the design of our experiment for which we investigated in detail layouts composed of two, three and four TV screens.

Participants

Ten volunteers (one female) participated in the experiment (mean age was 27.9 years, $SD = 3.7$ years). Participants' self-reported daily average time for watching television was 1.5 hours ($SD = 2.1$ hours). All participants had normal or corrected to normal vision.

Apparatus

TV screens were part of a large image (1.30×0.87 meters) that was projected on a wall with a standard projector (24.5 dpi). Participants were seated comfortably in a chair at a distance of 2.30 meters from the projection. Given the fact that the projected screens did not fill the entire projected image, the maximum visual angle was 25° on the x axis. The background of the projection was black, which gave participants the impression of multiple TV screens at the same depth on the same wall. Following the taxonomy of [17], our screen scenario possesses depth contiguity (*i.e.*, all screens are at equal distance from the observer) and visual

field discontinuity (*i.e.*, screens are located in the same vertical plane but are spatially separated, which makes them appear as distinct displays instead of a visual contiguous screen). The movies displayed by each screen lasted one minute each and were prepared in advance. The audio was turned off for all videos in order to isolate the effects of the visual information alone on attention. The FaceLab eye-tracking device[1] was employed during the experiment by following the practices of the visual attention community [8,19] and those of previous experiment designs investigating visual attention for TV [3,11,12].

Design

The experiment was a within-participants design with two independent factors:

(1) TV-COUNT, the number of distinct TV screens, with three values: 2, 3, and 4 screens.
(2) LAYOUT, representing the space arrangement of the TV screens and their sizes. For this factor we designed three distinct conditions: TILED, PRIMARY, and ARBITRARY (Figure 3). In the TILED condition all the screens have equal size and are arranged in a compact order. For PRIMARY, one screen acts as the main screen and is larger than all the rest, equally-sized satellite screens. The ARBITRARY condition shows the screens in arbitrary sizes with a random layout.

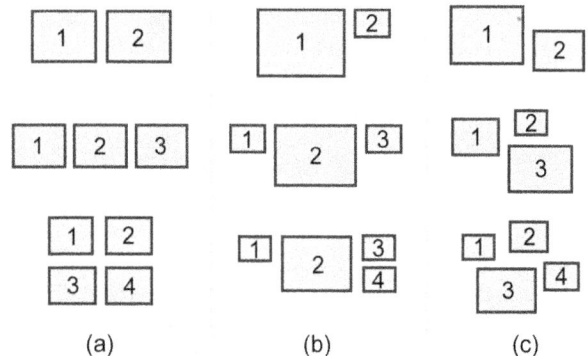

(a)   (b)   (c)

Figure 3. TV layouts for the TILED (a), PRIMARY (b), and ARBITRARY (c) conditions with two, three, and four screens.

TV layouts were created so that the total display area covered by constituent screens would be approximately constant for each layout (*i.e.*, the size of the TV screens was larger for layouts with fewer screens). In the preliminary experiment we displayed movie sequences that were cut from the same movie scene. At that point, we adopted such an approach in order not to bias the visual attention of our participants to only some, presumably more captivating screens. However, we found that people were trying to put the individual movie pieces together in order to understand the full story, generating therefore a different visual attention pattern from what one would normally expect when watching television.

---

[1] The FaceLab system is a head-free eye-tracker. We calibrated the tracker with a 9-dot grid and used it to record eye gaze at a rate of 60 Hz, http://www.seeingmachines.com/product/facelab/

For the full experiment, the TV screens displayed different content. However, we verified the content *a priori* by running a motion detector (frame-to-frame difference) to make sure that the motion level was roughly the same across screens of the same layout.

Task

Participants were asked to watch prerecorded movies for each combination of TV-COUNT and LAYOUT conditions, resulting in a total number of 9 experimental trials per participant corresponding to 9 minutes of watching TV (one minute per condition). Each participant watched the movies separately to eliminate any effect of social watching on attention. Participants were asked to watch the movies as if they were watching their TV at home, and were told they had to answer a questionnaire after each trial in order to ensure a minimal level of attention. Condition order was randomized across participants. After each trial, participants were administered NASA TLX tests[2] (using the computer version available on-line at[3]) to collect workload subjective ratings, and were handed questionnaires to evaluate their understanding of the content they had just watched. At the end of the experiment, participants filled a final questionnaire in which they reported the perceived comfortability (PC) of watching each layout on a 5-point Likert scale, with 1 being very uncomfortable and 5 very comfortable. Participants were also asked to specify the maximum number of TV screens they would feel comfortable watching at the same time (MAX-TV).

RESULTS #1: DISTRIBUTION OF VISUAL ATTENTION FOR MULTI-SCREEN TV

Discovery Time

Our participants systematically discovered all screens before committing to one screen to watch. In general, this process can be very fast and a single eye fixation is usually enough to roughly understanding the topic being watched [15]. Discovery time varied between 0.1 and 15.5 seconds, with a mean time of 2.4 seconds ($SD = 0.3$). We found a significant effect of TV-COUNT on discovery time ($\chi^2(2) = 43.400, p < .001$) showing that more time was needed by participants to visually fixate more screens until all have been discovered (Figure 4a). DT values ranged from 0.8 seconds for two screens up to 4.5 seconds for four screens. A second degree polynomial showed a perfect fit with observed data ($R^2 = 1$), suggesting that discovery time relates to the number of screens in a quadratic manner (DT = $0.70 \cdot$ TV-COUNT$^2 - 0.97 \cdot$ TV-COUNT$+1.10$). There was no significant effect of LAYOUT on DT ($\chi^2(2) = 2.867, n.s.$).

Discovery Sequence

The discovery sequence informs about the order in which screens are visually attended during the discovery time. For two screens, there are only two possible sequences, *i.e.*, 1,2 and 2,1, and we found our participants preferring the former for all layouts, with preference counts of 8 out of 10 for the

TILED layout, 10/10 for PRIMARY, and 9/10 for ARBITRARY. (For convenience, screen numbers are shown in Figure 3.) For three screens, there are 3! = 6 possible sequences, out of which 2,3,1 occurred the most for TILED (5 out of 10), 2,1,3 for PRIMARY (7/10), and no majority preference could be identified for ARBITRARY. For four screens, there are 4! = 24 possible sequences, out of which 1,2,4,3 occurred the most for TILED (4/10), 2,1,3,4 for PRIMARY (4/10) and, again, no majority preference for ARBITRARY (for which 8 different sequences were found among the 10 recordings). These results show that viewers discover screens from left to right for the two screen condition (sequence 1,2), are first attracted by the middle screen when three screens are present (sequences 2,3,1 and 2,1,3), and follow a counter-clockwise pattern (*e.g.*, 1,2,4,3) in the absence of a primary screen to attract attention first (2,1,3,4 for PRIMARY).

The discovery sequence mainly shows the impact of layout. For screens of equal size, a left-to-right model was adopted by our participants, which corresponds to the reading order in Western culture (which was the case for our participants). For the PRIMARY layouts, discovery begins with the larger screen despite it not being the left-most screen. This finding shows that participants immediately identified the largest screen as the main or primary one. The anti-clockwise pattern is also interesting, as it builds on the observed left-to-right model, but also exploits the shortest distance between screens. Consequently, it may represent an instance of the Z-shaped pattern observed during reading [18], but specific for multi-screen TV.

Screen Watching Time

The average percentages of visual attention shared between screens are illustrated in Figure 4e using color codes, with darker values showing more visual attention. We found significant differences for the TILED and PRIMARY layouts and three and four screens, while only the ARBITRARY layout had a significant effect on SWT for two screens. Results show that screen watching time is related to the size of the screen (*i.e.*, the large screen in all the PRIMARY conditions received more visual attention), but also with content, as we later found by asking participants (*e.g.*, participants' visual attention was more attracted by the right screen of the 2-ARBITRARY condition that displayed a bicycle race, instead by the first screen that showed news, resulting in 68% and 31% devoted attention, see Figure 4e).

SWT can be further visualized as heat maps (Figure 1) that use color codes to describe gaze density spatially along the screen area size. When all screens are of equal size, the gaze density reflects the SWT values exactly (*e.g.,* low color density for the first screen, larger for the central, and moderate for the third in the 3-TILED condition, see both Figures 1 and 4e). However, in the PRIMARY condition, the gaze density color of the largest screen has lower maxima, as gaze is distributed across a larger area (larger coverage).

Transition Count

The number of eye gaze transitions between screens varied from 11 to 200 for the entire watching time of one minute,

---

[2] http://humansystems.arc.nasa.gov/groups/tlx/
[3] http://www.keithv.com/software/nasatlx/

with a mean value of 64.8 transitions ($SD = 28.9$). We found significant effects (at $p < .001$) for both TV-COUNT ($\chi^2(2) = 41.667$) and LAYOUT ($\chi^2(2) = 10.237$, with no significant difference between TILED and PRIMARY for LAYOUT). Figure 4b reveals an expected yet strong positive correlation ($R^2 = 1$) between TV-COUNT and TC: more screens determine more transitions during the first minute of watching (TC $= 20.5 \cdot$ TV-COUNT $+ 23.9$). We also found that the ARBITRARY layout led to significantly less transitions. This may be explained by the fact that looking in the center of ARBITRARY layouts covers most of the screens that are close to this centered point of focus. Consequently, there is less need to actually transitioning to other screens, as the peripheral information is available to viewers' visual attention and is processed accordingly, as explained by the zoom-lens model [6].

Eye Gaze Travel Distance
During the one minute of each trial, participants' eye gaze travelled in average 39.7 meters (Figure 4c). Interestingly, the number of TV screens had no significant effect on EGTD ($\chi^2(2) = 1.667, n.s.$), but the way the screens were arranged in space did ($\chi^2(2) = 8.867, p = .01$). Post-hoc Wilcoxon tests (corrected at $p = .05/3 = 017$) revealed significant differences only between the PRIMARY and ARBITRARY layouts, but not between the other two layout pairs. Participants seemed to have travelled the same amount of distance in terms of eye gaze for both TILED and PRIMARY, but the large screen of the PRIMARY condition led to larger eye gaze travel distances to reach the secondary screens when compared to the ARBITRARY layout.

Switch Time
The switch time (Figure 4d) is the time required for eye gaze to travel between screens, and we found it to vary up to 29% of the total watching time, with an average of 2.5% ($SD = 5\%$). We found a significant effect of TV-COUNT on Switch Time ($\chi^2(2) = 8.824, p = .01$) with post-hoc tests showing significant differences only between two and four screens. There was no significant effect of LAYOUT on Switch Time ($\chi^2(2) = 2.867, n.s.$). Overall, this measure revealed that four-screen layouts are less efficient in terms of actually fixating TV content, as they unnecessarily consume eye gaze for transitions in-between screens.

RESULTS #2: COGNITIVE LOAD AND COMFORTABILITY FOR MULTI-SCREEN TV
Cognitive load
After each trial, participants were administered NASA TLX tests to collect their subjective ratings of the workload on a scale from 1 (low) to 100 (high). We found that the TLX value increased with the number of TV screens from 28.4 for two screens to 39.9 and 50.7 for three and four screens (Figure 5, left). More TV screens were perceived more difficult to follow, as shown by a Friedman test ($\chi^2(2) = 27.214, p < .001$). Post-hoc Wilcoxon signed-rank tests revealed significant differences (at $p = .05/2 = .025$) between two and three, and three and four screens, with medium to large effect sizes ($r = .42$ and $.50$). Significant effects of TV-COUNT were found for each dimension of the NASA TLX test (Figure 5, right). At the same time, there was no significant effect of LAYOUT on the perceived task load measured by TLX ($\chi^2(2) = 4.206, n.s.$), nor on any of the six dimensions employed by the NASA TLX test.

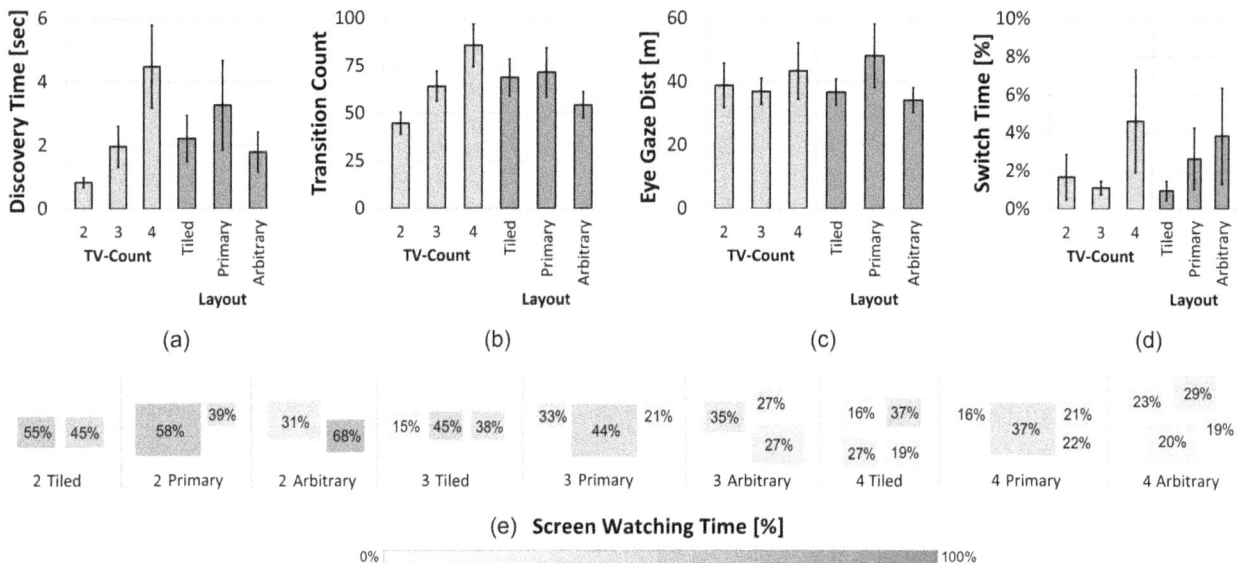

Figure 4. Visual attention measures for multi-screen TV: Discovery Time (a), Transition Count (b), Eye Gaze Distance (c), Switch Time (d), and Screen Watching Times (e). (Note that SWTs (e) do not always add to 100%; the remainder is the Switch Time.)

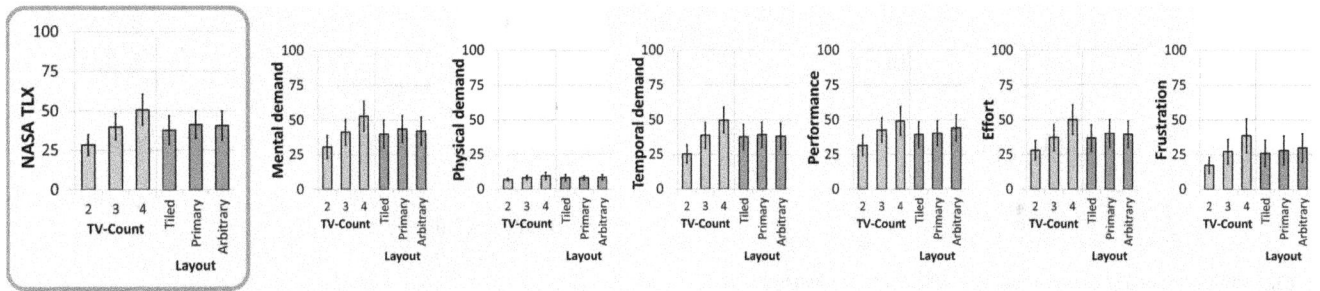

Figure 5. Participants' average workload ratings measured with the NASA task load test for each TV-Count and Layout (left). Note: The NASA TLX test employs six dimensions (right) to measure workload in the range [0, 100] corresponding to the subjective perceptions of Low/High (e.g., high mental demand, low physical effort), and Poor/Good for Performance.

Comfortability

At the end of the experiment, participants were asked to rate the perceived comfort (PC) of watching each screen layout on a 5-point Likert scale. They were also asked to specify the maximum number of screens they felt could be watched comfortably at the same time (MAX-TV).

The median PC rating over all trials was 2.5, in between of uncomfortable and neutral (Figure 6a). Maximum of comfortability was perceived for layouts with two screens (4, comfortable), and was 2 (uncomfortable) for layouts with more than two screens. We found a significant effect of TV-Count on PC ($\chi^2(2) = 39.244, p < .001$) that was further confirmed by post-hoc Wilcoxon signed-rank tests (at $p = .05/3 = .017$) for paired conditions (2,3) and (2,4) with large effect sizes ($r = .51$ and $.57$ respectively). No significant effect was detected between three and four screens. We also found a significant effect of Layout on perceived comfortability ($\chi^2(2) = 23.275, p < .001$). Post-hoc Wilcoxon signed-rank tests revealed significant differences (at $p = .05/3 = .017$) between Primary and Arbitrary ($r = .44$), and Tiled and Arbitrary ($r = .47$), but not between Primary and Tiled.

The median value of MAX-TV was 2 screens (Figure 6b). We found a significant effect of TV-Count on MAX-TV ($\chi^2(2) = 13.565, p < .001$), no significant difference between 2 and 3 screens, but significant between (3,4) and (2,4) with effect sizes $.36$ and $.40$. There was no significant effect of Layout on MAX-TV ($\chi^2(2) = 5.261, n.s.$).

RESULTS #3: CAPACITY TO UNDERSTAND CONTENT AND PERCEIVED SCREEN WATCHING TIME

Content understandability

After each trial, participants were administered multiple-choice questions about the content displayed by each screen (one question per screen). Each question had four possible choices with only one being correct. The last choice was always "I don't know the answer". We counted the number of correct answers as well as the number of "don't know" answers. We found that participants were able to remember content with an average accuracy of 75.2%, while the percentage of "don't know" answers was 16.3% (Figure 7). There were no significant effects of TV-Count or Layout on the mean number of correct answers ($\chi^2(2) = 4.000$ and

$\chi^2(2) = 0.970$ respectively, n.s. at $p = .01$), but we found a marginally significant effect of TV-Count on "don't know" answers ($\chi^2(2) = 6.645, p = .036$).

Perceived Watching Time

After each trial, participants estimated in percentages how much they watched each screen. When we correlated this perceived SWT with measured SWT, we found a Pearson coefficient of $r = .763$, significant at $p = .01$. This result shows a surprisingly good capacity of our participants to estimate what they were actually watching and how much. Correlation coefficients computed for each condition are shown in Figure 8, with a maximum of .892 for 2-Arbitrary.

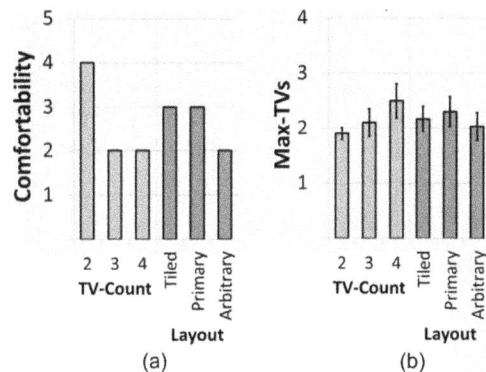

(a)   (b)

Figure 6. Participants' median ratings of Perceived Comfort (a) and the average of the maximum number of TV screens they felt could be watched comfortably at the same time (b).

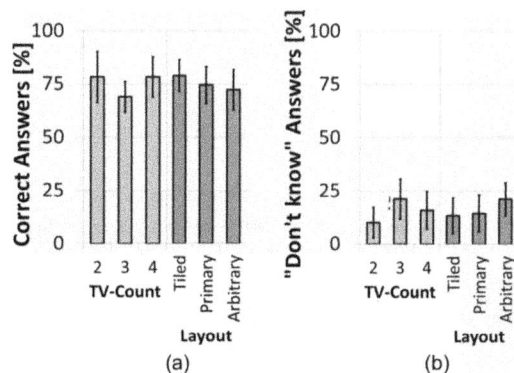

(a)   (b)

Figure 7. Participants' Content Understandability (CU).

117

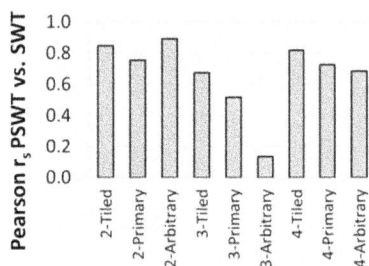

Figure 8. Correlations between perceived and measured SWT. (All significant at $p = 0.01$, except for 3-ARBITRARY.)

VISUAL ATTENTION TOOLKIT

We release our set of measures in the form of the Visual Attention Toolkit for TV (VATic-TV), which we make available to the community as open source software companion to this paper contribution (VATic-TV can be downloaded from http://www.eed.usv.ro/~vatavu). We also release all the data files (*i.e.,* movies of the experiment and eye gaze tracking data logs) collected and used in this study as a multi-screen eye gaze dataset to allow easy replication of results and encourage further investigation of visual attention phenomena for multi-screen TV applications.

CONCLUSION

We proposed in this work a set of nine general and reusable measures to characterize viewers' visual attention patterns for multi-screen TV, out of which the six objective measures can be computed automatically with the toolkit accompanying the paper. We applied our measures to evaluate multi-screen TV layouts and showed how the number of screens and their structure affect viewers' visual attention and cognitive load. We look forward to see how our measures will be employed by the community to understand more about viewers' visual attention patterns for emerging multi-screen TV applications.

ACKNOWLEDGEMENTS

The paper and research effort have been co-founded by the European Commission under project "NUBOMEDIA - An elastic Platform as a Service (PaaS) cloud for interactive social multimedia", reference FP7-ICT-2013.1.6 GA-610576.

REFERENCES

1. Anderson, J.R. 2004. *Cognitive psychology and its implications.* Worth Publishers, New York, USA
2. Cesar, P, Bulterman, D.C., Jansen, A.J. 2008. Usages of the Secondary Screen in an Interactive Television Environment: Control, Enrich, Share, and Transfer Television Content. *Proc. of EuroITV '08*, 168-177
3. Cummins, R.G., Tirumala, L.N., Lellis, J.M. 2011. Viewer Attention to ESPN's Mosaic Screen: An Eye-Tracking Investigation. *Journ. Sports Media* 6(1), 23-54
4. Courtois, C., D'heer, E. 2012. Second screen applications and tablet users: constellation, awareness, experience, and interest. *Proc. of EuroITV '12*, 153-156
5. Eriksen, C, Hoffman, J. 1972. Temporal and spatial characteristics of selective encoding from visual displays. *Perception & Psychophysics* 12 (2B), 201-204
6. Eriksen, C., St James, J. 1986. Visual attention within and around the field of focal attention: A zoom lens model. *Perception & Psychophysics* 40 (4), 225–240

7. Forlines, C., Shen, C., Wigdor, D., Balakrishnan, R. 2006. Exploring the effects of group size and display configuration on visual search. *Proc. of CSCW '06*, 11-20
8. Frintrop, S., Rome, E., Christensen, H.I. 2010. Computational visual attention systems and their cognitive foundations: A survey. *ACM TAP* 7(1), 39 pp.
9. Geerts, D., Cesar, P., Bulterman, D. 2008. The implications of program genres for the design of social television systems. In *Proc. of UXTV '08*. ACM, 71-80
10. Hawkins, R.P., Pingree, S., Hitchon, J., Radler, B., Gorham, B.W., Kahlor, L., Gilligan, E., Serlin, R.C., Schmidt, T., Kannaovakun, P., Kolbeins, G.H. 2005. What Produces Television Attention and Attention Style? Genre, Situation, and Individual Differences as Predictors. *Human Commun. Research* 31(1), 162–187
11. Holmes, M.E., Josephson, S., Carney, R.E. 2012. Visual attention to television programs with a second-screen application. In *Proc. of ETRA '12*. ACM, 397-400
12. Kallenbach, J., Narhi, S., Oittinen, P. 2007. Effects of extra information on TV viewers' visual attention, message processing ability, and cognitive workload. *Computers in Entertainment* 5(2). ACM, NY, USA
13. Miller, G. 1956. The Magical Number Seven, Plus or Minus Two: Some Limits on Our Capacity for rocessing Information. *Psychological Review* 63, 81-97
14. Posner, M.I. 1980. Orienting of attention. *Quarterly Journal of Experimental Psychology* 32, 3-25
15. Potter, M.C. 1976. Short-term conceptual memory for pictures. *Journal of Exp. Psychol.* 2, 509-522
16. Rashid, U., Nacenta, M.A., Quigley, A. 2012. The cost of display switching: a comparison of mobile, large display and hybrid UI configurations. *Proc. AVI '12*, 99-106
17. Rashid, U., Nacenta, M.A., Quigley, A. 2012. Factors influencing visual attention switch in multi-display user interfaces: a survey. *Proc. of PerDis '12*. ACM, 6 pages
18. Reichle, E.D., Rayner, K., Pollatsek, A. 2004. The E-Z reader model of eye-movement control in reading: Comparisons to other models. *Behav. Brain Sci.* 26, 445-476
19. Riche, N., Mancas, M., Culibrk, D., Crnojevic, V., Gosselin, B., Dutoit, T. 2012. Dynamic saliency models and human attention: a comparative study on videos. *Proc. of ACCV'12*, 586-598
20. Schwarz, J., Klionsky, D., Harrison, C., Dietz, P., Wilson, A. 2012. Phone as a pixel: enabling ad-hoc, large-scale displays using mobile devices. *CHI '12*, 2235-2238
21. Sohlberg, M.M., Mateer, C.A. 1989. *Introduction to cognitive rehabilitation: theory and practice.* Guilford Press
22. Tan, D.S., Czerwinski, M. 2003. Effects of Visual Separation and Physical Discontinuities when Distributing Information across Multiple Displays. *OZCHI'03*, 184-191
23. Theeuwes, J. 1991. Exogenous and endogenous control of attention - the effect of visual onsets and offsets. *Perception & Psychophysics* 49(1), 83–90
24. Vatavu, R.D., Mancaș, M. 2013. Interactive TV Potpourris: An Overview of Designing Multi-Screen TV Installations for Home Entertainment. *INTETAIN'13*, 49-54
25. Vatavu, R.D. 2013. There's a world outside your TV: exploring interactions beyond the physical TV screen. In *Proc. of EuroITV '13*. ACM, NY, USA, 143-152

The Effect of Cinematic Cuts on Human Attention

Christian Valuch
Cognitive Science Research
Platform, University of Vienna
christian.valuch@univie.ac.at

Ulrich Ansorge
Faculty of Psychology,
University of Vienna
ulrich.ansorge@univie.ac.at

Shelley Buchinger
Faculty of Computer Science,
University of Vienna
shelley.buchinger@univie.ac.at

Aniello Raffaele Patrone
Cognitive Science Research
Platform, University of Vienna
aniello.patrone@univie.ac.at

Otmar Scherzer
Faculty of Mathematics,
University of Vienna
otmar.scherzer@univie.ac.at

ABSTRACT
Understanding the factors that determine human attention in videos is important for many applications, such as user interface design in interactive television (iTV), continuity editing, or data compression techniques. In this article, we identify the demands that cinematic cuts impose on human attention. We hypothesize, test, and confirm that after cuts the viewers' attention is quickly attracted by repeated visual content. We conclude with a recommendation for future models of visual attention in videos and make suggestions how the present results could inspire designers of second screen iTV applications to optimise their interfaces with regard to a maximally smooth viewing experience.

Author Keywords
Attention; Eye tracking; Saccades; Editing; Continuity; Second screen applications; Evaluation

ACM Classification Keywords
H.1.2 [Models and Principles]: User/Machine Systems—human information processing; H.5.2 [Information Interfaces and Presentation (e.g. HCI)]: User Interfaces—evaluation/methodology; H.5.m. [Information Interfaces and Presentation (e.g. HCI)]: Miscellaneous

INTRODUCTION
Designing successful applications for online and interactive television (iTV) requires a proper understanding of the factors that determine the user's experience. Working towards this objective, HCI research has been using eye tracking as a means of evaluating user interfaces [11]. For instance, in multiple screen applications [1] users frequently shift their gaze between at least two locations [6]. The presence of the second screen can distract the viewer from the main content of the show [1]. Understanding which factors determine the viewer's attention in such situations would allow designers to optimize their applications in favor of a maximally smooth

viewing experience. To investigate these questions on a more general level – with a broad range of applications, such as video coding [13], or continuity editing [14] – we looked at gaze shifts after cinematic cuts. Human attention is closely related to eye movements. *Saccades* - abrupt gaze shifts between two locations - are a direct consequence of shifting attention to a new location [8]. Accordingly, by looking at the properties of saccades, it is possible to formulate and test theories about attention.

Current models of human attention and gaze behavior in videos emphasize the role of novelty, or *Bayesian surprise*. They assume that visual content that is maximally dissimilar from the viewer's prior visual experience is the best predictor of human attention and gaze direction. Indeed, eye tracking confirmed that human gaze direction in continuous videos is better explained by Bayesian surprise than by alternative models [7]. However, this is not necessarily true for cuts within edited videos. Existing evidence suggests that attention is attracted by repeated visual features in situations where location correlations between two successive images are low [2, 9].

Edited videos frequently contain hard cuts, i.e. visual discontinuities that require shifting attention from one location to another because object locations are uncorrelated across the cut. Moreover, making sense of narratives and content across cuts implicitly requires deciding whether the post-cut scene is a continuation of the pre-cut scene [14]. Here, *within scene cuts (WSCs)* continue with the same scene from a different angle; *between scenes cuts (BSCs)* continue with a different scene (see Figure 1). Orienting attention to repeated visual features could enable viewers' quick and efficient recognition of content that connects the cut images (in the case of WSCs).

The Present Study
We tested the hypothesis that after cuts, attention is more strongly attracted by repeated visual content than by novel, or surprising content. We conducted an eye tracking experiment, in which participants had to watch and keep their gaze on a video that was shown next to another, irrelevant video. Both videos contained hard cuts and unforeseeably kept or switched their locations at the cuts. This manipulation created a low correlation of object locations as is typical of cuts. Presenting two videos side by side also allowed us to measure influences of repeated versus novel content on saccades,

during which attention and eye movements are tightly coupled [8]. If locations switched, participants had to saccade to the new location of the video they were instructed to follow (similar to shifting gaze between two screens).

We analyzed *saccadic reaction time (SRT)* as a measure of viewers' re-orienting of attention to the post-cut scene after a location switch. Following our hypothesis, we predicted shorter SRT after cuts where much visual content was repeated (WSCs, or cuts with high image-image similarity) and longer SRT after cuts where less visual content was repeated (BSCs, or cuts with low image-image similarity).[1] In the remaining sections of this paper we give details on our method, results, and discuss implications for further research and improvements of iTV applications.

Figure 1. Example cuts. (A) Within scene cut (WSC). (B) Between scenes cut (BSC). Screenshots derived from videos by QParks.com, available under CC BY 3.0 at vimeo.com/89901459 and vimeo.com/89248621.

METHOD

Participants
Forty-two students (34 female) with a mean age of 23 years took part in an eye tracking experiment. Informed consent was obtained from all participants.

Stimuli
We used 20 sports videos in which we deliberately inserted new cuts. Each video showed the same sport throughout (e.g., *skiing*). Videos were edited in pairs, resulting in ten sets of two videos. The sport in the first video was always different from the sport in the second video (e.g., *skiing* vs. *surfing*). Cuts always occurred simultaneously in both videos. Average video duration was 2.5 minutes and the complete set contained 212 cuts. Cuts were assigned to either a WSC or a BSC condition. Whenever major visual changes, e.g. in scenery, actors, or ongoing actions occurred with the cut, the cut was coded as a BSC. In contrast, cuts that connected two images showing the same scene, action, and actors were coded as WSCs. Figure 1 shows examples. We assumed that more visual content is repeated after WSCs than after BSCs.

---

[1]This prediction is the opposite of that of the Bayesian surprise model which generally predicts a shorter SRT for less similar than for more similar image content.

To validate this, we compared the similarity of color histograms of the last pre-cut and the first post-cut frame and, based on this measure, assigned each cut to a *High similarity* or a *Low similarity* condition. We used color similarity because color contributes to gaze and attention preferences for repeated information [9], allows visual recognition after location and/or perspective shifts [15], and conveys information useful for cut detection [5].

Apparatus
Gaze data were recorded using an EyeLink 1000 Desktop Mount eye tracker (SR Research Ltd., Kanata, Ontario, Canada) at a sampling rate of 1000 Hz. The eye tracker was calibrated to each viewer's dominant eye using a 5-point calibration. Every time the videos switched locations, the exact timestamp was saved to the eye tracking data file, which allowed analyzing the latency of the first saccade to the target video with millisecond precision. Stimuli were displayed on a 19-in. color CRT monitor (Sony Multiscan G400) with a resolution of $1,280 \times 1,024$ pixels and a refresh rate of 60 Hz. The experimental procedure was implemented in MATLAB (MathWorks, Natick, MA, USA) using the Psychophysics Toolbox [3, 10] and the Eyelink toolbox [4]. Viewing distance to the monitor was 72 cm supported by chin and forehead rests. The viewable screen area subtended $28° \times 21°$. The apparent size of the 400×300 pixel videos was $8.75° \times 6.15°$ and they were shown vertically centered at a horizontal eccentricity of $6.56°$.

Procedure and Design
The experiment consisted of 20 blocks in which two videos were presented on the screen. Importantly, participants were instructed to view only one of the videos (the target video) while ignoring the other (the distractor video). At the beginning of each block, the starting location of the target video was announced by a green rectangle. Participants were informed that the videos switched locations at random intervals, and instructed to relocate their gaze as fast as possible to the target video's new location once the videos had switched locations. Throughout the experiment, each block was presented twice so that either of the videos was serving as the target in the first and as the distractor in the second half of the experiment (or vice versa).

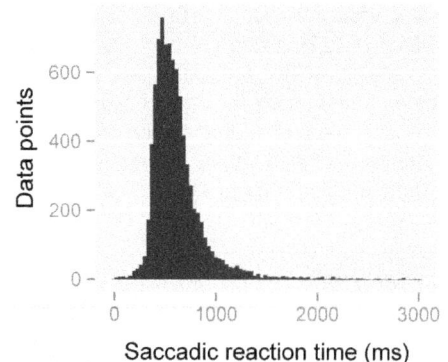

Figure 2. Distribution of valid saccadic reaction times (i.e. the latencies of the first saccade to the target video after a location switch).

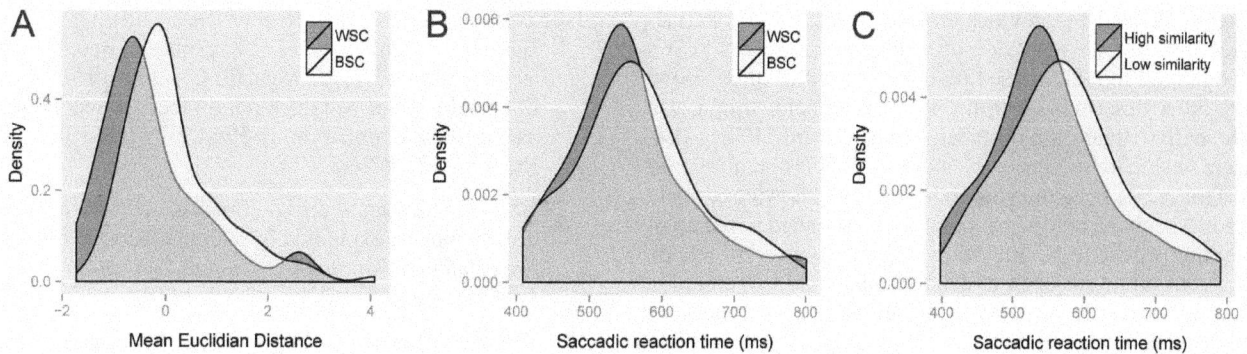

Figure 3. Results. (A) Distribution of mean Euclidian distances (*z*-transformed) of RGB color histograms of the last pre-cut and the first post-cut frame as a function of cut category. Values below 0 represent higher similarity, values above 0 represent lower similarity. (B) Distribution of individual median SRT as a function of cut category. (C) Distribution of individual median SRT as a function of color histogram similarity across the cut.

Data Analysis

Saccades were identified as sample periods where the change in gaze direction was larger than $0.1°$, eye movement velocity exceeded $30°/s$, and acceleration exceeded $8000°/s^2$. The main dependent variable was SRT, defined as the latency of the first saccade towards the target video after the videos switched locations. SRT was analyzed as a function of the type of cut (WSC vs. BSC) in the target video, and the similarity of RGB color histograms across cuts (High similarity vs. Low similarity) – for further details see Stimuli and Results. We expected shorter SRTs (faster gaze relocation) after WSCs than BSCs. Similarly, we expected shorter SRTs after High similarity than after Low similarity cuts.

Gaze data were preprocessed in MATLAB and statistical tests were run in R [12]. Out of 8,904 collected data points (i.e. 212 cuts for each of the 42 participants), 8,397 (94.3 %) contained valid SRTs and were subjected to statistical analyses. Data were excluded if no saccade to the target video was identified within a time-window of 3 s after the location switch or if gaze was already at the new location shortly ahead of the switch. Figure 2 depicts the distribution of valid SRTs. Individual median SRTs per condition were tested for within-participant differences by *t*-tests. We report Pearson correlation coefficients as measures of effect sizes. For all statistical tests, we set α at 0.05.

RESULTS

Image Similarity Across Cuts

To validate that more visual content is repeated after WSCs than BSCs, we calculated the mean Euclidian distance of the RGB color histograms between the final pre-cut and the first post-cut frame. For better interpretability, we *z*-transformed these values, so that values below 0 represent higher similarity (indicated by the smaller Euclidian distance), and values above 0 represent lower similarity (indicated by the greater Euclidian distance). A Welch two sample *t*-test indicated significantly higher color similarity in WSCs than BSCs, $t(148.3) = 2.86$, $p<.01$, $r = .23$ (see also Figure 3A).

Saccadic Reaction Time After Location Switches

In a first analysis, we tested whether the a priori categories of WSCs and BSCs could explain any variance in SRTs. Using a

paired *t*-test, we found that median SRT was on average 9 ms shorter in WSCs than BSCs, $t(41) = -2.03$, $p<.05$, resulting in a medium-sized effect of $r = .30$ (see also Figure 3B).

For a second analysis, we categorized the cuts into either a *High similarity* or a *Low similarity* condition, depending on whether the *z*-transformed similarity measure for these cuts was below or above 0. Again, we tested for significant differences in SRTs between these conditions. A paired *t*-test of median SRTs confirmed that on average SRTs were 23 ms shorter after High similarity than after Low similarity cuts, $t(41) = -6.83$, $p<.001$, representing a large effect of $r = .73$ (see also Figure 3C).

DISCUSSION

Our data suggest that after cuts viewers are able to re-orient their attention more quickly if visual content is repeated from the pre-cut scene: Following WSCs or High similarity cuts, saccades to the target video were initiated significantly faster than after BSCs, or Low similarity cuts. Results confirmed viewers' preference for repeated features during reorienting after cuts with low object-position correlations. The following limitations apply.

First, our results seem to conflict with the assumption that novel or surprising information is the best predictor of attention and gaze direction in videos [7]. However, we argue that an advantage for repeated information characterizes only a short time frame following cuts. During this period, viewers search for familiar visual content for deciding whether the previous scene continues, or not. Soon after, a preference for novel or surprising information should take over but future models should account for the effect of cuts on attention, too.

Second, in an effort to precisely measure the speed of attentional orienting after cuts we presented two videos simultaneously. This enabled us to elicit and record saccades of comparable start/end points for each cut. This is good because saccades are valid reflections of attention. However, the surprise model was supported during viewing of single videos. Viewing single videos is a situation that we ultimately also want to understand. Therefore, future research should aim to replicate our findings under single video viewing conditions.

Third, motivated by previous research [2, 9, 5, 15], we validated the stronger repetition of visual content across WSCs as compared to BSCs based on color similarity only. However, other descriptors that do not rely on color might also sufficiently explain the observed differences in SRTs. Also, we are unable to isolate color-repetition effects operating on a short timescale from the viewers' long-term knowledge about object-associated colors that possibly contributed to the color repetition effect (e.g., the knowledge that *snow* is *white*). These questions are open to debate and should be studied in future experiments, possibly by including control conditions with black and white videos.

Implications for iTV Applications

To conclude, we think a preference for repeated visual content applies in all situations in which the location of objects is uncorrelated across successive views. This is relevant for improving user interfaces in iTV. To give just one example, with second screen applications a second screen showing information that is visually unrelated to the main screen might distract the viewer [1]. Following from the present study, we would recommend that designers of second screen applications should include visual elements that repeat across both screens to minimize the time necessary for shifting attention between the two screens and assure a maximally smooth user experience. Even more interesting applications could become possible once eye tracking becomes widely available in consumer electronics. Then, it will be possible to dynamically adapt the content on a second device based on what was just looked at on the primary screen. Finally, we would like to stress that the methods presented in this paper can be easily adapted to study the effects of particular second screen iTV applications on human attention.

CONCLUSION

Our paper presents evidence that after cinematic cuts viewers quickly re-orient their attention to visual content that is repeated from the pre-cut scene. A preference for repeated visual content after cuts should be incorporated into models of human attention which currently assume that novelty or Bayesian surprise is the best predictor of human attention and gaze direction in videos. We also discussed implications of our results for the improvement of iTV applications.

ACKNOWLEDGMENTS

We thank the reviewers for their excellent comments on a previous version of the paper, as well as Melanie Szoldatics and Heide Maria Weißenböck for assistance with data collection, and gratefully acknowledge grant CS11-009 from the Wiener Wissenschafts-, Forschungs-, und Technologiefonds (WWTF, Vienna Science and Technology Fund) to Ulrich Ansorge, Shelley Buchinger, and Otmar Scherzer. We also wish to express our special gratitude to Dr. Anton Luger.

CORRESPONDENCE

Correspondence should be addressed to Christian Valuch, Cognitive Science Research Platform, University of Vienna, Liebiggasse 5, 1010 Wien, Austria.
Email: christian.valuch@univie.ac.at.

REFERENCES

1. Basapur, S., Mandalia, H., Chaysinh, S., Lee, Y., Venkitaraman, N., and Metcalf, C. Fanfeeds: evaluation of socially generated information feed on second screen as a tv show companion. In *Proc. EuroITV 2012*, ACM Press (2012), 87–96.

2. Becker, S. I. Can intertrial effects of features and dimensions be explained by a single theory? *Journal of Experimental Psychology: Human Perception and Performance 34*, 6 (2008), 1417–1440.

3. Brainard, D. The psychophysics toolbox. *Spatial Vision 10*, 4 (1997), 433–436. http://psychtoolbox.org//.

4. Cornelissen, F. W., Peters, E. M., and Palmer, J. The Eyelink Toolbox: eye tracking with MATLAB and the Psychophysics Toolbox. *Behavior Research Methods, Instruments, & Computers 34*, 4 (2002), 613–617.

5. Gargi, U., Kasturi, R., and Strayer, S. Perfomance characterization of video-shot-change detection methods. *Circuits and Systems for Video Technology, IEEE Transactions on 10*, 1 (2000), 1–13.

6. Holmes, M., Josephson, S., and Carney, R. Visual attention to television programs with a second screen application. In *Proc. Eye Tracking Research and Applications*, ACM Press (2012), 397–400.

7. Itti, L., and Baldi, P. Bayesian surprise attracts human attention. *Vision Research 49*, 10 (2009), 1295–1306.

8. Kowler, E., Anderson, E., Dosher, B., and Blaser, E. The role of attention in the programming of saccades. *Vision Research 35*, 13 (1995), 1897–1916.

9. Maljkovic, V., and Nakayama, K. Priming of pop-out: I. Role of features. *Memory & Cognition 22*, 6 (1994), 657–672.

10. Pelli, D. G. The VideoToolbox software for visual psychophysics: Transforming numbers into movies. *Spatial Vision 10*, 4 (1997), 437–442.

11. Poole, A., and Ball, L. J. Eye tracking in HCI and usability research. In *Encyclopedia of Human-Computer Interaction*, C. Ghaoi, Ed. 2006.

12. R Core Team. *R: A language and environment for statistical computing*. 2012. http://R-project.org/.

13. Salomon, D. *Data compression: The complete reference*. Springer, 2004.

14. Smith, T. J., Levin, D. T., and Cutting, J. A Window on Reality: Perceiving Edited Moving Images. *Current Directions in Psychological Science 21*, 2 (2012), 107–113.

15. Swain, M. J., and Ballard, D. H. Color indexing. *International Journal of Computer Vision 7*, 1 (1991), 11–32.

Storied Numbers: Supporting Media-Rich Data Storytelling for Television

Susan J. Robinson[1], Graceline Williams[1], Aman Parnami[1], Jinhyun Kim[1], Emmett McGregor[3], Dana Chandler[2], Ali Mazalek[1]

Synaesthetic Media Lab[1]	School of Social Work[2]	School of Communication[3]
Georgia Institute of Technology,	Georgia State University	American University
Atlanta, GA	Atlanta, GA	Washington, DC
{srobinson, racel.williams, aparnami, jinkim, mazalek}@gatech.edu	dchandler3@student.gsu.edu	blind9productions@gmail.com

ABSTRACT

The digital convergence of broadcast television, user-generated content from online and mobile sources, and interactive surfaces brings an opportunity for the development of platforms to support media-rich data storytelling for television audiences. In this paper, we report on a production model and system featuring a multi-touch interactive table with tangibles in the broadcast studio, on which performers use information visualizations to access and present media-rich content from viewers. The system uses content generated from a mobile application that couples close-ended survey items with rich media, such as video. The app is designed to increase opportunities for public debate on civic issues, but is also suitable for pure entertainment topics, such as sports and lifestyle. We present the results of an evaluation of our production model and the studio prototype in a lab setting with television production experts and on-air talent. Our results indicate that such systems must be designed with a flexible user profile in mind to accommodate performer capabilities and preferences, operational variations, program formats, and changing conventions in touch interaction.

Author Keywords

Data Storytelling; Information Visualization; Mobile Surveys; Interactive Surfaces; Interactive Television

ACM Classification Keywords

H.5.m. Information interfaces and presentation: Miscellaneous

INTRODUCTION

Today we are surrounded by more and more data, from environmental statistics to health trends, and presenting big data on television is a major challenge. How can quantitative data sets be presented to television audiences in an engaging and informative way? Successful television programs are visually engrossing, evoke human emotion,

offer suspense and surprise, and are salient to audiences. Numerical data should be enlivened and made "live" to meet these expectations from viewers. In investigating how this could be done, we found in our research that we had to create novel technologies on both the data *gathering* and *presentation* sides and combine these in a new way to adequately address this problem space. The primary goal of the research reported here was to assess the acceptability, feasibility, and usability of our overall production model and proposed technologies for broadcast studios to support media-rich data storytelling on television. For data gathering, we used the affordances of mobile media to combine two time-honored traditions in the media: the man-on-the street interview and the public opinion survey. To do this, we used mobile phones to create a novel survey format that *tightly couples* closed-ended questions with the ability to record video explanations of choices made. The result is a new type of content that we call "storied numbers," which become "storied data" when aggregated, lending itself to presentation using information visualization techniques.

On the presentation side, our studio system features an interactive anchor desk with multi-touch and tangible controls to support the exploration of data and stories. The set-up includes a screen display system around the table optimized for viewers to see the action, and from which program feed can be taken. This configuration supports roundtable discussion and debate programs by creating a shared information space on which experts can explore trends in the data and play out media-rich content, such as viewer video viewpoints, to spark debate. This enables audiences to see the developing analysis and to form their own insights as the narrative unfolds.

RELATED WORK

Cross-Platform Media and Television

Our system combines the strengths of mobile, networked and broadcast media with interactive surface technologies in a novel way to create an ecosystem capable of engaging audiences in the processes of generating media-rich data and its presentation in television programming. A 2013 study that collected over 600 responses on television viewer habits, dynamics, and behaviors, confirms that television is still a major platform despite other web offerings [1].

Television broadcasts provide a unique opportunity to use cross-platform/cross-client approaches to engage technologically-connected and -adept audiences, such as use of mobile video captured by citizen journalists [10], to live Twitter feeds during political events [13], the use of mobile devices for social interaction during TV shows [3], and support of social interaction during and after television programming [2].

Interactive Surfaces and Data Storytelling

The use of interactive surfaces and data visualizations are becoming more integral to and prevalent in television broadcasting, from John King's "Magic Wall" on CNN to SportsNation on ESPN. Our system is the first to move the data visualizations on interactive displays from the wall to a tangible/multitouch studio desk, partially in response to the performance challenges introduced by vertical displays. These include the performer occluding viewers' view of the visualization and having to turn a back to the audience [12]. Interactive tables have been used for storytelling and performance for over a decade. Tangible Viewpoints coupled tabletop tangibles with multiple character viewpoints to engage users in an interactive narrative [9]. reacTable [6] and mixiTUI [11] allow users to deliver live musical performances on tabletops that utilize both touch and tangible controls. An evaluation with 117 viewers of a live performance of mixiTUI found that TUIs enriched their musical viewing experience and that they wanted to understand how digital output was being manipulated [11]. These previous works indicated that there are several design decisions that need to be considered when developing a cross-platform interactive table application for television.

To guide our design decisions on the information visualization side, we consulted works like [4]. In particular, [5] examined data visualization on interactive surfaces, identifying some of the key research questions and design considerations with regard to collaboration.

Tangible and Touch Interaction

One of the main challenges of our project was deciding when to utilize touch versus tangible controls. Our work is informed by prior research on touch vs. tangibles in this respect, e.g., [7, 8, 14]. Hybrid surface systems, those with touch and tangible controls, are discussed in [7]. In [8],

touch and tangible interfaces are compared through a timed study asking participants to perform translation and rotation functions to create a space layout through either a touch or a tangible interface. Results showed that all participants completed the tasks faster with the tangibles and thought they were easier to use. This research found that leveraging real world metaphors could contribute to making the work easier with tangibles. The downside of tangibles was their lack of reusability. Another study [14] compared touch and tangibles in manipulation and acquisition tasks. Similar to [8], users found it easiest to manipulate tangibles. In our system, we used a combination of touch and tangibles, with an emphasis on using tangibles to add visual interest and make actions visible to studio cameras and thus audiences.

SYSTEM DESIGN

The Production Model

Our model identifies three stages in the television production process during which digital media affordances can bring about change (Figure 1): content generation (production), content presentation (editorial), and performance (program). At each stage, we designed and deployed specific technologies and techniques to support viewer-participants, producers, and on-air talent in generating and working with content that contains both multivariate data and rich media. The telling of stories is not just reserved for the performance stage; it is encapsulated at each turn.

For content generation, we created a mobile application, *SayWhyPoll*, which allows users to provide video responses in addition to closed-ended survey questions. The addition of video responses provides users with the opportunity to explain their choices, tell personal anecdotes, and even dispute the framing of the question. A database back-end enables producers to create surveys in minutes and to choose between two modes of releasing the survey: "man-on-the-street" or "remote" mode. "Man-on-the-street" mode allows a journalist to administer the survey multiple times in-person. "Remote" mode allows viewers to take the survey once on their own mobile device. Quantitative survey data and geographic coordinates can be sent immediately to the server, with video sent similarly or uploaded later when a high-speed connection is available.

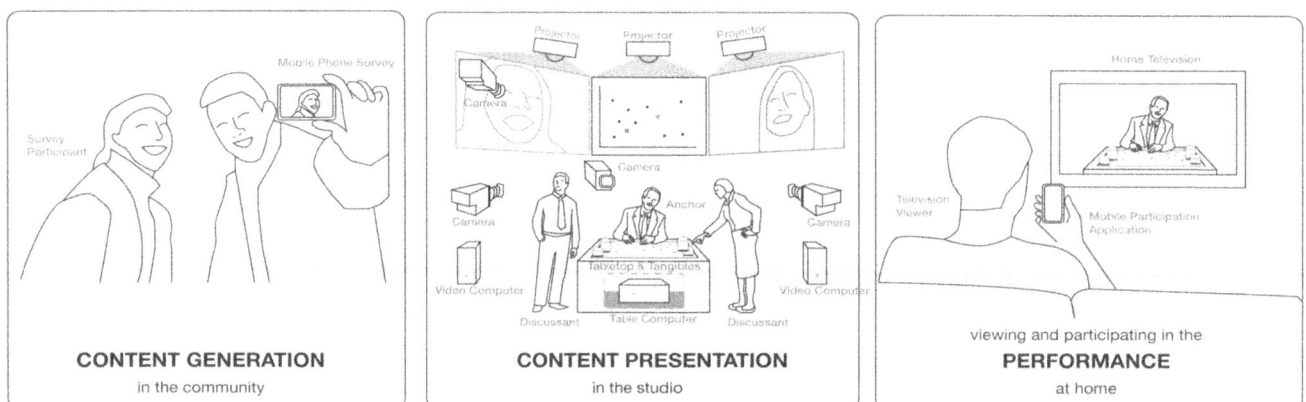

CONTENT GENERATION
in the community

CONTENT PRESENTATION
in the studio

PERFORMANCE
at home

Figure 1: Cross-platform ecosystem.

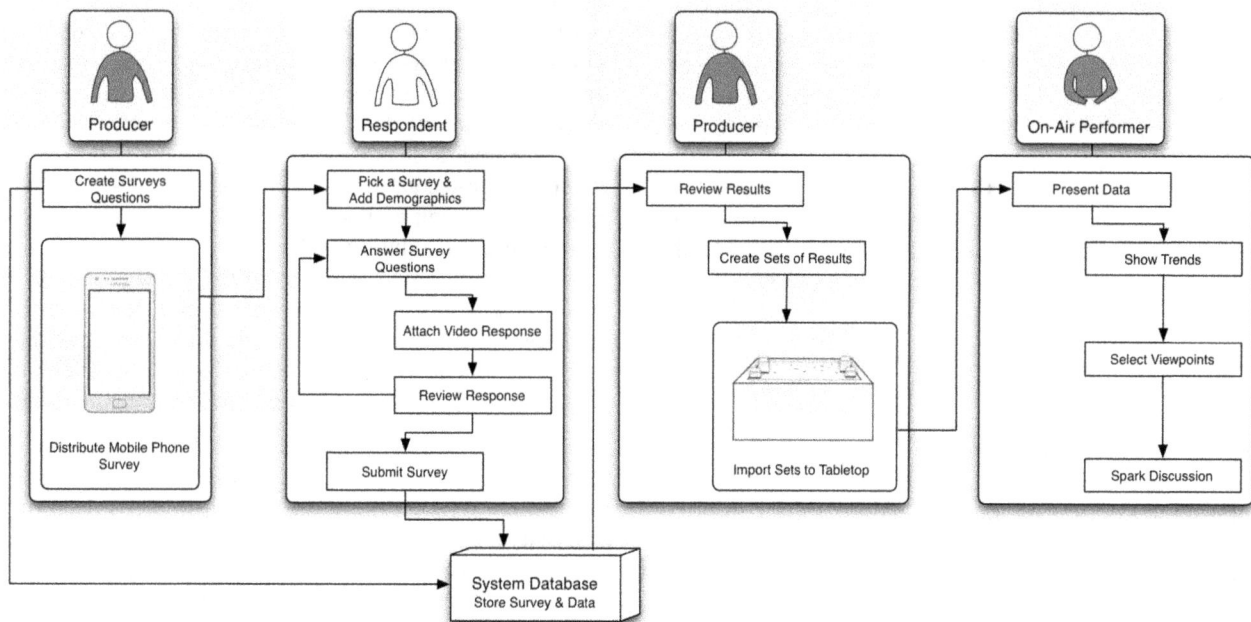

Figure 2: Cross-platform system to support data storytelling for television audiences.

For the content presentation stage, our production model inserts the human storyteller, in the form of an associate or producer who curates the content from the *SayWhyPoll* submissions to create a compelling story. While some parts of the editorial process can be automated using meta-data from the submission, such as answer values, the producer has the ultimate control. In our use case, the producer uses the same information visualization application utilized on the interactive table for on-air presentation to discover interesting content. If there are many responses, our model calls for this application to randomize the responses, so that contributors matching an item of interest have equal chances to be featured. The final step is for the producer to flag the best video viewpoints for on-air presentation indicated by visual markers, and, if desired, to note the top points to be presented in the rundown, cues, and scripts.

Deciding what type of information visualization to use is also part of the editorial processes in our model, as it shapes the story that can be told. We have previously experimented with maps and novel representations [12], as well as the scatterplots described here, and visual metaphors such as a game or race on which to plot responses. The visualization one might choose depends in part of the characteristics of the data. For example, one might visualize geographically-relevant data, like national election results, on a map, while health trends might be visualized using a scatterplot.

In the performance stage of our model, on-air talent is briefed by producers on the content highlights and the overall resulting narrative, with the level of improvisation to be determined by program format. A short segment in a structured news show would have the talent using the visualization primarily as a "player" device; but a hour-long

public issues program could have the talent using viewpoints from people from differing life situations to add depth to a policy debate.

Prototype System

Our prototype system is composed of the following components (Figure 2): 1) the *SayWhyPoll* mobile application as the content gathering method, and 2), a data visualization system dubbed *Tangible Anchoring*, currently running on a Microsoft PixelSense interactive table that is networked with machines controlling display screen output.

The *SayWhyPoll* application for smartphones is used to create customized polling surveys for use in remote or face-to-face mode. Each time a survey is delivered, the application receives a unique random-generated ID number from an online server that is attached to the poll data for indexing purposes. In addition to answering the survey questions, a respondent also has an option to attach a video, recorded through the smartphone camera, justifying their position on a particular question. On completion, the survey data—responses and videos— is uploaded to the server. Our systems' main presentation and storytelling platform is Microsoft's PixelSense, a commercially available interactive table that is rectangular and spans 40 inches diagonally. We set up the table to be high enough to be operated while standing or sitting on stools. In our scenario, the anchor and discussants sit around three sides of the table with the open side facing studio cameras. The PixelSense runs Windows 7 and is capable of multi-touch input, tangible object tag pattern recognition, and video output to projectors. It comes with a custom set of tag patterns for use with tangible objects on the surface, called ByteTags.

To visualize the storied data for the evaluation featured in this paper, our interactive table application, *Tangible Anchoring*, (Figure 3), implemented in the C# language with the use of the Surface SDK, was programmed to feature a scatterplot. Since our visualization aids in exploring survey data collected with *SayWhyPoll*, the data is downloaded from an online server apriori in XML format. An XML file also provides for configuration settings. The interactive table application reads the XML files and applies settings to generate a visualization.

To control the storied data on the PixelSense, several types of tangibles were developed, as shown in Figure 3. X- and Y-axis tangibles are used for sliding the visible axis window, to zoom in and out, and to rotate the categories featured along each axis. Q and A tangibles, shown in green, are used for selecting or filtering different question and answer choices. The Tagger tangible, shown in blue, enables highlighting of data points to enable persistence while changing dimensions of the visualization. Using these controls, users can explore data trends and play out videos to create a narrative about a topic of interest. For example, one can iterate through different survey questions and filter responses. Each question and filtered response presents individual survey responses with visual markers; in our prototype, these markers are either a square if a response has a video associated with it, or a circle if it does not. Using the multi-touch controls of the PixelSense, performers can drag a finger over markers to reveal meta-data about the responses such the name and age of persons featured. Performers tap on a square video marker to play out the corresponding video on one of two overhead screens; this could signal the control room to switch what is being viewed by the audience, in a production setting.

Figure 3. Interactive tabletop with scatterplot and tangible controls.

EVALUATION
The purpose of our lab study was to evaluate the feasibility and acceptability of combining data with video viewpoints for presentation to television audiences using an interactive table studio/set piece featuring information visualizations with tangible and touch controls.

Methods
Our protocol called for a cooperative think-aloud combined with an in-depth interview, followed by a user experience survey, to be administered by a researcher who was an expert in television studio production. The interview guide was structured to: 1) elicit feedback on the overall model of gathering rich-media survey content via mobile phones and presenting it using a tabletop information visualization; 2) prompt responses during and after the cooperative think-aloud on specific details of the user's experience; and 3) provide reactions to a scenario-of-use in a public opinion discussion show. Our scenario-of-use presented a talk show format with an anchor and two discussants reviewing responses from public opinion poll and debating the issues.

Due to the presence of international, regional, and local television operations in our city (Atlanta, GA, USA), we were able to successfully reach experienced television professionals using a snowball sampling technique. We had a total of 14 participants, who fell into three types of experts: 1) television professionals working or who had worked in television operations, production, or as on-air talent; 2) producers of digital media content associated with news (social and on-line media); and 3) entertainment industry experts. The study took 2 hours to complete and was recorded from three camera angles to capture user behaviors and discussion.

Following the lab study, the video record was analyzed for user interaction patterns and the sessions were transcribed and analyzed for themes by five members of the research team using a common codebook. All coded transcripts were reviewed by the lead researcher and the findings were discussed among the research team for concurrence. The findings reported here are themes found across at least three respondents and the quotes provided to illustrate these themes are from a number of participants.

RESULTS
The in-depth interviews and surveys indicated that our expert study participants, who work across a range of environments and roles, found the overall production model presented feasible. They expressed that the concept of coupling survey questions with video was worth pursuing. They most often framed the approach as a way to engage audiences, in the same vein as "man-on-the-street" interviews and user-generated content give viewers the opportunity to be seen and heard. All participants, except one, indicated that such an application could be used on-air in today's environment and would be helpful when working with user-generated survey content. The interviews also yielded specific insights into how the production model and system features could be refined during the content gathering, content presentation (editorial), and performance stages to support data storytelling in the context of studio broadcast production. In the next sections, we present our results according to the production model and the technologies and techniques evaluated.

If It's Good Tape, It's Good Tape

In general, reactions to the mobile application itself were positive, with respondents seeing it as a way to reach people in their viewing area when the cost of keeping reporters in the field across distances is prohibitive. While interacting with the tabletop, participants played video clips from a pilot *SayWhyPoll* survey, some of which had poor audio. This prompted them to comment that the most important factor in content for television is the quality of the clips, which they defined as going beyond just a good recording. As one expert put it, *"if it's good tape it's good tape."* The consensus was that for interviews, "good tape" shows an energetic person making concise points that are entertaining or incisive. One news expert stated that in the U.S., the average sound bite for news programs is 9 seconds, another remarked that for discussion shows, up to 20 seconds, and these estimates were repeated by others.

Respondents could see content gathering on a topic coming from multiple sources, rather than solely gathered remotely or through man-on-the-street intercept. One felt that additional content, including packages from professionals, and paid respondents, might be in a content set. For man-on-the-street interviews to be useful, participants representing news operations felt that some level of training is essential, e.g., *"there is a format ... you want the person to repeat the question and the answer ... whereas other people ... it's not a succinct answer."* For people who might receive surveys remotely, ease-of-use is critical, and limiting the recording to short bites. One participant noted that for the content gathering to be successful overall, the questions presented must be of interest to viewers, *"I think the question is going to have to be really compelling ... if it is a question I really don't care about ... no amount of technology can get me to watch this."*

Finding the Gems

"... that sifter, that curator, seems to me as just as important as the person who is doing this, who is performing the data."

If good answers start with good questions, identifying the best viewpoints and representing them in exciting ways is dependent on the human operator in our production model. Our participants confirmed the importance of this stage and role and said that the person overseeing this stage makes or breaks the show. They identified two main functions for this stage, for program producers: 1) to select the best visualization for the content under discussion, and 2) to screen, identify, and select the top sound bites and media to be featured during the program.

While current on-air programs often feature maps on large displays, our visualization for this study, a scatterplot, controlled by touch and tangibles, was completely novel to all our participants. This new interaction and visualization provoked lively discussion about what types of visualizations would work on television, and how complex or simple these should be in terms of the number of data points, graphics, and text, and potential viewer reactions. Most of the professionals emphasized that any visualization should be comprehensible at a glance and not overwhelm the viewer. They liked the idea of using a scatterplot, but often the conversation turned to more traditional images. One participant said, *"maybe you have a graph on one story, and a map on another story ..."*, and regarding the scatterplot, *"I think it works for me - when it's a big data set and you are trying to minimize it - but what if you are trying to do this with geography ... [such as] all casualties in Iraq...this might be difficult to control ...so you get to a level of sophistication [in the commentary] with it."*

For the second editorial function, identifying the best content to show, experts were in agreement that the *act of discovery* was a function of this stage of production, not to be done in performance. The feeling was summed up by one working anchor, who said, *"[presenters] don't want to stumble around, on the show, looking for video."* And another humorously remarked, *"so let's say that you're not so skilled at the board ... you're coming off a little more miniscule than you are pro."*

As with any temporal medium, experts emphasized the selection of particular content pieces to show depends not only on individual merits of each video or image, but expertise in how the data "dots" will make a dialogue in the flow of the program. Suggestions for adding interest included juxtaposing different types of people (e.g., men versus women), extreme views on either side that could lead to more moderate positions, and opposing political stances. Content that provokes emotion is important in making the data come alive: *"That's what makes data interesting ... the arguments and the human element to it,"* said one working professional.

Show Time

Given the participants' high level of expertise, it perhaps is not surprising that the key finding of the study can be summed up as "it depends." While there were concrete suggestions for improving the scatterplot visualization to support performance, there was less agreement on generalizing how data storytelling might play out in terms of potential program flow, how much storytelling action occurred either behind the scenes or in front of the camera, and the optimal balance of interaction between touch or tangible controls. These decisions, our professionals told us, depend on the type of show being produced and the strengths and preferences of individual performers.

Learning Curve

All participants noted that there would be a learning curve to using the interactive table, when first using the equipment and before each show, whether there was to be a short segment as a sidebar, or if the program featured the table. One participant summed this up by saying *"it's a trained motor skill"* overall. On-air talent felt that there would always be a short rehearsal prior to any show: *"... it's like a symphony, or some kind of choreographed [dance]. You are going to have to do this beforehand to figure out which hand is going to do it. Once you've figured out what routine is going to be, I don't think it's really a big deal."*

Scripted versus Improvised

" ... talent is funny. Some of them are total control freaks, and they want to do everything themselves, and others are like, 'all I want to do is sit up here and read ... don't tell me I have to do something.'"

Many participants agreed, that prior to program, the producer should--at a minimum--provide a rundown of the data and media identified through the editorial process as going on air, with sequences spelled out, and notes on content selected for the on-air performer. From there, the level of scripting could run from completely planned, such as a news read where only a few 9-second bites are featured, to improvised, e.g. a live, hour-long talk show, in which talent could select content based on the flow of the conversation.

Several participants pointed out that a talent's knowledge of the domain from which the data was generated would have a great effect on how much support the talent might desire for data storytelling. The political analyst John King of CNN, who pioneered the use of touch surfaces on U.S. television, was cited as an example of someone who *"you really think you can go to for real information"* due to his relative ease with using touch surface technology and his command of relevant facts without scripting.

Typically, some improvising in television performance is desired, as it increases the liveliness of the program. The dynamic nature of the data visualization was considered a plus in this regard. It was considered visually appealing and enabled the viewer to see how on-camera performers arrived at trends and particular viewpoints. However, many participants felt strongly that it was important to know the story in advance, so that talent could provide their own embellishments without being caught up in figuring out the next "plot point". One person observed, *"the anchor putting their own perspective on the story would come in is when they look at the material [in advance] and they find something interesting ... they find one of those questions and they want to pose it to someone who comes in."*

However, the format of the show will change the equation regarding the level of script support. The ability to improvise could be helpful in some formats, such as a morning talk show, where there are several people on camera at a time that need something of shared interest, for which the table could fill the function. One participant noted, *"One of the hardest things is about interactivity on set. How do you get all of those people on set at the same time doing something together...something they can all look at and talk about?"* But in a show featuring a single personality, using the table for focus could take away from viewers. As an experienced anchor put it, *"how much is the*

anchor going to be looking down ... and disconnected? .... One of the things you would have to work on is making that [the talent] is not looking away too much."

Hidden versus Visible Actions

"the charm of this device is seeing how you are taking control of it."

Another theme that emerged in our interviews was the degree to which "getting to the point" was on display in the actions of the performer. One serious challenge to using this technology on air is simply the expectation, by many audiences, of receiving information quickly. This has implications for the amount of functionality for direct manipulation featured on the interface. One performer advocated for a simpler design and less flexibility on the interface to support fast-paced performance. A producer repeated this sentiment, suggesting the addition of a "mini-screen" with pre-set views of the data that the performer could switch to with a simple touch.

There were a range of opinions on how much behind-the-scenes human and on-the-screen technical support should be provided to the performer, but most felt strongly the answer was: a lot. The extreme end of this view was one operations person who suggested the tangibles be controlled on the tabletop through remote means. On the other end, a number of people felt that having the talent perform actions was important, *"because the person wants to show the interactivity ..."* However, the way live television programs are directed particularly points out the challenge of transferring "where the action is" to the on-air performer. As one participant mentioned *"so many of the decisions are coming from the control room ... the anchors are just following what they say."* One of the key takeaways from our evaluation, in terms of supporting action on-air, was the need to improve the meta-data preview of the rich-media content provided when the data points are hovered over. Many participants thought key information to be displayed would include: name, age, location, runtime of clip, and a succinct five word summary of the point being made. This enables accurate verbal segues by the talent to the material: *"And now we have Marcie from Michigan who is forty-seven and she disagrees with our last gentleman."*

Tangible versus Touch Interaction

"My first inclination is to touch. That is part of being part of the smartphone culture." AND *"[The tangibles] make it look like a cool, new technology to me - as opposed to this is just a big iPhone."*

As the first quote above suggests, the use of touch surfaces has greatly evolved and this study strongly suggests that touch conventions have changed people's interest in and acceptance of tangible controls. Many of our participants could see replacing the X- and Y-axis tangibles with pinch, pull, or swiping motions; they were less resolved regarding the Q and A tangibles. The Tagger tangible, offering a specific function, received little comment. Touch was seen as more *"intuitive,"* and one person said the tangibles seem *"more gimmicky than anything."* With an emphasis on touch come other possibilities, for example, *"the new media [types] would say, how can we draw circles?"*

The second quote sums up the predominant counterpoint even the pro-touch participants voiced, that the tangibles provide visual interest and set the technology apart from everyday devices, i.e. their use was more in line with show business. One newsperson said *"...if I could put this on set and look at it through a camera I would probably have a very different perspective on just the aesthetics of all this ..."* Once again, our overall results suggest that the choice of interface is less about usability than the preferences of the performer and desired production values.

Fine Points
The participants offered many suggestions for refining the prototype. Art direction was a topic on which participants' views diverged greatly. Some participants argued for more intense graphics, while others felt a sparse look would help convey patterns and not overwhelm the viewer. The latter point is directly related to the complexity of a scatterplot graph. While offering great flexibility in information visualization operations, the format received mixed responses due to complexity. As one person put it, *"maybe there are too many elements to play with – but I think it makes for good TV."*

In terms of staging, participants thought that the simulated studio set up in our lab, with displays and typical studio camera angles, was well done. They counseled against having guest discussants perform any functions on the table, such as using a tangible to filter. Finally, there is a need to take into account the height of performers in sizing both the table and potentially any tangibles, as one participant had difficulty reaching all parts of the table.

DISCUSSION
During our study, we were struck by the diversity of operational environments, program formats, branding, budgets, personalities, and preferences we encountered, even in our partial sample of television professionals. These diverse aspects form the context from which designers and engineers construct specific problem spaces as they may seek to create effective technologies to support data storytelling for television. Our findings call for attention in tailoring solutions when designing for broadcast production environments and the systems of people and technologies found in each.

Tailoring for the Television Performer
Our system has two main components, a mobile application and an interactive table presentation system, which supports three stages in our model of data storytelling: content gathering, content presentation, and performance. It is the shaping of potential practices in the third stage, performance, that our findings may best inform decisions.

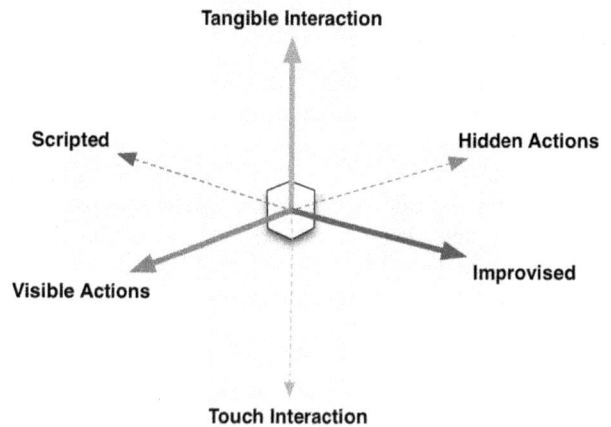

Figure 4. Three dimensions of the Flexible User Profile.

We found in our study a set of tensions in the problem space of designing interactive tables for the performance of media-rich data storytelling. Figure 4 arranges these themes in a 3-dimensional space as a tool to aid designers in working through the preferences of performers and the resources of their supporting environments. We intend for this model to be used to locate performers and their supporting systems along the continuums we identified as relevant to this problem space.

For example, during elections, national television news services often will run programs that remain on-air as results come in; there is a wealth of data to discuss, potentially visualize, and supplement with human-interest stories. This is easily a context in which the producer might decide that a high degree of visible analysis would be desirable. Due to the emerging situation, inefficiencies in improvisation would be tolerable and could even fill time.

Alternatively, daily primetime local news programs are highly structured and rapid-paced, with the need for short segments and less depth. In this situation, the interactive table may be used over a period of evenings to examine reactions to an event, such as a toxic spill, across a range of affected citizens relative to the affected area. In this context, a reporter might use a map visualization with preset views. This set-up would rely more on hidden action (analysis), scripted content, and touch interaction only.

FUTURE WORK

Additional Case Studies
While participants thought our production model was feasible and that the overall concept holds promise, there are limitations to our findings. We were only able to approximate a television studio in our lab and to speculate on how audiences might receive these programs. More study is needed in real production environments to see if the technologies proposed are truly feasible. We would like to produce pilot programs with datasets and test them with potential audiences to refine program scenarios. We also

need to test our design tool for tailoring data storytelling technologies for performers and their environments.

The use of a novel information visualization in our study was helpful in surfacing what our experts felt was missing or what they would immediately think of creating on-air, and this suggested a number of topical areas in television programming to which our practices could be applied. These areas included elections, *"to be able to gather questions from the community and pose them to the candidates,"* sports broadcasting, due to its wealth of statistics; or special news features, *"send the [survey] to the Red Cross ... in refugee camps and ask them to capture what people are thinking;"* to supplement current events, and certainly, in the generation of new types of public opinion data gathering and presentation.

Technical Directions
In terms of technical directions, our participants gave us a number of specific suggestions for each phase in our model of production. For example, we hesitated to limit the length of recorded sound bites during content creation generation, but this is important for saving time later. We also plan to develop additional utilities for the content visualization and editorial stage, including a way to input a quick summary of the content's main points, whether it is a sound bite or an image with critical information. Performance refinements might include options on the interactive tabletop for using tangible or touch controls on our current visualization, and enriching the graphics according to suggestions.

SUMMARY
To enhance data storytelling on television, it is first necessary to enhance the datasets by including the content elements necessary for television programs. The data must be made visual and plotted. Thus data storytelling should be facilitated at all stages of production: content generation, content visualization/editorial, and performance. To this end, our system for supporting data storytelling combined an experimental mobile survey data gathering application with the creation of information visualizations for interactive tabletop presentation for television. Our evaluation with television professionals validated our production model, but raised important issues about the variability of production environments and on-air talent preferences in terms of program control, visibility of action, and the use of our interactive table. Next steps include refining the production model and technologies and creating pilot programs featuring the use of our studio tabletop for storytelling and audience testing of programs.

ACKNOWLEDGEMENTS
We would like to thank John Stasko and Laurie Baird for input and encouragement, as well as our research teammates Basheer Tome, Paul O'Neill, Lauren Langley, Ramik Sadana, Megha Sandesh, Ravi Karkar, Derek Yeung, and Eva Artinger.

REFERENCES
1. Abreu, J., Almeida, P., Teles, B. and Reis, M. Viewer behaviors and practices in the (new) Television Environment. In *Proc. EuroITV '13*, ACM (2013), 5-12.
2. Antonini, A., Pensa, R.G., Sapino, M.L., Schifanella, C., Teraoni Prioletti, R. and Vignaroli, L. Tracking and Analyzing TV Content on the Web Through Social and Ontological Knowledge. In *Proc. EuroITV '13*, ACM (2013), pp. 13–22.
3. Geerts, D., Cesar, P. and Bulterman, D. The Implication of Program Genres for the Design of Social Television Systems. In *Proc. UXTV '08*, ACM (2008), pp. 71–80.
4. Hullman, J. and Diakopoulos, N., 2011. Visualization rhetoric: framing effects in narrative visualization. *Transactions on Visualization and Computer Graphics, IEEE 17*, 12 (2011), pp.2231–40.
5. Isenberg, P., Elmqvist, N., Scholtz, J., Cernea, D. and Hagen, H., 2011. Collaborative visualization: Definition, challenges, and research agenda. *Information Visualization 10*, 4 (2009), pp.310–326.
6. Jordà, S., Geiger, G., Alonso, M. and Kaltenbrunner, M. The reacTable: exploring the synergy between live music performance and tabletop tangible interfaces. In *Proc. TEI '07*, ACM (2007), 139-146.
7. Kirk, D., Sellen, A., Taylor, S., Villar, N. and Izadi, S. Putting the physical into the digital: issues in designing hybrid interactive surfaces. In *Proc. People and Computers: Celebrating People and Technology*, British Computer Society (2009), 35-44.
8. Lucchi, A., Jermann, P., Zufferey, G. and Dillenbourg, P. An empirical evaluation of touch and tangible interfaces for tabletop displays. In *Proc. TEI '10*, ACM (2010), 177-184.
9. Mazalek, A., Davenport, G. and Ishii, H. Tangible viewpoints: a physical approach to multimedia stories. In *Proc. Multimedia*, ACM (2002), 153-160.
10. Murray, J. H. Transcending transmedia: emerging story telling structures for the emerging convergence platforms. In *Proc. EuroITV '12*, ACM (2012), 1-6.
11. Pedersen, E. W. and Hornbæk, K. mixiTUI: a tangible sequencer for electronic live performances. In *Proc. TEI '09*, ACM (2009), 223-230.
12. Robinson, S. J., Mendenhall, S., Novosel, V. and Mazalek, A. Tangible anchoring: grasping news and public opinion. In *Proc. ACE '10*. ACM (2010), 75-78.
13. Shamma, D.A., Kennedy, L. and Churchill, E.F. Tweet the Debates: Understanding Community Annotation of Uncollected Sources. In *Proc. WSM '09*, ACM (2009) pp. 3–10.
14. Tuddenham, P., Kirk, D. and Izadi, S. Graspables revisited: multi-touch vs. tangible input for tabletop displays in acquisition and manipulation tasks. In *Proc. CHI '10* ACM (2010), 2223-2232.

Leap Gestures for TV: Insights from an Elicitation Study

Radu-Daniel Vatavu
University Stefan cel Mare of Suceava
Suceava 720229, Romania
vatavu@eed.usv.ro

Ionuţ-Alexandru Zaiţi
University Stefan cel Mare of Suceava
Suceava 720229, Romania
ionutzaiti@yahoo.com

ABSTRACT

We present insights from a gesture elicitation study in the context of interacting with TV, during which 18 participants contributed and rated the execution difficulty and recall likeliness of free-hand gestures for 21 distinct TV tasks. Our study complements previous work on gesture interaction design for the TV set with the first exploration of fine-grained resolution 3-D finger movements and hand pose gestures. We report lower agreement rates (.20) than previous gesture studies and 72.8% recall rate and 15.8% false positive recall, results that are explained by the complexity and variability of unconstrained finger gestures. Nevertheless, we report a large 82% preference for gesture commands versus TV remote controls. We also confirm previous findings, such as people's preferences for related gestures for dichotomous tasks, and we report low agreement rates for abstract tasks, such as "open browser" or "show channels list" in our specific TV scenario. In the end, we contribute a set of design guidelines for practitioners interested in free-hand finger and hand pose gestures for interactive TV scenarios, and we release a dataset of 378 Leap Motion gesture records consisting in finger position, direction, and velocity coordinates for further studies in the community. We see this exploration as a first step toward designing low-effort high-resolution finger gestures and hand poses for lean-back interaction with the TV set.

Author Keywords

Gesture interfaces; interactive TV; Leap Motion; motion gestures; elicitation study; hand pose; recall likeliness.

ACM Classification Keywords

H.5.2 User Interfaces: Evaluation / methodology; Input devices and strategies (e.g., mouse, touchscreen).

INTRODUCTION

Television represents a valuable component in our lives, not only for delivering information and entertainment [11,12], but also for creating premises for enriched social interaction [1,2,9]. Over the years, content type, content accessibility, and underlying TV technologies have evolved considerably.

Figure 1: Experiment setup for eliciting leap gestures for iTV.

We now witness and explore inhabited, interactive, and internet television systems [1,3,12,30,32] that are augmented by audio surround systems, ambient effects [33,39], and secondary-screen devices [6]. However, interacting with the TV set has remained virtually unchanged, because interactions are still bound to the use of the standard TV remote control. In the context in which researchers see television as a concept on a converging path to interactivity [5], better designs of input devices are required to meet users' expected level of experience unencumbered by the interaction problems frequently reported for standard TV remote controls [2].

We are interested in this work in understanding people's preferences for interacting with TV with free-hand gestures, and we investigate, for the first time in the context of the interactive TV, a new gesture acquisition scenario, *i.e.*, short-range hand pose and 3-D finger movements that we capture with the Leap Motion controller [23] (see Figure 1). We are thus able to provide insights on the use of fine-grained finger gestures for TV interfaces that complement existing research on gesture interaction for TV [4,8,14,17,40,44].

Our contributions are as follows: (1) we collect people's preferences for interacting with the TV set with 3-D finger movements and hand poses that we acquire with the Leap Motion controller (which are referred in this work as *leap gestures*); (2) we contribute a set of design guidelines for using such type of gestures for controlling various functions of the TV set, and release our collected dataset of gestures to the community for further studies. We see our exploration as a first step toward designing low-effort finger movements and hand pose gestures for lean-back control of the TV set.

RELATED WORK

We place our effort in a larger body of work originating from both academia [4,8,10,17,22,40,44] and industry [24,34,37] interested in designing gestural interfaces for the interactive TV, but also in the even larger community of researchers exploring people's preferences for gesture commands [19,21,25,27-29,36,42]. However, we direct our attention toward understanding the use of fine-grained finger movements and hand poses for executing tasks for the TV set. Such gesture types have not been explored before in the interactive TV context, probably because of the lack of accessible technology to capture them. However, the dexterity and multi-functionality of the human hand has been thoroughly studied in psychology [16]. It is our belief that such gesture types are more appropriate in the context of lean-back versus lean-forward interaction paradigms with television than are large body movements [38,40,44].

We connect our work to previous explorations of gesture interfaces for TV. For example, Freeman and Weissman [14] proposed the first TV gesture interface that mapped hand movements to a cursor displayed on the screen; Bobeth et al. [4] investigated the way older adults employ free-hand gestures for controlling TV functions; Dias et al. [10] were interested in designing gesture interfaces for specific applications running on TV; and Vatavu [39] introduced augmented TV spaces for the control of which they proposed pointing gestures captured with an augmented remote. Finally, the PalmRC work of Dezfuli et al. [8] approaches the most our rationale for exploring low-effort short-range gestures for TV. The authors employed the palm of the hand as a supporting surface for finger touch to enable eyes-free control of the TV set.

We conduct this work in the tradition opened by the guessability methodology of Wobbrock et al. [43] that has been successfully applied for gesture elicitation studies in various application domains [21,22,28,29,36,42] including the interactive TV [38,40,44]. For example, Vatavu [40] collected and analyzed free-hand gestures captured at coarse level with the Kinect sensor in what constituted the first gesture elicitation user study for the interactive TV. A follow-up exploration [38] extended the initial findings and gesture set with more discussion centered on people's preferences of gestures versus TV remotes. Wu and Wang [44] were also interested in hand and body gestures that they captured at the same coarse level of detail. Beyond this previous work, we believe there is much opportunity in leveraging the fine-grained dexterous movements of fingers for low-effort lean-back interaction with the TV set. To this end, we focus in this work on short-range finger movements and hand poses that we capture with the Leap Motion controller [23]. In doing so, we deliver the community with further insight on designing gestural interfaces with this so far unexplored category of gestures. It is our strong belief that such gesture types are likely to represent an optimal choice for lean-back TV control in the line of simple eyes-free alternatives to the TV remote [8].

EXPERIMENT

We conducted an elicitation experiment [7,42,43] to collect people's preferences for leap gestures in the context of iTV.

Participants

Eighteen (18) volunteers (4 females) participated in the study (mean age 25.0 years, $SD = 3.1$). All participants were right-handed. Ten participants had no previous experience with gestural interfaces, whereas the other eight had used Nintendo Wii and Microsoft Kinect controllers for games. All participants owned touch-screen phones, but touch gestures are different in nature from the mid-air finger movements and hand poses investigated in this work.

Apparatus

A 40-inch (102 cm) Sony TV was connected to a laptop running Microsoft Windows 8.1 and our custom gesture acquisition software collecting Leap Motion gesture data. The Leap Motion controller is a 3-D tracking device that is able to detect and track targets with a precision of up to 0.01 mm in a 3-D space of .227 cubic meters with a 150° field of view, and can report tracked data (i.e., position, direction, and velocity coordinates) for up to 10 fingers at a rate of over 200 frames per second [23]. The Leap controller was conveniently placed for our participants at comfortable arm reach (see Figure 1 on the previous page).

Referents

We selected 21 referents[1] common for television watching, but that also include new functions recently made available on Smart TVs, e.g., open browser. The referents list was divided into four categories: (a) nine basic TV commands (BASIC): open, close, next and previous channel, volume adjustments, and menu commands; (b) three generic commands (GENERIC): yes, no, and ask system for help; (c) six channel query commands (QUICK-CHANNEL): go to favorite and second favorite channels, access random channel, go back to last channel, and go to specific channels identified by their numbers, such as channels #7 and #27; and (d) three feature related commands (TV-FEATURE), such as show TV guide, channels list, and open web browser. Table 1 lists all referents. Our set of referents is similar to those used in previous studies, e.g., Vatavu [40] employed 12 referents (our BASIC and GENERIC); Wu et al. [44] used 18 referents (out of which 9 are our BASIC ones, while they focus more on content play, such as "fast forward" or "play song" functions); and Morris [29] used 15 referents (focused on the content displayed in a web browser). While we relied on these previous studies to inform our set of referents, we also considered new referents to understand the opportunity to employ gestures for other tasks. For example, we decided to include functions to quickly access important channels (i.e., the favorite channel), but also two referents to understand how participants will refer to channel numbers with hand gestures (i.e., "Go to channel #7" and "Go to channel #27").

---

[1]We follow the terminology of Wobbrock et al. [42] that used the word referent to denote the effect of a gesture command.

Table 1. Set of referents used for the elicitation experiment.

No.	Referent	Description
		BASIC referents (9)
1	Open	Open the TV set
2	Close	Close the TV set
3	Next	Go to next channel
4	Previous	Go to previous channel
5	Volume up	Increasing sound volume
6	Volume down	Decreasing sound volume
7	Volume mute	Turn off volume
8	Open menu	Open a generic contextual menu
9	Hide menu	Hide/close the contextual menu
		GENERIC referents (3)
10	Help	Ask system for Help (e.g., show Help screen).
11	Yes	Enter affirmative answer to a system elicited Yes or No question
12	No	Enter negative answer to a system elicited Yes or No question
		QUICK-CHANNEL referents (6)
13	Go to favorite channel	Quick access to user's favorite channel
14	Go to 2nd favorite channel	Quick access to user's second favorite channel
15	Go to random channel	Have the TV choose a channel to watch, at random
16	Go to channel #7	Quick access to channel #7
17	Go to channel #27	Quick access to channel #27
20	Last channel	Quick access to the last channel that the user watched
		TV-FEATURE referents (3)
18	TV Guide	Open the TV guide
19	Show channels list	Show the list of available TV channels
21	Open browser	Open web browser

Task

Participants were seated comfortably at approximately 2 meters from the TV set. The experimenter was present during the entire duration of the study with the role to introduce participants to the features of the Leap Motion controller and to supervise the data collection procedure. Before running the study, participants were given some time to familiarize with the equipment and discover its active sensing area, *i.e.*, the 3-D volume above the device in which the hand is detectable by the device. The elicitation experiment consisted in presenting each referent (Table 1) with a text message on screen followed by an instruction to suggest a suitable gesture command. Participants took as much time as they needed to propose gestures. Once they were confident about their gesture proposals, the experimenter asked participants to reproduce the gesture one more time so that it could be recorded by the Leap Motion controller and annotated by our software.

Referents were presented in a random order, resulting in 21 trials, one trial per referent. At the end of the experiment, participants filled in a questionnaire in which they went through all referents one more time and tried to recall their gesture proposals. For each proposed gesture, participants rated how well it fit to the referent on a 5-point Likert scale, with 1 denoting "no fit at all" and 5 "very well fit". During this process, participants were also asked to perform the gesture one more time so that the experimenter could rate

how easily they were able to remember their own gestures (which he did on a 5-point Likert scale with 1 denoting "immediate recall" and 5 "no recall"). If participants were not able to recall the previously proposed gesture, they were asked to propose a new one. Participants also rated their likeliness to remember gestures from 1 denoting "very easy to remember" to 5 "very difficult". They also rated on 5-point Likert scales whether they preferred the proposed gesture or a TV remote button (a TV remote was available for participants to consult at this stage). The experiment took on average 35 minutes to complete per participant.

RESULTS

Consensus between participants

We measured consensus by calculating *individual* agreement rates for each referent with the methodology of Wobbrock et al. [42,43], but also by computing *overall* Kendall's W coefficients of concordance [20]. In our case, agreement rates vary between $1/18 = .055$ (corresponding to the case with each participant proposing a distinct gesture for a given referent) and a maximum of 1 (perfect consensus between participants, all suggesting the same gesture for a given referent). We refer the reader to Wobbrock et al. [42,43] for the formula to calculate agreement rates and run-through examples. Kendall's coefficient of concordance [20] is a normalization of the Friedman statistic used to assess the agreement between multiple raters with a number ranging between $.0$ (no agreement at all) and 1 (perfect agreement).

The mean agreement rate across all referents was $.20$ ($SD = .15$), see Figure 2a. This result was confirmed by the value of the Kendall's W coefficient which was $.254$ ($\chi^2(20) = 91.439, p < .001$). As Kendall's coefficient is related to the average of Spearman rank correlation coefficients between pairs of rankings [20] (p. 276), we can interpret the magnitude of its effect as medium (*i.e.*, less than .30, but greater than .10) according to Cohen's suggested limits for appreciating effect size. The highest agreement rate was obtained for the "Next" and "Previous channel" commands ($.62$ and $.54$ respectively), for which participants proposed hand movements to left and right. The lowest agreement rates ($.07$) were obtained for abstract tasks, such as "Volume mute", "Open browser", and "Show channels list" (Figure 2a).

Figure 2c shows the average agreement rates calculated for each of the four categories of referents. The highest agreement rate was $.26$ for BASIC (Kendall's W $= .310$, $\chi^2(8) = 44.584, p < .001$), followed by $.17$ for GENERIC (W $= .082$, $\chi^2(2) = 2.943, n.s.$), $.18$ for QUICK-CHANNEL (W $= .161$, $\chi^2(5) = 14.504, p < .05$), and $.08$ for TV-FEATURE (W $= .094$, $\chi^2(2) = 3.391, n.s.$). These results are explained by the fact that the BASIC category includes referents with embedded scale range information (*e.g.*, up and down, next and previous, etc.), while TV-FEATURE includes abstract tasks. For reference, we list all participants' gesture proposals for the entire set of 21 referents under the Appendix section.

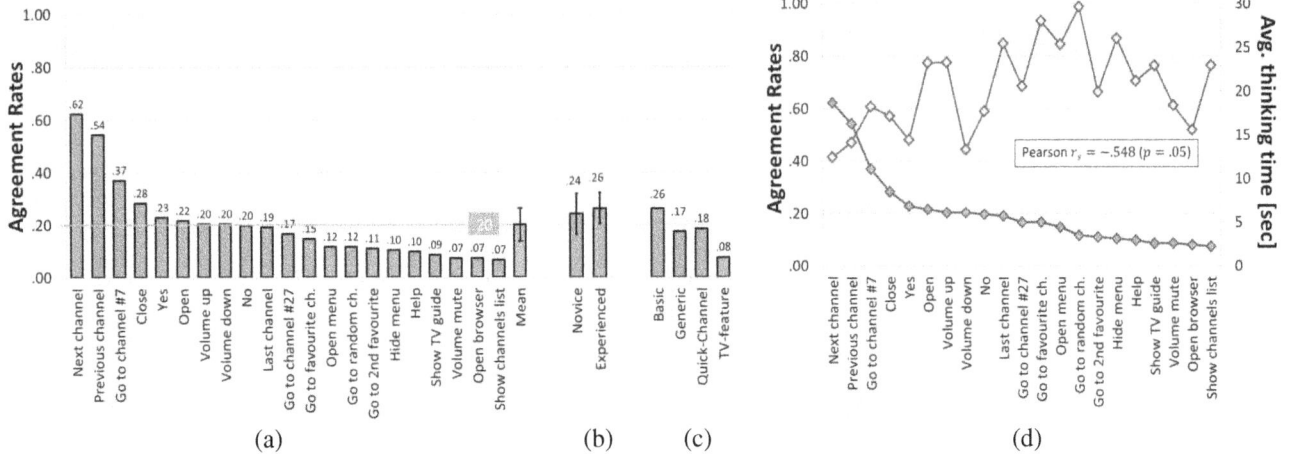

Figure 2: Agreement rate results for the 21 referents in our set (a), comparison between novice and experienced users (b), between referent categories (c), and correlation between agreement and average thinking times (d).

Experienced versus novice users

Eight participants had previously used gestures for video games. To understand the effect of previous experience on elicited gestures, we calculated agreement rates distinctly for the two groups. Results showed higher agreement for the experienced group, .26 versus .24, see Figure 2b. However, the difference was not significant ($U = 172.000, Z = -1.223, n.s$), showing that previous freehand and body gesture practice (from other application domains, such as gaming) had no influence on consensus for TV gestures.

Agreement rate and thinking time

Participants spent in average 20.5 seconds ($SD = 5.0$) to search suitable gesture commands. We found a significant negative correlation between agreement rates and thinking time (Pearson $r_{(N=21)} = -.548, p = .05$), see Figure 2d. This result is surprising, showing that the more time participants took to think about gestures, the less agreement resulted. This finding can be interpreted in two ways. First, the more time participants allocated to the task, the more creative they wanted to be generating gesture commands less likely to be proposed by others. Second, participants' first choice (*i.e.*, the gesture choice after a minimum thinking time) was likely to be found by other participants as well, probably due to some internal mechanism of understanding referent actions, *e.g.*, move hand to left and right for moving to the next or previous item in a list.

Gesture goodness

Participants used a 5-point Likert scale to rate how fit their gesture proposals were for each referent (gesture goodness), with 1 denoting "no fit at all", 2 "less fit", 3 "moderate", 4 "good fit", and 5 "very good fit". Overall, the median rating was 4 showing good confidence in proposed gestures. A Friedman test revealed a significant effect of referent type on self-reported goodness ($\chi^2(20) = 67.761, p < .001$). Four commands were rate "very well fit": "Next channel", "Previous channel", "Volume up" and "Volume down", while the lowest rated gestures (3, "moderate fit") were "Go to favorite", "Go to 2nd favorite channel", "Volume mute", "Open browser", and "TV guide".

Preference for gestures versus the TV remote

We were also interested in participants' preferences for gestures versus the TV remote control. Participants rated their preferences using an 11-point Likert scale going from 5 to 0 and back to 5 with the left-most 5 levels encoding preference for gestures, 0 a neutral state, and the right-most 5 preference for the remote. Results were in favor of gestures that were preferred for 82% of all ratings versus 12% for the remote, while 6% were neutral (Figure 3a). The intensity of the preferences measured on a 5-point scale showed a median score of 4 for gestures and 3.5 for the remote (Figure 3b).

Recall rate

Participants were also asked how easy they found recalling gestures they had just proposed (recall likeliness), which they answered using a 5-point Likert scale from 1 "very easy" to 5 "very difficult". The median rating across all participants and referents was 3, "moderate difficulty". At the same time, while running through the questionnaire, participants had to perform once more each gesture, and the experimenter observed their reaction time and encoded it on a 5-point Likert scale as well, with 1 corresponding to "instantaneous recall" and 5 being "no recall at all". The experimenter's median rating was 1 as the majority of the participants recalled their gestures instantly. However, when further analyzing this data, we found that only 72.8% of the participants' replay of gestures were correct (out of all 18×21=378 gestures), while in 11.4% cases participants could not remember their gesture proposal, and in 15.8% of all cases they "recalled" the wrong gesture (a gesture that we referred to as a *false positive*). Figure 4 illustrates the recall results for each referent. A Friedman test showed a significant effect of referent type on the experimenters' rating ($\chi^2(20) = 53.391, p < .001$). Best recalled gestures were found for "Next channel" and "Volume up", while lowest recall rates occurred for "Open menu" and "Open browser". We also found a significant Pearson correlation between agreement rates and recall likeliness ($r_{(N=18)} = .618, p = .01$), showing that gestures with large consensus are also more likely to be recalled easier.

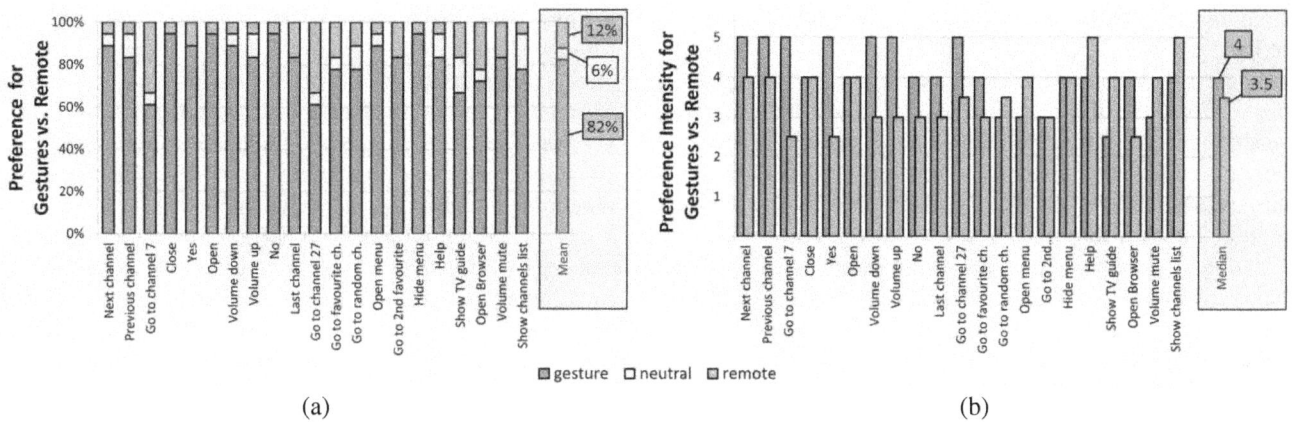

(a)   (b)

Figure 3: Participants' self-reported preferences for using leap gestures versus the TV remote, shown overall as percentages (a) and intensity of preference (b). NOTE: referents are listed in descending order of their agreement rate (as in Figure 2a).

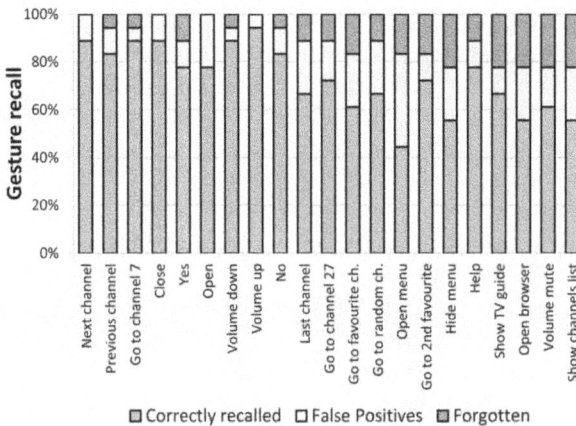

Figure 4. Leap gesture recall. NOTE: referents are listed in descending order of their agreement rate (as in Figure 2a).

GESTURE SET

We collected 378 gestures (=18 participants × 21 referents) with corresponding fit-to-function ratings. Based on the agreement rate results (Figure 2), we assigned each referent with the gesture that received the highest agreement. For references with low or no consensus at all, we selected one of the participants' gesture proposals that we believed best matched the referent based on our previous experience in gesture interface design. Results are listed in the Appendix, where we highlighted gestures that made it into the final set. Please note that this gesture set is by no means the definite set to use. Its main goal is rather to inspire gesture interface designs for the TV than to stand as a standard. For example, practitioners may opt for a combination of fine-grained finger movements and large arm gestures as in previous work [38,40,44], in which case they would only use some of our findings. However, besides the "winning" gesture for each referent, we believe there is also value in the other, lower rated gestures as well. For this reason, we decided to list in the Appendix all participants' gesture proposals. We also make available our set of recorded leap gestures to the research community for further studies, such as developing gesture recognizers to support such interfaces (http://www.eed.usv.ro/~vatavu).

IMPLICATIONS FOR DESIGN

Our results give insights on the way people define, rate and evaluate, and later recall fine-grained resolution 3-D finger and hand pose gestures. By using our findings, we are able to provide several guidelines for practitioners interested in designing TV interfaces employing such gesture types.

1. Finger and hand pose gestures are preferred to remotes, but there is low agreement between users. We found an overwhelming preference for using gestures instead of the TV remote control. For 82% of all responses, participants preferred gestures over the remote. The result is surprising given the low agreement rate we found for gesture preferences (.20). This finding shows that finger gestures tend to be highly personalized and suggests user-dependent training in order to avoid poorly designed interfaces [26,31] with less intuitive mappings between gestures and functions.

2. Users fall back on previously acquired gesture interaction models. During the experiment we observed one interesting behavior emerging when participants were thinking about gestures. When having to execute a more difficult task, users tended to propose gestures using a strategy that appeared as design iteration until they reached a simple and familiar gesture command. For example, users sometimes noted the similarity of the gesture they executed with touch gestures, such as directional swipes for "Next" and "Previous channel". This behavior originates from previous practice with touch-screen devices [18].

3. Preference for 2-D gestures. We found that users mostly employed the 3-D gesture-sensing device to articulate 2-D gestures. Most of the gestures we collected can be executed in 2-D without any major loss. For example, directional movements of the hand and drawing letters and symbols occurred mostly in a vertical plane in front of the user. For some gestures, users imagined a 2-D plane above Leap Motion that they used as a support for drawing gestures.

4. Users prefer either motion or hand pose gestures, and combinations of these two are less likely. To find out more about our participants' gesture preferences, we analyzed the resulted gesture dataset by classifying gestures into four classes as per the taxonomy of Vatavu and Pentiuc [41]:

simple static (*i.e.*, hand poses), simple dynamic (sequences of hand poses, but no motion), complex static (only motion is important), and complex dynamic (both motion and hand pose). For 40% of our participants' gestures only motion was relevant, followed by 38% of hand gestures involving only postures, either static or combinations of postures. Of all gestures, 22% involved combinations of hand pose and motion. Figure 5 shows the distribution of gestures.

5. Users associate gestures and commands in a way that helps maximize recall rate. This behavior was revealed by the recall percentages (see Figure 4) that show similar values for dichotomous leap gestures. When encountering referents with opposite effects (*e.g.* "Next" and "Previous channel", "Volume up" and "Volume down"), most participants considered gestures should also be similar.

7. Preference for culture-specific leap gestures. We observed many such gestures, *e.g.*, thumbs-up, hand wave, fingers closing in shut-up gesture, etc. The gestures we report in this work are common for Western cultures and they may prove inappropriate for other cultures. Also, the right-to-left and left-to-right movements for "Previous" and "Next" are also probably connected with the left to right reading order.

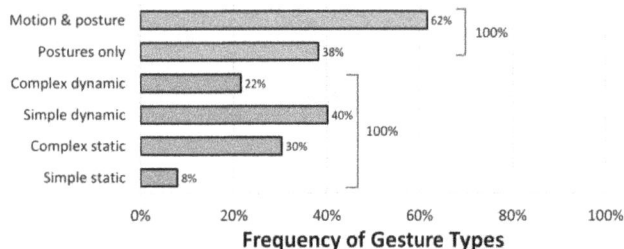

Figure 5. Frequency distribution of participants' leap gestures according to the gesture taxonomy of [41].

With our results we also confirm findings reported in a previous study focusing on large free-hand gestures [40]:

8. Exploit hand pose to distinguish between different commands. Hand pose is important to differentiate between gestures with similar motion. For instance, the colloquial gesture "come to me" was executed with all fingers to denote "Help" but only with three fingers to "Go to the favorite channel". Vatavu [40] also reported the importance of hand pose to differentiate between free-hand gesture commands.

9. Users show preference for drawing letters in mid-air to execute tasks whose names start with those letters. In many cases participants suggested letters to identify tasks, especially abstract ones, such as "Open Menu" (letter "M"), "TV Guide" (letter "G"), "Open Browser" ("B"), etc. There were multiple letter suggestions for the same command, such as both "C" and "L" for the list of channels. We also encountered the use of symbols, such as drawing "@" to open the browser, or the universal quantifier symbol "∀" to access a random channel. Users drew digits to specify channels by their numbers, *e.g.*, "Go to channel #27". We believe this behavior is also explained by participants' previous experience with touch-screens on which they can easily produce letters and symbols with stroke gestures.

We also witnessed cases in which users performed gestures with the support of the non-dominant hand, approaching the idea of the PalmRC prototype of Dezfuli et al. [8], which allows us to derive yet another design guideline:

10. Make use of concrete or imaginary support surfaces to assist users to articulate gestures. We observed situations in which participants employed part of their hands as an active sensing area (*i.e.*, a button). In other cases, participants performed gestures in a vertical plane in front of the body. Yet in other situations, participants imagined a horizontal plane above the Leap Motion controller that they used as a reference for their gestures.

CONCLUSION

We presented results of the first study on fine-resolution gestures for the interactive TV. We delivered guidelines for working with such fine-resolution gesture types for iTV scenarios employing a Leap Motion or similar device. We compared our results with previous studies on free-hand gestures [40] and complemented their findings. To encourage further exploration of such gesture types for iTV, including recognition and interaction techniques, we provide our user-defined dataset composed of 378 gestures with recorded position, direction, and velocity coordinates for hand and fingers. We hope that this first exploration on fine-resolution gestures will attract the community attention toward designing viable gesture alternatives for the remote in the context of lean-back TV interaction.

ACKNOWLEDGMENTS

This research was supported by the project liFe-StaGE, "Multimodal Feedback for Supporting Gestural Interaction in Smart Environments", project no. 740/2014, co-funded by UEFISCDI, Romania and OeAD, Austria.

REFERENCES

1. Barkhuus, L. 2009. Television on the internet: new practices, new viewers. In *Proc. of CHI '09*, 2479-2488

2. Bernhaupt, R., Obrist, M., Weiss, A., Beck, E., Tscheligi, M. 2008. Trends in the living room and beyond: results from ethnographic studies using creative and playful probing. *Comp. in Entertainment* 6(1), Art 5

3. Benford, S., Greenhalgh, C., Craven, M., 2000. Inhabited television: broadcasting interaction from within collaborative virtual environments. *ACM TOCHI* 7(4), December 2000, 510-547

4. Bobeth, J., Schmehl, S., Kruijff, E., Deutsch, S., Tscheligi, M. 2012. Evaluating performance and acceptance of older adults using freehand gestures for TV menu control. In *Proc. of EuroiTV '12*, 35-44

5. Cesar, P., Chorianopoulos, K. 2009. The Evolution of TV Systems, Content, and Users Toward Interactivity *Found. and Trends in HCI* 2(4), April 2009, 373-95

6. Cesar, P, Bulterman, D.C., Jansen, A.J. 2008. Usages of the Secondary Screen in an Interactive Television Environment: Control, Enrich, Share, and Transfer Television Content. *Proc. of EuroITV '08*, 168-177

7. Cooke, N.J. 1994. Varieties of knowledge elicitation techniques. *Int. Journ. Hum.-Comput. St.* 41(6), 801-849

8. Dezfuli, N., Khalilbeigi, M., Huber, J., Müller, F., Mühlhäuser, M. 2012. PalmRC: imaginary palm-based remote control for eyes-free television interaction. In *Proc. of EuroiTV '12.* ACM, NY, USA, 27-34

9. Dezfuli, N., Khalilbeigi, M., Mühlhäuser, M., Geerts, D. 2011. A study on interpersonal relationships for social interactive television. In *Proc. of EuroITV '11*, 21-24

10. Dias, T., Variz, M., Jorge, P., Jesus, R. 2013. Gesture interaction system for social web applications on smart TVs. In *Proc. of OAIR '13,.* Paris, France, 225-226

11. Elsweiler, D., Mandl, S., Lunn, B.K. 2010. Understanding casual-leisure information needs: a diary study in the context of television viewing. In *Proc. of IIiX '10*, 25-34

12. Fanciulli, M. 2008. Principles of entertainment in inhabited television. In *Proc. of AVI '08*, 5-12

13. Freeman, D., Vennelakanti, R., Madhvanath, S., Freehand pose-based Gestural Interaction: Studies and implications for interface design. In *Proc.of IHCI '12*,1-6

14. Freeman, W.T., Weissman, C.D. 1995. Television Control by Hand Gestures. In *Proc. of the IEEE Int. Workshop on Automatic Face and Gesture Recognition*

15. Jeong, S., Song, T., Kwon, K., Jeon, J.W. 2012. TV remote control using human hand motion based on optical flow system. In *Proc. of ICCSA '12*, Springer-Verlag, Berlin, Heidelberg, 311-323

16. Jones, L.A., and Lederman, S.J. 2006. *Human Hand Function.* Oxford University Press, Inc., New York

17. Juhlin, O., Önnevall, E. 2013. On the relation of ordinary gestures to TV screens: general lessons for the design of collaborative interactive techniques. In *Proc. of CHI '13.* ACM, New York, NY, USA, 919-930

18. Holzinger, A., Finger instead of mouse: touch screens as a means of enhancing universal access. In *Proc. of ERCIM '02*, No.235. 387-397

19. Kane, S.K., Wobbrock, J.O., Ladner, R.E. 2011. Usable gestures for blind people: understanding preference and performance. In *Proc. of CHI '11*, 413-422

20. Kendall, M.G., Babington Smith, B. 1939. The Problem of m Rankings. *Annals of Math. Statistics* 10(3), 275–287

21. Kray, C., Nesbitt, D., Dawson, J., Rohs, M. 2010. User-defined gestures for connecting mobile phones, public displays, and tabletops. *Proc. of MobileHCI '10*, 239-248

22. Kühnel, C., Westermann, T., Hemmert, F., Kratz, S., Müller, A., Möller, S. 2011. I'm home: Defining and evaluating a gesture set for smart-home control. *Int. Journ. Hum.-Comput. St.* 69 (11), 693-704

23. Leap Motion, https://www.leapmotion.com/

24. Magic Remote, http://www.lg.com/global/magicremote/

25. Lim, J.H., Jo, C., Kim, D-H. 2012. Analysis on User Variability in Gesture Interaction. In *Proc. of ICHIT '12.* Springer LNCS 7425, 295-302

26. Malizia, A., Bellucci, A. 2012. The artificiality of natural user interfaces. *Commun. ACM* 55(3), 36-38

27. Mauney, D., Howarth, J., Wirtanen, A., Capra, M. 2010. Cultural similarities and differences in user-defined gestures for touchscreen user interfaces. In *Proc. of CHI EA '10.* ACM, New York, NY, USA, 4015-4020

28. Morris, M.R., Wobbrock, J.O., Wilson, A.D. 2010. Understanding users' preferences for surface gestures. In *Proc. of GI '10*, 261-268

29. Morris, M.R. 2012. Web on the wall: insights from a multimodal interaction elicitation study. In *Proc. of ITS '12.* ACM, New York, NY, USA, 95-104

30. Nadamoto, A., Tanaka, K. 2005. Complementing your TV-viewing by web content automatically-transformed into TV-program-type content. In *Proc. of MULTIMEDIA '05.* ACM, New York, NY, USA, 41-50

31. Norman, D.A. 2010. Natural user interfaces are not natural. *Interactions* 17(3), May 2010, 6-10

32. Olsen, D.R., Partridge, B., Lynn, S. 2010. Time warp sports for internet television. *ACM TOCHI* 17(4), Art 16

33. Phillips Ambilight, http://www.philips.co.uk/c/televisions/33092/cat/#/hue

34. Philips uWand, http://www.uwand.com/

35. Ren, G., O'Neill, E. 2013. Freehand gestural text entry for interactive TV. In *Proc. of EuroITV '13*, 121-130

36. Ruiz, J., Li, Y., Lank, E. 2011. User-defined motion gestures for mobile interaction. *Proc. of CHI '11*, 197-206

37. Samsung Smart TV: TV Gesture Book, http://www.samsung.com/global/microsite/tv/common/guide_book_5p_vi/waving.html

38. Vatavu, R.D. 2013. A Comparative Study of User-Defined Handheld vs. Freehand Gestures for Home Entertainment Environments. *Journ. Ambient Intell. Smart Environments* 5(2). IOS Press, 187-211

39. Vatavu, R.D. 2013. There's a World outside Your TV: Exploring Interactions beyond the Physical TV Screen. In *Proc. of EuroITV '13.* ACM, NY, USA, 143-152

40. Vatavu, R.D. 2012. User-defined gestures for free-hand TV control. In *Proc. of EuroiTV '12*, 45-48

41. Vatavu, R.D., Pentiuc, S.G. 2008. Multi-Level Representation of Gesture as Command for Human-Computer Interaction. *Computing and Informatics* 27(6). Slovak Academy, 837-851

42. Wobbrock, J.O., Morris, M.R., Wilson, A.D. 2009. User-defined gestures for surface computing. In *Proc. of CHI '09.* ACM, New York, NY, USA, 1083-1092

43. Wobbrock, J.O., Aung, H.H., Rothrock, B., and Myers, B.A. 2005. Maximizing the guessability of symbolic input. In *Proc. of CHI EA '05*, 1869-1872

44. Wu, H., Wang, J. 2012. User-Defined Body Gestures for TV-based Applications. In *Proc. of ICDH '12*. IEEE Comp. Society, Washington, DC, USA, 415-420

APPENDIX A. COMPLETE SET OF PARTICIPANTS' GESTURE PROPOSALS

We present the full list of gestures proposed by our participants for all the referents. The first | highlighted | gesture in for each referent was the one that received the highest agreement rate. However, some referents received low consensus, and for these cases we selected one gesture from all proposals as the authors' choice for that referent, which we | highlighted | as well.

No.	Referent	Participants' gesture proposals
1	Open	**Open palm** , hand waving, move hand upward, move fist upward followed by wrist rotation, move hand downward, move palm away from the body, thumbs-up, move hand downward and backward then and forward and downward
2	Close	**Close palm** , hand waving, closing into a pinch all (all finger tips touching), move hand downward, fist moving up and down twice, move fist upward followed by wrist rotation, hand performing the "go away" cultural gesture, draw "X", perform click in mid-air with the index finger
3	Next channel	**Move hand right to left** , **Move hand left to right** , thumbs-up with moving to the right, "ok" cultural pose with thumb and index fingers, moving the index finger from left to right and then clicking in mid-air. Please note the two options in terms of movement direction (left-to-right and right-to-left) that correspond to two metaphors: moving the viewing window (as it happens with scrolling actions and traditional GUI) and moving the items themselves [31].
4	Previous channel	**Move hand left to right** , **Move hand right to left** , thumbs-up with moving to the left, perform double click in mid-air with the index finger, draw circle clockwise. Please note the two options in terms of movement direction (left-to-right and right-to-left) that correspond to moving the viewing window (as it happens with the scrolling action and traditional GUI) or the items themselves [31].
5	Volume up	**Move hand upward** , hand in pinch pose expanding fingers, thumbs-up with moving to the right, thumbs up moving upwards twice, move hand upward, rotate imaginary button to the right, draw "+", opening hand from thumb-index pinch, draw triangle pointing up, open palm, draw circle clockwise, hand performing the "go away" cultural gesture
6	Volume down	**Move hand downward** , from open palm to index-thumb pinch, thumbs-up with moving to the left, thumbs up moving downwards twice, rotate imaginary button to the left, move hand from left to right, draw triangle pointing down, closing into a pinch all (all finger tips touching), draw circle counter-clockwise, hand performing "come closer" cultural gesture
7	Volume mute	**Closing fingers into pinch** , fist followed by extending little finger, open palm, thumbs-down to thumbs-up, draw "X", close fist, open palm to index-thumb pinch, thumb-little finger pinch, open palm facing down move left to right, draw crossed zero, draw circle counter-clockwise, move hand downward, move hand left to right, move hand right to left, move palm away from body
8	Open menu	**Draw letter "M"** , draw small "o" small "m", rotate wrist down to up, move hand up, opening hand from thumb-index pinch, perform click in mid-air with the index finger, hand in pinch pose open fingers, hand waving, move hand down.
9	Hide menu	**Hand wave** , closed fist open index and little finger, close fist, open hand rotate upward to downward, from open palm to index-thumb pinch, move hand upward, hand performing the "go away" cultural gesture, rotate palm left to right, hand performing "come closer" cultural gesture.
10	Help	**Draw letter "H" or symbol "?" in mid-air** , hand performing "come closer" cultural gesture, hand in "peace sign" cultural gesture, wave fingers, finger snapping, move hand toward body, wave, pinch and wave
11	Yes	**Thumbs-up hand pose** , draw "check" sign, three fingers down, draw letter "Y", thumbs-up rotated 90 degrees to the right, perform a click in mid-air with the index finger, open palm, pinch followed by thumbs-up
12	No	**Hand wave** , close fist, three fingers down, move hand up, thumbs-up rotate from right to up, draw "X", move hand down
13	Go to favorite channel	**Show index finger** , thumbs-up, perform "come closer" cultural gesture, pinch between the thumb and little finger, move index finger down and upward, draw "check" sign, open palm, fingers snapping, draw star, thumbs-up rotated to right, move hand downward and backward then and forward and downward
14	Go to 2nd favorite channel	**Show two fingers (index and middle)** , thumbs-up rotated 90 degrees to right, thumb ring finger pinch, two fingers up, peace sign left to right, fingers snapping twice, draw digit "2", two fingers up followed by thumbs-up, move hand in front two times
15	Go to random channel	**Rotate palm facing down to palm up** , draw circle clockwise, draw circle anti-clockwise, draw circle anti-clockwise for three times, close fingers, open palm rotating down to upward, wave with fingers, perform a click in mid-air with the index finger, perform "so so" cultural gesture, open palm, draw letter "R", hand waving, drawing universal quantifier symbol (∀)
16	Go to channel #7	**Draw digit "7"** , various finger configurations to indicate "7" as a preferred channel
17	Go to channel #27	**Draw number "27" in mid-air** , various finger configurations to indicate "27" as a preferred channel
18	Show TV guide	**Draw letter "G"** , move hand upward, thumbs-up, draw letter "M", move palm in front of the body, move hand downward, perform "so so" cultural gesture, move hand left to right, show index finger, pinch followed by wave, open palm
19	Show channels list	**Draw square** , four fingers move down, open palm, draw letters "C" and "L", move hand downward, hand performing "come closer" cultural gesture, wave, move hand upward, pinch followed by wave, perform double click in mid-air with the index finger, move hand toward the body, draw letter "L", draw circle anti-clockwise
20	Last channel	**Draw circle anti-clockwise** , index and middle fingers moved to the left, fingers snapping, two fingers up, thumbs-up moving back, hand rotating imaginary button to the left, wave
21	Open Browser	**Draw symbol "@"** , move palm downward twice, close fist, draw letter "W" three times as in "WWW", hand performing "go away" cultural gesture, pinch twice, pinch followed by thumb ok, moving index finger from left to right, move hand from right to left, move hand downward, move palm in front of the body, show three fingers.

Tablet, Gestures, Remote Control? Influence of Age on Performance and User Experience with iTV Applications

Jan Bobeth*, Johann Schrammel*, Stephanie Deutsch*, Michael Klein*,
Mario Drobics°, Christina Hochleitner°*, Manfred Tscheligi°*†

*CURE – Center for Usability Research & Engineering, Modecenterstraße 17/2, 1110 Wien, Austria

°AIT – Austrian Institute of Technology GmbH, Donau-City-Straße 1, 1220 Wien, Austria

†ICT&S Center, University of Salzburg, Sigmund-Haffner-Gasse 18, 5020 Salzburg, Austria

{bobeth, schrammel, klein, deutsch, hochleitner, tscheligi}@cure.at

ABSTRACT

Due to recent development of TVs in the direction of highly interactive multimedia platforms, interactive TV (iTV) applications gain popularity. In terms of control possibilities a variety of input modalities have become available, though effects on performance and user experience of different age groups when controlling different iTV applications remain unclear. We present an empirical investigation comparing three input modalities (tablet, freehand gestures, remote) for controlling two iTV applications (Photo Browser, Nutrition Tracker) used by older and younger adults. Results show that all three independent variables had significant influence on performance, while we did not find influence of age or application on user experience. Overall tablet input based on a mirrored TV screen showed the best performance and was preferred by both age groups. Older adults were overall slower and showed a particularly large performance gap with the remote in comparison to younger adults.

Author Keywords

Touch; tablet; freehand gestures; remote; iTV; older adults.

ACM Classification Keywords

H.5.2 [**Information Interfaces and Presentation**]: User Interfaces – *Evaluation, Input devices and strategies.*

INTRODUCTION

Driven by recent advancements of TVs, typical practices of using TVs have undergone many changes. Nowadays, these practices range from passive media consumption to highly interactive TV applications [32]. A variety of input modalities has been suggested to control diverse iTV applications [7,30]. Despite these developments, traditional remotes remain the preferred interaction means for TV-based media usage [27]. Nevertheless, empirical evidence exists showing that input modality influences the performance outcome for different tasks and should be chosen accordingly [23].

By using interactive TV applications older adults can benefit from various services at home based on a familiar device [26]. With advanced age, cognitive, perceptual and motor abilities can deteriorate, while at the same time affecting the motivation in handling new technology [25]. On the interaction level, direct manipulations can reduce the effects of age-related functional decline, and on the motivational level, older adults are able to adapt to new technology if they perceive obvious benefits [13]. Thus, iTV applications might become more attractive for older adults when appropriately designed and benefits are clear. The plethora of different approaches for controlling iTV applications such as advanced remote controls [1,6], touch interactions [8,27], and various forms of gesturing [9,31] leads to the question of which input modality best matches the input requirements of a given iTV application, and which age effects apply. To our knowledge no empirical research has been conducted that directly compared performance and user experience characteristics of these input modalities for different iTV applications.

In this paper, we present an empirical study that compared a standard remote, freehand gestures, and a tablet showing the mirrored TV screen used by older and younger adults controlling two different iTV applications. The two iTV applications differed in terms of data and required input information: a list-based photo browser and a dialog-based nutrition tracker. The goal of this study was to assess performance and user experience of the input modalities with these applications to better support design of iTV applications, especially for older adults. Before describing our study in detail, we present related work that influenced its setup and the development of the prototypes.

RELATED WORK

Input devices for TV control

Various techniques have been developed to control TV applications over a distance. With regard to our study, we focus on touch-based interaction and freehand gestures.

Touch-based interaction

Preliminary work providing a concept for touch-based interaction on a remote control was suggested by Enns and MacKenzie [10], who attached a touchpad to a remote device. Choi et al. [6] adopted this idea and tracked the users thumb on and above the surface of an optical touchpad. In their approach, a shadow representing the user's thumb is presented on the TV and used for pressing a button or drawing simple strokes. With the emergence of touchscreens, the concept of using a second screen was embraced, either for parallel usage such as sharing or transferring content, or for controlling iTV applications [4]. One of the first such systems was a PDA application to manipulate interactive content on a TV [29]. Cruickshank et al. [8] developed a PDA application to control various iTV functionalities and showed significant improvement in interacting with iTV interfaces. More recent application areas for touch-based remote control are e.g. to participate in interactive TV shows [20] or to track meals [30].

Freehand gestures
Early work on freehand gestures for TV control [15] transferred the point and click experience known from the computer mouse to the TV by tracking hand movements to control a cursor. Stenger et al. [31] enhanced this approach by adapting the trigger and the execution command (e.g. a grab gesture). Chen et al. [5] dispensed with the visible cursor and controlled TV channel and volume settings by moving the left or the right arm upwards or downwards. Dezfuli et al. [9] assigned interactions to specific regions of the users´ non-dominant hand, triggered when tapped with the dominant hand which facilitates to control the TV blindly. The system of Freeman et al. [14] interprets eight static hand postures and allows to control iTV applications like photo browsing in laid-back situations.

Comparative studies on input devices
In the context of interactive TV an early comparison found that the mouse interaction outperformed two different remote controls and was strongly preferred by users [21]. Comparing a standard remote with a same-shaped touch-enabled remote (arrow keys vs. swipe gestures) Pirker et al. [27] found that the touch-based interaction provided a better overall user experience although performance was worse. Rashid et al. [28] studied the costs of display switching by comparing the control of a large display with a touchpad, a hybrid approach (with content parts displayed on a mobile device) and a pure mobile device interaction. Although participants performed worse with the hybrid approach they preferred it. A previous study with a similar setup using a movie search application showed that users preferred a remote over a hybrid tablet interface [18]. Regarding gesture-based interaction a recent study compared motion gestures and freehand gestures for home entertainment and showed that familiar point and click as well as drag and drop techniques are naturally reused in this domain [32].

Age effects and input devices
When comparing the performance during the interaction with different input devices, task completion time has been shown to be significantly lower for older than for younger adults (e.g. [11,16]). In contrast, error rates often do not

differ between younger and older users [13]. Findlater et al. [11] revealed that older users in particular benefit from touch screens compared to mouse usage: touch interaction reduces the performance gap between older and younger adults. In contrast, Ng et al. [24] found that older adults preferred a trackball over mouse and touch interaction, and that the latter could moderate only parts of age-related performance differences. In a multi-dimensional analysis comparing three input modalities (direct touch, a remote touchpad and gesture input) and two age groups for wall-sized displays Heidrich et al. [17] found the highest scores in performance and hedonic quality for touch input. In a study on motion-based game controllers [16] older adults performed worse than younger adults in motion-based games without age-related differences in device comfort or enjoyment. Bobeth et al. [3] compared four approaches for using freehand gestures to navigate TV menus. Results showed that directly transferring hand movements to control a cursor achieved the best performance and was preferred by older adults.

Given the growing popularity of iTV applications and the quantity of available input modalities, more research is needed to understand the specific needs of older adults in order to support designers in creating usable and enjoyable iTV applications for this audience. In contrast to existing research, our study compared the input modalities remote, tablet, and freehand gesturing for controlling two different navigation concepts of iTV applications. We examined performance and user experience differences between these applications and the three input modalities, and which age effects apply. Because of the commercial success of tablets and gesture-based interactions, we omitted other input modalities for interactive TVs such as touchpad [6] or motion-recognizing remotes [1].

METHOD

Research Questions
The following two research questions and accordant hypotheses formed the basis of our study.

Q1: How does the performance of older and younger adults differ when controlling two interactive TV applications with different input modalities (tablet, freehand gestures, remote control)?

We expect a low number of errors with the remote for both age groups, as they are already well acquainted with this form of interaction. We expect shorter task completion times for the interaction with tablet and gestures; especially older adults should benefit of direct manipulation means. Because of different functionalities we expect performance differences between the two iTV applications.

Q2: Is there a difference in the user experience of older and younger adults when using different input modalities, in terms of usability, effectiveness, satisfaction, and efficiency?

With respect to age effects in user experience we do not expect significant differences following previous findings [16]. Due to the novelty and direct-manipulation aspect of touch interaction and freehand gestures we expect higher satisfaction rates for these means compared to the remote. We expect positive ratings for the remote in terms of usability, as both age groups are accustomed to it.

Study Design
Our study was based on a 3 (input modalities) x 2 (iTV applications) x 2 (age groups) mixed between-within subjects design. Our dependent variables were performance (task completion time, number of errors) and different indicators for user experience (usability, effectiveness, satisfaction, efficiency). Additionally, qualitative comments and a preference ranking of input modalities were collected.

Participants
Our study involved 30 participants of two age groups: (i) 15 older adults (8 women and 7 men) between 66 and 80 years old (M=71.3, SD=3.9), and (ii) 15 younger users (8 women and 7 men) between 19 and 38 years old (M=26.8, SD=4.4). We deliberately omitted participants between those two age groups in order to enhance differentiation of age-related effects. To avoid experience-based biases we focused on right-handed participants who frequently watch TV and who have first experiences with touch-based devices but do not own a smart phone or tablet. In a pre-study all participating older adults had gained experience with gesture-based interactions. For younger participants having first experiences with the Microsoft Kinect was a recruitment criterion. We controlled frequency of use for 16 other technical devices (ranging from TV and PC to tablet and camera) to prevent group differences in technical expertise. There was no significant difference in frequency of use between older adults (M=3.28, SD=.13) and younger participants (M=3.09, SD=.08, t_{28}=-1.24, p <.05).

Apparatus and Input Modalities
We based the comparison on two iTV applications with different navigation concepts: a Nutrition Tracker (NT) and a Photo Browser (PB).

Nutrition Tracker: This application provides a nutrition diary on TV. The start screen contains 2 large buttons: one to open the input dialog for beverages and one for tracking meals. After opening the dialog for meals users could enter

the type and amount of food intake in a simple two-step procedure by selecting one or more of 6 food categories which were arranged in a 2x5 grid layout (see Figure 1 right) and then canceling or saving the input. For drinking behavior, 3 different drink categories could be selected.

Photo Browser: In this application 30 photos are presented either in an overview view, which consists of 5 pages of 6 photos and can be scrolled horizontally like a list (see Figure 2), or in a detail view (1 large photo). Switching back from detail to overview was possible via a button at the bottom of the screen. In order to prevent any emotional biases based on the photo content, we only selected pictures with a neutral rating of the IAPS (International affective picture system) [19]. Each photo could be identified clearly with a simple phrase like "the photo with the coffee cup".

The basic interactions with the three input modalities worked the same way for both applications (see Figure 1). Interfaces and tasks were designed by taking into account and avoiding the "fat finger" problem for touch devices or fatigue for gesture-based interactions.

Tablet: Because of reported interfering effects of hybrid user interfaces [18,28] (see Related Work section), the TV interface was mirrored on the tablet which allowed users to focus only at the input device during interaction. Afterwards, focus switches back to the TV. Therewith, we also adhered to the recommendation of Nichols et al. [25] stating that the need to focus at different distances (i.e. between input and output device) should be minimized for older adults as much as possible. A selection was done by tapping on the desired element on the touch screen. Within the Photo Browser, scrolling horizontally was realized by a swipe gesture.

Freehand gestures: We used a point-and-click approach as it performed best and was preferred by older adults [3]. The user's hand was tracked and its position was translated to screen coordinates to control a cursor. Selection was accomplished via a Wizard-of-Oz action carried out by the supervisor whenever the user performed a grab gesture.

Remote: the four arrow keys were used for changing the focus between interaction elements and the OK button was used for selecting the currently highlighted element. By this means, we followed the recommendation of Bernhaupt et al. [2] to focus only on the remote's main buttons.

Figure 1: The three input modalities: remote (left), tablet interaction (middle), and freehand gestures (right).

The Photo Browser was developed with Adobe Flex/AIR, with communication between devices over WiFi; the Nutrition Tracker was developed using Java Swing (TV) and the Android SDK (tablet), with communication between devices via Bluetooth. Despite the differences in technologies, efforts were made to ensure that the two applications looked similarly to avoid accordant biases. The TV was a 32", 1080p Samsung LCD TV with a refresh rate of 100 Hz. The gesture tracking was developed using the Kinect for Windows SDK. The mouse cursor was replaced with a large hand icon within both applications. The remote was a standard Windows-compatible infrared device (Hauppauge! Media Center remote). The tablet was a 7" Archos 70 internet tablet with 800x480px resolution.

During the evaluation, participants were asked to sit in front of the TV while performing the various selection tasks. The participants sat on a firm office chair in a comfortable upright position. The Kinect sensor was placed on top of the TV and angled so that the participant's right shoulder was located in the center of its field of view. A constant shoulder-to-TV distance of 2 meters was maintained for all modalities. This standardized setup was designed to keep potential interference from positioning effects constant. The tablet and the remote were placed on a coffee table in front of the user. The supervisor took a seat to the side of the coffee table (see Figure 2). To prevent any supervisor-caused biases the same person led all study sessions.

Figure 2: Setup of the study with TV, supervisor and a participant using the tablet to control the Photo Browser.

Procedure

Before starting the actual study we asked the participants about their use of technology. Subsequently, they conducted a simple motor test measuring manual dexterity adapted from the standardized Box and Block test [22]. By this means, we wanted to better understand the performance results. The task for participants was to move as many enwrapped pralines as possible with the dominant hand out of a box and into the corresponding space in an adjacent box, while crossing a 15cm obstacle, within 60 seconds.

Next, participants received an introduction for each of the six sessions (3 input modalities x 2 applications). They should spend up to two minutes to understand how the

prototype works and how they could control it with the given input modality. For practicing purposes the supervisor asked them to conduct up to five test tasks. For the actual study participants were asked to conduct 12 tasks with each input device (3x12) and both iTV applications. Thus, each participant performed 72 tasks in total. The instruction for a task with the photo browser was e.g.: "Please navigate to the photo of the train and open it in detail view." Similarly, for the nutrition tracker participants were asked: "Please enter that you had a glass of water." If an error occurred (e.g. the wrong photo has been opened) it was documented and the task was repeated.

After conducting the 12 tasks with one input modality for one iTV application, participants rated their user experience with the help of the standardized 4-item questionnaire UMUX [12]. Afterwards, the participants conducted 12 different tasks with the same application using the next input device. This procedure continued until all input devices had been tested and rated for both iTV applications. To avoid biases based on the order of input devices or applications, both independent variables (application and input modality) were counterbalanced between all participants. The tasks and the order of tasks stayed constant for each combination of input modality and application, in order to assure the same conditions for all participants. At the end of study, all participants ranked the three input devices according to their own personal preference for both iTV applications.

RESULTS

The main analysis instrument was mixed ANOVA. For every analysis the assumption of sphericity was tested using Mauchly's Test; we only report the results of this test explicitly in case the assumption was violated and corrections had to be applied. For post-hoc comparisons t-tests with Bonferroni corrected alpha levels were used.

Motor test. On average, older adults had worse motor skills (M=28.67, SD=1.28) than younger participants (M=34.14, SD=1.37), t_{27}=2.93, p<0.01. There are significant correlations between motor skills and task completion time for all input modalities: tablet, r=-0.46, p<0.01, gesture, r=-0.47, p<0.01, and remote, r=-0.50, p<0.01. The better the motor skills, the lower the task completion time.

Performance:

Task completion times were analyzed using mixed ANOVA with *age* as between subjects and *input modality* and *application* as within subjects' factor (see Figure 3). For the performance measurement all task completion times where users made an error were removed. The measurements of every experimental condition (i.e. each combination of factor levels) were checked for outliers by use of boxplots. Outliers were removed in case they lay more than three times the length of the box (i.e. the interquartile range) from either end of the box. Altogether five measurements had to be removed.

The ANOVA showed significant main effects for all three independent variables. Task completion times were significantly faster for the *Nutrition Tracker* than for the *Photo Browser*, $F_{1,28}$=149.28, p<0.001. *Input modality* also had a significant influence on task completion time, $F_{2,56}$=37.27, p<0.001. Post-hoc comparisons showed that the tablet was significantly faster than both freehand gestures and remote. There was no significant difference between gesture and remote. As expected also *age* showed a significant influence on performance, $F_{1,28}$=54.32, p<0.001. Older users were slower than younger ones.

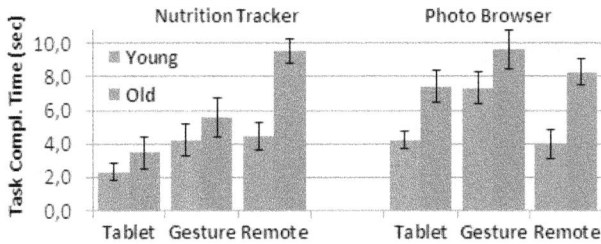

Figure 3: Task completion times for all experimental conditions. Error bars show 95% CI.

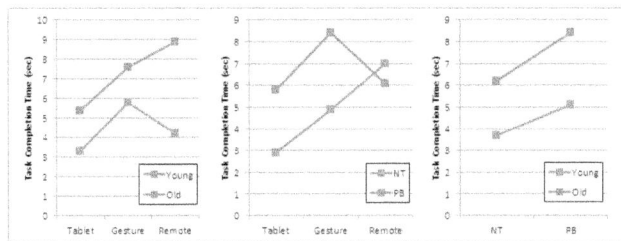

Figure 4: Interaction graph for Interaction Modality x Age (left), Interaction Modality x Application (middle) and Application x Age (right).

We also found significant interactions between the independent variables. There is a significant interaction effect between *input modality* and *age* $F_{2,56}$=13.62, p<0.001. This indicates that the used input modalities had different effects on task completion times depending on the users' age (see Figure 4 left). Whereas for tablet and gestures a similar trend in task completion time can be identified, the remote did perform well with younger users but comparatively poor for the elderlies.

The analysis also showed a significant interaction effect for *application* and *input modality*, $F_{2,56}$=53.67, p<0.001. Whereas for tablet and gestures we see a better performance in the *Nutrition Tracker*, in the case of the remote this aspect is reversed and the *Photo Browser* has the shorter task completion times (see Figure 4 middle).

We also found a significant interaction between *application* and *age*, $F_{1,28}$=5.31, p=0.029 (see Figure 4 right). Both age groups showed an increase in task completion times for the *Photo Browser*; however this increase is more distinctive for older adults.

Error rate. For every condition the number of errors was recorded. An error was counted when a participant selected an incorrect element. Overall error rates were rather small, and most tasks could be completed without errors. ANOVA shows a significant main effect for the *application*, $F_{1,28}$=19.06, p<0.001. Overall the error rate was higher for the *Nutrition Tracker* (Mean number of errors per condition i.e. 12 tasks: 1.06) than for the photo browser (0.42 errors). Also, we found a main effect for a*ge,* $F_{1,28}$=11.03, p=0.002 with older adults (Mean number of errors: 1.18) making significantly more mistakes than younger users (0.30). The analysis also showed a significant interaction between *application* and *age*, $F_{1,28}$=10.85, p=0.003. Whereas the error rate for the younger adults only shows a medium difference for the two applications (*Nutrition Tracker*: 0.38, *Photo Browser*: 0.22), the error rate for the older adults was approximately three times higher in case of the *Nutrition Tracker* (1.733) compared to the *Photo Browser* (0.622).

User Experience

All measures for user experience express a positive attitude of participants. The lowest-scoring measure of our study was efficiency (UMUX4) of gesture-based input in the *Nutrition Tracker* with a mean of 3.73, which is still slightly better than a neutral rating of 3.5 (see Table 1).

Both, the analysis for **Overall Usability** (UMUX1) and **Effectiveness** (UMUX2) does not show an effect of *application* or *age*, only *input modality* has a significant influence on the users rating of usability, $F_{2,56}$=14.98, p<0.001 and effectiveness, $F_{2,56}$=15.43, p<0.001. Post-hoc comparisons show that in both cases gesture is rated significantly lower than the two other modalities.

A similar significant influence of *input modality* was found for **Satisfaction** (UMUX3), $F_{2,56}$=8.08, p=0.001 and post-hoc test showed again that gesture-based input is rated worse than the other modalities. Also two interaction effects were found: First, the interaction of *application* with age is significant, $F_{1,28}$=11.46, p=0.002. Whereas the *Nutrition Tracker* was perceived different by the two user groups (satisfaction rating of 6.27 by the older versus 5.16 by the younger) the *Photo Browser* was rated similar (5.69 vs. 5.56). Second, there is a significant interaction between *application* and *input modality*, $F_{1.66,46.40}$=6.28, p=0.006. As Mauchly's test indicated that the assumption of sphericity has been violated ($\chi^2(2)$=6.26, p=0.04) degrees of freedom have been corrected using Greenhouse-Geisser estimates of sphericity (ε=0.829).

Analyzing the results for **Efficiency** (UMUX4) similar patterns as observed previously emerge. ANOVA shows a significant main effect for *input modality*, $F_{2,56}$=16.40, p<0.001 with the gesture-based approach rated significantly less efficient than the two other modalities. Also, the efficiency rating shows an interaction effect between *application* and *input modality* similar to the performance and satisfaction measurement, $F_{2,56}$=4.49, p=0.016.

			UMUX1	UMUX2	UMUX3	UMUX4
Nutrition Tracker	Tablet	Young	6.53	6.20	6.47	6.20
		Old	6.20	6.13	6.53	6.33
	Gesture	Young	4.93	4.20	4.33	3.73
		Old	5.53	5.00	5.87	5.00
	Remote	Young	6.07	5.27	4.67	5.40
		Old	6.00	5.60	6.40	5.80
Photo Browser	Tablet	Young	6.33	5.60	5.73	6.00
		Old	5.67	5.87	5.53	5.13
	Gesture	Young	5.13	4.27	4.80	4.27
		Old	5.00	5.00	5.27	4.53
	Remote	Young	6.53	5.93	6.13	6.00
		Old	5.93	6.07	6.27	6.20

Table 1: Mean ratings on the user experience scales ranging from 1 (bad) to 7 (good).

User Preferences

Asked to rank the input modalities older adults and younger adults put for both applications the tablet on rank 1, the remote on rank 2 and gesture on rank 3 (see Figure 5). None of the older adults ranked the modality gesture first. Many participants could imagine to use more than one input modality to control iTV applications which is in line with the findings of Coelho et al. [7].

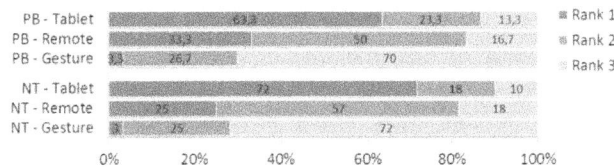

Figure 5: Ranking of the input modalities in percentage for Photo Browser (PB) and Nutrition Tracker (NT).

DISCUSSION

The discussion first focuses on the performance measurements and then analyses the user experience results.

Task completion time. The observation that older adults needed significantly more time to complete tasks was expected and confirmed findings of previous research (e.g. [11]). Lower task completion times with the Nutrition Tracker could be explained by the fact that tasks in the Photo Browser application required the navigation between several pages, while the Nutrition Tracker was based on one page and dialogues. The better performance of the tablet might be caused by the higher motor costs of moving the upper limb for gesture-based interactions and the necessity of numerous button presses in combination with button switches at the remote.

The effect of *age* on *input modality* is in particular interesting for the remote as the performance gap between older and younger adults was greatest and not in line with the trends for tablet and freehand gestures. One reason for this effect might be the different usage patterns of the remote. While younger adults used the remote mostly with one hand and without looking at it, the majority of older adults used both hands (see Figure 1 left) and looked at the remote for each button switch. Various explanations for this behavior difference are possible [13]: (i) Age-related decline of fine motor control leads to problems when using buttons on the remote. Thus, the buttons were too small for blind usage. (ii) Age-related loss of dexterity might lead to a higher expenditure of time per button press, which adds up with every button press. (iii) Older adults seem to be more anxious about making errors and want to be sure to press the correct button. The tablet is able to mitigate all of these age-related differences as it features larger targets, a lower number of needed interactions and direct feedback about whether the correct picture is being opened. Freehand gestures, meanwhile, require good motor abilities but not the same degree of precision as pressing small buttons on a standard remote. In addition, the cost of display switching between devices is avoided.

The measured interaction effect between *application* and *input modality* emphasizes the influence of the interaction concept for iTV applications. While navigating linearly through a two-row list of photos worked well with the remote, the dialog-based navigation concept of the Nutrition Tracker led to problems. This unusual interaction concept for controlling TVs was possibly more cognitively demanding for participants when using an indirect input device. In contrast to the repetitive button presses needed when using the Photo Browser, the Nutrition Tracker required users to switch between buttons more often, which also cost more time. The direct manipulation approaches of tablet and freehand gestures seem to be better candidates for the control of two-level dialog-based iTV applications. In summary, our hypothesis on shorter task completion times for tablet and gestures was only true for the tablet, while our hypothesis on performance differences between the applications could be verified.

Error rate. The number of errors was low in general and no significant influence of input modalities was measured. Therewith, our expectations on a low number of errors with the remote were confirmed. The identified impact of *application* might be caused by the unusual dialog-based user interface of the Nutrition Tracker. The more complex two-level selection approach seemed to be more error-prone and cognitively demanding than the more linear user interface of the Photo Browser. The higher general error rate of older adults in comparison with younger ones may be attributed to the slightly reduced motor skills that impact all three input modalities. With the remote two buttons were occasionally pressed at the same time, while with the tablet the swipe gesture led occasionally to accidently performed taps, and with the freehand gestures the tendency to overshoot targets occurred more often. Nevertheless, the low overall number of errors suggests that the applications could be controlled without major problems with all three input modalities.

User Experience. A positive user experience was reported for all measured items (UMUX1-4). As hypothesized and analog to previous research, no significant differences were found between *age* groups [16]. Similarly, the choice of *application* did not influence user experience factors. More polarizing or personal content in the iTV applications could have had a greater impact on user experience than a Photo Browser that shows neutral photos and a Nutrition Tracker that records arbitrary non-personal meals. Together with the low error rates, these positive results suggest that the two iTV applications were designed appropriately and that both age groups enjoyed using them. All three input modalities were rated as being easy to use.

Nevertheless, *input modality* had a significant influence on all measured items (UMUX1-4). The lower rating of freehand gestures might be caused by the longer task completion times but also by technical problems related to functional issues of the prototype (see Limitations section). Although tablet interaction showed better performance results than remote both input modalities received similar results in the user experience ratings. This might be caused by the fact that participants were able to accomplish all tasks with both devices without major problems. However, when asked to rank input modalities preferences could be identified. A clear preference was found for the mirrored TV screen on the tablet, probably because of the overall best performance and the advantage of direct manipulation. In summary, our hypothesis of higher satisfaction with tablet and gestures could not be verified but the one on positive usability ratings for the remote was confirmed.

Measures for Satisfaction (UMUX3) showed *age* effects on *application* and an influence of *input modality* on *application*. While both age groups showed a similar level of satisfaction with the Photo Browser, older adults were more and younger adults less satisfied with the Nutrition Tracker. Ratings of younger adults might reflect the worse performance which occurred using the Nutrition Tracker, while older adults might have rated more with regards to its content. Nutrition tracking might be more relevant for older adults. Further, the effect of *input modality* on *application* might be explained by the different navigation concepts of the two iTV applications. The rather linear interactions with the Photo Browser could be achieved comfortably and almost blindly with the remote. For the two-level dialog-navigation of the Nutrition Tracker direct manipulations per touch seemed to be more comfortable.

LIMITATIONS
In our setup the freehand gesture recognition sometimes produced short delays of some hundreds of milliseconds. Participants needed to correct their movements and lost some time. Hence our study might not directly be applicable to gesture recognition systems that perform in real time. Occasionally more serious freezes occurred; in these cases performance for the given task was not measured, but they may have influenced the perceived user experience negatively. Interestingly, the Kinect had more problems detecting hand movements of older adults than of younger adults. Maybe the tendency of older adults to sit in more hunched or crooked postures contributed to this trend, as the Kinect software attempts to identify the full-body skeleton to be able to track individual limbs.

CONCLUSION
In this paper, we examined the influence of *age*, *application* and *input modality* on performance and user experience when controlling iTV applications. We observed younger and older adults using a list- and a dialog-based iTV application with the input modalities tablet, freehand gestures and remote. While all three independent variables had a significant influence on performance, user experience differences were only found for *input modality*.

The results show that a mirrored TV screen on a tablet is the most promising of the assessed alternatives to control iTV applications for both younger and older adults. Direct manipulations and the reduction of display switches for conducting selection tasks seems to be advantageous in this context, especially for older adults. Accordingly, we recommend designers targeting older adults to avoid unnecessary display switches e.g. by mirroring the TV screen on a tablet. Also, using freehand gestures seems to be a promising approach, but requires improvements on the technical side towards higher accuracy and robustness. If a system can assure accurate real-time tracking, short point-and-click gestures should provide comfortable means for selection tasks without grabbing a physical control device. The remote works well for linear tasks, while older adults had problems with the non-linear user interface and showed a particularly high performance gap compared to younger participants. For linear use cases (e.g. zapping) the remote works equally good whereas designers should keep the amount of needed button changes reduced, thus for more complex input they should design the navigation in a series of linear task or consider omitting the remote for older adults completely.

Overall, older adults are easily able to adopt alternative input modalities to control iTV applications. The presented work lays the foundation for further investigations about the control of iTV applications, e.g. including further input modalities or multimodal usage scenarios.

ACKNOWLEDGMENTS
This work has been partly funded by the AAL JP projects FoSIBLE (AAL-2009-2-135), AALuis (AAL-2010-3-70).

REFERENCES
1. Bailly, G., Vo, D.-B., Lecolinet, E., and Guiard, Y. Gesture-aware remote controls: guidelines and interaction techniques. *Proc. ICMI'11*, (2011), 263–270.
2. Bernhaupt, R., Obrist, M., and Weiss, A. Trends in the living room and beyond. *Proc. EuroITV'07*, Springer (2007), 146–155.

3. Bobeth, J., Schmehl, S., Kruijff, E., Deutsch, S., and Tscheligi, M. Evaluating performance and acceptance of older adults using freehand gestures for TV menu control. *Proc. of EuroITV'12*, ACM (2012), 35–44.

4. Cesar, P., Bulterman, D., and Jansen, A. Usages of the secondary screen in an interactive television environment: control, enrich, share, and transfer television content. *Proc. EuroITV'08*, (2008), 168–177.

5. Chen, M., Mummert, L., Pillai, P., Hauptmann, A., and Sukthankar, R. Controlling your TV with gestures. *Proc. of MIR'10*, ACM (2010), 405–408.

6. Choi, S., Han, J., Lee, G., Lee, N., and Lee, W. RemoteTouch: Touch-Screen-like interaction in the TV viewing environment. *Proc. CHI'11*, (2011), 393–402.

7. Coelho, J., Duarte, C., Biswas, P., and Langdon, P. Developing accessible TV applications. *Proceedings of ASSETS'11*, (2011), 131–138.

8. Cruickshank, L., Tsekleves, E., Whitham, R., Hill, A., and Kondo, K. Making interactive TV easier to use: Interface Design for a Second Screen Approach. *The Design Journal 10*, 3 (2007).

9. Dezfuli, N., Khalilbeigi, M., and Huber, J. PalmRC: imaginary palm-based remote control for eyes-free television interaction. *Proc. EuroITV'12*, (2012), 27–34.

10. Enns, N. and MacKenzie, I. Touchpad-based remote control devices. *Proc. of CHI'98*, (1998), 229–230.

11. Findlater, L., Froehlich, J.E., Fattal, K., Wobbrock, J.O., and Dastyar, T. Age-related differences in performance with touchscreens compared to traditional mouse input. *Proc. of CHI '13*, ACM (2013), 343–346.

12. Finstad, K. The Usability Metric for User Experience. *Interacting with Computers 22*, 5 (2010), 323–327.

13. Fisk, A.D., Rogers, W.A., Charness, N., Czaja, S.J., and Sharit, J. *Designing for older adults: principles and creative human factors approaches*. CRC Press, 2009.

14. Freeman, D., Vennelakanti, R., and Madhvanath, S. Freehand pose-based Gestural Interaction: Studies and implications for interface design. *Proceedings of IHCI'12*, IEEE (2012), 1–6.

15. Freeman, W.T. and Weissman, C.D. Television Control by Hand Gestures. *IEEE Intl. Wkshp. on Automatic Face and Gesture Recognition*, (1995).

16. Gerling, K., Dergousoff, K., and Mandryk, R. Is Movement Better? Comparing Sedentary and Motion-Based Game Controls for Older Adults. *Proc. of GI'13*, (2013).

17. Heidrich, F., Ziefle, M., Röcker, C., and Borchers, J. Interacting with smart walls: a multi-dimensional analysis of input technologies for augmented environments. *Proc. of AH'11*, ACM (2011).

18. Johnston, M. and Haro, L.D. A multimodal interface for access to content in the home. *Proc. of ACL'07*, (2007).

19. Lang, P., Bradley, M., and Cuthbert, B. International affective picture system (IAPS): Affective ratings of pictures and instruction manual. *Tech. Rep. A-8*, (2008).

20. Lin, C.-L., Hung, Y.-H., Chen, H.-Y., and Chu, S.-L. Content-aware smart remote control for Android-based TV. *2012 IEEE International Conference on Consumer Electronics (ICCE)*, IEEE (2012), 678–679.

21. MacKenzie, I. and Jusoh, S. An evaluation of two input devices for remote pointing. *Engineering for Human-Computer Interaction*, (2001), 235–250.

22. Mathiowetz, V., Volland, G., Kashman, N., and Weber, K. Adults Norms for the Box and Block Test of Manual Dexterity. *The American Journal of Occupational Therapy 39*, 6 (1985), 386–391.

23. McLaughlin, A.C., Rogers, W. a, and Fisk, A.D. Using Direct and Indirect Input Devices: Attention Demands and Age-Related Differences. *ACM transactions on computer-human interaction 16*, 1 (2009), 1–15.

24. Ng, H., Tao, D., and Or, C.K.L. Age Differences in Computer Input Device Use: A Comparison of Touchscreen, Trackball, and Mouse. *Advances in Information Systems and Technologies 206*, (2013).

25. Nichols, T.A., Rogers, W.A., and Fisk, A.D. Design for Ageing. In G. Salvendy, ed., *Handbook of human factors and ergonomics*. John Wiley & Sons, Hoboken, N.J., 2006, 1418–1458.

26. Obrist, M., Bernhaupt, R., and Tscheligi, M. Interactive TV for the Home: An Ethnographic Study on Users' Requirements and Experiences. *International Journal of Human-Computer Interaction 24*, 2 (2008), 174–196.

27. Pirker, M., Bernhaupt, R., and Mirlacher, T. Investigating usability and user experience as possible entry barriers for touch interaction in the living room. *Proc. of EuroITV'10*, ACM (2010), 145–154.

28. Rashid, U., Nacenta, M., and Quigley, A. The cost of display switching: a comparison of mobile, large display and hybrid UI configurations. *Proc. of AVI'12*, ACM (2012), 99–106.

29. Robertson, S., Wharton, C., Ashworth, C., and Franzke, M. Dual device user interface design: : PDAs and interactive television. *Proceedings of CHI'96*, ACM Press (1996), 79–86.

30. Simon, H. Enrichment of Interactive Digital TV using Second Screen. *International Journal of Computer Applications 64*, 22 (2013), 58–64.

31. Stenger, B., Woodley, T., Kim, T.K., and Cipolla, R. A vision-based system for display interaction. *Proc. British HCI'09*, British Computer Society (2009).

32. Vatavu, R.-D. A comparative study of user-defined handheld vs. freehand gestures for home entertainment environments. *Journal of Ambient Intelligence and Smart Environments 5*, 2 (2013), 187–211.

How to Lose Friends & Alienate People: Sharing Control of a Single-User TV System

Mark McGill[†]
m.mcgill.1@research.gla.ac.uk

John Williamson[‡]
jhw@dcs.gla.ac.uk

Stephen A. Brewster[†]
stephen.brewster@glasgow.ac.uk

[†] Glasgow Interactive Systems Group   [‡] Inference, Dynamics and Interaction Group
School of Computing Science, University of Glasgow, Glasgow, G12 8QQ, UK

ABSTRACT

The single physical remote control, paired to a media system, is no longer necessarily the only (or indeed primary) mechanism of control, with new input modalities (e.g. gesture) and mechanisms (e.g. mobile devices) allowing anyone to contribute to the input and control. This paper investigates the potential for extending single-user interfaces in order to support multi-user use, as a means of utilizing new inputs without having to abandon the familiar interfaces, control management behaviours and mental models that users have established. A survey was conducted investigating existing behaviours for managing control in terms of prevalence and acceptability. These behaviours and potential new ones were then incorporated into a multi-user system where management of control was virtualized, using mobile devices for input. We found that behaviours derived from existing ones (e.g. passing/taking control) were at worst functionally equivalent to, and in some cases superior to, managing a single physical remote control. We suggest that sharing single-user TV systems implementing these behaviours offers a viable alternative to concurrent use TV systems.

Author Keywords

Shared control; multi-user; media systems; mediation of control; single-user;

ACM Classification Keywords

H.5.m. Information Interfaces and Presentation (e.g. HCI): Miscellaneous

INTRODUCTION

Since 1955, interaction with the television has iterated upon a single device that is now considered a *de facto* standard: the remote control. It is a device of ubiquity in the living room and has a host of associated management behaviours; it can be passed, taken, shared, relinquished, hidden, denied. However, it is in the process of being supplemented with new interfaces relying on previously under-used input modalities (such as gesture or voice) and mechanisms (such as every mobile device in the room) for exerting control. In addition, it is becoming commonplace for modern SmartTVs to bundle multiple remotes (e.g. a standard button remote and a touchpad or gestural remote), whilst Android devices are now available with IR blaster support, thus potentially vastly increasing the number of devices capable of controlling a given media system.

As such, the constraint of "one user at a time" is being eroded, with new possibilities for seamless multi-user use (be it discrete or concurrent) becoming a reality; for example consumer televisions (e.g. Samsung SmartTVs[1] with gesture/voice/touchpad control) and set-top boxes (e.g. the Xbox One[2] building on previous work regarding voice and gesture controls [10]) feature the technological capability for multi-user use. However, existing behaviours and familiar interactions are potentially being discarded without due consideration. These new systems introduce two issues: concurrency of use and management of use.

Concurrency of use: In providing systems that support concurrency, we may be introducing additional complexity and undermining users' mental models of the media systems they interact with. This could have an affect on groups such as visually impaired people (with the state of the system changing outwith their control) or older adults (with concurrent multi-user use often enabled through multi-pointer/cursor approaches which both require a degree of dexterity and coordination, whilst increasing visual complexity; this is in contrast to systems reliant on discrete events for navigation for example). Additionally, there exists a significant legacy of single-user set-top boxes (cable/satellite receivers etc.) that do not support concurrency but could support a system mediating between given inputs.

Management of use: In facilitating ubiquitous control and moving away from traditional behaviours for managing control, we may be undermining the users' capability to manage who can interact with these systems, for example parents taking the remote away from a child. Whilst systems such as the Xbox One have the capability to identify users, and thus the crude physical management of control could be supplanted by a more reactive and programmed form of management, there are a number of issues e.g. privacy concerns regarding always-on sensors in the living room. As such, there is scope for arguing that traditional behaviours for managing use be preserved in some fashion, and furthermore that we identify

---

[1] http://www.samsung.com/us/2013-smart-tv/
[2] http://www.xbox.com/en-US/xbox-one/entertainment

the components of these traditional behaviours that are most important (in terms of usage and acceptability).

This paper investigates how systems designed for control by one user at a time can be used my multiple users, examining how existing and new behaviours might fare in a system where the bottleneck of a physical remote control no longer exists, whilst retaining the single-user interface users are familiar with.

RELATED WORK

Sharing Single-User Systems

In 1990, Greenberg *et al.* [6] demonstrated a means of sharing single-user applications through view-sharing and turn-taking, and this concept has been frequently extended and re-implemented since. For example, two decades later, Abe *et al.* [1] examined tolerant sharing of single-user applications amongst multiple users. The idea of adapting single-user systems represents a pragmatic approach, one that is often deployed due to some constraint preventing the redesign of the underlying single-user system. Often it is a wish to retain the mental model and learned behaviours users have developed, or an acknowledgement that systems are often targeted at the single-user model, even though there will be use cases where multi-user use is likely to occur.

Concurrent Interaction

Concurrent use interfaces are either managed (e.g. You *et al* [18] used computer vision techniques to detect users and partition and rearrange personal space on a shared display), self-managed (e.g. Tse *et al* [17] demonstrated how users were found to self-partition shared workspaces in order to achieve optimal collaboration), or achieved through the combination of the two. This is a common feature of tabletop interaction, for example LunchTable [11] integrated a multi-touch display table with a large, vertical display for rich information, allowing the sharing of content among a whole group, whilst control of the display was managed concurrently via the multi-user table.

Outwith tabletops, Single-Display Groupware [16] multi-pointer systems are perhaps the most relevant example of concurrency [3], to the extent that strategies for multi-pointer management are becoming increasingly relevant [15].

However, the multi-pointer approach is not without its flaws, requiring greater dexterity/continual adjustment when manipulating said pointer (moving away from the discrete, button based controls traditional in remote controls), increased visual noise, and potentially decreased performance [9].

Mediated Interaction

There have been a number of papers proposing shared-use media systems. For example, Ballendat *et al.* [2] developed a system whereby a large vertical display enabled media related tasks (browsing, viewing), adapting the presentation based on the angle and proximity of the user, and pausing when the user was no longer engaged with the system. In this scheme, the user closest to the system was considered most engaged with it, thus essentially sharing the system through a hierarchy of proximity.

Pohl *et al.* [13] proposed that interaction could be defined by the extent to which the user was engaged in a task. They suggested that there was a set of scenarios where casual interaction might be better suited for a given task, and that determining this level of engagement (and thus which form of interaction, casual or focused/engaged) be up to the user. The system would then adapt depending on how much attention and effort the user chose to invest. They too discussed proximity, for example pointing to the fact that the bandwidth of user interactions decreases proportional to distance to the device with which the user is interacting, thus mapping engagement to proximity.

However, these approaches may not be appropriate for collocated groups in shared spaces interacting with media systems. For example, the proxemic approach does not take into account the fact that proximity to a media system is dictated not by engagement, but by seating arrangement: it might be just as likely to be fully engaged in the system, without being the closest person to said system, as being entirely disengaged from the system at close proximity, given the variety of seating arrangements in living spaces.

In contrast, approaches have been undertaken to design "seamless" interaction techniques such that, regardless of proximity, the same mechanics for interaction would be retained. Clark et al. [5] proposed a proximity-based interface that allowed users to interact with a media system both within range of touch, and at a distance, transitioning to pointing or device input when far away. Of note here was the fact that in the evaluation of this system, the proximity-based interaction was not frequently used; additionally, having the interface change depending on distance via zooming was found to be counter-intuitive.

This raises some important discussions regarding whether an interface should be adaptive within the domain of the living-room: is there enough space typically available such that the interface becomes unusable at a distance and thus needs to adapt? And how is shared use facilitated? If a group of users is currently attending to the display, with one user browsing through available media, to whom should the display be targeted?

Group interaction with media systems overlaps with these techniques, but is fundamentally different in many ways. Proximity is in all likelihood rendered irrelevant in static seated contexts, whilst attentional interfaces are muddled by the fact that many users may be attending to the display, and all may intend to interact with it at some point.

Additionally, attempting to adapt to attention is fraught with difficulty: if a user looks away from the screen, perhaps to talk to someone, that does not give sufficient justification that they might want their media paused: in providing interaction techniques that are low effort and seamless, both casual and engaged interaction are potentially adequately facilitated.

Finally, there are also social and cultural issues: any given interaction technique may contradict societal norms (e.g. undermining the control of the head of the household) or cultural norms (e.g. a particular gesture set being inappropriate).

Summary

Shared use of media systems by co-located groups occurs frequently, and as such these media systems should be able to flexibly facilitate such usage, whilst taking advantage of new modalities and input mechanisms available to users. Schemes have been proposed that implement new behaviours and interfaces, supporting concurrent or mediated usage, which have had some success. However, they do not adequately take into account the breadth of reliance on single-user media systems, and the existing behaviours for explicitly managing use or control of these systems that have been developed over a considerable period of time.

EXISTING BEHAVIOURS SURVEY

To gain an understanding of existing behaviours for sharing control in home media systems and their acceptability, a short survey was conducted, reaching 156 respondents in all (for demographics see Figure 1). The survey was sent out to available University mailing lists (covering staff and students) as well as online forums/social media, with printed copies distributed to respondents in demographics less likely to be reached via email.

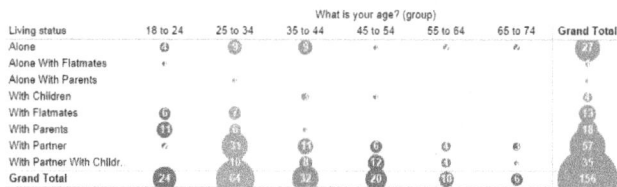

Figure 1. Demographics of respondents, broken down by age and living status (gender omitted, however split was approximately 60-40 biased towards males).

Its intention was exploratory, consisting of questions (predominantly 5-point Likert-type) constructed to explore control methods, decision making and media consumption activities across various different intimacy groups (groups of friends, family, colleagues etc.). Full survey results are available on request.

Control Is A Commodity

The most relevant and interesting result of this survey was in two questions regarding how control was shared in home media systems and how acceptable these methods were (see Figures 2 and 3).

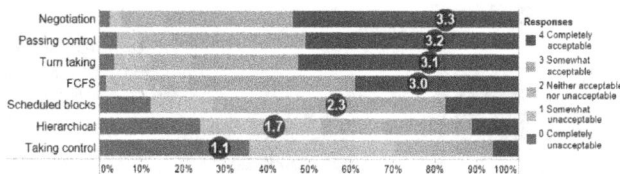

Figure 2. Responses to the question "How acceptable do you find the following ways of controlling media systems?". Responses were Likert-type five point scale, ranging from completely unacceptable to completely acceptable, and converted into 0-4 scale for mean acceptability (labeled in grey circles, higher is better) for relative comparisons.

We asked participants to rate hypothesised control management behaviours (and suggest their own if not appropriate). Of these, "first come, first serve", "passing control around", "negotiation e.g. asking for control" , and "turn taking" were the most used strategies, with "hierarchical (an individual is

typically in control)" , "scheduled blocks for sharing control of the TV", and "taking the control from whomever currently has it" falling behind. This supported the view that control of these systems is a commodity or resource in and of itself. As the person currently in control plays a large part in dictating events, if you acquire control, you might be reticent to relinquish it; societal norms of fairness may, however dictate that strategies be introduced to accommodate other's wishes and uses, hence passing control, turn taking and negotiation feature.

Of these frequently used control schemes, in terms of acceptability they were largely similar (see Figure 3). We would suggest that the behaviours that have developed around control of these media systems have evolved towards ones that are broadly acceptable. They may not be perfect (for example, first come first serve featured ~60% of respondents in the somewhat acceptable or lower category), but people are familiar and comfortable with passing control, and negotiating amongst themselves, an indicator of the social nature of managing these systems.

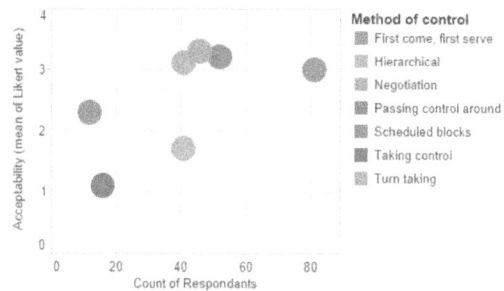

Figure 3. Plot of acceptability (mean of converted five point Likert scale to 0-4 scale for scoring, higher is better) against count of respondents that had previously responded to using that method of control often.

Of the less frequently used schemes, taking control was deemed unacceptable (~70% of respondents considering it somewhat to completely unacceptable), as was hierarchical control (~50% considering it somewhat to completely unacceptable).

From this survey, we arrived at an understanding of current behaviours for managing control: whilst these behaviours ranked highly in terms of acceptability, their suitability in scenarios where the token of the single remote control was removed (e.g. gesture or device control) would be questionable - are these acceptable behaviours (such as passing control) to be marginalised in the face of allowing anyone control at any time, and how will we design systems that can handle such an eventuality?

STUDY: MEDIATION OF CONTROL

Given the findings of the survey and the literature review, we elected to develop a system for virtualizing control, such that it could be managed in software by users, in order to investigate the following questions:

1. How relevant are existing behaviours for managing control, given the eventual removal of the bottleneck of a single remote control?

2. Can users self-mediate control, in the case where everyone is in control? Is mediation of control necessary?

3. What new behaviours can we facilitate given a virtualized control and how do these compare to existing behaviours?

We chose to examine these behaviours on a TV media system designed for use by one user at a time. This allowed us to retain the interface and mental models that users are familiar with, whilst also examining the potential for facilitating multi-user use of existing single-user media systems. Furthermore, this provided the added benefit of being able to examine our virtualized management of control without the potentially confounding effect of a concurrent use, multi-user interface (for which there is as yet no established standard).

Thus, our control scheme was to be similar to that of a standard remote, with the ability to move left/right/up/down, and select items of interest. Multi-user use was to be facilitated through virtualized management of control.

Proposed Control Schemes

For this study, 10 different control schemes were proposed (see Table 1 for details), broadly categorised as either "one user in control at a time" (hereafter "one user"), and "multiple users concurrently" (hereafter "everyone"). The "one user" schemes were based on existing behaviours: **passing**, **taking** and **turn taking**. Additionally, a variant of passing/taking was introduced: *lending*, essentially a hierarchical means of managing control where control could be lent out, and revoked, from an individual with authority. The **control** condition also fell into this category, being one remote control physically shared amongst participants.

The "everyone" schemes were introduced on consideration that, if everyone could potentially be in control of a single-user interface, would an amount of self-organisation/mediation take over, thus demonstrating that system-based mediation of control was not necessary? As such, conditions were added allowing for **everyone** in control, **subsets** of control (where different group members had control of different functions, thus requiring cooperation), **hierarchy** (where one member's input would override that of the others), **plurality** (where selection decisions were based on majority votes but navigation was concurrent) and **blocking** (where members could selectively and temporarily block each other from control).

Participants

Three person intimacy groups (2 groups of friends, 1 group of cohabitants, 1 family group (siblings), 1 group of colleagues) were recruited, five groups in all, fifteen participants total (male=7, female=8, mean age=21.2, SD age=3.5). These participants were to be evaluated across two sessions in a repeated measures (within-subjects) design, with five conditions in one session, and five in the second.

Each session was one hour long, with conditions assigned to sessions in a pseudo-random manner. Additionally, participants were given time to trial each mediation of control scheme until they felt comfortable in its operation.

Task Design & Implementation

The task was to schedule what programs the group wished to record for a given 3-hour time period (once per condition),

using an Electronic Programme Guide (EPG). For each condition, they were assigned a three hour block in which they were to pick and choose programs to record for viewing.

The program listing was generated from scraped listings of UK and New Zealand television, and randomly assigned into hour long or half hour long blocks. Conditions were assigned pseudo-randomly to time-periods, with no condition using the same time period more than once. The EPG used for this task was Windows Media Center (WMC)[3]. This was done primarily to ensure ecological validity using an interface comparable with home media systems.

In terms of the virtualized management of control, Android phones with a basic remote interface were used (see Figure 4). These devices provided users with the ability to browse through the EPG, confirm recordings and manage control through two "special" buttons whose function changed depending on the mediation of control scheme being used.

For example, in the passing control conditions, these two buttons would refer to the other two participants by name, allowing the user to select to whom to pass control. Additionally, the devices gave feedback as to who was in control and an overview of the main display (the WMC interface). The WMC EPG itself was presented on a projector display, with participants arranged sociopetally around the display in a mock living room (see Figure 5).

For implementation details for each condition, see Table 1. Task duration was enforced through the use of 3 hour blocks in the EPG (which took from ~3min to schedule, with an additional unlimited time for training that usually lasted for around ~3 min). As such each control scheme was typically used for ~6min (so ~30min per session, ~25min for questions, ~5 for briefing). There was no time pressure; participants carried out the task to completion at their own pace.

This task duration was deemed acceptable because people interact with EPG interfaces often, but for short intervals; it is the nature of both the time-series data, the narrow range of time they are interested in, and the aim of the task. The task

---

[3]http://windows.microsoft.com/en-GB/windows7/ products/features/windows-media-center

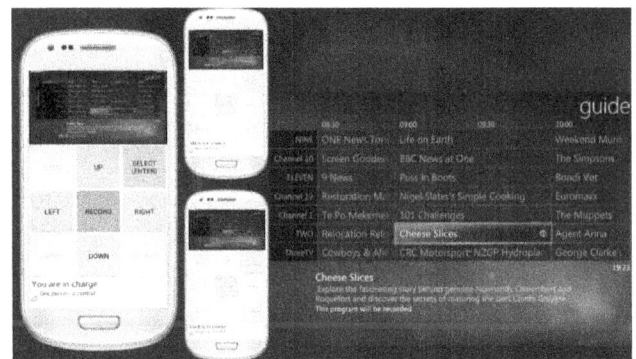

Figure 4. The user interface for controlling the system, and managing control. Three Android devices were used as remote controls to a Windows Media Center interface (pictured right). The bottom left/right buttons change function depending on the condition being evaluated.

Condition	Description	Implementation Details
		One user at a time
A: Control condition	One person in control	*A single device placed on the table with participants instructed to use it as they would a normal remote*
B: Lending	Ability to lend control and take it back	*Two buttons were used to explicitly lend/retrieve control*
C: Passing	Control can be passed around	*Two buttons were used to explicitly pass control to the other participants*
D: Taking	Control can be taken off them	*Two buttons were used to explicitly take control from the other participants*
E: Turn-taking		*Control was passed every 10 seconds*
		Multiple users (Everyone contributes to control)
F: Everyone	Everyone has control	*All devices in control at all times*
G: Plurality	Majority rules voting for selections	*When a selection was made participants were blocked from browsing, and would have 5 seconds to respond positively to confirm the selection or it would be denied*
H: Hierarchy	Designated individual outranks the others and can override their control	*One participant was randomly selected to outrank the others, when they used the system the others were blocked from control*
I: Subsets	Everyone has a subset of control	
J: Blocking	Can block other people temporarily	*Two buttons were used to selectively block participants for periods of 4 seconds*

Table 1. Experimental conditions by category. "One user at a time" denotes one person in control at any one time, while "Multiple Users" denotes everyone being in control simultaneously.

itself is well understood by users, short to conduct, and provided motivation for multiple users to interact concurrently (conflicting media interests), suiting our usage as a novel and ecologically valid task.

For the purposes of this experiment, ecological validity was strived for in a number of ways: the use of WMC ensured an ecologically valid single-user EPG interface, representative of media systems used in the home currently. A laboratory room was mocked up to resemble a living room, with natural lighting, comfortable sociopetal seating and a large display.

Figure 5. Living-room-like space used for conducting evaluations. Left: sociopetal seating arrangement. Right: Projector display with WMC.

Measures

Participants were recorded for the duration of the experiment, while instrumented system usage metrics (action counts: number of button presses per user) were also captured to measure intra-group dominance: the disparity between users within their groups i.e. to what extent did one user dominate usage of the system.

Users were presented with questionnaires on the completion of each condition, including workload (NASA TLX [7]), usability (System Usability Scale (SUS) [4]), and 5-item Likert-scale questions covering the acceptability of control schemes and preferences regarding their use.

Additionally, users were asked to rank the conditions in order of preference at the end of the study, with post-condition and post-experiment interviews used in order to further understand user preferences and dislikes regarding control schemes.

Results

Unless otherwise stated, a repeated measures ANOVA (conducted using linear mixed-effects model fit by maximum likelihood (*lme()* in R) was performed with a *post hoc* Dunnett's test (comparison of every condition with the control, which was analogous to a single physical remote control). Conditions found as significantly different ($p < 0.05$) from the control in the Dunnetts test are listed in each Figure. Boxplots show quartiles (25th, 50th, 75th), with means indicated by the dark circles.

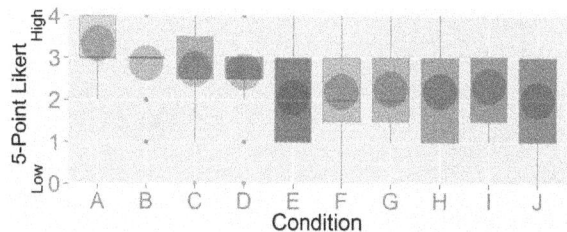

Figure 6. "I was satisfied with my experience using the system to accomplish the task" - $\chi^2(9) = 24.0994, p < 0.01, \eta^2 = 0.143$ Dunnetts: E, F, G, H, I J (letters refer to conditions in Table 1). Blue shades: "one user" conditions. Red shades: "everyone" conditions.

"One User" Schemes Are Functionally Equivalent

The "one user" schemes appeared to be functionally equivalent across a variety of metrics, with comparable SUS scores (see Figure 9), TLX scores (see Figure 8), and action counts (a measure of how much effort was required in order to use the system, see Figures 7 and 10).

Additionally, Conditions B, C, and E all achieved superior mean rankings than A (see Figure 11). Indeed, these Conditions could rarely be separated from the control.

"Everyone In Control" Fared Poorly

Conversely, the "everyone in control" conditions were broadly found to be significantly worse than the Control in SUS scores, TLX mental demand, temporal demand, effort, frustration, and self-rated satisfaction with using the system.

Additionally, the "everyone" schemes were rated poorly in terms of acceptability as a means of sharing control with others, fairness, and the extent to which users felt "in control". This trend continued in the instrumented metrics, with higher

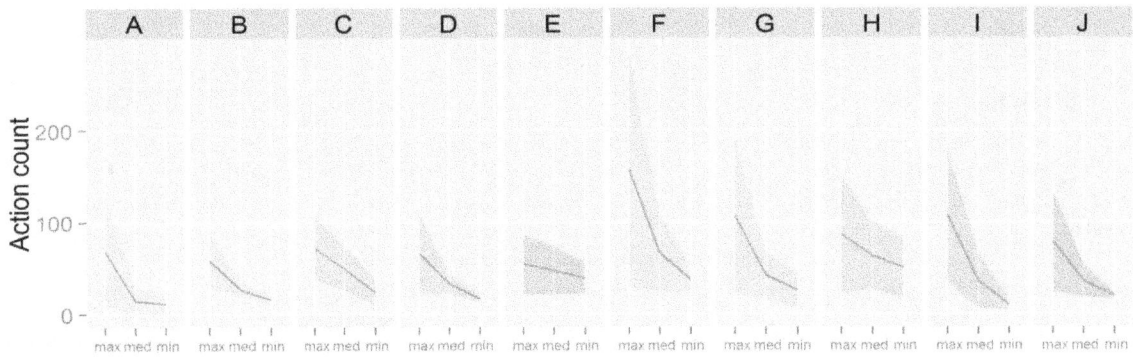

Figure 7. Dominance by actions - Plot of three values per condition: mean of (max / median / min) action counts across groups, with shaded standard deviation - $\chi^2(9) = 21.11, p < 0.01, \eta^2 = 0.233$ Dunnetts: F. Blue shades: "one user" conditions. Red shades: "everyone" conditions.

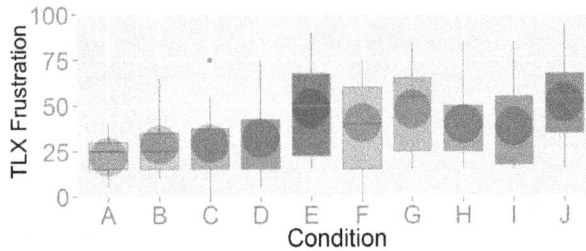

Figure 8. TLX Frustration Question by condition, lower is better - $\chi^2(9) = 33.93, p < 0.01, \eta^2 = 0.103$ Dunnetts: E, F, G, J. Blue shades: "one user" conditions. Red shades: "everyone" conditions.

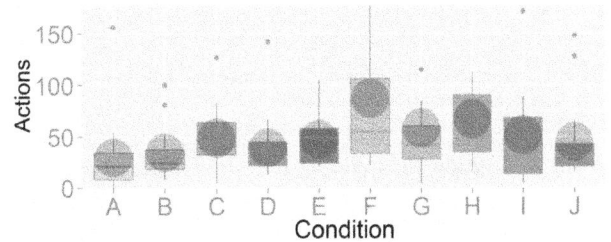

Figure 10. Mean actions across users by condition - $\chi^2(9) = 23.30725, p < 0.01, \eta^2 = 0.104$ Dunnetts: F. Blue shades: "one user" conditions. Red shades: "everyone" conditions.

mean action counts (see Figure 10), indicating that instead of self-mediation, users were having to expend greater effort in order to counteract each other's inputs.

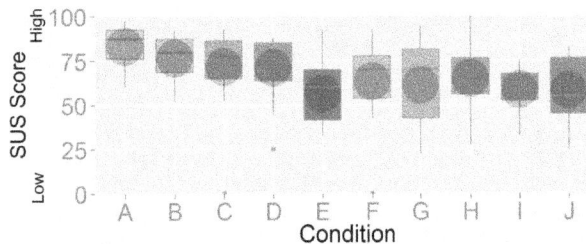

Figure 9. Overall SUS Score (a ten-item Likert-type questionnaire for assessing usability, higher is better) - $\chi^2(9) = 36.80, p < 0.01, \eta^2 = 0.181$ Dunnetts: E, F, G, H, I J. Blue shades: "one user" conditions. Red shades: "everyone" conditions.

Dominance

Dominance here refers to the disparity between users within their groups, in terms of instrumented metrics, specifically action counts (button presses). This was examined as a potential metric for measuring fairness: to what extent did one user dominate usage of the system. Shareability [8] has been shown to be important in terms of impacting equity of control [14]; barriers preventing shareability thereby foster interpersonal dominance within groups (as seen for example in [12]).

In Figure 7 we can see that by action count, condition E (turn taking) exhibited the least dominance, which is to be expected when each participant is given the same amount of time in which to operate. Compared to our control condition, the "one user" conditions exhibited lower dominance behaviour, in contrast to the "everyone" conditions.

The "one user in control" conditions by and large exhibit low dominance, a level that is perhaps socially acceptable

or even necessary for a group task. The results for condition D partially confirm this: in this condition, participants were allowed to take control whenever they wished, therefore it might be reasonable to presume that if one participant was dominating to the detriment of the experience, the others might have taken control, given their familiarity with their fellow participants.

In contrast the "everyone in control" conditions exhibited greater dominance behaviour than the "one user" conditions, an indicator of their chaotic nature (reported in most post-condition interviews), with one user effectively being required to actively and continuously assert control over the system in order to counteract the discordant nature of multiple simultaneous inputs.

Caveats & Edge Cases

There were some notable exceptions to these observations. For example, Condition G (majority rules for selections) came out favourably in subjective metrics; participants indicated that although they disliked the underlying "everyone" scheme they enjoyed the fairness of voting to make a selection; this was a confound where we evaluated mediating selection, not control.

Similarly, Condition E (turn taking) frequently fared poorly (e.g. featuring the highest mean TLX temporal demand). Enforced fairness via time-slicing may have been confounded by the necessity to time-slice at small intervals in order to allow participants to experience the control scheme within the duration of the task.

Additionally, questions are raised regarding the acceptability of taking control (condition D), whose mean ranking was the only ranking of the "one user" conditions to be worse than the control.

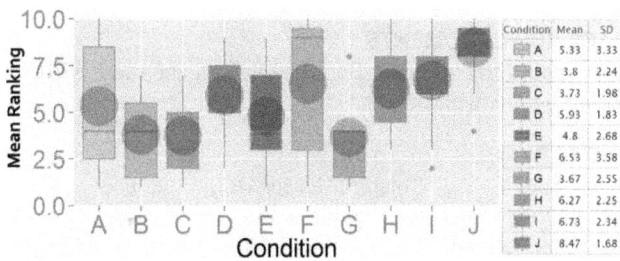

Condition	Mean	SD
A	5.33	3.33
B	3.8	2.24
C	3.73	1.98
D	5.93	1.83
E	4.8	2.68
F	6.53	3.58
G	3.67	2.55
H	6.27	2.25
I	6.73	2.34
J	8.47	1.68

Figure 11. Ranking (lower is better) - Friedman test $\chi^2(9)$ = 37.20 p < 0.01, Wilcox pairwise sign rank test with Bonferroni correction showed no statistically significant differences (p > 0.05)

Interview Feedback

Control: Some Want It, Some Don't

For some, being in control was important and not being in control disquieting (G: refers to group, C: refers to condition):

> "I liked the ones where I was in control, I liked being the one in control" G:2, C:Debrief

Conversely, in some of the groups there were participants that had no interest in being in control, for example because of a disinterest in making decisions or even a dislike in sharing viewing:

> "I don't like being in charge, so I'm happy to let someone else have the responsibility" G:2, C:F
> "I liked it because he was in control, and can watch what he wants to watch" G:2, C:A
> "I don't want to share TV with them!" G:3, C:D

"Everyone In Control" Encourages Dominance

Three groups provided similar complaints regarding the discordant nature of the everyone in control conditions, with participants explicitly noting the presence of dominance behaviour in this condition:

> "I always find this a bit annoying in computer games where you both have control and you invariably hit the wrong thing, because you both go down at the same time, so you make mistakes more trying to get to the same thing" G:2, C:F
> "One person has to take the lead because you can't all operate at the same time" G:3, C:F

"One User At A Time" Preferred

Again, most groups noted and preferred the simplicity of the "one user in control" schemes and their associated management schemes, e.g.:

> "It was good to be able to transfer the remote" G:2, C:D
> "One person in control is the best, because we can all talk to each other and just one can pick" G:4, C:Debrief

However there were concerns regarding the usefulness of some of these schemes:

> "I feel like this is just mechanising something you can do naturally" G:2, C:G
> "I think in the end everything is too tiring for me, I prefer to give control to anyone, quite a lot of things are interesting to watch." G:3, C:Debrief

SUMMARY AND DISCUSSION

"One user at a time" is superior to "everyone in control"

The "one person" conditions exhibited statistically better SUS ratings and mean rankings (aside from Condition G) confirming the view that the primary differentiator between conditions was whether they allowed concurrent inputs versus allowing one user to interact with the underlying media system at a time.

Lending, passing, and taking control are, at worst, comparable to having one physical shared remote

These conditions exhibited comparable TLX, SUS, and dominance behaviour (with no statistically significant differences) whilst mean user rankings were moderately better than that of the control (Condition A). That these schemes approach the usability of the single remote control users are familiar with suggests that we can build mediation of control schemes that are on par with, and superior to in functionality, the existing standard of a single remote control for input.

"Everyone in control" is poorly suited to concurrent use

These conditions exhibited worse mean rankings, poor SUS scores, higher TLX frustration, as well as greater dominance behaviour (excluding Condition G). This suggests that single-user media systems should not be opened up to concurrent use, and places a question mark over the usability of new input mechanisms such as phones with IR support if there is no means of mediating between multiple concurrent inputs.

Design Implications

Currently, there are a number of ways in which TV media-system user interfaces can accommodate multi-user use e.g.:

- Multi-pointer/cursor UIs
- Split-screen/screen division
- Offloading interaction onto other devices or screens
- Mediating control through proximity or attention

However, these approaches may have issues regarding moving away from existing interfaces and their associated mental models and behaviours. We propose that, given the increasing range of input modalities (e.g. mobile phones with IR support or remote apps, or multiple users employing gestural controls etc.) mediation of control schemes might provide an alternative to redesigning familiar interfaces, allowing use of these new input modalities and mechanisms without coupling them to new and potentially confusing user interfaces, by retaining familiar single-user interfaces and interactions. As an example, consider a TV which can be controlled by every smart phone in the room; mediation of control would allow users to achieve concurrent use, where destructive inputs (e.g. both attempting a navigational event simultaneously) would be prevented.

Additionally, we propose an initial set of mediation of control schemes (passing/taking/lending control), based on existing control management behaviours, that can facilitate this usage.

Future Work

We foresee a number of areas in which further work would be required in order to determine both the viability and suitability of mediation of control schemes.

Appropriateness of Mediation of Control

Establishing the generalisability of this approach e.g. what tasks are suited to more simplistic single-user interactions (and thus are suited to mediation of control schemes) would aid in designing multi-user smart TVs whose more basic or ubiquitous functionality is still readily accessible to users of all ages and capabilities. Navigation, 1-dimensional controls (e.g. volume or channel switching), or contexts where the complexity of higher bandwidth input controls (such as pointer input) is unnecessary (e.g. grid-based views navigated via cursor) might all be areas where mediation of control is of use. Additionally, facilitating management of control might provide additional social benefits, for example being able to take control from children, or have parental inputs prioritised, that would be worth investigating in longitudinal studies in the home.

Further Mediation of Control Schemes

Our study looked at existing behaviours as the primary inspiration for our mediation of control schemes, suggesting thus far that there is no one scheme that should become the defacto mediation of control scheme. There are other potentially useful ways in which mediation of control could be applied, for example:

- Inferring when a user is no longer interacting
- Prioritising user inputs and modalities
- Employing timeouts to automatically relinquish control

Future work should look to examine both their acceptability, their suitability across different tasks and contexts, and appropriate feedback for communicating availability for interaction, whilst establishing what set of mediation of control schemes should be used, and when.

CONCLUSIONS

Our capability to enable shared use of TV media systems in the home has increased substantially in the last few years, with new input mechanisms (e.g. smartphones) and modalities (e.g. gestures) allowing for anyone in the living room to contribute to the input and control of a media system.

Concurrent use interfaces may be inappropriate for a number of reasons (e.g. visual complexity, undermining existing mental models regarding interaction). Additionally, we suggest that concurrent use of single-user media systems is inappropriate as users are ineffective at self-mediation of control, with inputs combining destructively. As such, we propose that single-user media systems be augmented with mediation of control schemes; this combination offers a potential alternative to concurrent use systems, allowing for users to retain the familiar interfaces and mental models they have developed over time, whilst allowing new input mechanisms and modalities to be utilized in an effective and useful way.

Finally, we offer an initial set of mediation of control behaviours (passing, taking and lending control) derived from existing behaviours for managing control that are at worst functionally equivalent to, and in some cases better than, in terms of dominance and subjective ratings, managing the single physical remote control, to serve as a baseline for examining future mediation of control schemes.

ACKNOWLEDGMENTS

We would like to thank Bang & Olufsen and the EPSRC for funding this work.

REFERENCES

1. Abe, Y., et al. Tolerant sharing of a single-user application among multiple users in collaborative work. In *Proc. CSCW 2010* (2010), 555–556.

2. Ballendat, T., Marquardt, N., and Greenberg, S. Proxemic interaction. In *Proc. ITS 2010*, ACM Press (2010), 121–130.

3. Birnholtz, J. P., et al. An exploratory study of input configuration and group process in a negotiation task using a large display. In *Proc. CHI 2007*, ACM Press (2007), 91–100.

4. Brooke, J. SUS-A quick and dirty usability scale. *Usability evaluation in industry* (1996).

5. Clark, A., et al. Seamless interaction in space. In *Proc. OzCHI 2011*, ACM Press (2011), 88–97.

6. Greenberg, S. Sharing views and interactions with single-user applications. In *ACM SIGOIS Bulletin*, vol. 11, ACM (1990), 227–237.

7. Hart, S., and Staveland, L. Development of NASA-TLX. In *Human mental workload* (1988).

8. Hornecker, E., et al. From entry to access. In *Proc. DPPI 2007*, ACM Press (2007), 328–342.

9. Lalanne, D., and Lisowska Masson, A. A Fitt of distraction. In *Proc. CHI EA 2011*, ACM Press (2011), 2125–2130.

10. Morris, M. R. Web on the wall. In *Proc. ITS 2012*, ACM Press (2012), 95–194.

11. Nacenta, M. A., et al. The LunchTable. In *Proc. PerDis 2012*, ACM Press (2012), 1–6.

12. Oya Aran, et al. A multimodal corpus for studying dominance in small group conversations. In *Proc. LREC MMC 2010* (2010), 2223–2232.

13. Pohl, H., and Murray-Smith, R. Focused and casual interactions. In *Proc. CHI 2013*, ACM Press (2013), 2223–2232.

14. Rogers, Y., et al. Equal Opportunities: Do Shareable Interfaces Promote More Group Participation Than Single User Displays? *Human-Computer Interaction 24*, 1 (2009), 79–116.

15. Schmid, O., et al. Collaborative web browsing. In *Proc. EICS 2012*, ACM Press (2012), 141–150.

16. Stewart, J., et al. Single display groupware. In *Proc. CHI 1999*, ACM Press (1999), 286–293.

17. Tse, E., et al. Avoiding interference. In *Proc. CSCW 2004*, ACM Press (2004), 252.

18. You, W., et al. Studying vision-based multiple-user interaction with in-home large displays. In *Proc. HCC 2008*, ACM Press (2008), 19–26.

Off-Screen Media: Spatial Display and Interaction in Augmented Television

Dale A. Herigstad

SeeSpace Ltd

Abstract

A study in the evolution of spatial considerations in media, looking at how we navigate and design for more complex media consumption. A new model will be presented for pairing information in the TV viewing space.

Categories and Subject Descriptors

H.5.1 Multimedia Information Systems (Video)

Keywords

Interactive Television; spatial interaction; gesture; AR; augmented television; stereo 3D TV

Short Bio

Now living in London, Dale Herigstad spent 30 years in Hollywood as a Creative Director for motion graphics in TV and film. His mission has been to apply the principles of rich media design to interactive experiences. He began designing interfaces for Television more than 20 years ago, and was a founder of Schematic, which grew and merged with other digital agencies to form the global agency POSSIBLE.

Dale has developed a unique spatial approach to designing navigation systems for various screen contexts. He was a part of the research team that conceptualised digital experiences in the film "Minority Report," and is now leading development in gestural navigation for screens at a distance. Screens have always defined unique spaces, and with advancements in stereo 3D projection and new AR, information can occupy these spaces. Spatial context is becoming increasingly important in screen design. Virtual space and place are new frontiers of design.

He has an MFA from California Institute of the Arts, where in 1981 he taught the first course in Motion Graphics to be offered to designers in the United States. He served on the founding advisory board of the digital content direction at the American Film Institute in Los Angeles, and also was an active participant in the development of advanced prototypes for Enhanced TV at the American Film Institute for many years. Dale has 4 Emmy awards.

More recently, Dale co-founded the company SeeSpace, which will deliver its first product, inAiR, later this year. InAiR places dynamic Web content in the space in front of the Television, perhaps the first Augmented Television experience.

TVX'14, June 25–27, 2014, Newcastle Upon Tyne, UK.
ACM 978-1-4503-2838-8/14/06.
http://dx.doi.org/10.1145/2602299.2603001

Author Index